STUDIES IN AMERICAN POLITICAL DEVE

C000053218

An Annual

Volume 3

Studies in American Political Development will publish theoretical and empirical research on political development and institutional change in the United States. A diversity of subject matters and methodologies is invited, including comparative or international studies that illuminate the American case. Manuscripts of up to 75 pages in length, excluding footnotes, will be considered. There is also a Notes and Exchanges section for shorter presentation of research perspectives and findings, comments on earlier articles, and review essays on bibliography of unusual interest.

Submissions will be accepted until December 1 for publication in the next volume. Authors should send three copies of the manuscript (double-spaced), which will not be returned. After initial screening by the editors, selected manuscripts will be reviewed anonymously. Publication decisions will be made with regard to the total contents of each annual volume.

Please address all correspondence to: *Studies in American Political Development*, Department of Political Science, University of California, Los Angeles, California 90024.

The editing of *Studies in American Political Development* is assisted by funds from the College of Letters and Science, University of California, Los Angeles and the Institution for Social and Policy Studies at Yale University.

STUDIES IN
American
Political
Development

An Annual

VOLUME 3

Yale University Press
New Haven and London

Designed by Nancy Ovedovitz
and set in Baskerville type with Avant Garde for display
and printed in the United States of America by
Vail-Ballou Press, Binghamton, N.Y.

Library of Congress catalog card number: 86–40192
International standard book number: 0–300–04486–0 (cloth)
0–300–04487–9 (paper)

The paper in this book meets the guidelines for permanence and
durability of the Committee on Production Guidelines for Book
Longevity of the Council on Library Resources.

10   9   8   7   6   5   4   3   2   1

Contents

RESEARCH NOTES

STUDIES IN AMERICAN POLITICAL DEVELOPMENT

An Annual

Volume 3

FORUM

Editors' Note

As interest in the history of political institutions has rebounded, arguments have moved from the assertion that "institutions matter" to the analytic and normative implications of different approaches. In this volume, we air two such debates in a new section called Forum. The first raises the problem of locating the state, in this case in the urban setting. At issue is whether recent studies have effectively broken with an earlier generation of scholars or whether they have trapped themselves in the discourses of functionalism.

The second takes as its point of departure the claim that the "new institutionalism" provides a basis for unifying normative and empirical concerns, in this case in the field of public law. The question raised is whether such unification as is proposed will only reinforce existing liberal values and practices, while insulating them from serious philosophical criticism.

TERRENCE J. MCDONALD
University of Michigan

The Burdens of Urban History:
The Theory of the State in
Recent American Social History

Louis Hartz summed up the mission of his historical generation when he wrote, as part of the rationale for *The Liberal Tradition* in 1955, that "the way to fully refute a man is to ignore him . . . and the only way you can do this is to substitute new fundamental categories for his own, so that you are simply pursuing a different path." Hartz was referring to the influence of Charles Beard and what Hartz called the "frustration that the persistence of the Progressive analysis of America has inspired." He was arguing that his generation had to stop honoring the progressives by contending with them; the key to destroying their interpretation of American history was the reinvention of American history by means of new conceptual tools.[1]

The so-called progressive analysis of America, which so frustrated Hartz, held that conflict—economic, social, regional—was the key to understanding its past. Although none of the versions of this view was exactly like another, Richard Hofstadter felt that the overall thrust of this interpretation of American history—predominant during the years 1910 to 1950—was best summarized in a passage written by Vernon Louis Parrington:

> From the first we have been divided into two main parties. . . . On one side has been the party of the current aristocracy—of church, of gentry, of merchant, of slave holder, or manufacturer—and on the other the party of the commonalty—of farmer, villager, small tradesman, mechanic, proletariat. The one has persistently sought to check and limit the popular power, to keep the control of

This essay was originally presented at the 1987 meeting of the Social Science History Association. It was greatly improved by detailed comments by the editors of this journal, by professors Margaret Somers and Michael Dawson of the University of Michigan, and by Professor J. Morgan Kousser of the California Institute of Technology. The time for writing the essay was provided by a fellowship from the John Simon Guggenheim Memorial Foundation.

1. Louis Hartz, *The Liberal Tradition in America* (New York: Harcourt Brace Jovanovich, 1955), 28.

the government in the hands of the few in order to serve special interests, whereas the other has sought to augment the popular power, to make government more responsive to the will of the majority, to further the democratic rather than the republican ideal—let one discover this and new light is shed on our cultural tendencies.[2]

Hofstadter's quotation of this view was part of an obituary for the progressive interpretation of American history that he wrote less than fifteen years after Hartz's book appeared. According to Hofstadter, the "tide began to run out" on the progressive interpretation during the 1950s when "conflict as a vitalizing idea began to be contested by the notion of a pervasive American consensus." What had "toppled" the progressive interpretation—perhaps better, allowed his generation to topple it—were new concepts and methods that facilitated replacement of the "simple-minded" dualism of the progressives with a new appreciation for the complexity of the American past. Among these new theoretical frameworks and methodological approaches, he wrote in 1968, were Freudianism, the sociology of knowledge, functionalism—especially as presented in the works of Robert Merton—and quantification. Together these permitted the introduction of "the entire sociological penumbra of political life" into historical writing.[3]

Although Hartz and Hofstadter were undoubtedly among the most brilliant and wide-ranging of the generation of so-called consensus historians, they were by no means the only ones who recognized that the supplanting of one historiographical tradition by another requires battles at the theoretical and methodological as well as the substantive fronts. In fact, perhaps the most important accomplishment of their generation was the borrowing from the social sciences of new ways of constructing their interpretation of the American past. Some of the most important historiographical "products" of the postwar period were based upon middle-range social scientific concepts such as latent functions and reference groups from sociology, pluralism from political science, status anxiety from social psychology, information and transaction costs from economics, and so on. Moreover, as Ian Tyrell has recently pointed out, it was this postwar turn to the social sciences that, in function if not intent, both rescued American history from "more reactionary forms of empiricism" and inoculated it for some time against more radical types of analysis such as Marxism.[4]

Historians, however, did not "invent" consensus, as historiographers so often propose. Consensus history was merely the historian's moment of a more general transformation of the social sciences that began before World War II and was consolidated soon after it. Beginning in the 1930s political science and

2. Richard Hofstadter, *The Progressive Historians* (Chicago: University of Chicago Press, 1969), 438.

3. Ibid., 443.

4. Ian Tyrell, *The Absent Marx: Class Analysis and Liberal History in Twentieth Century America* (Westport, Conn.: Greenwood Press, 1986), 101. This is an excellent consideration of some of the same issues raised in this essay that is marred only by its ahistorical assumption that the problems in liberal historiography would have been solved by a dialogue with Marxism.

sociology, too, began a shift from an institutionally based and reform-oriented social science to one that was focused more on culture and concerned more with stability than reform. While historians shifted from conflict to consensus as a central theme in American history, sociologists and political scientists shifted their focus from the ways in which American society was problematic to the ways in which it was normative. Moreover, the simultaneity of these shifts across the social sciences and their attachment to the development of a prestigious empirical social science gave these views of American society past and present enormous legitimacy and staying power.

For the most part, however, historians have failed to think very carefully about how these theoretical frameworks have shaped and limited their ability to apprehend and interpret American history. This failure originates in the tendency of many historiographers to write about transformations in historical interpretations in relative isolation from parallel transformations in the social sciences. The problem has persisted because, until relatively recently, most historians have been notoriously reluctant to engage in explicit theoretical debate. Therefore, they are sometimes simply unaware of the intellectual legacy of their middle-range concepts, or, in the worst cases, they are committed to what David Hackett Fisher has pointed out is the historian's version of the "Baconian" fallacy, which is the belief that they deal only in the "facts," without the need for organizing theoretical frameworks.[5]

One might have expected that the rise of historically oriented social science would have brought these issues to the fore, but for the most part it has not. Although sociologists and political scientists have begun to work with historical data, they have not, on the whole, been especially concerned with either the histories of their own disciplines or the historiography of the secondary historical sources on which they base their accounts. In fact, historical social scientists have tended, ironically, to commit their own version of the error of historians by appropriating what they think are "facts" from the works of historians without examining the frameworks within which those alleged facts are embedded.

Together, then, the relative lack of interest among historians in theory and among social scientists in historiography have set up an unproductive intellectual exchange. Historians have "borrowed" middle-range theory from the social sciences and used it to structure their "facts." But then political scientists and sociologists have "borrowed" these "facts" to construct the historical accounts on the basis of which they hope to theorize.

This would be a point of purely epistemological interest were it not for the role of such a set of exchanges in the construction of the current conception of the relationship between class and politics in the American city. Because it was the cockpit of important social, economic, and political change and perhaps also the location of the most active of the branches of the state in American history before the New Deal, the American city is rightly perceived as one important locus for the attempt to "bring the state back in" or put "politics"

5. David Hackett Fischer, *Historians' Fallacies: Toward a Logic of Historical Thought* (New York: Harper and Row, 1970), 4.

back into social history. However, after two decades of the "new" social history—most of it urban community studies—that has reintroduced the vocabulary of class, conflict, and ideology into American history, the conception of urban politics remains one of ethnicity, patronage, and nonideological machines, a view constructed in the 1950s. Moreover, this view of urban politics is characteristic of newer work not just in history but also in political science and sociology, and it plays a role in recently developed theories of both class formation and state building.

The intellectual history of the construction and appropriation of this view of urban politics is a case study of the process outlined above—of the power of the theoretical frameworks of one generation to structure the discourse of another. Both by ignoring politics and by failing to examine critically the theoretical frameworks within which they have perceived it, members of a new generation of historical social science have so far failed in their task of substituting new fundamental categories for those of their predecessors. What some have called the "neoprogressive" view of American society continues to carry the burden of a remarkably consensual view of American politics.

THE EXCEPTIONABLE HISTORY OF AMERICAN EXCEPTIONALISM

Symptoms of a lack of fit between the "social" and "political" history of the last two decades are apparent in a recent series of essays on the process of class and state formation by historians and historically oriented political scientists and sociologists. These essays, undertaken for the most part within a framework of a revived interest in American "exceptionalism," reveal that the work of the so-called new social history has, for the most part, undermined the social and ideological bases of traditional claims of exceptionalism but, to a great extent, has retained those parts having to do with politics.

For historically oriented social scientists writing in the era of Hartz and Hofstadter the relationship between class and politics in America was relatively unproblematic. For a variety of reasons, including the absence of feudalism, economic abundance, rapid social mobility, or essential ideological consensus, there was no consciousness of class in America. Compared to other countries, then, America was "exceptional" because there, as Seymour Martin Lipset has argued for almost thirty years now, "the development of working class political consciousness . . . required an act of intellectual imagination."[6]

Armed with both new analyses of American social history and a more supple theory of ideology, the new social and labor historians have argued, in contrast, that in both structure and ideology the United States and Europe have not been as different as exceptionalists might have thought. These studies suggest that structural opportunities for occupational mobility in the United States were not as great nor was agreement on fundamentals as widespread as the old

6. Seymour Martin Lipset, "Why No Socialism in the United States?" in S. Bialer and S. Sluzar, eds., *Sources of Contemporary Radicalism* (Boulder, 1977), and Lipset, "Radicalism or Reformism: The Sources of Working-class Politics," *American Political Science Review* 77 (March, 1983): 1–18.

exceptionalists argued. Most Americans lived and died in the class of their birth, economic dislocation and inequality were at least as obvious as the promise of abundance, and, as a result of these social and economic facts, an implicitly anticapitalist "producer" ideology of "equal rights" was both fairly widespread and fairly well institutionalized. Moreover, this ideology was prominent in conflicts both at the point of production and in the political arena.[7]

These arguments have essentially shifted the terrain from social to political exceptionalism. A new generation of commentators on this issue has formulated a rough consensus on class formation in America in which, as Sean Wilentz has put it, "politics mattered a great deal." Taken together the contributors to this view, including, among others, Wilentz, Eric Foner, Jerome Karabel, Ira Katznelson, Amy Bridges, and Martin Shefter, contend that in contrast to Europe where economic inequality was joined with a long struggle for political equality, in the United States, as Foner has put it (following Alan Dawley), the messages of the economic and political sectors were contradictory. Here economic inequality was accompanied by political equality; what Perlman called the "free gift" of the suffrage antedated the emergence of capitalist economic institutions.[8]

More important than the possession of this free gift, of course, was the way that it was organized. Here, too, a surprising unanimity has emerged in this literature. It argues that the ballot box was "the coffin" of class consciousness in America because of the apparent openness and equality of the political system; the organization of politics on the basis of ethnicity, territoriality, and patronage; and the institutionalization of politics in political machines that rewarded ethnic particularism with divisible material incentives.

For example, the decline of artisanally based class consciousness is now thought to have been brought about in large part by the appearance of ethnic political machines. As part of a nonideological party system, they exploited locality-based ethnic divisions "more than anything else" and thus produced a

---

7. This discussion of the "exceptionalism" framework is based primarily on the following works: Eric Foner, "Why Is There No Socialism in the United States?" *History Workshop Journal* 17 (1984): 57–80; Sean Wilentz, "Against Exceptionalism: Class Consciousness and the American Labor Movement, 1790–1920," *International Labor and Working Class History*, no. 26 (1984): 1–24 (and responses by Nick Salvatore and Michael Hanagan); Ira Katznelson, *City Trenches: Urban Politics and the Patterning of Class in the United States* (Chicago: University of Chicago Press, 1981); Katznelson, "Working-Class Formation and the State: Nineteenth-Century England in American Perspective," in P. Evans, D. Rueschemeyer, and T. Skocpol, eds., *Bringing the State Back In* (Cambridge: Cambridge University Press, 1985), 257–284; David Montgomery, "Labor and the Republic in Industrial America, 1860–1920," *Le Mouvement social* 111 (1980): 201–15; Jerome Karabel, "The Failure of American Socialism Reconsidered," *Socialist Register* (1979): 204–27. These works summarize the findings of the new social history that are relevant for this argument. For a recent crossnational survey of the prospects for social mobility in the United States and Europe which finds them similar, see Hartmut Kaeble, *Social Mobility in the 19th and 20th Centuries: Europe and America in Comparative Perspective* (New York: St. Martin's Press, 1986).

8. Alan Dawley, *Class and Community: The Industrial Revolution in Lynn* (Cambridge: Harvard University Press, 1976).

split between radical politics at the workplace and the politics of ethnic bargaining and accommodation in the neighborhood. The maintenance and manipulation of this split throughout the nineteenth century was one of the factors in the post-Civil War disruption of what David Montgomery has called the "sense of moral universality among 'the producers'" that provided the language of militancy for the nineteenth century working class.[9]

What is striking about the new political consensus, however, is the disjunction between its conception of class and its conception of politics. Both in their essays on exceptionalism and in their own substantive writings, these authors and others consider class to be not a category but a process, and class consciousness to be not an attribute but a project; class formation in general is complex, contingent, and historical. This supple understanding of class contrasts with an ascriptive and functionalist understanding of politics in these same essays. In the work of the labor historians, in particular, while class is a project, ethnicity seems primordial; while class formation is a complicated process, party formation is almost automatic; while labor leadership is courageous, farsighted, and self-conscious, political leadership is craven, manipulative, and nonideological. The construction of class consciousness is rooted in the mutuality of the everyday realities of work and neighborhood; this same mutuality—apparently—disappears in the voting booth where nonideological particularism takes over and the favor, the city permit, the patronage job prevail.

In the works of the historically oriented political scientists, the political aspects of the relationship between class and politics are handled more deftly. In particular, these authors underline the challenges of party building at the institutional and ideological levels. Bridges, for example, has emphasized both the necessity of party leaders to mobilize majorities and the need of workers to pursue political goals through the parties in her account of the way class and politics intersected in the antebellum period. Shefter has included the decentralized nature of the American state and the relative accessibility of its local branch in his explanation of the way in which trade unions and political machines organized working-class life in the later nineteenth century.[10] In the end, however, for both it was the political machines that played the key role. For Bridges "the institutions of machine politics coordinated an accommodation between the working classes and their social betters." For Shefter, "at least in the major cities . . . machines consolidated their position as the most important vehicle through which the working class participated in politics."[11]

This interpretation now also plays an important role in considerations of the exceptionalism of the American state. Building on the accounts of Katznelson and Shefter, for example, Theda Skocpol has emphasized the "crucial conse-

---

9. Montgomery, "Labor and the Republic."

10. Amy Bridges, "Becoming American: The Working Classes in the United States before the Civil War," and Martin Shefter, "Trade Unions and Political Machines: The Organization and Disorganization of the American Working Class in the Late Nineteenth Century," in Ira Katznelson and Aristide Zolberg, eds., *Working Class Formation: Nineteenth Century Patterns in Western Europe and the United States* (Princeton: Princeton University Press, 1986), 157–278.

11. Bridges, "Becoming," 189; Shefter, "Trade Unions," 267.

quences" for public policy-making of the subordination of government functions to the patronage needs of the political parties. According to Skocpol, a
factor in the relatively late development of the American welfare state was the
role of "patronage democracy" including the "urban political machines based
on the ever-renewed streams of immigrants flowing into the American industrial working class." Because of patronage democracy, politics served primarily
"symbolic-expressive and entertainment functions" and was not a matter of
using parties to articulate demands for policies in the collective interest of wage
earners as a class. Instead nineteenth-century politics involved "getting out the
vote" within "the various ethnically and religiously based local residence communities that formed the remarkably stable building blocks of grassroots support for the major party organizations."[12]

Somewhat surprisingly, these understandings of the role of ethnicity, patronage, and machines are almost identical to those of the so-called consensus
historians. For them, for example, the patronage-based politics of the urban
political machine was the perfect response to both the functional needs of
urban society and the nonideological character of American politics. For the
generation of the fifties, political machines extended social exceptionalism into
politics; for current commentators the political machines blocked the transmission of radicalism from society into politics. In both cases the conception of
politics is society-centered, nonideological, and functionalist. For reasons having to do primarily with its middle-range theories, much of the new history has
simply rediscovered the political propositions of the old.

THE LIBERAL MATRIX FOR POLITICAL ANALYSIS

Most current interpretations of urban and community politics in American
history have been deeply influenced by middle-range theoretical propositions
drawn from sociology and political science. These emerged out of what David
Ricci has called the "liberal matrix" of political analysis that was constructed in
the years immediately following World War II. To understand the contin-
gency—and contestability—of these frameworks, it is necessary to begin with a
brief look at the intellectual history of this era and the elements of this matrix.[13]

For the first three or four decades of the twentieth century a reform-oriented
"progressive" social science paralleled—indeed included some of the same

12. Theda Skocpol and John Ikenberry, "The Political Formation of the American Welfare
State in Historical and Comparative Perspective," *Comparative Social Research* 6 (1983): 87–
148. See also Theda Skocpol and Ann Shola Orloff, "Why Not Equal Protection? Explaining
the Politics of Public Social Spending in Britain, 1900–1911, and the United States, 1880s–
1920," *American Sociological Review* 49 (1984): 726–50.

13. Useful overviews of the intellectual history of these years include Edward A. Purcell, *The
Crisis of Democratic Theory: Scientific Naturalism and the Problem of Value* (Lexington: University of
Kentucky Press, 1973); Alan Wald, *The New York Intellectuals: The Rise and Decline of the Anti-
Stalinist Left from the 1930s to the 1980s* (Chapel Hill: University of North Carolina Press, 1987);
Robert Booth Fowler, *Believing Skeptics: American Political Intellectuals, 1945–1964* (Westport,
Conn.: Greenwood Press, 1978); Richard Pells, *The Liberal Mind in a Conservative Age: American
Intellectuals in the 1940s and 1950s* (New York: Harper and Row, 1985).

persons as—progressive history. As Edward Purcell has written, these political scientists and sociologists believed in the ultimately rational nature of the universe and thought that science could lead men to a full understanding of the social process and "an intelligent reordering of American institutions in a spirit of social harmony." Somewhat ironically, both their own work and the events of the 1930s and 1940s began to undermine these views. Empirical studies began to reveal "irrational" aspects of personality and behavior within the United States, and the rise of fascism and the onset of war seemed to confirm these findings outside of it. By the late thirties and through the war years, both intellectuals at large and social scientists within their disciplines turned toward a more "realistic" evaluation of both the possibilities of and need for "reform" in America.[14]

In his recent book *The Liberal Mind in a Conservative Age* Richard Pells has described aspects of the process by which liberal intellectuals writing in the 1950s consolidated this new view of American politics and society. Convinced that it was necessary to chasten the naivete, simplistic dualism, and rationalism of their predecessors, these intellectuals—including, of course, Hartz and Hofstadter, but also many others—attempted to invent a new liberalism that was based on a more realistic view of human nature in general and American society in particular. It would, therefore, be less likely to unleash a moralistic urge to fanaticism and more likely to recognize the remarkable degree of real social and political progress in the United States.[15]

Finding less conflict and more complexity in American society, these intellectuals argued that it was both the reality and the glory of American history that politics was based upon the voluntary group rather than the card-carrying party; ad hoc, cross-class, group political alliances rather than class alliances; and the pragmatic search for specific individual or group economic gains from politics rather than a moralistic call for the reconstruction of society itself. In this new liberal view of American politics, candidates were properly brokers, and parties agencies of mediation. The system as a whole was incremental, rather than totalistic, and inefficient, but it was less likely to destroy itself in pursuit of messianic goals. Like most of those who have written about the intellectual history of the postwar generation, Pells has abstracted these thinkers from currents in the disciplines within which many of them worked, and he has ignored the theoretical contributions of enormously influential social scientists who do not fit his definition of "intellectual." Therefore, the way that the social sciences operationalized these ideas is not altogether clear in his account.

Fortunately, Ricci's thoughtful book *The Tragedy of Political Science* provides a case study of this process in that discipline. His analysis is important because it emphasizes that the change in political science occurred not just in terms of its propositions about American politics but also in terms of its ways of defining social "science," theory, and method. The components of what he calls the "matrix" of liberal discourse were the redefinition of politics—both as practiced and as analyzed—from a matter of results to a matter of "method," the

14. Purcell, *Crisis*, 24.
15. Pells, *Liberal Mind*, 117–82.

redefinition of theory from "grand" to "behavioral" (or "middle range"), and the refocusing of political analysis from what should be to what is.[16]

Like their representatives in the broader intellectual stream political scientists in the postwar period were also worried about the extravagant claims of their prewar liberal predecessors. Whereas prewar political scientists believed that men could be the best judges of their own interests and, therefore, that responsible mass democratic government was both desirable and possible, postwar scholars developed the theory of elitist democracy on the basis of precisely the opposite propositions. Worldwide depression, fascism, and war underlined the "truth" that men were not necessarily the best judges of their interest, that only better trained and politically disciplined elites should participate in politics, and that politics should involve narrow and nonideological conflict. At its most ideological edge, this change of view shifted the agenda of political science from the question "how can American institutions be changed to facilitate democracy?" to "how do American institutions facilitate democracy?"

Among the discoveries of such analyses were those contending that many apparently nondemocratic aspects of American politics were functional for democracy. Thus, in these years, the positive aspects of inequality, apathy, declining voter participation, and the absence of political ideology were stressed: elites were more likely to support democracy, thus some inequality was beneficial; the ignorant were less likely to vote, thus declining participation was not all bad; agreement on the rules of the game was less likely to produce fanaticism than was argument over first political principles, thus the absence of such argument was a plus; and so on. In the writings of some political scientists, in short, everything that seemed manifestly dysfunctional to democracy to their predecessors was now determined to be latently functional.

THE REHABILITATION OF THE POLITICAL MACHINE

The changing status of the political machine in the literature of social science was a bellwether of this broader change. From the publication of Bryce's *American Commonwealth* in 1888 the machine had been the scourge of American politics and the reason that municipal government was the infamous "one conspicuous failure of the United States." For Bryce—who was president of the American Political Science Association in 1908—the master conflict in urban politics was between the rich, well educated, and the good on the one side, and the corrupt and ignorant on the other. In *The American Commonwealth* the machine linked together the venal and the pliable. The boss "sat like a spider, hidden in the midst of his web," with the power to dispense places, reward the loyal, and punish the mutinous because he was the best among the "knot" of

---

16. David M. Ricci, *The Tragedy of Political Science: Politics, Scholarship, and Democracy* (New Haven: Yale University Press, 1984), 99–208. Another powerful and important analysis of the postwar transformation of theories of politics is Michael P. Rogin's *The Intellectuals and McCarthy: The Radical Specter* (Cambridge: MIT Press, 1969).

political operators that "pulled the wires for the whole city," and thereby riveted their "yoke" upon it.[17]

This view of the political machine—which focused on its power and corruption in order to speed its removal—was characteristic of most writing on it by political scientists until its rehabilitation in E. Pendleton Herring's influential 1940 book *The Politics of Democracy*. Herring's book was essentially a paean to American political institutions and an antidote to what he called "the application of critical standards too high for human attainment" that tended to produce a sense of frustration and cynicism about American political institutions.[18]

Viewed against the threatening rise of totalitarianism, it was the reformer, not the politician—Herring minimized the use of the term boss—that was the problem. Reformers failed to understand the truth that men were not rational, but rather passionate and greedy. Because they were, a political "adjuster" was needed to stand for "relativity in the struggle of absolute values." Machine politicians performed the vital function of ensuring continuity and cohesion in an ethnically and economically divided community both by providing services and by maintaining a political moderation that avoided "the barricades of intransigence." Rather than deserving moral opprobrium, they merited more credit than they received. In his review of Herring's book, E. E. Schattschneider noted that "confronted with the prospect of losing our institutions, we look at them with new eyes." The transformation of the boss from moral scourge to human relations expert was certainly symptomatic of this attitude.[19]

A similar transformation was going on in sociology, where, as Robert Friedrichs has pointed out, a prewar reform-oriented focus on social institutions was replaced by a postwar focus on the functional necessities of the "social system." Again the changing status of the political machine reflects this transformation. For the "social engineers" of the early decades of the century, the machine was part of a vicious circle that could be broken by an informed electorate; for their critics in the fifties, its "latent functions" were critical to the urban "system."[20]

The reform view of the machine predominated when, in 1935, the distinguished sociologist F. Stuart Chapin undertook to systematize the institutional

17. James Bryce, *The American Commonwealth* (London: Macmillan, 1888), 2:75–76. For useful studies of this generation of political science, see also Bernard Crick *The American Science of Politics: Its Origins and Conditions* (Berkeley: University of California Press, 1959), 73–118, and Raymond Seidelman and Edward J. Harpham, *Disenchanted Realists: Political Science and the American Crisis, 1884–1984* (Albany: State University of New York Press, 1985), 60–158. David Hammack discusses the thought of this generation of urban analysts in "Problems in the Historical Study of Power in the Cities and Towns of the United States, 1860–1960," *American Historical Review* 83 (1978): 323–49.

18. E. Pendleton Herring, *The Politics of Democracy: American Parties in Action* (New York: W. W. Norton, 1940), x.

19. Ibid., 136; for brief accounts of the impact of this book see Purcell, *Crisis*, 190, and Ricci, *Tragedy*, 110–111. Schattschneider's review is quoted in Purcell.

20. Robert W. Friedrichs, *A Sociology of Sociology* (New York: Free Press, 1972), 11–56; For another discussion of this change, see Richard J. Bernstein, *The Restructuring of Social and Political Theory* (Philadelphia: University of Pennsylvania Press, 1976).

approach in sociology in his *Contemporary American Institutions: A Sociological Analysis*. For Chapin a sophisticated institutional approach to local government required consideration of not only the "legalistic" pattern of government reflected in law and charter but also the pattern of the less obvious "quasi-legal" world of the boss and the political party and the "extra-legal" world of patronage, bribe, and corruption. In his view, the need of political parties for funds, business for privileges, and criminals for protection led to a sinister link between these worlds. Understanding of the interlock between these institutions could lead to the breakage of this "vicious circle" by means of increased voter participation and the expansion and professionalization of public services.[21]

Robert K. Merton took precisely this set of institutional linkages, but reversed their moral charge in his classic analysis of the "latent functions" of the political machine which first appeared in 1949. The successive editions of *Social Theory and Social Structure* (in 1949, 1957, and 1968) played an enormous role in the redefinition of the social sciences in terms both of theory and of research agenda. Merton, as is well known, used the term *middle-range theory* to apply to that category of theory that lay between working hypotheses on the one hand, and unified systems theories on the other—in essence the same thing as behavioral theory in political science. Moreover, he made major contributions to such theory, popularizing the concepts of latent functions, reference groups, and locals and cosmopolitans, to mention only those that were to play an important role in the reconstruction of American political history.[22]

Merton offered his famous distinction between "manifest" and "latent" functions in an attempt both to codify and exemplify functionalist thought and to extol its advantages to the other social sciences. Such a distinction, he said, clarified the analysis of seemingly irrational social patterns and directed attention to theoretically fruitful fields of inquiry. It also precluded "the substitution of naive moral judgments for sociological analysis," and in this way the distinction also tied him tightly to the overall intellectual and political mission of his generation, which was, as we have seen, the replacement of "naive" reformism with "realistic" science.[23]

Indeed, as Alan Ryan has pointed out, like other members of his intellectual generation, Merton was "impressed with the unlooked for goodness of the consequences of much social life in America." According to Ryan, the only reason for using the term *latent function* was to emphasize that "the good results he is looking at are not those which gratify the actors, but those that gratify

21. F. Stuart Chapin, *Contemporary American Institutions: A Sociological Analysis* (New York: Harper Brothers, 1935), 27–48.

22. In spite of—perhaps because of?—his influence in the construction of recent American social science, Merton's work has been very little evaluated. See Robert Bierstadt, *American Sociological Theory: A Critical History* (New York: Academic Press, 1981), 443–89; and Piotr Sztompka, *Robert K. Merton: An Intellectual Profile* (London: Macmillan, 1986). Merton, *Social Theory and Social Structure: Toward the Codification of Theory and Research* (Glencoe, Ill.: Free Press, 1949).

23. Merton, *Social Theory*, 61–81.

other people." But this equation of "function" with "good consequence" had a deleterious effect on the sociology of this period, when "articles on such topics as 'Some Social Functions of Ignorance' turn out to be articles on 'Some Unthought of Good Effects that Ignorance Produces for almost Everyone.' "[24]

In this spirit Merton opened his analysis of the functions of the political machine with a critique of his predecessors' moralistic approaches to it, which did not, in fact, explain its vitality so much as hope for its extinction. According to Merton, the recognition that, in spite of its apparently manifest corruption, the machine was satisfying basic latent functions was the beginning of a scientific analysis of the phenomenon. In fact, he argued, the machine historically had fulfilled such functions, including the organization of power in an atmosphere in which political authority was legally fragmented, the humanizing and personalizing of assistance to what Merton called the "deprived classes," the provision of a route of social mobility for those with limited opportunities elsewhere, and the provision of political privileges to business which stabilized the economic situation. Failure to recognize such functions led reformers to indulge in "social ritual rather than social engineering."[25]

IMPORTS AND EXPORTS

For a generation of historians who were, as Richard Hofstadter was to write in 1955, "far more conscious of those things they would like to preserve than they are of those things they would like to change," Merton's apparently scientific assault on the moralism of prewar reform was a useful tool in the construction of a usable past for New Deal-style liberalism. Therefore, the classic accounts of urban politics in Oscar Handlin's 1951 book *The Uprooted* and Hofstadter's 1955 book *The Age of Reform* imported these conceptions into history. It was these conceptions that were exported into political science to bolster the opinions of Herring which underlay the accounts of machine politics written in the early 1960s by Theodore Lowi and Edward C. Banfield and James Q. Wilson.[26]

For Handlin the urban machines were the crucial link in the immigrants' political acculturation. The boss had usually arisen from among the immigrants and "remained one with them," championing the little man against the big and seeing to ward and neighborhood issues, such as housing and employment, that affected the immigrants' day-to-day existence. For Hofstadter, who based his account of machine politics entirely on Handlin, the easygoing and pragmatic boss understood the immigrant's desire for concrete personal gains from political participation because he worked within a political ethos which

24. Alan Ryan, *The Philosophy of the Social Sciences* (London: Macmillan, 1970), 189–90.

25. Merton, *Social Theory*, 73. Merton noted there that he took his understanding of these functions from Chapin. I have discussed Merton's theory of latent functions and its effects on American urban political history in more detail in Terrence J. McDonald, "The Problem of the Political in Recent American Urban History: Liberal Pluralism and the Rise of Functionalism," *Social History* 10 (1985): 323–45.

26. Richard Hofstadter, *The Age of Reform: From Bryan to FDR* (New York: Vintage, 1955), 14; Oscar Handlin, *The Uprooted* (New York: Grosset and Dunlap, 1951).

sprang from the "urgent needs [of the immigrants] that so often grew out of their migration." For both historians, the focus of reformers on the alleged corruption and fiscal extravagance of the bosses was misplaced "moralism." More important was the fact that through the functions they fulfilled, the bosses placed human needs above "inherited notions and inhibitions," and in so doing, according to Handlin, they prevented socialism and radicalism from taking root among the immigrants.[27]

It was no coincidence, of course, that these bosses looked a lot like Franklin D. Roosevelt. Merton himself had exemplified the way the machine "humanized and personalized" aid to the needy with a footnote referring to a story about Harry Hopkins's work under Roosevelt. Handlin argued that it was the machine that "opened to the immigrants the prospect that the state might be the means through which the beginnings of security could come," although it was not until the New Deal that immigrants were no longer "divided by the necessity of choosing between their own machines and reform," because by then reform had changed so that it could "swallow up their machines, bosses and all." Hofstadter's admiration of the boss's "pragmatic talents" was paralleled in his praise of FDR's opportunistic virtuosity and the ability of the New Deal to put human needs above "inherited notions." Like the machines the New Deal avoided moralism and simply went about the business of dealing pragmatically with politics and society as it found them. Meanwhile, the opponents of the New Deal shared with the opponents of the political machine an inability to accept the changes in their status brought about by industrialization, immigration, and urbanization, and their political movements were, in fact, "moralistic binges."[28]

The description of machine and reform "political style" presented by Theodore Lowi in his 1964 book At the Pleasure of the Mayor was based entirely on the categories of Handlin and Hofstadter, as was that in City Politics, published by Edward C. Banfield and James Q. Wilson in 1965. Banfield and Wilson turned the "political ethos" argument on its head by approving of the "middle-class" ethos that Hofstadter and Handlin scorned. They did not follow this with a condemnation of the machine, however, because of their concern for the machine's centralization of urban authority. Whatever its ethical faults, they argued, the machine was apparently able to overcome the decentralization of urban political authority that blocked the undertaking of public projects. For this reason, it was never to be compared to "ideal" alternatives, and, in some instances, it was preferable to any alternative likely to appear on the urban political scene. Lowi argued somewhat similarly that an "honest" machine that centralized authority for the public good might be the solution to the crisis of urban government.[29]

---

27. Handlin, *Uprooted*, 210–13, 226; Hofstadter, *The Age*, 183, 9, 316. Cf. McDonald, "The Problem of the Political," 331–33.

28. Merton, *Social Theory*, 372n97; Handlin, *Uprooted*, 226; Hofstadter, *Age*, 5–22.

29. Theodore Lowi, *At the Pleasure of the Mayor: Patronage and Power in New York City, 1898–1958* (Glencoe, Ill.: Free Press, 1964), 179–80; Edward C. Banfield and James Q. Wilson, *City*

SOCIAL SCIENCE HISTORY AND THE REVIVAL OF ETHNICITY

For the first generation of postwar brokers between history and the social sciences like Handlin and Hofstadter, the social sciences were a grab bag into which historians could reach for ideas without necessarily transforming the discipline itself. Although both were open to the instruction of the social sciences, they were not convinced that history should become one. Moreover, both were more deeply involved in the reconstruction of American history along the lines of the new liberalism than in the reconstitution of history as a social science.

For the first generation of their more social scientific successors, however, like Lee Benson and Samuel P. Hays, the goal was to use the social sciences to transform history itself, to develop a "social scientific" history that focused on the structure of social and political behavior and avoided the focus on "episode and ideology" in the naive political narratives of their predecessors. For the most part, these historians were oblivious to the politics of either "empirical social science" itself or the specific middle-range frameworks they borrowed. Benson turned to Merton's theory of reference groups as a way of understanding how there could be any meaningful political conflict in an economically consensual society; Hays inserted Merton's conception of "locals and cosmopolitans" into a modernization framework as a way of explaining the change in consciousness brought about by the modernizing thrust of American social development.

For Benson and Hays the work of the generation of Handlin and Hofstadter was both insufficiently "scientific" and, for Hays at least, too closely tied to the "liberal" interpretation of American politics. Both argued that political history was episodic and too little concerned with the "structure" of political behavior over time or across space. Both also felt that this focus on "episode and ideology" turned American history into what Benson referred to as a "Hobbesian" world in which every historian worked for himself and there was little hope for the development of a properly "professional" (read scientific) community that could produce cumulative empirical results. Their turn to the "empirical" social sciences for a model of professional reorganization was, therefore, predictable and, on the whole, beneficial, if somewhat naive. But both their historiographical indebtedness to their predecessors and their selection of models and ideas from the social sciences kept their revolution from being more than "halfway."[30]

Politics (Cambridge: Harvard University Press, 1965), 126. The influence of these authors on the conception of urban politics among political scientists has been powerful. One prominent political scientist who has resisted aspects of the machine framework is Paul E. Peterson. See Peterson, *The Politics of School Reform, 1870–1940* (Chicago: University of Chicago Press, 1985).

30. Their programmatic statements—essays written in the period from the late fifties through the sixties, for the most part—are collected in Benson, *Toward the Scientific Study of History* (Philadelphia: University of Pennsylvania Press, 1972), and Hays, *American Political History as Social Analysis* (Knoxville: University of Tennessee Press, 1980). Benson's social

Benson, for example, predicated his well-known work *The Concept of Jacksonian Democracy* on the search for the bases of political conflict in a society lacking fundamental economic conflict. This work, which is rightly perceived as one of the founding texts of the "ethnocultural" interpretation of American political history, is often wrongly remembered as a "test" of the relative ability of class and ethnicity to explain political behavior. In fact, Benson defined the former out of his inquiry, declaring this work to be an extension of "the complementary theses" of consensus presented by Hartz and Hofstadter. According to Benson, Hofstadter had "enlarged and sharpened our vision" with the insight that no significant group had challenged the legitimacy of a capitalist system of political economy in the United States and Hartz had revealed the same about political theory.[31]

In spite of this agreement on some fundamentals, Benson argued, conflict could and did occur in the series of stages best illuminated by Merton's theory of reference groups: ethnocultural "issues" like temperance or sabbatarianism created groups, groups became reference points (either positive or negative), reference points became continuing political roles. This view, according to Benson, was superior to that which held that disagreements arose from "the simultaneous existence of different stages of society" or "clashing economic interests." As he was later to explain, "cultural attributes have much greater potential than economic attributes to function as the basis of social groups . . . [because they] tend strongly to function as the *primary* reference groups that men 'naturally' turn to when they engage in the myriad types of conflict endemic in the capitalist epoch."[32]

This argument, too, however, was influenced to a great extent by the theoretical framework within which it was framed. Benson's turn to Merton was a turn, as others have noted, to an essentially voluntaristic theory of action, a nonstructural theory of group formation, and a system in which the role of power was relatively underdeveloped. Merton's theory of reference groups was based upon the theory of relative deprivation and contended that attitudes and action were more influenced by the groups with which one identified—positively or negatively—than by one's social structural situation. As Piotr Sztompka has pointed out, what is important in this theory is "clearly the idea of reference (i.e., relativisation), and not the idea of group." In fact, it is not completely clear in Merton's account what a group is or from where groups come. Merton's theory was well matched with Benson's assumption that there were no funda-

---

scientific mentor was Paul Lazarsfeld; Hays reports he was most influenced by Merton. Both Lazarsfeld and Merton were at the famous Department of Sociology at Columbia in these years.

31. Lee Benson, *The Concept of Jacksonian Democracy: New York as a Test Case* (Princeton: Princeton University Press, 1961), 272–73.

32. Ibid., 276, 281; Benson, "Marx's General and Middle Range Theories of Social Conflict," in Robert K. Merton, James S. Coleman, and Peter H. Rossi, eds., *Qualitative and Quantitative Social Research: Papers in Honor of Paul F. Lazarsfeld* (New York: Free Press, 1979), 189–209. Merton's essays on reference groups were included in the 1957 edition of *Social Theory and Social Structure*, 225–387.

mental economic structural differences in American society. But this framework did not, could not, permit a test of the relative political salience of class
and ethnicity.[33]

Reflecting his interest in social history, Hays's work was more social "structural" than that of Benson. Moreover, Hays blasted the work of Hofstadter for
its emphasis on the role of the middle class in urban reform and its reliance on
the analysis of middle-class ideology in its theory of progressivism. Structurally
generated struggles for power were the centerpiece of the works of Hays and
the reason for his popularity among those who attacked consensus history.[34]

As I have written elsewhere, however, the cutting edge of Hays's work was
dulled by its definition of *structure* in essentially structural-functional terms. In
a 1965 essay on the social analysis of American political history, Hays called for
attention to the "systematizing and organizing processes inherent in industrial-
ism as the dynamic force in social change in modern life" and the structure of
relationships—between "locals and cosmopolitans"—which those processes
generated. More than just these terms were borrowed from Merton, however;
so also was Merton's explanation of the "relative proportions" of locals and
cosmopolitans in different communities as resulting from "characteristic forms
of environing social structure with their distinctive functional requirements."[35]

By 1974, in Hays's essay on the political structure of the American city, this
structuring process had blossomed into a "constant tension between forces
making for decentralization and forces making for centralization in human
relations and institutions," and a political system "shaped and reshaped" according to the "inner dynamic" of the changing economic and social order. If in
Benson politics was detached from structure, in Hays politics was overwhelmed
by it; "structures" and "processes" generated reified worldviews that took the
place of conflicting political actors.[36]

The successors to Benson and Hays in the new political history, including
most prominently Paul Kleppner and Richard Jensen, extended both the
historical claims and the empirical reach of ethnocultural political history,
arguing flatly that "partisan affiliations were not rooted in economic class
distinction," and "religion was the fundamental source of political conflict in
the Midwest." But as Jensen himself has written, the theoretical framework
within which these authors worked was essentially a functionalist one. Their
question was what was the function of politics in nineteenth-century America.
Assuming, like the founders of the field, that it was not to advance economic
interests, they argued that it was to solidify those that were "cultural."[37]

33. Sztompka, *Merton*, 230; Bierstadt, *Theory*, 443–89.

34. Hays's criticism of Hofstadter is in "The Politics of Reform in Municipal Government in
the Progressive Era," *Pacific Northwest Quarterly* 55 (1964): 157–69.

35. Hays, "The Social Analysis of American Political History, 1880–1920," *Political Science
Quarterly* 80 (1965): 373–94. Merton's essay on local and cosmopolitan influentials was also
included in the 1957 edition of *Social Theory and Social Structure*. I have considered Hays's use
of these categories in more detail in McDonald, "The Problem of the Political," 339–342.

36. Hays, "The Changing Political Structure of the City in Industrial America," *Journal of
Urban History* 1 (1974): 1–32.

37. Richard Jensen, *The Winning of the Midwest: Social and Political Conflict, 1888–1896*
(Chicago: University of Chicago Press, 1971), 58; Paul Kleppner, *The Cross of Culture: A Social*

Moreover, within this framework even apparently economic issues, such as the tariff, were viewed as really only culturally symbolic—flags, as it were, so that voters motivated primarily by local ethnocultural issues knew for which party to vote. The reinterpretation of "economic" issues as "cultural" was important to this framework because, as Richard L. McCormick has pointed out, only a small fraction of public policy in the nineteenth century involved distinctively ethnocultural issues; the majority of public policy-making involved clearly economic issues.[38]

The possibility that these issues have been wrongly interpreted as cultural is raised by a series of penetrating essays on the methodology of these—and other—works in the ethnocultural political school by J. Morgan Kousser and Allan J. Lichtman which have undermined their quantitative infrastructure. In essence, these authors contend that the ethnocultural historians either have not conducted the multivariate tests of ethnicity and class that they claim to have done or have not conducted them properly. Historians who have seen these critiques as so much hair-splitting among quantitative historians—for whom they feel little sympathy in any event—not only misunderstand the gravity of the criticism but belie their own commitment to historical "facts," as well as the ethnocultural historians' often repeated claim to social scientific status.[39]

THE PERSISTENCE OF PLURALISM IN THE NEW SOCIAL HISTORY

The construction of a social analysis of politics by Benson and Hays was contemporaneously accompanied by a broader turn to social history by the so-called new urban historians beginning with Stephan Thernstrom. These analysts focused primarily on "society"—actually social mobility—rather than politics, and employed the community study as both object and method. The implicit and explicit theory of these studies was pluralist; pluralism both rationalized their separation of politics and society and explained the—usually poorly examined—links between social and political mobility.

Because of its role in the community power debates of the 1960s, pluralist theory is often thought of as primarily a set of statements about "who governs" in contemporary America. In the work of Robert Dahl it was this, of course, but

Analysis of Midwestern Politics, 1850–1900 (New York: Free Press, 1970), 35. Richard Jensen, "Historiography of American Political History," in Jack P. Greene, ed., *Encyclopedia of American Political History* (New York: Scribners, 1984), 1:1–25

38. Richard L. McCormick has made this point in a thoughtful review of this literature, "Ethnocultural Interpretations of Nineteenth-Century American Voting Behavior," in McCormick, *The Party Period and Public Policy: American Politics from the Age of Jackson to the Progressive Era* (New York: Oxford University Press, 1986), 29–63.

39. These critiques include J. Morgan Kousser, "The 'New Political History': A Methodological Critique," *Reviews in American History* 4 (1976): 1–14; Kousser and Allan J. Lichtman, "'New Political History': Some Statistical Questions Answered," *Social Science History* 7 (1983): 321–44; Lichtman, "Political Realignment and 'Ethnocultural' Voting in Late Nineteenth Century America," *Journal of Social History* 16 (1983): 55–82; Kousser, "Voters Absent and Present," *Social Science History* 9 (1985): 215–27.

also much more. It was a dynamic and historical theory of politics, which attempted to explain the relationship between political ideology and institutions, economic and political development, individual mobility and political consciousness, and, ultimately, "society" and the "state."[40]

In his *Preface to Democratic Theory*, published in 1956, Dahl laid down a fundamental principle of his work—and his generation—in the argument that institutions like the Constitution were less important guarantors of American democracy than the widespread consensus that underlay them. "Prior to politics, beneath it, enveloping it, restricting it, conditioning it, is the underlying consensus on policy that usually exists in the society among a predominant portion of the politically active members." Acting on this belief, Dahl embarked upon the construction of what today would be regarded as a society-centered theory of politics to explain the role and reproduction of this consensus in his more widely read 1961 book, *Who Governs?*[41]

The famous "Book I: From Oligarchy to Pluralism" in Dahl's *Who Governs?* presented a sophisticated, apparently empirical, resolutely behavioral, and easily generalizable theory of the development of American local politics that was to have an enormous impact on historians. At a high level of generality, Dahl argued that in the eighteenth and early nineteenth centuries New Haven—and by invited extension, American communities everywhere—had been ruled by interlocked socioeconomic, political, and at times religious elites. The effects, however, of large-scale social changes like industrialization, immigration, and population growth were to destroy the socioeconomic basis of this elite by creating new sources of economic power, generating greater social complexity, and permitting population growth. All these changes multiplied the bases of political power and, thereby, the number of political elites. As society became a mosaic of groups, the rational approach to politics was one rooted in political conflict among self-interested groups—or their leaders—whose goals were short term, pragmatic, negotiable, and capable of being fulfilled within the existing framework of social and political institutions of American society. Agreement on these conditions formed a consensus on the rules of the game, and competition among the many groups maintained a rough political equilibrium.[42]

This socioeconomically driven shift from "cumulative" to "dispersed" inequality in American society was facilitated by the expansion of the state produced by a linkage between political integration and social mobility. In New

40. Again, volumes have been written about pluralism but much less on Dahl himself, who was, arguably, the political scientist most read by historians of this generation. Edward Purcell considers him to be "perhaps the most influential and persuasive advocate of a more realistic democratic theory" (Purcell, *Crisis*, 260.)

41. Robert A. Dahl, *A Preface to Democratic Theory* (Chicago: University of Chicago Press, 1956), 132.

42. Robert A. Dahl, *Who Governs? Democracy and Power in an American City* (New Haven: Yale University Press, 1961). These arguments are not original with Dahl or restricted to his work. But they were presented in a way that had particular appeal for historians because it was both historical and, apparently, empirical.

Haven, new socioeconomic groups—especially ethnic groups—entered society at the bottom and experienced an initial period when their "proletarian" status prevented them from engaging in political activity. But as members of the group began to achieve lower-middle-class economic status and therefore had the leisure to work in politics, they began to experience political mobility as well; as more members of the group became active, the public sector grew in response to their needs through a patronage-based process similar to the latent functions described by Merton.

This was not, however, the only similarity to Merton's analysis. Another, and equally important, was Dahl's theory of psychological mobility. For Dahl, to begin with, there was "no distinctive working class outlook that could be formed into an ideology and program different from that already expressed in middle class ideals." This was because of the social mobility process, in which "each generation of workers was enormously more prosperous than its parents in a seemingly endless expansion of gains." Even if there had been such an outlook, of course, the process of ethnic mobility outlined above would have undercut it. Ethnics entered as "proletarians"—thereby fragmenting class— but soon moved up the class ladder in his three-stage explanation of political assimilation which ended when the ethnics "have middle class ideas, adopt a middle class style of life, . . . and look to others in the middling strata for friends, associates, marriage partners." Or, in other words, both workers as workers and workers as ethnics had middle-class reference groups.[43]

In Stephan Thernstrom's classic 1964 book, *Poverty and Progress: Social Mobility in a Nineteenth Century City*, the relationship between politics and social structure was mediated so explicitly by Dahl's theory that the book made a powerful political statement almost in spite of its location in the new *social* history. Ostensibly an analysis of the life chances of immigrant laborers in nineteenth-century Newburyport, Massachusetts, Thernstrom's book was also a test of the rags-to-riches thesis in American history. Its argument that the range of occupational mobility was distinctly narrower than the conventional framework suggested was delivered as a criticism of the "consensus" assumption of ever increasing abundance. Its claim, however, that a "mobility ideology" was widespread in American society and its linkage of social mobility and political integration—a linkage taken directly from Dahl—turned it into the social historical equivalent of Dahl himself.[44]

It cannot be said that without Dahl there would have been no Thernstrom because the book was deeply influenced by the work of Handlin, who was Thernstrom's adviser. Handlin had long been concerned with the impact of mobility on social integration, and, as Ian Tyrell has pointed out, his books were organized around the question of how society can be reintegrated after it

43. Ibid., 30, 35.

44. Stephan Thernstrom, *Poverty and Progress: Social Mobility in a Nineteenth Century City* (Cambridge: Harvard University Press, 1964). This analysis of the political framework of Thernstrom's book helps clarify a point on which there has been much confusion among historians: how a work of avowedly "history from the bottom up" could have such consensual implications.

is decomposed by mobility or rapid social change. The fact that the narrative structure of Thernstrom's book, therefore, goes from an integrated Federalist Newburyport, disruption through industrialization, population growth, and immigration, to a final stage of social and political reintegration is attributable, in part, to Handlin's influence.[45]

This framework, however, not only recapitulated that of Dahl's from a New Haven ruled by the "Patricians" to one ruled by the "Ex-plebes"—as Thernstrom fully acknowledges in his footnotes—but also made a very similar connection between social and political mobility. Following Hofstadter and Hartz explicitly, Thernstrom argued that in Newburyport—as in Dahl's New Haven—party politics were consensus politics to begin with because of the relative absence of conflict over social and economic policy. As in New Haven, the interlocking elite of Federalist Newburyport was smashed by industrialization and immigration and replaced with a variety of overlapping voluntary groups. As in New Haven, the local political arena was "open to ambitious [immigrant] men of talent" and the Irish-born who rose in politics were "precisely those who had risen dramatically in the occupational and property spheres"—the "entrepreneurs" in Dahl's scheme. And just as important, Thernstrom believed he had found the "social roots of consensus politics" in what he called the "mobility ideology." Even at the bottom of the class ladder there were abundant opportunities for modest self-advancement, and, therefore, "Horatio Alger was a primary symbol of the American political tradition." Consensus politics in Newburyport was based on the genuine absence of "the desperate economic grievances and the rigid social barriers which fed the class-based parties . . . of the old world."[46]

Thernstrom thought he had discovered the social correlate of Dahl's "democratic creed" in his notion of the "mobility ideology." In fact the process was the opposite; Thernstrom worked from Dahl's conception of consensus as articulated in *Who Governs?* in 1961 to construct both the social function and political implications of the mobility ideology in 1964.

PLURALIST NEO-MARXISTS

Under the influence of the British Marxist labor historians like E. P. Thompson, American social historians after Thernstrom transformed the study of mobility into the study of class formation. In so doing, they demonstrated that the mobility ideology was an inadequate description of the ideology of the American working class just as the process of mobility in no way captured the entire experience of capitalist industrialization.[47]

In effect, in response to the pluralist separation of economy and polity the historians of the working class rejoined these spheres by politicizing production, arguing effectively that the "economic" is "political" in the sense that the relations of production produce with them certain relations of domination and ideological justifications for that domination. Their careful reconstructions of

45. Tyrell, *The Absent Marx*, 102–03.
46. Thernstrom, *Poverty and Progress*, 181–82; 271n41.
47. E. P. Thompson, *The Making of the English Working Class* (New York: Vintage, 1966).

the patterns of work and their detailed exegesis of a wide variety of sources for understanding working-class culture revealed the interweaving of economics, politics, and ideology in the sphere of production. Similar attention was not, however, lavished on the workings of politics; in many of these studies, in fact, politics was a crucial but residual category explained in recognizably pluralist terms.

This pattern was set in one of the first direct responses to the work of Thernstrom, Alan Dawley's *Class and Community: The Industrial Revolution in Lynn*, which was published in 1976. By means of the techniques described above, Dawley successfully challenged the understanding of class, mobility, and ideology characteristic of the social historical mobility studies since Thernstrom. In his brief analysis of politics, however, which lacked entirely the care and subtlety of his analysis of production, he "discovered" what he called the "same process" in Lynn as Dahl had described in New Haven. In Lynn "local politics provided a convincing demonstration to wage earners that men from their own ranks could rise to the highest position in honor in their community," and this reinforced the ideological legitimacy of the political system while, at the same time, "pork-barrel temptations" lured most working-class voters away from a workingmen's party and back to the two regular parties. In his view, contrary to Thernstrom, Horatio Alger was out: "every mass action, every collective expression of opinion identifies Horatio Alger as an outcast in the minds of Lynn workers. Electoral politics, not faith in occupational success or property ownership, was the main safety valve of working class discontent." Ironically, however, the ballot box was, in Dawley's now famous phrase, "the coffin of class consciousness" because Robert Dahl had said it was.[48]

This "new" framework for the understanding of class and politics was to be repeated in many studies influenced by Dawley's. For example, Daniel Walkowitz's *Worker City, Company Town* found that "the dominant liberal social and political ideology of progress undermined labor's class consciousness, while social mobility and the political process both provided experiences that confirmed that ideology." In Troy, New York, class and ethnicity reinforced each other among the Irish in the 1850s and 1860s, but by the 1880s an Irish bourgeoisie and political machine emerged. Irish politicians—still an important symbol of immigrant mobility, success, and power—"circumscribed class politics." In Susan Hirsch's study of antebellum Newark, *Roots of the American Working Class*, the first generation of workers used politics as an arena for cultural conflict, and, thereafter, increased immigration blocked the development of class politics by extending the hold of ethnic politics. "The urban political machine organized immigrant working class voters into ethnic blocks, socializing them to an American politics that gave them symbolic achievements . . . as well as personal aid."[49]

48. Alan Dawley, *Class and Community: The Industrial Revolution in Lynn* (Cambridge: Harvard University Press, 1976), 219. For Dawley's use of Dahl, see 293n6.

49. Daniel Walkowitz, *Worker City, Company Town: Iron and Cotton Worker Protest in Troy and Cohoes, New York, 1855–84* (Urbana: University of Illinois Press, 1978), 253–55; Susan Hirsch, *Roots of the American Working Class: The Industrialization of Crafts in Newark, 1800–1860* (Philadelphia: University of Pennsylvania Press, 1978), 109–31.

These neo-Marxist community studies—and others like them—ended with pluralist understanding of politics for reasons having to do both with Marxian theory and their own historical practice. As Erik Wright, among others, has pointed out, the understanding of "the political" in Marxian theory was not one of its most fruitful formulations. Politics entered Marxist analysis primarily in two ways: in the moment at which and process by which a class shifted from its purely economic existence "in itself" to its political existence "for itself," and in the political institution that was essential for reproducing the structure of capitalist economic relations. In crude hands the process of class formation was completely teleological, and the pattern of state action, wholly instrumental; as late as 1977 Ralph Miliband complained about both of these problems in the Marxian theory of democratic politics.[50]

This theoretical problem was compounded by both the amount and the type of attention these studies devoted to politics. Because the focus of all of them was on class formation, not political formation, politics was invariably considered in a seemingly obligatory, but always brief and inadequate single chapter. Moreover, the analytical style of the chapters on politics was remarkably different from those dealing with class. Whereas the latter were usually structural, quantitative, and detailed, the "analysis" of politics resorted to the "old" political history with a vengeance: a narration of personalities, intrigue, and manipulation with barely a nod to systematic analysis of the behavior of the electorate or the polity itself. This tendency has been carried to an extreme in Sean Wilentz's widely praised new book on the formation of the New York City working class. There the politics of the Workingmen's parties are rendered in loving detail, while the representatives of the "regular" parties lurk in the background only as shadowy opportunists and manipulators.[51]

Ironically, in all these studies this barely analyzed, essentially residual, and traditionally related category then becomes the most compelling reason for the failure of class consciousness to move from the shop floor to the ballot box or beyond. Lacking a well-developed alternative, the connection between economy and polity is, as we have seen, made by means of a jury-rigged version of Dahl's framework. Dahl's theory was, after all, "base" driven—the shift from cumulative to dispersed inequalities was brought about in large part by socioeconomic change—and it maintained that political interests were generated outside the political arena and then brought into it where they were disciplined, perhaps combined, and adjudicated. The simple addition of an instrumental theory of the state and a hegemonic interpretation of consensus allowed its transformation.[52]

50. Erik O. Wright, "The Status of the Political in the Concept of Class Structure," *Politics and Society* 11 (1982), 321–341; Ralph Miliband, *Marxism and Politics* (New York: Oxford University Press, 1977).

51. Sean Wilentz, *Chants Democratic: New York and the Rise of the American Working Class, 1788–1850* (New York: Oxford University Press, 1984).

52. For a useful consideration of the problems of such conflation of theories, see Robert R. Alford and Roger Friedland, *Powers of Theory: Capitalism, the State, and Democracy* (Cambridge: Cambridge University Press, 1985).

TAKING POLITICS SERIOUSLY

Theda Skocpol, among others, has noted the important ways in which pluralist, functionalist, and Marxist theories parallel one another in their "society-centeredness." In each of these frameworks—which, of course, overlap and interact—politics and the state are constituted by, rather than constitutive of, society. At one level, therefore, the construction of a conception of American politics emphasizing ethnicity, patronage, and machines represents only this tendency toward the subsumption of the state by society in the social sciences since World War II. Recognition that states are "weighty actors" with their "own" histories may in due course correct this problem.[53]

This essay has tried to point out, however, that the problem is more complicated than that. Across the social sciences the effort to use historical and institutional means to "bring the state back in" is contaminated by the conceptual residues of a particular moment in American history when the identities of and connections among social science, history, liberalism, and the state were redefined. It is said that hegemony is accomplished when the views of one class become the "common sense" of another. Few would deny that it is just common sense that American urban politics involves ethnicity, patronage, and machines.

Of course, no one would argue that either ethnicity or patronage was irrelevant to nineteenth-century American politics, nor would anyone claim that there were no political machines. The question is whether or not these foci enrich or impoverish the conception of the state at the subnational level. A brief review of the contributions and limitations of the literatures we have considered here demonstrates the ways in which they interact to narrow the consideration of the state.

The contribution of the ethnocultural political literature has been the rediscovery of the breadth and significance of political participation in nineteenth-century America. The problem of this work has been its failure to connect participation and policy formation; its reduction of politics to cultural symbolism has produced a state that does not act to produce an authoritative allocation of resources or play an active role in the economic constitution or transformation of society.[54]

The contribution of the neo-Marxist community studies has been the reintroduction into American history of class and conflict as social and political realities. Moreover, this work suggests that political economic issues—from the control of police to the maintenance of common lands—were of great importance. However, acceptance of a view of the state as primarily an arena of symbolism, ideological manipulation, or pure and simple pork-barrelism has led this literature to a sort of imperialistic economism in which the process of

---

53. Skocpol has made these points in various places; see "Political Response to Capitalist Crisis: Neo-Marxist Theories of the State and the Case of the New Deal," *Politics and Society* 10 (1980): 199–200; and Skocpol, "Bringing the State Back In: Strategies of Analysis in Current Research," in *Bringing*, 4–6.

54. McCormick, *Party Period*, 55–63.

production has been the *only* or at least the most important location for the production of political ideology. This has led these historians either to ignore or to trivialize the power of political ideology to shape social and economic ideologies.[55]

The contribution of the historically oriented political scientists like Katznelson, Shefter, and Bridges has been a shift from the social to the political roles of machine politics; from machines as uncritical respondents to needs of the urban masses to political organizations with their own imperatives. The problem of this literature is the centrality and inevitability of machine politics itself, the assumption that the machines are the key to American political development.

Taken together, these approaches shrink the state. Taking politics seriously requires its expansion, the recognition of the manifold ways in which politics helped to constitute nineteenth-century American society. The legislative and judicial branches at the state and local levels of the American system were fundamentally and continuously involved in the definition and redefinition of *public* and *private* in terms of property, interests, and realms of action, and those activities were continuously salient politically.

In its everyday actions the state was continuously conferring privileges and creating—or extracting—resources and thereby constituting conflicting political actors and their ideological representations of their actions. Both these actions and the role of the state itself were enormously controversial. By doing some damage to the subtleties of their thought, one can range nineteenth-century state ideology on a continuum from Federalists, Whigs, and Mugwump Republicans on the one hand to the Jeffersonian Republicans and Jacksonian and Bourbon Democrats on the other. For the former, an active state was a guarantor of stability, economic development, and, ultimately, social harmony. For the latter, it presaged corruption and the disruption of a natural social harmony as well as the domination of those favored by political-economic privileges over those without those privileges. Ironically, whatever other socioeconomic changes were to transpire in nineteenth-century America, these ideological poles in the debate over the role of the state would persist.[56]

Furthermore, positions on the state and political democracy were linked unpredictably. Throughout the nineteenth century, those who professed to place their faith in "the People" objected to the expanding state, whereas those who tended toward political elitism lauded such expansion. Whigs before the Civil War and Mugwumps afterward favored an expanding state but limited suffrage; pre–Civil War Jacksonian Democrats and post–Civil War Bourbon Democrats favored mass political mobilization and a small state. Those, therefore, whom one might have expected to expand the state purely for patronage

55. For a useful survey of the issues these studies raise for political history, see Richard L. McCormick, "The Social Analysis of American Political History—After Twenty Years," in McCormick, *Party Period*, 89–140.

56. For general surveys of these issues, see, among others, M. J. Heale, *The Making of American Politics 1750–1850* (London: Longman, 1977), and Morton Keller, *Affairs of State: Public Life in Late Nineteenth Century America* (Cambridge: Harvard University Press, 1977).

reasons did not necessarily do so on ideological grounds, and those who favored expanding the state objected to political patronage beyond a certain level.

In the course of these battles, the "agrarians" and "aristocrats," "producers" and "drones," "people" and "monopolists" were groups whose material reality and ideological status were created in and by the state. Only by ignoring political ideology can labor historians contend that the producer ideology emerged at the point of production to become the language of class in America. In fact this ideology emerged out of *political* combat and was appropriated by working-class organizations. Its origin explains its ability simultaneously to facilitate and obstruct radical action. Moreover, it is in part for this reason that labor historians have avoided detailed comparisons of "labor" and "party" ideology: they contain many of the same ideas.[57]

Against this background of contentious state action, battles over the so-called ethnocultural issues—the enforcement of temperance, sabbatarianism, and so on—were also battles over the extension—or retention—of state authority over society. Moreover, the political alignments on these issues were similar to those on others; Whigs and Republicans favored state action on ethnocultural issues and in other areas; Democrats opposed the former and campaigned actively for retrenchment at both local and state levels. Ethnocultural political alignments were not necessarily, therefore, just symbolically expressive; they were also linked to prior positions on economically related activities of the state.

In fact, the post–Civil War political era at the state and local levels opened with assaults on the activities of the prewar and wartime state in the public debt limitation campaigns conducted in state after state following the war. When the 1880 census surveyed these limitations on the state and local public sector for the first time, it found that fifteen of the thirty-eight states had added debt restriction provisions to their constitutions, and three others had authorized legislatures to do so. Twenty-four of the thirty-eight states had restricted the right of cities to invest in railways; twenty-five barred them from investing in private corporations. All but three of the constitutional debt ceilings were adopted before 1877, indicating that they were not just responses to the panic of the mid-1870s but had to do with more deep-seated reactions to state economic and fiscal activities. Historians have, for the most part, ignored these movements, in spite of their rich potential for revealing the sense of the state in these years.[58]

57. Studies emphasizing party ideology include, among others, John Ashworth, *'Agrarians' and 'Aristocrats': Party Political Ideology in the United States, 1837–1846* (Cambridge: Cambridge University Press, 1987); Eric Foner, *Free Soil, Free Labor, Free Men: The Ideology of the Republican Party before the Civil War* (New York: Oxford University Press, 1970).

58. For background to these conflicts, see C. K. Yearley, *The Money Machines: The Breakdown and Reform of Governmental and Party Finance in the North, 1860–1920* (Albany: State University of New York Press, 1970); J. Mills Thornton, "Fiscal Policy and the Failure of Reconstruction in the Lower South," in J. Morgan Kousser and James M. McPherson, eds., *Region, Race, and Reconstruction: Essays in Honor of C. Vann Woodward* (New York: Oxford University Press, 1982), 349–94; Eric Monkkonen, *America Becomes Urban: The Development of U.S. Cities and Towns, 1790–1980* (Berkeley: University of California Press), forthcoming.

In addition to creating resources, of course, the state extracted them; state activity was controversial in part because it was costly. Statistics on property ownership and geographical mobility suggest that it is probable that the highly mobilized post–Civil War electorate was constituted both as voters and as taxpayers especially in the urban areas, but, again, the latter identity has been almost ignored. Nationwide the level of nonfarm homeownership—and thus eligibility for property taxation—was about 37 percent in 1890. Moreover, this homeownership spread remarkably deeply down the class structure, as it was not unusual for immigrants to own homes at a higher rate than the native born and for as much as 40 percent of skilled workers to own homes. It is also the case in mobility studies that those who accumulated property were those most likely to stay in one place and that homeownership was age specific—those who aged in one place were very likely to own homes.[59]

Because the most important qualification for suffrage in the late nineteenth century was residence and those most likely to stay in one place were also likely to accumulate real property and thus pay property tax, it is very likely that the relationship between spreading tax liability and increasing political participation was not coincidental. For example, throughout the nineteenth century the most highly mobilized ethnic group was the Irish, who were also the ethnic group with the highest rate of homeownership in many cities. As Stephan Thernstrom has pointed out, however, this property accumulation was achieved by means of what he calls "ruthless underconsumption," and the hold of immigrants on their property was tenuous at best. This new work suggests that groups that have been thought to be proponents of the expansion of government had more interest in stopping that expansion since the only guaranteed result of such expansion was an increased tax bill.[60]

The question of resources and costs brings us back to the literature on the political machine, which has been blissfully unaware of these issues. The functional model of the political machine provided a license for historically oriented social scientists to "discover" machines in city after city by ripping urban politics out of its institutional, ideological, and fiscal contexts. More recent historical and comparative work has produced abundant evidence that the all-powerful urban boss rarely, if ever, existed. In fact, urban politics was simply too contested, urban policy-making too complicated, and urban policymakers—believe it or not—too responsible to support such an image of the urban boss.

59. I have discussed the issue of urban fiscal politics more extensively in other places, including Terrence J. McDonald and Sally K. Ward, eds., *The Politics of Urban Fiscal Policy* (Beverly Hills: Sage Publications, 1984); McDonald, *The Parameters of Urban Fiscal Policy: Socioeconomic Change and Political Culture in San Francisco, 1860–1906* (Berkeley: University of California Press, 1986); McDonald "The History of Urban Fiscal Politics in America, 1830–1930: What Was Supposed to Be versus What Was and the Difference It Makes," *International Journal of Public Administration*, forthcoming. Cf. Monkkonen, *America Becomes Urban.*

60. For discussions of the rates and implications of homeownership, see Thernstrom, *Poverty and Progress*; Olivier Zunz, *The Changing Face of Inequality: Urbanization, Industrial Development, and Immigrants in Detroit, 1880–1920* (Chicago: University of Chicago Press, 1982); McDonald. *Parameters.*

There were, of course, politicians at precinct, ward, and city levels who were called bosses, and some of these men headed political and other organizations that could dispense patronage of widely varying amounts and types and could at times deliver some votes. But there were remarkably few machines that controlled citywide political offices for long periods of time, there is remarkably little evidence that political organizations either wanted or had the resources to meet the needs of the urban masses, and there is no evidence that the presence of machines fundamentally affected patterns of political mobilization.[61]

All these problems and more are revealed, for example, by reading back-to-back the accounts of New York City politics written by Wilentz, Bridges, Shefter, and David Hammack,[62] in which there is almost *no* agreement on when the machine became the machine, or exactly what difference that made. The variety in these accounts, testifies to the ability of these authors to discover the complexity of politics in New York City; the problem is the attempt to jam that complexity into the machine straitjacket.

When one considers the various ways that the subnational state helped to constitute society by acting or refusing to act, the various issues around which political mobilization occurred or failed to occur, and the various ideologies that these actions generated, the most damning thing that can be said about viewing politics from the perspective of ethnicity, patronage, and machines is simply that it is an extraordinarily narrow way of viewing the relationship between state and society in America. This narrowness is not surprising given the circumstances out of which this view emerged; its persistence is, however, given the wealth of tasks entailed in "bringing the state back in" to American history.

61. Examples of this new work in urban political history would include Jon C. Teaford, *The Unheralded Triumph: City Government in America, 1870–1900* (Baltimore: Johns Hopkins University Press, 1984); Teaford, "*Finis* for Tweed and Steffens: Rewriting the History of Urban Rule," *Reviews in American History* 10 (1982): 143–53; M. Craig Brown and Charles N. Halaby, "Bosses, Reform, and the Socioeconomic Bases of Urban Expenditure, 1880–1940," in McDonald and Ward, eds., *The Politics of Urban Fiscal Policy*, 69–100; McDonald, *The Parameters of Urban Fiscal Policy*. For another call for a more general restoration of political history, see J. Morgan Kousser, "Toward 'Total Political History,'" Social Science Working Paper no.581, Division of the Humanities and Social Sciences, California Institute of Technology.

62. David C. Hammack, *Power and Society: Greater New York at the Turn of the Century* (New York: Russell Sage Foundation, 1982).

IRA KATZNELSON
New School for Social Research

"The Burdens of Urban History": Comment

How, if at all, can studies of the city help us understand the distinctive qualities of the American regime? In "The Burdens of Urban History," which refines and elaborates his earlier paper "The Problem of the Political in Recent American Urban History," Terrence McDonald, a historian who has written on urban fiscal policy and conflict,[1] argues that students of the city have focused their work too narrowly on bosses and machines, patronage and pluralism. In so doing, they have obscured other bases of politics and conflict, and, trapped by liberal categories of analysis, they have perpetuated a self-satisfied, even celebratory, portrait of American politics and society. This unfortunate directionality to urban research in some measure has been unwitting because historians and social scientists have been unreflective about the genealogies, and mutual borrowings, of their disciplines. Even recent critical scholarship in the new social history and in the social sciences under the banner of "bringing the state back in" suffers from these defects. As a result, these treatments of state and society relationships, and of the themes that appear under the rubric of American "exceptionalism," are characterized by an epistemological mishmash, a contraction of analytical vision, and an unintended acquiescence in the self-satisfied cheerleading of the academy that began in the postwar years.[2]

This is a spirited account. Its main themes are interlaced with important

---

1. Terrence J. McDonald, "The Problem of the Political in Recent American History: Liberal Pluralism and the Rise of Functionalism," *Social History* 10 (October 1985); Terrence J. McDonald, *The Parameters of Urban Fiscal Policy: Socioeconomic Change and Political Culture in San Francisco, 1860–1906* (Berkeley: University of California Press, 1986); Terrence J. McDonald and Sally K. Ward, eds., *The Politics of Urban Fiscal Policy* (Beverly Hills: Sage Publications, 1984).

2. A critique of the new state-centered tendencies in American and comparative politics for their conservatism in implicitly supporting a strong state and for being insufficiently attuned to the values of the liberal tradition can be found in Leonard Binder, "The Natural History of Development Theory," *Comparative Studies in Society and History* 28 (January 1986). I take up these questions below in my discussion of the distinctive aspects of the nineteenth-century state.

subthemes, including reservations about the functionalist strain that Robert K. Merton introduced into studies of the city, an interpretation of the creation of social science knowledge in the Truman and Eisenhower years, and a powerful critique of ethnohistory. As an assertive and artfully constructed polemic, the essay provokes and entertains with such biting turns of phrase as "pluralist neo-Marxists."

"The Burdens of Urban History" is worth attending to not because I think it is always right—indeed, it frequently is wide of the mark—but because it raises fundamental questions about the trajectory of American political development and its special characteristics and about the ways social scientists who work in a historical mode practice their craft.

Here, not without self-interest, I take up the challenge of McDonald's essay. I turn first to a critique of his critique. Later, I situate the analysis of important features of city politics in the nineteenth century—including ethnicity, territory, patronage, and pluralism—as important aspects of studies of American political development. In so doing, I hope not only to show that many of McDonald's objections to the focus on political machines and to the manner in which they have been studied are ill considered but to indicate how in fact such studies can contribute to the analytical goals he wishes to promote.

I

McDonald rightly laments the failure of historians to think carefully about the frameworks they have imported from the social sciences and the failure of social scientists to examine carefully enough the factual material they have appropriated from historians. He challenges both groups to be more self-conscious about the histories and implications of their disciplines. He is especially concerned that scholars, by taking too much for granted, may allow "the power of the theoretical frameworks of one generation to structure the discourse of another." Such, he maintains, has been the case in the relationship between urban studies and treatments of the American state.

How convincing is this sociology of knowledge and history of ideas? It is based on three strongly argued points. First, McDonald characterizes the late 1940s and early 1950s as *the* formative moment of postwar inquiry. Given the effects of generational transmission, the characteristics of this era for scholars in later periods are basic, and McDonald finds them doleful. Second, he objects to functionalism as an approach to studies of institutions and collective action in general, and to studies of urban political organizations in particular. Third, he maintains the relationship between social scientists and historians has resembled a game of leapfrog, with each jump leading the players, unwittingly, in precisely the wrong direction. Let us take each of these points in turn.

Like most students of American political development, McDonald begins his essay with a retrospective look at Louis Hartz and his contemporaries who challenged the Progressive historiographical tradition's emphasis on conflict between the haves and have-nots as the leitmotif of American history. Breaking free from the patrician aloofness of histories written in the Gilded Age and from the pessimism implicit in the closing of the frontier, such leading Progressives as Charles Beard and Vernon Parrington instead had pictured American history as a recurring battle in which popular forces strive consistently for an extension of democracy against elites and special interests of various kinds. Hartz and his fellow critics rejected this portrait as a simplification. Their complaint was less with the empirical description of various popular struggles than with the limits of these struggles and the framing of these descriptions. The consensus school sought to identify the ideas and institutions that define the terrain on which the conflicts that have marked the American past have taken place. For them, the exceptional markers of the American experience have been its liberalism and its pluralist political institutions. The conflicts vividly described by the Progressives, they argued, have inhered in these values and practices.

Like McDonald, I disagree strongly with important aspects of the portrait painted by the consensus historians, especially with the notion that the liberalism of the American Founding fixed the limits of the regime once and for all and the related idea that American liberalism is surrounded by an unbridgeable moat. Moreover, in their zeal to correct for Progressive overstatement, the consensus school underplayed the scope for agency and the significance of the histories of blacks, women, workers, and immigrants. The reductionism of the Progressives was more than matched by the condescension of their critics. They had little to say about victimization and resistance. Nonetheless, it is possible to differ with many, even most, of the features in the work of Hartz and others in the consensus school yet still appreciate sympathetically the analytical significance of their effort. This McDonald does not do. Instead, he caricatures their critique by conflating the central analytical thrust of the consensus school with the warm appreciation many of its practitioners had for the values and institutions of American liberalism.

This ellipsis is not a small flaw. McDonald's criticism of the consensus historians provides a vital underpinning for his own analysis. He wishes to establish that their work provides the sustaining roots of the family tree of recent urban political studies (and, by indirection, the roots of recent scholarship on American political development). In McDonald's account, the generative importance of consensus history implicates these later works in the shift of Hartz and his generation away from history and social science written in the service of reform to a conservative scholarship smugly satisfied with the stable social order of the United States, a move McDonald characterizes as leading "from the ways in which American society was problematic to the ways in which it was normative."

By their failure to recognize this patrimony, he argues, students of city politics, especially those who have stressed the integrative qualities of local political machines, have compromised their own aims of building a new social history and of reintroducing the state into political analysis. Thus, the limitations of consensus history continue to characterize recent scholarly trends, often behind the backs of critical scholars. One of the main contributions of the essay is McDonald's attempt to unmask this inheritance by tracing the influence of the anti-Progressive postwar trend in history and the social sciences on scholars who came of age in the 1960s and after.

My objections to McDonald's account of the consensus school are at two levels. The first, and more general, is that he commits the theoretical fallacy of opposing conflict and consensus. Just as it is possible to generalize that all societies (except perhaps the most primitive) are structures of competing groups and interests actually or potentially in conflict, so it is also the case that such conflicts ordinarily get played out within restricted fields of ideas and institutions, at least some of which are accepted, deeply or provisionally, knowingly or tacitly, by the actors as the rules of the contest. Even during moments of rebellion and revolution, conflict is shaped by the formal and tacit rules of institutions and social relations. Power and domination are structured; so is resistance. From this standpoint, it is just as important to say something about the structuration of a given contest as it is to take note of its tumult. In *this* respect, in the debate between the Progressive and consensus schools, the latter won hands down.

My second objection is McDonald's identification of this emphasis of the consensus school with the celebration of the existing order. To be sure, more than a few consensus historians were delighted to discover the mainsprings of stability for a regime they admired. This, however, was a matter of their preference, not an analytical necessity. Richard Hofstadter (whom McDonald places squarely in the consensus camp even though he was profoundly ambivalent about its orientation, approach, and achievements) made just this point when he wrote:

> It is a mistake to assume that the consensus idea is intrinsically a *prescriptive* one which commits us to this or that particular arrangement. It is part of the *descriptive* task of the historian or political scientist to find and account for the elements of consensus in any situation, but he is not required to endorse what he finds. . . . If the matter is seen this way, I believe it will be understood that the idea of consensus is not intrinsically linked to ideological conservatism. In its origins, I believe it owed almost as much to Marx as to Tocqueville, and I find it hard to believe that any realistic Marxist historian could fail to be struck at many points by the pervasively liberal-bourgeois character of American society in the past. Many aspects of our history, indeed, seem to yield to a "left" consensus interpretation, and some radical historians have in fact begun to see it that way.[3]

Hofstadter further underscored that the consensus idea is not an empirical tool but a counterassertion to a fixation on conflict as such. "It has somewhat the same relation to historical writing as a framework to a painting: it sets the boundaries of the scene and enables us to see where the picture breaks off and the alien environment begins."[4] Of course (and this, much of the consensus

3. Richard Hofstadter, *The Progressive Historians: Turner, Beard, Parrington* (New York: Vintage Books, 1970), 451–52.

4. Hofstadter, *The Progressive Historians*, 453. Hofstadter observes in a footnote that "my own assertion of consensus history in 1948" in *The American Political Tradition* "had its sources in the Marxism of the 1930's" (452). Elsewhere in this chapter, he makes clear his own ambivalences about the work of the consensus historians, especially their timelessness, their lack of institutional specificity, and their tendency to celebrate what they describe. Hartz

school did not see, or at least did not acknowledge), such frameworks themselves may be contested, and they are never neutral. They rarely are static, but
may expand or contract. Nevertheless, as Gramsci understood just as well as
Hartz, the analysis of conflict without attention to the distinction between a
framework and a field of action, and to the actual content of the field within this
frame, is something of an analytical (and political) absurdity. Further, without
attention to just these issues comparative analysis would be meaningless.

I have no quarrel with McDonald's description of the emergence of a group
of scholars within the academy in the postwar years who linked the ideas of
consensus and pluralism to a celebration of American political, economic, and
social arrangements. But this joining of analysis and satisfaction was conjunctural and contingent, not structural or necessary. To inquire, as Werner
Sombart did, about the absence of socialism in America or, as Hofstadter did,
about the remarkable combination of violence and relative political stability in
the United States, where insurgencies (with the grand exception of the Civil
War) have been controlled, localized, isolated, and partial, is to ask fundamental questions about the regime regardless of one's ontology, normative perspectives, or political preferences.[5]

The conflation of analysis and celebration in McDonald's evaluation is not a
limited problem because it underpins much of his subsequent analysis: "Across
the social sciences the effort to use historical and institutional means to 'bring
the state back in' is contaminated by the conceptual residues of a particular
moment in American history when the identities of and connections among
social science, history, liberalism, and the state were redefined." At the core of

---

makes much the same point as Hofstadter in rejecting the antimony of conflict and consensus:
"So one cannot say of the liberal society analysis that by concentrating on national unities it
rules out the meaning of domestic conflict. Actually it discovers that meaning, which is
obscured by the very Progressive analysis that presumably concentrates on conflict . . . The
argument over whether we should 'stress' solidarity or conflict in American politics misleads
us by advancing a false set of alternatives" (Hartz, *The Liberal Tradition in America* [New York:
Harcourt Brace, 1955], 20). At the same time, as Hofstadter notes, "it is a valid comment on
the limits of consensus history to insist that in one form or another conflict finally does remain,
and ought to remain, somewhere near the center of our focus of attention. . . . Certainly,
American history, even without feudalism and socialism, has been far from bland" (458, 462).

5. Werner Sombart, *Why Is There No Socialism in the United States?* (White Plains, N. Y.: M. E.
Sharpe, 1976); Richard Hofstadter, "Reflections on Violence in the United States," in Richard
Hofstadter and Michael Wallace, eds., *American Violence: A Documentary History* (New York:
Vintage Books, 1971.) Certainly this is how Michael Rogin, who is praised by McDonald for
his "powerful and important analysis of the postwar transformations of theories of politics"
(fn. 16), understood the contribution of Hartz. Rogin wrote that he considered *The Liberal
Tradition in America* to be a "thoroughgoing, creative analysis of American political culture"
that helps explain these distinctive features of working class formation in the United States:
"The uprooted, conservative European peasants who migrated to European cities produced a
politics of revolutionary socialism. For those who settled in American cities, that same uproot-
ing migration from farms to cities resulted in a narrow, self-concerned machine politics"
(Michael Paul Rogin, *The Intellectuals and McCarthy: The Radical Spector* [Cambridge: MIT
Press, 1969], 35–37).

this argument is the idea that because the descriptive emphasis on political machines, ethnicity, and patronage and their analytical treatment in functionalist terms came onto the scholarly scene under the broad aegis of a consensual celebration, subsequent generations of scholars *necessarily* carry *all* the analytical and normative baggage of the generative moment.[6]

If, for McDonald, consensus history is emblematic of a more general scholarly thrust, functionalism, especially as practiced by Robert K. Merton, is more directly implicated in his account of how the genesis of postwar urban studies has been compromised. Fuctionalism is central to his history of ideas because of the influence he ascribes to Merton's 1949 essay on "Manifest and Latent Functions," especially the brief section that deals with "Some Functions of the Political Machine."[7] In McDonald's account, Merton's rehabilitation and appreciation of the machine informed Oscar Handlin's 1951 volume, *The Uprooted*. In turn, Hofstadter based his account of the machine in his 1955 *Age of Reform* on Handlin. From there, Mertonian conceptualizations entered political science via the influence of Hofstadter and Handlin in Robert Dahl's *Who Governs?* (1961), Theodore Lowi's *At the Pleasure of the Mayor* (1964), and Edward Banfield and James Q. Wilson's *City Politics* (1965). The influence of Merton continued with Lee Benson's *The Concept of Jacksonian Democracy* (1961) and other ethnohistories. In turn, these various books informed the new urban political science of the 1970s and 1980s, including work by Shefter, Bridges, and myself. Finally, the Mertonian perspective has afflicted the "bringing the state back in" perspective in the scholarship of Theda Skocpol because (in spite of her overt antifunctionalism) she relies on these urban studies to characterize the diffuse party and patronage characteristics of the nineteenth century American state.

To a considerable degree this history of ideas is persuasive. In "Burdens," however, it is grounded more on the authority of the essay's author than on the marshaling of supportive material.[8] Even if the evidence he presents is sparse, McDonald succeeds in showing that studies of city politics have been influenced strongly by Merton's rejection of the machine-reform antinomy as a reason to extol middle- and upper-class reformers at the expense of working class politicians and voters and, instead, to consider local political party organizations in terms of their activities and functions in mobilizing voters, providing services, defining the character of local politics, and brokering economic as well as political bargains. Unfortunately, McDonald suggests that the influence of

6. McDonald has singled out my own work for this criticism in "The Problem of the Political," 344–45.

7. Robert K. Merton, *Social Theory and Social Structure*, rev. ed. (New York: Free Press, 1957), chap. 1, esp. 72ff.

8. Some of the works said to build on the others hardly make reference to them, if at all. Lowi, for example, cites Merton and Handlin perfunctorily, but he does base some pages on Hofstadter's distinction between the Yankee and immigrant styles, and these categories recur in modified form in Banfield and Wilson. Dahl cites none of these authors. Although there are traces of functionalist language in some of the work of the various authors cited, the evidence for the linear transmission of influence presented in these pages is weak.

Merton is the dirty secret of urban studies, as if the borrowing and learning that have taken place occurred either in simple linear fashion, independently of research and evidence (he writes, for example, of Dahl's "apparently empirical" study), or without taking alternative, competing interpretations into account.[9]

Merton's contributions have been appreciated by urbanists at least as much for their resurrection of an important empirical subject and for providing a welcome counterpoint to the moralism of earlier class-interested analysts as for their functionalist theoretical perspective. On the latter subject, McDonald has nothing good to say. He dismisses functionalism as simply an expression and legitimation of the status quo. He laments the influence of Merton principally because of the implicit conservatism of functionalism which equates "function" with beneficial outcome and thus echoes consensus history by warmly reaffirming the positive aspects of American life.

McDonald's reading of Merton is unreasonable in two related ways. First, it is at odds with Merton's text. The early part of "Manifest and Latent Functions" is a rejection of a number of functionalist postulates (the postulates of functional unity, universal functionalism, and indispensability) that would necessarily make functionalist accounts a conservative defense of the existing order. Immediately upon his dismissal of these approaches, Merton underscored his opposition to functionalism as conservatism in a section on "Functional Analysis as Ideology." There, he wrote, "functional analysis in sociology is threatened with a reduction to absurdity, once it adopts the postulate of all existing social structures as indispensable for the fulfillment of salient functional needs." Not only did Merton clearly abjure the link between functionalism and conservatism; he devoted a long discussion to an attempt to show similarities between functionalist analysis and Marxism, an argument that subsequently has found its way into Marxist scholarship. Functionalism, Merton argued, involves "no *intrinsic* ideological commitment although, like other forms of sociological analysis, it can be infused with any one of a wide range of ideological values." As for his treatment of urban politics, Merton stated that what he was trying to do was substitute detached analysis for moralism.[10]

Now, such claims should always be greeted with skepticism; whatever his intent, Merton may be wrong to think that functionalism has no ideological or normative implications. Certainly there is a significant critical tradition that faults it on just this score.[11] Yet without any direct textural warrants, McDonald

---

9. Thus, the important differences between the various authors cited, as, for example, the important ways in which Bridges's and Shefter's analyses differ from Banfield's and Wilson's, for example, are never considered. Further, although McDonald mentions Pendelton Herring's 1940 contribution, he misses out on the more influential 1937 volume by Harold Gosnell, *Machine Politics, Chicago Model* (Chicago: University of Chicago Press, 1968), which was reissued with an introduction by Theodore Lowi.

10. Merton, *Social Theory and Social Structure*, 38–45, 71. On Marxism and functionalism, see G. A. Cohen, *Karl Marx's Theory of History: A Defense* (Princeton: Princeton University Press, 1978), especially chaps. 9 and 10.

11. This kind of criticism is mounted with great passion and effect in Alvin Gouldner's *The Coming Crisis of Western Sociology* (New York: Basic Books, 1970). As part of his larger enter-

labels Merton an apologist for the status quo. To demonstrate this point, he quotes the British political theorist Alan Ryan's opinion that Merton, impressed by the goodness of America, used the term *latent function* to equate *function* and *good result*. When Alvin Gouldner sought to make a comparable case, he did so not by trying to figure out how much Merton appreciated American arrangements but by developing the analytical argument that Merton's claim to value-freedom is misleading because of its rootedness in a concern with order: "In saying that Functionalism's ideology is conservative, I mean to suggest, primarily, that its fundamental posture toward its surrounding society entails an acceptance of its master institutions, but not that it is *necessarily* procapitalist and antisocialist. Committed as it is to the value of order, it can do no other than accept the kind of order in which it finds itself."[12]

Gouldner's claim accurately identifies an unreflective tendency among many structural functionalists, but it does not succeed in making its case against either Merton's middle-range theorizing or functionalist tools more generally. Social scientists may wish to understand the ways a social order is reproduced without necessarily accepting either the given specific order or the value of order itself. Referring to functionalism, Gouldner claims that "it is not disposed to a public criticism of the master institutions of the larger society".[13] The absence of a subject in Gouldner's sentence is telling: functionalists may or may not be disposed to a politics of criticism and opposition. Middle-range functionalism is a tool of analysis compatible with the entire range of political preferences.

My first objection, then, is that McDonald's consideration of Merton is unreasonable in its textual reading and interpretation. My second concerns the absence of any serious discussion of functionalism as a tool of explanation in the social sciences in general or for the study of urban politics in particular. McDonald might have argued, as Jon Elster has, that the consequentialism of the functionalist approach produces bad social science because it lacks agency and substitutes the association of variables for coherent mechanisms of cause and effect. But "The Burdens of Urban History" lacks this kind of argumentation. Nor does McDonald refute the claim on behalf of functionalism that this mode of analysis is no more, but also no less, than an attempt to suggest plausible relationships between features of social reality that appear to co-vary.

---

prise of a critical investigation of Parsonian structural functionalism, Gouldner takes Merton to task for promoting an ascetic, depoliticized version of social utilitarianism. He argues that this type of theorizing is a substitute for politics, and that it turns basic normative questions into technical ones. I think it necessary to distinguish between the Grand Theory of Parsons that presents a contentless portrait of the social order as a substitute for a macroanalytic and historical vision of social organization and the middle-range theorizing of Merton, whose tools can be put to use within alternative macroanalytic understandings of the modern world, and of social order and social change. How effective they are as tools, of course, may be another question, but their suitability for use is a matter largely independent of their original grounding within the Parsonian framework.

12. Gouldner, *Coming Crisis*, 335.
13. Ibid. 335–36.

On this rendering, the considerable merit of functionalism is that it is a summons to the formulation of scholarship that can show how a proposed functional relationship actually works, whether by the direct intent of actors or by specifiable nonpurposive mechanisms.[14] Instead of an analytical discussion at this level, functionalism is rejected out of hand by McDonald as a part of the insidious "liberal matrix" of the late 1940s and early 1950s.

Although his dismissal of consensus history and functionalism is too facile, McDonald is quite right to identify the immediate postwar period as a formative intellectual and political period. This was a moment of the invention of a liberal "vital center"[15] in political life and of influential conceptual elaborations in the social science disciplines—pluralism in political science, reference group theory and functionalism in sociology, and dissonance theory and status anxiety in social psychology. Incontestably, there was an affinity between the new liberal politics and the new social science. Taken whole, this remarkable moment of creativity, especially at the level of middle-range theory, defined the field of scholarly play not only for the social scientists and historians of that generation but for their successors, even those who were at odds with the scholarly and political imperatives of the new liberalism.

McDonald's insistence that we reckon with the legacy of the postwar years is entirely appropriate, for if "science is tooled knowledge,"[16] a disproportionate share of the tools in the kitbag of social science and history were forged then. Alas, by aiming his focus nearly exclusively on the shift by this scholarly generation from criticism of the regime to satisfaction with it, McDonald misses the chance to fully portray this time of intellectual ferment as I believe he should: as characterized both by a contraction of scope and a deepening of focus. The former is to be regretted, the latter to be applauded.

This is hardly the place for an extended treatment of the shifts in the university and knowledge communities in the 1940s and 1950s. In shorthand, I think the first hallmark of this scholarly time is that it was a moment of a substantive reduction of the scope of the subject matter under investigation in the social sciences. In discipline after discipline, older subjects disappeared from view: constitutionalism, the law, and the state from political science; classical considerations of capitalism as a system from economics; the normative and textual emphases of the history of philosophy from academic philosophy; macrohistorical treatments of social organization from sociology. The focus shifted, respectively, to interest group analysis and political behavior under the banners of pluralism and behaviorism, to technical debates between Keynesians and anti-Keynesians that resulted in a neoclassical synthesis, to logic and language analysis, and to segmented studies of social reality joined

---

14. For discussions, see Arthur L. Stinchcombe, *Constructing Social Theories* (New York: Harcourt Brace and World, 1968); Jon Elster, *Ulysses and the Sirens* (New York: Cambridge University Press, 1979); Cohen, *Karl Marx's Theory*; and the symposium, "Marxism, Functionalism and Game Theory," *Theory and Society* 11 (July 1982).

15. Arthur Schlesinger, Jr., *The Vital Center* (Boston: Houghton Mifflin, 1948).

16. Joseph Schumpeter, *A History of Economic Analysis* (New York: Oxford University Press, 1954), 7.

together under the aegis of structural functionalism. The reasons for these contractions are to be found mainly outside the academy, in the experiences and legacies of depression and war, and in the apparent ability of the Western intellectuals in the postwar period to avoid having to choose between liberty at the cost of economic trauma or prosperity at the cost of statism. No doubt, success in winning the war and forging a prosperous aftermath, against expectations, produced a good deal of self-satisfaction. But what is more important for us is that it led to a narrowing of the attention span of history and the social sciences which we are still struggling to overcome.

At the same time, this reduction went hand in hand with important analytical advances that should not be swept aside or assimilated into the less desirable features of the period. These advances in technique (as in the sophistication of quantitative methods), in the richness of description (as in accounts of the dense interest group formations in American politics), and in middle-level tools of analysis (including dissonance theory, game theory, and other forms of social choice, and the lamented functionalism and pluralism) produced for the too limited set of questions on which they were brought to bear striking advances in analysis and understanding. Like McDonald, I deeply regret the narrowing of terrain in this period; unlike him, I think the major advances in history and in the social sciences are not simply barriers to be overcome but tools that, with appropriate care and within different frameworks, can be put to use on precisely those questions their developers put aside. My complaint with the history and the social science of this formative period, in short, is not so much that it was celebratory or wrong but that it was radically insufficient. David Ricci has called the middle-range social science of this period a "liberal matrix,"[17] and McDonald argues that most recent interpretations of urban and community politics in the social sciences and in history are trapped within it. I disagree. For even if we accept Ricci's label, scholars who utilize the analytical tools elaborated at that moment need not be bound by the thematic or analytical limits of that time. The tools are there for us to use, thoughtfully and critically, for other purposes. And so, I will argue, they have.

II

McDonald appears to think that because he shows that recent students of cities have focused on the same problems as scholars in Hartz's and Merton's generation—particularly issues of patronage, political organization, and ethnicity—and that they have worked on them with some similar tools—including variants of functional analysis and attention to questions of social order—he has made the case that this body of scholarship is badly tainted. "Somewhat surprisingly, these understandings of the role of ethnicity, patronage, and machines are almost identical to those of the so-called consensus historians." At best, this is a descriptive claim, not an argument. McDonald continues: "For the generation of the fifties, political machines extended social exceptionalism into poli-

17. David M. Ricci, *The Tragedy of Political Science: Politics, Scholarship, and Democracy* (New Haven: Yale University Press, 1984).

tics; for current commentators the political machines blocked the transmission of radicalism from society into politics. In both cases the conception of politics is society-centered, nonideological, and functionalist." This indictment does not stand up to close scrutiny. It assumes, wrongly, that continuities in theories of the middle range imply a uniformity or constancy in the problematics of research and the terms of analysis. More important, it underappreciates the achievements of the body of urban political scholarship and the ways it has, and can, inform studies more broadly cast of the American regime.

Before turning to these issues, there is a prior question to be addressed: the very status of the traditional subject matter of urban political studies. McDonald is not entirely consistent about the significance of urban political machines as an object of analysis. At some points he reluctantly acknowledges there might be something of importance here. "No one would argue," he writes, "that either ethnicity or patronage was irrelevant to nineteenth-century American politics, nor would anyone claim that there were no political machines." Near the conclusion of the essay, however, he debunks the importance of a focus on machines for nineteenth-century city politics, claiming among other things that all-powerful machines "rarely if ever existed" and that "there is no evidence that the presence of machines fundamentally affected patterns of political mobilization." There is a good deal of disagreement among urban scholars about these claims, and debates about them fill the relevant journals. I will not take them up here because they are secondary to McDonald's purpose. At issue is whether there is much to gain by focusing on this dimension of the American regime, and whether those who have done so have had a positive or deleterious effect on studies of American political development. On these points, McDonald is unequivocal: the focus on the political machine impoverishes "the conception of the state at the subnational level," and "a brief review of the contributions and limitations of the literatures we have considered here demonstrates the way in which they interact to narrow the consideration of the state" in the American regime as a whole. These criticisms would be much more persuasive if offered as hortatory injunctions to avoid certain analytical pitfalls than as repudiations of important and promising bodies of literature.

McDonald certainly is justified in arguing that the city has been more than a forum for ethnic conflicts over spoils presided over by political bosses. For the past two centuries, cities have been locales for different and contested kinds of collective action and political mobilization, disputes about real estate and land use, transportation, education, and a host of other subjects. Cities have been venues for labor organization, repression, and strife. He is also right in saying that some students of the city have focused on machine politics to the exclusion of many of these topics and that a broadening of focus would be desirable.

Who would disagree? Certainly not most of the scholars McDonald criticizes. Merton, for example, draws our attention not just to the latent functions of the machine in securing the political integration of urban residents but also to the ways machines served the business community. For local capitalists, they provided access points to government contracts and eased the recruitment of labor, they brokered relations with local bureaucracies, and they provided a buffer between the business community and the largely working-class population of the city. To take a much more recent instance, Amy Bridges's important

book on nineteenth-century New York stresses how an ethnic politics of assertive immigrant and ethnic loyalties was put to work by public policies, and even,
after Tweed, on behalf of fiscal responsibility. She also shows how machines
accommodated very different styles of politics, from militant confrontations
between groups and classes to a politics of mutualism, stressing collaboration
across these divides.[18]

Within these readings of the history of machine politics, the choice is not
whether to focus on the machine or on other urban topics but to come to an
understanding of the linkages joining them. And the issue is not whether to
treat the local machine as a surrogate for American political development
elsewhere in the federal system but to be able to trace the relationships between
the large themes of American political development and machine politics as the
characteristic American form of political participation at the local level in cities
where the majority of the American working class resided. McDonald seems to
want to press a choice between subject matters when the important challenge is
to connect them.

The progress that has been made in achieving this end is minimized in
"Burdens" as a result of the essay's overstated demonstration of continuities in
the history of urban studies. McDonald claims that recent students of machine
politics treat ethnicity as primordial, and party formation as an automatic
process. There is a tight linkage, he claims, between studies of the city and
pluralist understandings of politics, especially in terms of the separation of the
economy and the polity. Further, analysts of urban machines have produced
"society-centered" analyses, and they assume that studies of the machine are
"the key to American political development." My reading of this literature is
quite different. The recent work of such scholars as Bridges and Shefter make
ethnic and class formation contingent matters; they place their analyses within
state-centered and nonpluralist frameworks; and, rather than assume that the
machine is the main instrument of American political development, they ask
how an understanding of local politics can inform our comprehension of the
larger American regime.[19] Nevertheless, whether my interpretation or Mc-
Donald's provides the more accurate reading of specific texts is secondary.
More interesting is why, and how, studies of political machines can contribute to
understanding the distinctive features of the state in American political development.

III

Even the best recent urban political studies, McDonald avers, impoverish our
understanding of American political history by sins of omission and commis-

18. Merton, *Social Theory and Social Structure*, pp.75–77; Amy Bridges, *A City in the Republic:
Antebellum New York and the Origins of Machine Politics*. Cambridge: Cambridge University Press,
1984.

19. Amy Bridges, "Becoming American: The Working Classes in the United States before
the Civil War," and Martin Shefter, "Trade Unions and Political Machines: The Organization
and Disorganization of the American Working Class in the Late Nineteenth Century," in Ira
Katznelson and Aristide Zolberg, eds., *Working Class Formation: Nineteenth Century Patterns in
Western Europe and the United States* (Princeton: Princeton University Press, 1986).

sion: they shrink conceptions of the state, fail to link participation and the making of public policy, pay too little attention to fiscal decision making and taxation, deflect our attention away from the judicial and legislative activities that define state-market relations in the federal system, understate controversy and overstate political integration, and lack adequate treatments of group formation and ideology. Students of political machines have been "blissfully unaware of these issues." As a consequence, they have presented "an extraordinarily narrow way of viewing the relationship between state and society in America."

I am perplexed at how one can read the works of such scholars as Shefter and Bridges and reach these various conclusions, but this is a secondary matter. Much more important is the welcome challenge McDonald poses to locate the place of urban politics, and the machine in particular, as an aspect of the larger story of American state building and group formation, and to theorize this relationship in a manner that contributes not only to an intrinsic understanding of state-society relationships but to the insertion of the American experience within a comparative frame of reference. Unfortunately, McDonald's excessively polemical stance leads him away from a discussion of how scholarship on urban machines potentially can contribute to his own objectives. Even where students of the city are narrowly focused, their work can be utilized as constitutive elements of explanations of key features of the nineteenth century-American regime, including a national state with relatively low salience and a pattern of class formation that has distinguished starkly between the political identities of citizens as laborers and as members of households and communities.

Studies of political machines can assist our understanding of these matters by helping to construct the United States as a complex political and social formation within the emergent universe of nineteenth-century liberal democratic states in capitalist societies. These states differed in kind from their predecessors by specific sets of transactions, and rules to guide them, that linked states to their citizens and to their economies in new ways. Political participation and representation as matters of the rights of citizens and the organization of the capitalist markets of labor, money, and land by legal codes and public policies defined the fundamental challenges for nineteenth-century state builders. Only with the American and French revolutions did the modern category of the citizen, armed with rights, appear on the scene as a potential possession of every adult, and only with the supercession of the mercantilist political economy did the relationships of state and market come to be defined in a way that is still broadly familiar. The central problems of nineteenth-century state building concerned the way national states would organize these sets of transactions. At stake was the character and scope of the state itself and the rules and institutions that would link it to capitalist markets and to its population. The degree of autonomy, centralization, and capacity of given states and the character of the institutionalized transactions between states, citizens, and markets defined the issues of political contestation throughout the West in the early and middle nineteenth centuries. Moreover, the formation of modern working classes, a fundamental dimension of the new industrial, heavily urban capitalism, was shaped in contingent ways in specific countries by the characteristics of these linkages and transactions.[20]

There was a freshness and specificity to these challenges of state building and class formation. They were not unrelated. For if workers in the new unfettered labor markets were also citizens, they posed potential challenges in both the economy and the polity. State managers in the nineteenth century had to find ways to incorporate the participation of citizens without undermining the economic order on whose surplus they depended. This dynamic politicized the issues of state structure, political participation, and public policy concerned with the organization of markets and the mitigation of market outcomes.

The solution to these challenges in the establishment of institutions and norms in given national settings constituted the country's political regime. In the United States, the period from the Founding to Reconstruction may be understood as one of basic conflict over the formation of a regime consistent with the Constitution. In this long nineteenth century, the modern political party, judicial review, and the practice of federalism became the key markers of the polity's links to the economy and to its citizens, and, within this framework, so did the urban political machine.

How should these linkages be assessed? The most common way in the literature on states and political development is that of judging the capacity of states as strong or weak. A state is strong if it erects clear boundaries between the public and the private domains (indeed, in part, by establishing, maintaining, and legitimating these boundaries); if it succeeds in capturing for itself functions that previously or elsewhere belonged to civil society; if it develops an administrative bureaucracy that has coherent rules, boundaries, and instrumentalities of rule. But might it not be argued that a state is strong precisely to the extent that it erases the boundaries between the state, economy, and civil society, and between public and private; if it fuses with and penetrates economic and societal institutions to carry out the functions of production and reproduction in their fullest sense; and if a bureaucratic organization of society radiates out from the state to these other spheres?

Actually, these different criteria have been applied to quite different historical moments and locations. The first set has become the conventional wisdom in thinking about the Western state in the transition from feudalism; the second in thinking about modern totalitarianism. But what about the specific situation of western liberal capitalist democratic states? In this setting, the relevant issues are less concerned with the state as predator than with the terms of law, power, and representation that link the state, markets, and citizens. Under these circumstances, the condensed and bulky quality of the weak-strong dichotomy is apparent. Is a state strong when it is capable of imposing the wishes of the dominant classes on the rest of society, or when it is capable of resisting such domination? Is a state strong to the extent that it develops steering and planning mechanisms for the economy and society or when it empowers the economy and society with a vigorous autonomy? Is a state

20. This is one of the central organizing themes of Katznelson and Zolberg, eds., *Working Class Formation*.

stronger when its activities rest on a basis of mass political participation, mobilization, and consent, or when it can override or atomize individual and collective action? Further, we think we are sure a state gets stronger to the extent that it can extend its sovereignty over all the territory it claims to legitimately control, but just such an extension may impel it to govern by "weaker" decentralized forms of administration and organization. The history of state building in the United States is particularly well suited to examine just this set of fundamental questions. But how? Where does urban politics fit in? To see, we need first to take an analytical detour.

IV

The law, constitutionalism, and the state, which had disappeared as themes in political science in the late 1940s and 1950s, have been reintroduced into American political studies recently in such notable books as Stephen Skowronek's exploration of the development of national state administrative capacity in the late nineteenth and early twentieth centuries and Richard Bensel's treatment of sectional divisions and congressional representation between 1880 and 1980.[21] This new turn to the state at the national level so far has not explored how the city level of politics might be integrated into the wider American political experience. We shall see that this work, nevertheless, can help provoke just this kind of analytical integration.

Two works stand out as having provided the impetus for the scholarly movement to "bring the state back in" of which these recent studies of American political development have been a part: J. P. Nettl's 1968 article, "The State as a Conceptual Variable," and the 1975 collection of essays edited by Charles Tilly on *The Formation of National States in Western Europe*. They define a perspective and tools of analysis capable of situating the peculiarities of American political development within the universe of Western states. At the same time, the analytical thrust of Nettl's and Tilly's work eluded important issues concerning the specificity of the new genre of liberal state that developed in Western countries in the nineteenth century and, by so doing, obscured important strategic and normative questions associated with the new challenges of state-market and state-citizen transactions. Once rescued from the shadows of state theory, however, these issues can help us define a place for the city and its politics in the larger tale of American political development.

Nettl opened his paper with the observation that "the concept of the state is not much in vogue in the social sciences right now," and it aimed to integrate considerations of the state "into the current primacy of social science concerns and analytical methods." His central aim was to construct the concept of state in such a way as to make it amenable to comparative historical analysis. In this goal, the paper manifestly succeeded. More than any other single publication it

---

21. Stephen Skowronek, *Building a New American State: The Expansion of National Administrative Capacities, 1877–1920* (Cambridge: Cambridge University Press, 1982); Richard Bensel, *Sectionalism and American Political Development*. (Madison: University of Wisconsin Press, 1984).

provoked the reintroduction of the state into macroanalytical social science and history.[22]

For Nettl, the state has four central characteristics. It is, simultaneously, the irreducible unit of international relations, "a collectivity that summates a set of functions and structures in order to generalize their applicability," "an autonomous collectivity" that is "in a functional sense a distinct *sector* or arena of society," and "a sociocultural phenomenon." Leaving aside the first feature in this discussion, it is clear that the other three represent important domains of variation—state functions, the degree of state autonomy, and in the character of given cultural characterizations of stateness in specific times and places.[23] What the state actually does, how independently it performs its activities and pursues its goals, and how it is more widely viewed and understood are matters that have provided definition to the restoration of the study of the state to a central location within the social sciences.

These three lines of variation have been portrayed frequently in covariations in which weak states are juxtaposed to the strong. The latter, we have seen, are portrayed as states that capture more and more functions from civil society, construct clear lines of demarcation between the public and private domains, and develop the administrative capacity to manage state functions and secure the goals of the managers of the state. The Tilly volume showed how in the postfeudal era this process of state building was contingent and contested; and it stressed the importance of finance and tax policies, war and the military, and the development of public bureaucracies as key elements in the emergence of the modern nation state, which it understood primarily in terms of the institutionalized concentration of coercion. The key governmental variable, Tilly writes, is "the degree of 'stateness' of the governmental structure. Borrowing from J. P. Nettl, I mean the degree to which the instruments of government are differentiated from other organizations, centralized, autonomous, and formally coordinated with each other." For Nettl, what is remarkable about the American experience in just these terms is the low stateness of the regime in both structural and cultural senses. The federalism of the political system, the permeability of the state through the Congress, and the relatively small centralized bureaucratic establishment has produced a situation in which the very word *state* has no ordinary language meaning except as a second-tier level of government.[24]

This perspective provided the point of departure for Skowronek's treatment of American state building. "After all," he writes, "it is the absence of a sense of the state that has been the great hallmark of American political culture," and it

22. J. P. Nettl, "The State as a Conceptual Variable," *World Politics*, 20 (July 1968): 559; Charles Tilly, ed., *The Formation of National States in Western Europe* (Princeton: Princeton University Press, 1975).

23. Nettl, "The State," 562–66.

24. Tilly, *Formation*, 32. The Nettl-Tilly perspective on state building and stateness is grounded in the postfeudal separations of property, sovereignty, and civil society, which under feudalism, had been fused in the segmented units of the mode of production (Nettl, "The State," 568–72, 577–81).

is the "apparent stateness" of the nineteenth-century American state of courts and parties that provides the baseline for his study of the "systemic change in relations between an established state and its society" in the late nineteenth and early twentieth centuries.[25] The centerpiece of his study is the conflictual process of the extension of central state capacities during the period of the second industrial revolution. Even after four decades of vigorous, assertive state building in the Gilded Age and the Progressive Era, he argues, the American state remained comparatively underdeveloped, with an administrative body that was large by previous central state standards but that was losing the directive intelligence of assertive courts and capable political parties.

Like all works that change the nature of the conversation in a given field, Skowronek's book, both by what it says and by what it does not, provokes questions he does not write about. In the international arena, the state in a meaningful way is a unitary actor. Its competitors are other states. The state is assumed to have interests. Its "strength"—that is, its capacity to realize its interests—is tested in game-like transactions with other states in the competition for control over territory, populations, trade routes, and other valued resources and ends. By contrast, the very unitariness of the domestic state is a variable, not just its strength or weakness. The metaphor of strength requires the specification of the other (the economy and the various institutions and networks within civil society) against which the state may be either strong or weak in at least two dimensions: the "weight" of the state vis-a-vis other domestic macrostructures, and the state's capacity to affect and shape these other macrostructures. In liberal democratic states, these linkages are politicized; they provide the main conduits and content of political life.

Considerations of such transactions require a portrait of the social, organizational, and technical relations in the economy and civil society as much as they demand rich descriptions of the state apparatus and its capacities. Skowronek focuses almost exclusively on the latter task.[26] In this partial emphasis, he shares a lacuna of the Nettl-Tilly state-building tradition on which he draws that follows from its treatment of the development of modern states as a singular kind of phenomenon from the sixteenth century to the present. By making state building synonymous with the enhancement of central state administrative capacity, this body of work does not give theoretical recognition to the emergence of the new and problematical ties between states, citizens, and markets that made the environment so treacherous for state building in the nineteenth century. The consequence is a singular focus on increases or decreases in what Nettl called stateness. Missing is the subject matter of the patterning and rationality of the circuits of power and exchange that link the state to key others and, in consequence, the capacity to evaluate the desirability

25. Skowronek, *Building a New American State*, 3, 8.

26. His construction of a baseline antebellum state is thus shadowy and elusive only in part because it is not his manifest object of analysis; and he treats the "patchwork" and "hapless giant" successor without much content being ascribed to the society or to the economy with which they are in interaction.

of what the state is and does in terms of such valued objectives as justice, freedom, and equality.[27]

Bensel, by contrast, makes state-society and state-economy transactions the focus of his analysis of the comparatively unmediated representation of regional interests in national politics before the New Deal. His reconstruction of these relationships demonstrates how the division of the United States into separate sectional civilizations helped shape a national regime that had no distinctive interests or presence of its own, retained strong ties to citizens who were represented mainly in terms of the dominant economic interests of their regions, and yet demonstrated the capacity for economic policy making that nationalized the priorities of the industrial heartland and forced the rest of the country to pay the price of rapid industrial development. In presenting this analysis, Bensel points implicitly to issues that remain to be dealt with: patterns of group formation and conflict within the various regions, and the organization of capitalism and its markets by the state at subnational levels of government.

To deal with the questions suggested by Skowronek and Bensel that are not directly taken up by them, we need to expand the scope of inquiry. Only by understanding the conjoined development of the American state at each level of the federal system can we discern what Roger Benjamin and Raymond Duvall call "the state as the *organizing principles* that give 'totality,' or an underlying structural coherence, to . . . the myriad and diverse institutions of governance." As such, the state is, simultaneously, a unit of decision-making authority, a set of social relations of power and social control, a normative order, and a legal and institutional order that represents, shapes, and manages conflict, and that organizes a framework for the market economy while acting to alter market outcomes.[28] Taking the state as a whole, the American formula for dealing with these challenges in the nineteenth century was not the development of a "weak" state (though, taken on its own, this is a reasonable appellation for the national state), but the development of a diffuse and complicated, but nevertheless supple and capable, state apparatus. This regime had three main elements: a balance between center and periphery in a continental state, the vesting of most state-market transaction rules at the state and city levels, and the creation of a strong set of localistic linkages to the state for white male voters. Like any other, this political regime embodied a mix of incentives and

27. On the former point, see Phillipe Schmitter, "Neo-Corporatism and the State," European University Institute Working Paper no.106, 1984. Schmitter stresses a level of rationality that is neither at the systemic nor the individual level, but at a middle level linking the interests of classes, groups, and sectors and the interests of actors in the state located at organizationally specific places. On the latter point, see Binder, "The Natural History of Development Theory."

28. Roger Benjamin and Raymond Duvall, "The Capitalist State in Context," in Roger Benjamin and Stephen L. Elkin, eds., *The Democratic State* (Lawrence: University of Kansas Press, 1985), 22–27. These authors present these dimensions of stateness as alternative conceptualizations of the state. I do not see why this is the case, since the one I have put first can encompass the others.

disincentives shaping patterns of class and group formation in civil society and the character of collective action.

In his recent Russell lectures, Jack Greene shows how the new Republic faced many of the same dilemmas of state building that confronted the rule of the British Empire in North America in the seventeenth and eighteenth centuries. For the British, the American problem was one of defining a relationship between the metropolis and the colonies that could balance the goal to make the periphery more dependent on the center while accommodating considerable pressures for autonomy by the colonists. The American Revolution was testimony to the failure of the various constitutional schemes attempted by the British to manage their colonial relationship. Greene argues that after the revolution, the newly independent state found itself faced with precisely the same dilemma to solve, now in the guise of the problem of a republican empire. The postcolonial state was strong enough to create a continental union, but not strong enough to make such a union other than a federal one. The powerful tensions in the allocation of authority between center and periphery continued to threaten the cohesion of the American regime, and this prescription for governance survived the Civil War only by imposition. And yet, it is hard to see how the American state could have persisted at all without this kind of formula for balancing center and periphery in light of the immense differences in economic and societal relations between the regions.[29]

Capitalist development is impossible without the organization of the marketplace by the state. Until quite late in the nineteenth century, the key transactions between the state and the market took place not at the national but primarily at the state and secondarily at the local level. As Theodore Lowi has emphasized, under the doctrine of "reserved powers" the key laws affecting property, labor rights, and corporate regulation were not national in existence or scope. And, as William Brock has stressed, at this level the American state was robust and capable. State governments were assertive vis-a-vis the marketplace in their regulation of property and in the provision of miniwelfare states in the areas of public health and charity. Within this framework, "each of the states was a dynamic political and economic arena," Lowi argues. "Even as the economy became national, through national markets and exchanges, the states remained the source and the focus of politics."[30]

If the national state was dissociated for much of the nineteenth century from many of the most important transaction rules of state and market, these exchanges were insulated to a large degree, especially in the case of the working classes, from patterns of political mobilization and participation in the new mass franchise democracy. In the medium-size and large cities that were the loci of capitalist industrialization and of the concentration of the native and immigrant working classes, political identities and incorporation were fash-

29. Jack Greene, *Peripheries and Center: Constitutional Development in the Extended Politics of the British Empire and the United States, 1607–1788* (Athens: University of Georgia Press, 1986).

30. Theodore J. Lowi, "Why Is There No Socialism in the United States?" *Society* 22 (January-February 1985): 39; William R. Brock, *Investigation and Responsibility: Public Responsibility in the United States, 1865–1900* (Cambridge: Cambridge University Press, 1984).

ioned by highly localistic political organizations that were joined to the state and national levels in organizationally complex and much mediated fashion. Neither the form nor the content of these "machines" (I use the quotation marks because in some times and places they were centralized in hierarchical fashion under the leadership of a citywide boss, but in other times and places there was a plethora of relatively uncoordinated and competing neighborhood-based party organizations) was a primordial given. Indeed, the "classic" political machine, stressing territoriality and ethnicity, and segmented from labor organizations and class rhetoric, never existed in pure form, and where it approximated the norm it did so only after contests with other modes of political participation, including various nativist and laborist alternatives. Nevertheless, as a broad generalization, American nineteenth century urban politics was characterized by the machine's definition of its subject matter as territoriality and ethnicity in a manner that was distinguishable from the politics of labor at the workplace. This divided pattern has been a hallmark of American working-class formation. Elsewhere, I have tried to show how this outcome was shaped decisively by the organization and policies of the American state at different levels of government.[31]

The political machine thus helped manage the existence of a mass franchise democracy in a capitalist society by separating the most direct and intense level of political participation from the level of state-market organization, and by defining the identities of political actors in such a way as to minimize the challenge to state-market relations. Politics came to be defined at this level not as one of a working class versus capitalism and the state but as a politics of distinctive clusters of ethnic groups (with ethnicity understood as a complex constellation of cultural, class, and territorial markers) competing for the distribution of governmental services and spoils. This politics of patronage was noisy, real, and contested.

But it was not the only kind of political activity fostered by machine politics. For the political machine was a complicated organizational structure that, simultaneously, was highly decentralized (given the checkerboard social geography of big cities, the machine manifested itself in the wards as "us" for each local group) and centralized (at the city level the leaders of the local organizations could join together to make deals and contracts with business and labor leaders). Lowi has taken note of the role of local politics as it concerned state-market relations:

> The local governments were given considerable discretion to adapt state laws to local needs. As a consequence, local governments operated under consider-

---

31. Ira Katznelson, *City Trenches: Urban Politics and the Patterning of Class in the United States* (New York: Pantheon Books, 1981); also see Ira Katznelson and Margaret Weir, *Schooling for All: Race, Class and the Decline of the Democratic Ideal* (New York: Basic Books, 1985); Ira Katznelson, "Working Class Formation and the State: Nineteenth Century England in American Perspective," in Peter Evans, Dietrich Rueschemeyer, and Theda Skocpol, eds., *Bringing the State Back In* (Cambridge: Cambridge University Press, 1985); and the treatment of late nineteenth-century America by Martin Shefter, "Trade Unions," in Katznelson and Zolberg, eds., *Working Class Formation*.

able advantages in that their city councils and county legislatures were spared the burden of making fundamental social choices but were left relatively free to adapt general state laws to local demands. State regulatons became patronage in the hands of local officials, again in the original sense of the verb *to patronize*. If some particular conduct—such as using a private home as a boardinghouse or operating a restaurant or cab—was forbidden or restricted under state law, it could be handed back as a matter of privilege through local licensing. By definition, a license is a permission by a government to do something that is otherwise illegal. Licensing was an almost never-ending source of patronage in the hands of local governments. Other patronage included the letting of contracts for public works and the granting of access and rights-of-way in the use of public and private property.[32]

"Out of this," he continues, "emerged the local political machines." Not quite out of this, but with this set of resources. The machines that made these arrangements and distributed the resources they garnered defined what the state was—an engine of distribution—to most citizens, and it did so in such a way as to minimize class definitions and class consciousness.

Contemporary critics of the nineteenth century regime of state-market and state-citizen transactions focused a good deal of their ire on political machines. For an emerging Progressive intelligentsia they represented inefficiencies and a diffuse state. For many businessmen, they represented an expensive form of double taxation and elusive regulation and responsibility,[33] and for left-wing movements and parties they represented barriers to class organization and collective action. Thus the politics of Reform versus the machine, which has long been a favorite theme of urban political studies (including Dahl on New Haven and Lowi on New York), is important not just for the light it sheds on local disputes but as an important arena of conflict concerned both directly and indirectly with basic contours of the regime.

If hegemony is defined, as David Laitin does in an elaboration of Gramsci, as "the political forging . . . and institutionalization of a pattern of group activity in a state and the concurrent idealization of that schema into a dominant symbolic framework that reigns as common sense",[34] then the importance of the political machine was its capacity to create hegemony, that is, to define the institutional and symbolic framework of participation and political identities at key moments of transition and stress. The machines did not eliminate conflict; they channeled conflict. And if urban machines certainly were not the only political vehicle of this kind, they did provide for a time the key instrumentalities of hegemonic incorporation in cities undergoing rapid industrialization with large, and potentially insurgent, working-class populations.

---

32. Lowi, "Why Is There No Socialism," 39–40.

33. This point is argued in the regrettably neglected volume, Clifton Yearley, *The Money Machines: The Breakdown and Reform of Governmental and Party Finance in the North, 1860–1920.* (Albany: State University of New York Press, 1972).

34. David Laitin, *Hegemony and Culture: Politics and Religious Change among the Yoruba* (Chicago: University of Chicago Press, 1986), 19.

To be sure, there is a similarity between hegemonic analyses of machine politics of the kind Lowi, Bridges, Shefter, and I have presented in our work and the functionalism of Merton that McDonald so dislikes. There is also a continuity with the consensus historians' search for mechanisms of integration and the domestication of conflict. There is, too, a significant overlap between virtually all the studies of machine politics of the past four decades in their stress on ethnicity, patronage, and local territory. McDonald judges all these family resemblances to be misguided. Thus, writing about my work on urban politics, he argues,

> This description of the machine is a page torn directly from the book of Handlin, Hofstadter, and Merton. Katznelson has simply taken the functional model from the liberal pluralist framework and injected it into a neo-Marxist one. Such a strategy is always epistemologically risky because a model deduced from the first principles of one theory cannot necessarily be grafted onto a theory with different assumptions. In this case, the functional model of the machine is based upon an assumption of economic opportunity and political integration; the marxian theory assumes economic appropriation and political hegemony. The insertion of the functional model of the machine into a neo-Marxist analysis of urban politics does not strengthen the latter but, on the contrary, dilutes its analytical power considerably by making the achievement of political hegemony look relatively easy. The ease of this accomplishment is, however, less the reality of urban political history than the assumption of liberal pluralist theory.[35]

But why easy? No one who has studied political machines seriously would claim it was so—but if not easy, an accomplishment with which to be reckoned. And, as any literary critic knows, it is not possible to tear a page from one book and insert it into another without changing the meaning of each in fundamental ways. This may be a risky course, but it has paid some dividends already, and promises more, by identifying the patterning and character of conflict in American political development. What is now needed is not a return to the Progressive antinomy of conflict and consensus or a rejection of functionalism *tout court*, but systematic and comparative attention to the contingent and contested state-citizen and state-economy transaction rules that have character-ized the American regime and its peculiar state. Without such a careful chart-ing, both the analysis of politics and political strategy will prove elusive, and no amount of stress on conflict alone or critical incantations about consensus, functionalism, and hegemony will produce more than notes without a tune.

TERRENCE J. MCDONALD

Reply to Professor Katznelson

Professor Katznelson's essay deserves a lengthy reply, but space limitations require me to keep my response brief. I strongly disagree with the way that he

35. McDonald, "The Problem of the Political," 344–45.

has characterized the thrust of my essay, the point of my other work, and the implications of recent work by other urban historians. But rather than hash over these misinterpretations, I will focus instead on the issue between us that I think has the most relevance for future work on the role of urban politics in American political development: the utility of a focus on the urban political machine.[1]

Katznelson is absolutely right that the "new turn to the state at the national level so far has not explored how the city level of politics might be integrated into the wider American political experience." I agree with him, too, that, among other things, "what is now needed is . . . systematic and comparative attention to the contingent and contested state-citizen and state-economy transaction rules that have characterized the American regime." This agreement is no coincidence. It was in part the stimulating work of Katznelson himself that led me to begin my inquiries into the intellectual barriers to movement in precisely these directions.

The main point upon which we disagree is whether we can get "there" from "here," whether, as he puts it, "studies of political machines can contribute to understanding the distinctive features of the state in American political development." As I hope I made clear in my essay, I do not think that studies focused on *political machines* can contribute to such understanding, and Katznelson's essay has not swayed me on this point. On the contrary, his essay is a case study of the process by which that concept directs inquiries toward a "peculiar" understanding of the role of the state in American life.

As Michael Frisch has pointed out, the American city had barely stopped being portrayed as a "boil" on the body politic when it was transformed in the writings of Progressive Era reformers and academicians into the "hope" of democracy. Reconstructed as "the crux of civilization, where modern problems must be engaged and where, through triumphant engagement, American democracy would be redeemed," the study of the city became part of a larger discourse on the problems and potential of liberal democracy in general and the liberal state in particular. From Bryce to Banfield and beyond, much of what has passed for intellectual commentary on urban politics has really been part of this larger discourse.[2]

My essay attempts to analyze the grammar of this discourse, the means by which writing about urban politics has been transformed into statements about the liberal state and statements about the liberal state have been transformed into writing about urban politics. This is a complicated, interactive process involving changes in intellectual history, liberal politics, and the theoretical and methodological agendas of social science. More work needs to be done on this process both by me and by others, but at this point two things can be said about it with some certainty. First, this discourse has had the power to pull writing on

---

1. Assuming that the reader is familiar with the preceding essays, I do not cite here works that have already been discussed there unless my reference to them is specific.

2. Michael Frisch, "Urban Political Images in Search of a Historical Context," in Lloyd Rodwin and Robert M. Hollister, eds., *Cities of the Mind: Images and Themes of the City in the Social Sciences* (New York: Plenum Press, 1984), 197–232.

urban politics far from the more mundane details of urban politics itself, and, second, changes in the agenda of urban historical social science have had a great deal more to do with changes in this discourse than with the application of new techniques to new data in the field of urban political history.

The functional model of the political machine, itself, is a good example *not* of the "discovery" of new information about urban political history but of the "rereading" of the same information according to new discursive rules. Although proclaimed as an example of science, complexity, and realism, this concept is a better example of ideology, reductionism, and wishful thinking.

To begin with, the functional model of the political machine was constructed in part to legitimize a particular *version* of the role of the state in American political development. In that version all of the indexes of stateness that Katznelson borrows from Charles Tilly were minimized. The boundary between state and citizen was intentionally dissolved and the state subordinated to the citizen (or group of citizens), therefore the autonomy of the state was minimized; the legitimacy of the state was exaggerated, therefore the coercive powers of the state were ignored; the distributive function of the state was highlighted, therefore its need to extract resources was downplayed. This "disappearance" of the state went hand in hand with the apotheosis of the ward boss. It was the boss after all, who personified the state, embodying its lack of differentiation from society; it was the boss who subordinated the state to the citizen, winking at various violations of ordinances and laws, and so on; it was the boss who organized the relationship between the state and economy in such a way that things "got done" with enough resources left over to hand out the jobs and privileges that convinced the citizen the state was an engine of distribution.[3]

However, this image of the machine—which required a radical reduction of the multiple points of contact between the citizen and the state in urban America—was shaped as much by the desiderata of the mid-twentieth century liberal state as by the realities of the state in the nineteenth century. By focusing on the ward boss rather than the tax assessor, the precinct captain rather than the police captain, the party hack rather than the party ideologue, this view reconfigured the past in the shape of the present. Like America in the 1950s, urban politics in the nineteenth century became a time of resource abundance, high political legitimacy, and no ideology.

Now to make this point is in no way to attempt to reveal the "dirty secret" of urban studies or to trivialize the work of men like Hofstadter, Hartz, Merton, or Dahl. They helped revolutionize academic disciplines, reshape intellectual discourse, and even profoundly influence the broader political discourse. They were not always overjoyed at what they thought they found in the American past, and their intellectual and political energy and commitment are models for us all. Precisely because of their importance we owe them the same high level of critical engagement that they maintained with their predecessors. In this spirit

3. Charles Tilly, "Reflections on the History of European State-Making," in Tilly, ed., *The Formation of National States in Western Europe* (Princeton: Princeton University Press, 1975), 3–83.

it must be said about these authors, as Hofstadter himself said about his progressive predecessors, that consciously or unconsciously "many of their interpretative ideas rested on some kind of identification of the past and present that we could easily see through, not because we were cleverer but because *their* present was no longer ours."[4]

Indeed, if there is any dirty secret of urban studies, it may lie less in the commitments of this generation than in the epigonism of the succeeding ones who have, on the whole, mechanically applied this framework. In so doing, they have failed to see how much of the weight of the imposing edifice of American exceptionalism rests on the brawny shoulders of the boss and have failed to understand that the sense of statelessness that historical social scientists think they have *discovered* in nineteenth-century America was to a great extent *invented* in mid-twentieth-century America. Because the functional model of the political machine is both constitutive of and evidence for these views, a focus on it cannot offer a route to a new understanding of American political development. It is, instead, part of an endless loop back to an old one.

Studies of the multiple points of contact between citizen and state in America may lead in new directions, however. The starting point of such work might be the recognition that neither the federal system nor the early achievement of nearly universal white male suffrage exempted the American state from the tasks of state building. Like other states, to use Tilly's terms again, the American state, too, had to extract resources, differentiate itself from society, obtain a monopoly on legitimate coercive force, and maintain its own political legitimacy. The federal system determined the *location* in which those tasks were accomplished and the suffrage established some political *boundaries* on the techniques that could legitimately be used for accomplishing those tasks. They did not, however, predetermine the *means* by which these tasks were accomplished.

Now if—for the sake of argument at least—we give the political machine a vacation from its herculean labors, we see that in the "real" world of American city and state government there was no magic path to the accomplishment of these tasks. Extraction of resources from a population that had just fought a revolution in part against taxation was enormously difficult. Urban police forces struggled to wrest the means of coercion from ethnic gangs, elite vigilantes, and the private armies of industrialists. Acting in complete contradiction of the machine model, urban politicians professionalized police and fire departments, routinized the tasks of municipal bureaus, and successfully provided a wide range of public goods. Embedded in each of these areas of political struggle are the microdramas of a contingent, contentious, and fascinating state-building process in which ideology played a greater role than patronage, and fiscal scarcity a greater role than abundance; resistance to the process was as interesting as its completion. In the aggregate, the multiplicity of these conflicts underscores the absurdity of the belief that a "political machine" mediated all these issues.

4. Richard Hofstadter, *The Progressive Historians: Turner, Beard, Parrington* (New York: Alfred A. Knopf, 1968), xv.

We know about these conflicts because recent historical works have both reconsidered the reality of political machines and focused instead on the myriad ways in which the state intersected with society at the state and local levels in nineteenth-century America. There is no need to repeat here what I wrote in my essay about these works, but I must add that, contrary to Katznelson's reading of them, there is almost *no* disagreement that the power, competence, and centrality of the political machine have been exaggerated. For example, in a careful recent survey of this issue that is by no means hostile to the conception, M. Craig Brown and Charles N. Halaby conclude that the idea of rewriting the "history of urban politics has merit," because much of that history is either "missed or misrepresented" in conventional studies of political machines.[5]

Against the central thrust of this new work Katznelson offers not the record of achievement under the aegis of the functional model but the prospect of all the things that studies of political machines "could" do. He knows full well that the former would be a weak reed to lean upon. Although anything "can" happen, we know that thirty years of focus on the political machine has yet to take us close to the goals for urban political history that Katznelson and I share. I think I have explained satisfactorily why it hasn't.

Katznelson grudgingly concedes that some of my history of ideas is "persuasive," but then dismisses it with an epistemological claim that is happy-go-lucky, indeed: "as any literary critic knows, it is not possible to tear a page from one book and insert it into another without changing the meaning of each in fundamental ways." I guess we don't read the same critics. The ones I read focus on the formative power of political and academic discourse. Their work leads me to say, in conclusion, that Katznelson and others may be flattering themselves to think that they have "used" the functional model of the political machine. It is likely, on the contrary, that the functional model of the political machine—with all the political claims it entails—has "used" them.[6]

5. M. Craig Brown and Charles N. Halaby, "Machine Politics in America, 1870–1945," *Journal of Interdisciplinary History* 7 (1987): 587–612.

6. For a useful introduction to some of the issues raised by recent literary criticism, see Edward Said, "Criticism between Culture and System," in Said, *The World, the Text, and the Critic* (London: Faber & Faber, 1984), 178–225.

SOTIRIOS A. BARBER
University of Notre Dame

Normative Theory, the "New Institutionalism," and the Future of Public Law

In 1982 a panel of the Western Political Science Association meeting in San Diego took stock of postwar developments in the study of public law among American political scientists. The *Western Political Quarterly* has published the papers as a symposium intended to "revive a dialogue" among political scientists about the future of public law.[1] The participants in this symposium generally take for granted the decline among political scientists, academic lawyers, and legal philosophers of the belief that judicial decision can be or even ought to be free of "political" considerations. All seem to agree about the justified triumph of something called "political jurisprudence." Yet no consensus unites the symposium participants regarding all that political jurisprudence is or ought to be. The participants agree that political jurisprudence should be more than simply teaching and research that confines itself to the legal categories and research methods that dominate lawyers' legal briefs and judicial opinions. They also agree on the need for inquiry into the social-psychological factors of judicial choice, impact studies, alternative methods of conflict resolution, and the like. But the symposium reveals conflicting views regarding the philosophic questions of moral value that enter into legal judgments. Two views in particular stand out.

Austin Sarat welcomes what he sees as a growing "pluralism" of approaches to legal phenomena among political scientists. "Those who do political jurisprudence are able to bring to their scholarship, indeed combine in their scholarship, philosophy, history, sociology, and legal analysis as well as political science," he says. Therefore, he adds, political scientists should continue to read a range of writers from Dworkin and Unger to Riker and Shepsle (553). "Leaving the [old behavioralist] pretense of science behind has opened and enriched our study," says Sarat. And "one can hardly imagine good graduate

---

1. Harry Stumph, "Whither Political Jurisprudence: A Symposium," *Western Political Quarterly* 36 (December 1983): 533–70; page numbers hereafter cited in the text.

training today that ignored any approach," including "historical, doctrinal, descriptive, institutional, [and] normative approaches" (552).

Sarat gives a rather straightforward and compelling reason for his approval of the prevailing pluralism in public law: with the decline of behavioralist exclusivity and the advent of pluralism, we political scientists have "more to say about a considerably broader range of legal subject matters than we did ten years ago." In particular, pluralism gives scope to an active concern for justice. "Ours is a hope," says Sarat, "that by understanding the process through which justice is dispensed that injustice can, if scholarship makes a difference, be minimized." Pluralism helps make "ours . . . a place within political science where questions of fact and value go together; empirical and evaluative or prescriptive analysis both find a home where the concern for state responses to specific cases is so central" (555).

In marked contrast to Sarat's view is that of Martin Shapiro, a second symposium participant. Shapiro is especially unhappy about what he calls the recent appearance of a new "jurisprudence of values" which finds Ronald Dworkin playing "Godfather" to a movement that "rejects the notion that moral values are simply undebatable matters of personal preference such as 'I like vanilla'" (542). Unlike Sarat, Shapiro sees no place in political jurisprudence for a jurisprudence of values. "Political jurisprudence sprang from the same basic positivism that inspired [the] behavioral political science" of figures like "Key, Dahl, [and] Truman." The "basic premise" of that political science was that "in a world in which there were no objective values, but only personal preferences, the politically and legally 'right' or 'rational' could only be defined as whatever the democratic process ground out" (543). Because, according to Shapiro, values really are grounded in "personal preference," the new "jurisprudence of values" joins "old fashioned constitutional law" in a class of activity that is little more than a "mixture of doctrinal manipulation, literary criticism, selective history, and seat-of-the-pants policy analysis" (543). The persistence of this "pre-1950s" sort of thing was "understandable among the elderly" scholars "who had nothing better to do." But when "the young folks" do it (Shapiro recalls "a truly crazy APSA panel session when people under 35 were bothering me about the 'craftsmanship' of the Burger Court"), we have to blame "bad graduate education by obsolescing senior scholars" and "the fact that some young people still [enter] the law field of political science from old-fashioned normative political theory rather than new-fashioned American political behavior" (543).

Looking back on the symposium and doubtlessly stung by the portentous content of Shapiro's remarks, Rogers Smith sees a threat of "renewed clashes between 'behavioralist' and 'normative' public law scholars, now perhaps compounded by inter-generational divisions."[2] In a recent paper Smith argues that political scientists can head off a revival of these "pointless and avoidable" feuds by recasting public law scholarship in light of "recent directions in research in a number of fields, of a sort dubbed the 'new institutionalism' by James March

2. Rogers Smith, "Political Jurisprudence, the 'New Institutionalism,' and the Future of Public Law," *American Political Science Review* 82 (March 1988): 90.

and Johan Olsen."[3] More specifically, Smith proposes that public law scholarship should "unify many of its longstanding descriptive and normative concerns" "by explicitly designing their studies as explorations of what Theda Skocpol has termed 'the dialectic of meaningful action and structural determinants.'"[4]

I am critical of Smith's proposal. The approach he recommends cannot achieve his stated objective of unifying normative and empirical concerns. Yet I'm not troubled by this particular defect, for I'm far from convinced that unity in public law is a worthy end, and failure to achieve unity leaves matters no worse than they may presently be. My interest is the survival of the jurisprudence of values that Shapiro opposes. I'm persuaded that normative theory is an essential part of public law as a branch of political science, and I don't want a reversal of recent gains for normative theory in public law. From my perspective, Shapiro's position is a clear threat; Smith's instrumental failure is not. Failing to unify normative and empirical concerns could still leave unchallenged the intellectual importance and disciplinary status of each.

The problem with Smith's approach from the perspective of those who would defend a role for normative theory is that if Smith's proposal matures according to its logic, it will not just fail to unify diverse concerns; it will eventually expel the most important normative concerns from public law in political science. Even worse, it will banish these concerns while appearing to accommodate them. I contend here that, knowingly or not, Smith has built a Trojan horse in which to hide Shapiro's threat to normative theory in public law.

I try to expose the true character of Smith's proposal here, and in the process I offer some suggestions about the limitations of Smith's understanding of the new institutionalism in public law. I argue also that it is much better for all sides of the normative/empirical divide to live in open conflict with one another than to accept the peaceful arrangement Smith proposes. Although I find even a clashing pluralism to be of greater scientific value than any likely form of unification, I nevertheless conclude by sketching an institutionalist approach that might accommodate all sides.

SMITH'S PROPOSAL FOR UNITY IN PUBLIC LAW

To summarize my problems with Smith's article at the outset: he begins with a promise to elaborate an approach to the study of public law that can "address" and "unify" normative and empirical concerns in the field, but he does not deliver on this promise. The article not only fails to address normative concerns; it depreciates their status in a way that will enervate the most powerful of normative concerns, and it obscures that fact in a way that can only aid an assault on normative theory. To political scientists of the behavioralist main-

---

3. Ibid., 90, citing James G. March and Johan P. Olsen, "The New Institutionalism: Organizational Factors in Political Life," *American Political Science Review* 78 (1984): 734–49.
4. Ibid., 2, citing Theda Skocpol, *Vision and Method in Historical Sociology* (Cambridge: Cambridge University Press, 1984), 4.

stream, Smith presents himself as a messenger from an alien yet still authoritative place called modern philosophy, a messenger reporting on an alien but unauthoritative activity called normative theory or moral-political philosophy. Smith reduces normative concerns to empirical concerns, and he also reduces moral-philosophic activity to acts of "faith." He supports his position by creating the impression that modern philosophic authority is united against the possibility of "ideal theory" or reasoned inquiry into a moral reality beyond mere social convention. This impression is a false one. Smith simply fails to report all the relevant views among modern philosophers. In the end, he leaves us with an approach that banishes philosophic activity from public law without ever giving a compelling reason.

Smith's Promise to Address Normative as Well as Empirical Concerns

Smith begins with a call for some sort of unity or "synthesis" of existing approaches in the field of public law.[5] Unification seems necessary, as we have seen, to head off "renewed clashes between 'behavioralist' and 'normative' public law scholars." Beyond reporting Shapiro's aggressive statement of regret that some younger scholars are moving away from the behavioralist mainstream and back to an "old-fashioned 'jurisprudence of values,'" Smith offers no evidence that "renewed clashes" are likely. At no point, moreover, does he examine his assumption that a clashing multiplicity of approaches is counterproductive of theoretical or practical progress. He just assumes that "synthesis" and "unity" are good for an intellectual community.

Whence this assumption? We need to know because synthesis, unity, and intellectual harmony are hardly self-evident goods. The act of unifying diverse and clashing elements means either banishing some elements or establishing the hegemony of some over others. So Smith is proposing someone's regime here, and the question is whose. Are academic peace and quiet simply ends in themselves? Is Smith offering us a peace lover's hegemony, then? Connected, perhaps, to the hegemony in American political thought of Hobbes—notoriously a peace lover—and his successors, like Locke? I mention this possibility because Smith has grounded his own contribution to normative constitutional theory partly in Locke;[6] and by proposing the hegemony of empirical over normative concerns, which I will show later that he does, Smith reinforces a social science positivism that reflects the values of bourgeois liberalism while insulating them from attack simply by denying the meaningfulness of philosophic activity that goes beyond rationalization of prevailing social belief or synthesis of powerful social doctrines.[7] But Smith knows, of course, that the

---

5. Ibid., 89–90.

6. Rogers Smith, *Liberalism and American Constitutional Law* (Cambridge: Harvard University Press, 1985), chaps. 1, 8–9; for the centrality of peace as a value to both Hobbes and Locke, see ibid., 18–19. See also Walter Berns, "Judicial Review and the Rights and Laws of Nature," in Philip Kurland, Gerhard Casper, and Dennis Hutchinson, eds., *1982 Supreme Court Review* (1983): 49–83.

7. For a connection between classical bourgeois liberalism and the eventual abandonment of moral and political philosophy in constitutional theory, see Sotirios Barber, "The New

bourgeois liberal tradition of Hobbes and Locke has its critics. And the question here is what Smith offers to scholars who see more to philosophy and science than the alleviation of the human condition as conceived by classical liberalism. Peace at the expense of progress toward truths that lie beyond those of bourgeois liberalism may be acceptable to those who see no truth beyond the existing or emerging science and morality of the established social order—for these people no longer quest for philosophic foundations of any sort. But how does Smith accommodate those who place the highest value on philosophic activity because they see knowledge beyond convention as a basic, unfulfilled but not altogether hopeless, aspiration? How, in particular, does Smith accommodate the normative concerns of scholars who incline toward viewing philosophy the way Socrates did?

Socrates, we recall, considered dialectic the heart of scientific method and likened it to combat. He depicted the scientist par excellence (the philosopher as opposed to the sophistic defender of convention) as a truth lover, not a peace lover. Socrates was constitutionally incapable of accepting the community's answers to philosophic questions that he knew to be open questions, and could not believe that one could just will their closure. He considered the conventionalist closure of open questions a kind of death because he was driven by the possibility of genuine knowledge, not just conventional knowledge, and he understood human nature in terms of openness to that possibility. A Socratic understanding of knowledge and its quest may not enjoy mainstream status in American political science today. But it has by no means disappeared, especially among normative theorists and public law scholars.

I mention a Socratic moral realism not to launch an inquiry into its debate with philosophic conventionalism. I want only to suggest that whether intellectual harmony and consensus are desirable or not depends utterly on controversial philosophic judgments or assumptions regarding the nature of nature and our relationships to it, including the nature of our individual and collective selves. If nature is elusive yet progressively knowable, and if progress toward truth is good, then consensus is bad because consensus preserves what must be less than true.[8] Consensus in the face of nature conceived as real, yet elusive but progressively knowable, risks nominalism in the face of a reality that, confronted in an honest way, corrodes formulas, paradigm cases, canonical conceptions, and other forms of conventional authority.[9] Science, on this philosophically realist hypothesis, is incorrigibly open-ended and revisable because nature is knowable only through progressively better theories.

Right Assault on Moral Inquiry in Constitutional Law," *George Washington Law Review* 54 (1986): esp. 266–75. For a general account of social science positivism as a conservative political force, see Brian Fay, *Social Theory and Political Practice* (Winchester, Mass.: Allen Unwin, 1976), 57–64.

8. For the implications of this proposition for constitutional choice, see Sotirios Barber, *On What the Constitution Means* (Baltimore: Johns Hopkins University Press, 1984): 116–21, 141–42, 224n43.

9. See Michael Moore, "A Natural Law Theory of Interpretation," *Southern California Law Review* 58 (1985): 288–301.

Because Smith is a philosophic conventionalist,[10] he joins other conventionalists who say that there is either no real nature to be known or no escape to a reality beyond social conventions regarding nature. This frees the conventionalist to value consensus in and of itself (though, logically, a thoroughgoing conventionalist can have no real reason to value consensus or anything else) without regard to its "truth" or "falsity." Thus, a conventionalist like Robert Bork insists that convention is all that constitutes "truth" and "falsity," there being no accessible natural things and relationships to which our beliefs can correspond.[11] Smith contends much the same when he says in another work that "prevailing community standards" determine "what constitutes minimally rational, deliberative conduct and . . . what preserves the ability to engage in it."[12]

Smith's brand of unity promises an approach that addresses the existing concerns of normative theory, and, presumably, addressing these would entail preserving them. But Smith's approach neither addresses nor preserves the essential concerns of moral and political philosophy. What he promises in the beginning, he cancels by article's end.

In an all but penitent tone Smith "acknowledg[es]" at the outset of his article that "much of my previous work falls squarely within what Shapiro labels, rightly, as the 'jurisprudence of values.'" Smith now says he shares Shapiro's concern that "public law scholarship will not flourish if all scholars focus simply on spinning out their own normative legal theories."[13] Smith's characterization of normative theoretic activity does not quite replicate the mind set of many who practice it. Theorists who seek objectively better conceptions of general normative ideas deny that real moral authority can attach to beliefs consciously held supportable solely because they are "my own," "his or her own," or even "our own." Even the expression of maxims like "Be Thyself!" and "Love It or Leave It!" (variations on attaching moral authority to "one's own") requires links to beliefs held to be moral truths.[14] From this perspective, one who conceives normative theory as mere spinning of one's own views cannot take normative theory very seriously.

That there is more involved here than an unfortunate rhetorical choice on Smith's part is clear from the remainder of his article. Smith elaborates an understanding of the new institutionalism in public law that differs in no discernible way from standard empirical social science. Surely there is no one, behavioralist or otherwise, who would argue against the value of the proposed research—as far as it goes—treating the normative beliefs of a given population as independent variables in causal research and in interpretations of

10. See Smith, *Liberalism and American Constitutional Law*, 187, 213, 222, 226, 238, 305; see also Smith's embrace of Rorty, discussed below.

11. See Robert Bork, "Neutral Principles and Some First Amendment Absolutes," *Indiana Law Journal* 47 (1971): 25, 30–31.

12. Smith, *Liberalism and American Constitutional Law*, 213.

13. Smith, "Political Jurisprudence," 90.

14. See Ronald Dworkin, *Taking Rights Seriously* (Cambridge: Harvard University Press, 1977) 134–37; *Law's Empire* (Cambridge: Harvard University Press, 1986), 130–39.

institutional change. But this hardly runs all the way to normative theory. Normative theory is not essentially concerned with the causes or likely consequences of a given belief, or with how a given population understands or assesses a given change in the world. Opposed on the one hand to those who study the history of normative theory, and on the other to ideologues who seek primarily the implementation of their conclusions, the active normative theorist is engaged in an open-minded quest for real or interpretive knowledge of justice and the common good, for what these mean simply (or by nature) and in changing circumstances, and for what our best current hypotheses about such primary questions suggest about discrete events and institutional change, accomplished or proposed. None of this is addressed by Smith's unity proposal.

Smith does accept the view that value beliefs can actually motivate action and institutional change.[15] After affirming that "neither . . . mutually self-interested behavior nor the leading deterministic sociologies seem adequate to describe political life," Smith nevertheless thinks it "wise to identify other relatively lasting structures or patterns of behavior, institutions of various kinds, that shape and constrain political choices and conflict," including Braudel's " 'geographical frameworks, certain biological realities,' and even 'spiritual constraints [and] mental frameworks.' "[16] Smith acknowledges, however, that following Braudel risks reducing political choice to something "epiphenomenal." In public law it risks "downgrad[ing] the significance . . . of genuine judicial discretion . . . that is traditionally at the heart of public law analysis."[17] Smith believes we can avoid such reductionism by recognizing that the contextual elements of choice (for example, "economic relations . . . ideological outlooks . . . ethnic alliances") underdetermine choice. This means that decisions "are in part traceable to the creative political skill, judgment, and artistry of the actors involved," and that the "values of political actors may be altered by deliberate reflection."[18] Smith's desire to avoid what he himself regards as an indefensible positivist reductionism soon leads him to recognize the non-reducibility or "relative autonomy" of social institutions (state, economy, ideology) generally *and* a corresponding plurality of approaches in public law as a field.

Thus, in honoring "relative autonomy," Smith finds himself heading toward a situation in which scholars have different orientations and no compelling reason to regard their orientations as epiphenomenal of something else. These diverse scholars seek accounts of the way "interest groups place demands on courts, of how dominant coalitions and realignments affect judicial behavior,

15. For general accounts of the rise and decline of an older social science positivism which treats values as rationalizations for behavior and activities caused by subrational determinants, see Edward Purcell, *The Crisis of Democratic Theory* (Lexington: University Press of Kentucky, 1973), chaps 3, 6, 10; Fay, *Social Theory and Political Practice*; Edward Bernstein, *Restructuring Social and Political Theory* (Philadelphia: University of Pennsylvania Press, 1976); *Beyond Relativism and Objectivism* (Philadelphia: University of Pennsylvania Press, 1983).

16. Smith, "Political Jurisprudence," 99, quoting Fernand Braudel, *On History* (Chicago: University of Chicago Press, 1980), 31.

17. Smith, "Political Jurisprudence," 100; page numbers hereafter cited in text.

along with qualitative probings of legal ideology and major decisions, and quantitative studies of how judicial attitudes correlate with results" (101). But then on the same page Smith suddenly realizes that this pluralistic situation is the very situation he wanted to avoid in the first place. And when he awakens to this conflict of purposes his initial impulse to "unify" the field quickly over-powers his disapproval of reductionism. He can't tolerate a plurality of approaches because "it is not clear how we would tell which accounts [that is, approaches or governing questions] were more decisive, or whether the others really mattered at all." Since, for some reason, we political scientists should not tolerate open questions at the fundaments, "we should try to see how these difficulties [with a plurality of approaches] might be overcome." Having opened the question of which approach matters most, Smith now closes it (or closes himself to it) by going back to his previous invocation of Skocpol and asserting—not arguing—that "the fundamental methodological question is how students of politics, and in particular of public law, can give greater specificity to the precept that the 'interplay of meaningful acts and structural contexts' should be central to their analyses" (101).

With this choice of what the fundamental question for public law is, Smith proposes a broad approach that excludes normative analysis from its purview. As Smith would apply it in public law, Skocpol's "precept" would require that "students of legal ideology" would "take certain ongoing elements" of a particular ideology as "starting points for analyzing" judicial decisions. These "students of legal ideas would have to present more explicit models of the key mental or rhetorical structures they wished to explore than is often the case." (Shades of operationalism?) They would be alert to how "structures or institutions . . . may have arisen from past controversial political choices." This should make them and their readers less likely to see existing patterns as "writ into the nature of things." "All analysts . . . should identify as fully as possible their dependent variables, the set of 'meaningful acts,' such as judicial decisions, they claim to help explain." They must be prepared to settle for properly limited "interpretive narrative[s]" and representative cases where data elude statistical methods and aims. They should show how decision makers other than those under investigation might have responded differently in the same "structural contexts," taking care not to deny the causal influence of "judicial creativity." And finally they should ask how the choices of judges in turn affect the institutions in the background of those choices. Thus, "we must not only try to explain *Dred Scott*; we must also consider what developments *Dred Scott* helps to explain" (101–03).

This agenda omits activities specific to normative theory. It contains no programmatic recommendations fully responsive to Smith's stated belief that values that "may be altered by deliberate reflection" may motivate action that can "reshap[e] the world" (100). Nothing here accommodates the sense that political actors can have fundamentally better and worse reasons for acting, a sense that pervades the sphere of political action. This sense is the predicate for the activity of considering whether there are better or worse reasons for our ultimate choices; it is the predicate for moral-political philosophy.

When Smith says that behavioral factors underdetermine choice he moves in the right direction. But "choice" for Smith seems little more than a name attached to events that fall between the cracks of available environmental hypotheses—the accidental or "unexpected" element in our empiricist accounts and interpretations of what has happened and is likely to happen. So we can indeed talk about *Dred Scott*. We can attempt accounts of what came before and after. But there's nothing on Smith's new institutionalist agenda concerning whether decisions like *Dred Scott* are morally right or wrong. Nor is there anything on his agenda about what political systems we should try to establish or preserve in our quest for better answers to moral questions like those that figured in *Dred Scott*. There's nothing about whether an institution that could produce *Dred Scott* is compatible with our best current understanding of what the quest for justice entails or what democracy ought to be. Questions like these, however, make up most of the existing normative concerns in public law.

The last section of this essay offers some suggestions of what a serious address of normative concerns would require of an agenda for public law. But I must first discuss a few problems in Smith's understanding of moral philosophy.

On Smith's Understanding of Normative Concerns

To my contention that Smith reneges on his promise to outline an approach that addresses normative as well as empirical concerns, his article suggests some likely responses. He says, to begin with, that "normative debates . . . might be more attentive to the problem of the empirical generalizations they rely upon tacitly" (105). This probably means that people making practical arguments should try to verify the empirical propositions that are embedded in the minor premises of those arguments. To this all sides will agree, although empirical research confined to minor premises hardly addresses the background normative questions to which the major premises stand related as answers. Yet Smith may have something else quite controversial in mind, something far different from bringing empirical research to bear on generally acknowledged empirical premises. He comes close to proposing that empirical research can test the major premises of moral arguments. Whether he intends to or not, he will suggest to many of his readers that empirical research can answer questions of public right and wrong and the legitimate ends of government—questions we confront in deciding how best to interpret provisions like the commerce clause and the due process and equal protection clauses.

The startling prospect of answering such questions through empirical methods flows from Smith's reading of a group of modern philosophers whom he describes as "mov[ing] away from 'ideal theory' to more empirically-oriented 'pragmatist' approaches." Smith includes in this group names like Rorty, Walzer, MacIntyre, and Herzog (105). He finds these theorists successfully denying the existence of a moral reality beyond social convention—a simple, natural or real justice, and an objectively true understanding of the common good, as opposed to various opinions and conventions about such things. Smith agrees with these modern conventionalists, and this influences his conception of what moral philosophy is properly all about. Moral philosophy, it seems, is properly concerned with finding, reporting, and applying empirical generalizations about certain social conventions of particular communities. Thus, he says moral philosophy should "begin with the empirical and historical realities of our moral tradition." Moral philosophy should seek the "historical roots" of "our inherited principles" and "attend carefully to the role—great and small— they have played politically, attempting to judge their characteristic tendencies, strengths, and weaknesses in the crucible of social life" (105). Smith defends his rejection of "ideal theory" and his preference for pragmatic conventionalism with no more than personal assurances to his readers that it "seems to me largely sound"—that "it simply seems true that our moral outlooks are largely the products of past tradition, whether we are conscious of that fact or not" (105).

"Largely the products of past tradition," he says. But not entirely? Is this a hedge? Is there room here for a conception of distinctly human events as something other than movement that is either environmentally determined or accidental? Movement that occurs when reflection and argument go against habit, inclination, and convention? Although it is not as pronounced as one might want, Smith takes a big step toward an affirmative answer when he says:

> Pragmatism must indeed prove unsatisfactory if we use it to conceal from ourselves the necessity to criticize the current array of normative dispositions and to make reasoned choices among them. Those choices may have to be defended in turn by appeals to what seem to us to be more lasting aspects of our condition, in the manner of natural law theorists. (105)

But then he pulls back, for in the paragraph immediately following he refers to the "transcendental" or nonconventionalist "validity" of particular values as mere matters of "faith," not reason. And this reference returns us to the conventionalist denial that reason has access to a moral reality beyond convention. I don't see how Smith leaves us with more than (1) ideologies and other institutional determinants perceived by political actors as "tradition," (2) undetermined events perceived by observers as "creative acts and judgments," and (3) "faith" in our conventions and inventions. If convention, chance, and faith are all we have, we can never have reasons for believing that moral standards run deeper than established or emerging institutions. A further suggestion that right collapses into history and that empirical methods can decide moral questions is present in Smith's statement that "research that identifies actual patterns of legal and political discourse . . . should enable public law scholars to argue more powerfully about the values American law has really embodied historically" (105).[18]

Smith would thus bring us to a place where we could not say that we are ever moved to act for the sake of some general value like justice. Justice—justice itself, as opposed to both our idiosyncratic and our conventional versions of justice—moves us, if at all, only when we either reaffirm our old beliefs or

---

18. For arguments that judgments of this kind are inseparable from moral philosophic activity, see Barber, *On What the Constitution Means*, 84–85; Ronald Dworkin, *A Matter of Principle* (Cambridge: Harvard University Press, 1985), chap. 2; Moore, "A Natural Law Theory of Interpretation," 322–38.

affirm better beliefs about justice in the context of philosophic inquiry that reflects an awareness of the defeasibility of all concrete conceptions of justice. Because such inquiry must be a matter of self-critical striving—for we are interested, ex hypothesi, in *justice*, not our conceptions of justice—it can hardly rest in faith or commitment. If we ever do move, we move in the direction favored by a balance of the continuing arguments about what justice is and requires. Remove moral philosophy from the agenda and you reduce action for the sake of justice to what Smith himself recognizes as "ideological outlooks" that fall into the same class as "economic relations," "ethnic alliances," and other "contextual elements" of choice, elements that "underdetermine choice" (100).

Smith is, of course, entitled to stand where his best thinking or even his feelings tell him to stand on the old conflict between nature and convention, moral philosophy and history. But he is not entitled to omit important information about his sources of authority. And he does just that by the way he tells his readers about the philosophic developments on which he relies. By giving play to the recency of the pragmatic conventionalist turn from "ideal theory," Smith leaves the typical mainstream behavioralist to whom his article is addressed with the impression that he stands with the latest philosophic developments and against the old "natural law" theorists. Yet the pragmatic conventionalists are hardly without critics in the fields of moral philosophy, jurisprudence, and metaphysics.[19] I am not referring primarily to Straussians who are defending the New Right's historicist and antiphilosophical conceptions of tradition and "framers' intent."[20] Rather I point to the best of the current natural law theorists in public law, Michael Moore, who is altogether modern in his analytic and scientifically informed method. Important contemporary theorists who are either solidly in or close to the conventionalist position in public law take Moore's arguments seriously.[21] Smith hints at none of these developments, and one can only conclude that he ignores them because he is simply closed to arguments for a moral realist approach to the normative problems in public law.[22]

If Smith is closed to realism as an option, however, that may not mean he's closed to moral philosophy altogether. Smith's reliance on pragmatic conventionalism suggests an answer he might give to my argument that his agenda for public law is exclusively behavioral. If such an agenda is itself the dictate of a correct philosophic position, as Smith holds pragmatic conventionalism to be, then that agenda unifies empirical and normative concerns *properly understood*. And if each of us has a right to his conception of normative concerns, then

19. See Rorty's reply to some of his realist critics in *Consequences of Pragmatism* (Minneapolis: University of Minnesota Press, 1982), xxi–xxxvii.

20. See Gordon Wood, "The Fundamentalists and the Constitution," *New York Review of Books* 33 (February 18, 1988); Barber, "The New Right Assault."

21. See, for example, David A. J. Richards, "Interpretation and Historiography," *Southern California Law Review* 58 (1985).

22. See Sotirios Barber, review of *Liberalism and American Constitutional Law*, by Rogers M. Smith, *Political Theory* 15 (November 1987): 657–61.

Smith might be entitled to claim that his agenda satisfies these concerns. By adopting one particular philosophic teaching, Smith can banish what he calls "natural law" and "ideal" theorists while still claiming to accommodate normative concerns.

This, I submit, would be a false claim as applied to the most fundamental concerns of normative theory. A glance at current debates in the "jurisprudence of values" reveals at least two broad kinds of issues: conflicts over substantive conceptions of justice and other principles of constitutional morality (including appropriate institutional arrangements) and metatheoretical conflicts about the best approaches to these issues. Smith removes all live philosophic issues of both varieties from his agenda for public law. By removing the first group Smith cancels any hope he might have created about an approach that would address what many in public law now regard as the most fundamental of normative concerns, those regarding better conceptions of general normative ideas like justice, democracy, and so forth. Here he swaps live philosophic questions for essentially empirical questions about who believes what and how those beliefs should be efficiently administered. But that choice could still leave the second class of fundamental concerns, those involving questions of the proper approach to normative questions of the first type. In other words, a pragmatic conventionalist could still value the debate among conflicting interpretive approaches and related metaphysical and epistemological questions that for almost two decades have enriched the field of public law.[23] For it is only through such debates that one can reaffirm the merits of pragmatic conventionalism itself. That this class of questions is also missing from Smith's agenda suggests the transformation of pragmatic conventionalism from a philosophic position—one that exists in a context of philosophic debate—to an ideology.

If Smith acts consistently with the advice he gives others in his new institutionalism article, he will have removed himself from all philosophic debates by treating metaphysical issues as settled and normative issues fundamentally less than rational, and by calling for the hegemony of an approach that excludes all philosophic questions from its agenda. I would not criticize Smith for not honoring normative theory were he not pretending to do normative theory or because he had decided that normative theory was not as important to him personally as other pursuits. But one can criticize Smith's pretended address of normative theoretic concerns, and one can criticize his misrepresentation of his reasons for abandoning those concerns, namely, that a modern philosophic consensus militates against them.

THE PROBLEMS OF UNITY IN PUBLIC LAW: SHOULD MORAL PHILOSOPHY BE SOVEREIGN?

Because I have criticized Smith's agenda for public law, some readers may expect me to propose a better agenda. I outline something of the sort in the

23. For an overview, see Walter F. Murphy, James E. Feming, and William F. Harris III, *American Constitutional Interpretation* (Mineola, N.Y.: Foundation Press, 1986), chap. 8.

concluding section of this essay. But I cannot turn to the question of a better agenda without responding, albeit reluctantly, to Smith's assumption that unity would be good for public law. I don't think it would be. Unity risks intellectual hegemony, and hegemony risks intellectual reductionism and stagnation. If, however, those on what I regard as the right side of the issues don't accommodate the desire for unity, those on the other side will.

It may seem ironic for a moral realist (a "natural law" theorist, in Smith's terms) to be concerned with avoiding hegemony and stagnation. Those who suffer this sense of irony simply attest the general misinformation about the moral realist position. Michael Moore is, as I have noted, the leading realist in the current debate. His writings provide ample basis for concluding that moral realism actively excludes dogmatism in all its forms.[24] Stephen Macedo, another realist in the current debate, links realism with liberal toleration in areas of personal morality.[25] My own writings describe a posture of endlessly self-critical striving for presupposed moral truths we can never fully grasp.[26] I have also argued that liberalism must tolerate illiberal private associations as part of its logically compulsory obligation continuously to challenge its own presumed foundations, acting, when it must, only on "conclusions" tentatively held (140–44).

Realism, as I see it, even entails doubts about realism itself; hence its constitutional openness to conventionalism as an option. Realism properly contends that there is a moral reality to be known, not because of affirmative proof, but because all of us seem to hold by ineluctable presupposition that, although moral positions are always debatable, there are better and worse moral arguments. But as unshakable as our presuppositions of better and worse moral arguments might be, we can always wonder about the status of those presuppositions. It is that wonder that keeps us open to conventionalism. Open questions should be treated as open questions. From the perspective of what Smith calls "ideal theory," each approach in public law has an important place, including approaches that challenge the value of ideal theory as an enterprise. Empirical research is valuable to ideal theory in public law because constitutional theory and policy involve norms that are expected to work in practice. Conventionalist challenges to ideal theory are valuable to ideal theory because they aid the continuous process of self-examination favored by the ontological and epistemological hypotheses of philosophical realism.

So I would prefer to avoid talk of unity in public law. Yet if forced into such a discussion, I would make the following remarks. One can question whether or how Smith could, in the end, concede any place at all to normative theory, for by relegating its central judgments to "faith" and denying a moral reality beyond established or emerging convention, he can't understand normative issues as they are understood by those who take them seriously. Smith all but

24. See, for example, Michael Moore, "Moral Reality," *Wisconsin Law Review* (1982): 1098, 1143.

25. Stephen Macedo, "Liberal Virtues of Constitutional Community," *Review of Politics* 50 (Spring 1988): 215–40.

26. Barber, *On What the Constitution Means*, 117–24.

admits this when he says that "it simply seems true that our moral outlooks are largely the products of past traditions, whether we are conscious of that fact or not" (105). Moral theoretic activity based on a rejection of the pragmatist closure to the realist option would "simply seem false." If both false and beyond the new institutionalist pale of unification, why tolerate any theoretic inquiry that resists the pragmatist closure? Just to be nice to our misguided realist friends? What would that conception of friendship say about us and such things as our obligations to our students? Despite the way he's packaging his proposal, and assuming he's thought things through, Smith isn't serious about unifying existing concerns in public law. Those who still want to unify will have to elevate the most inclusive of existing approaches; and that is and can only be moral realism, or normative theory as a moral realist understands it.

The association, however, of moral realism with dogmatism of the ideological right and left is long-standing and widespread.[27] This perception is not only grounded in misunderstanding, as I have already indicated; it is also unfair, for positivists like Shapiro occupy the best strategic positions in American political science, and they currently pursue a policy of exclusivity more vigorously and successfully than anyone else. (How else can one explain the hegemony of positivism in political science some two decades after its collapse in the philosophy of science, whence it originally came?)[28] Nevertheless, the prejudice against moral realism persists, and if anything should ever succeed in domesticating zealous behavioralism for citizenship in a pluralist discipline, realists should then rededicate themselves to correcting perceptions that link realism to dogmatism. Realists must free themselves from association with claims to have successfully concluded the quest for moral truth and its equivalents (like "framers' intent") or to have transcended the problem of moral truth through sheer willfulness to power, existential commitment, or other means. True realism entails openness and excludes hegemonic dogmatism—even its own; it is the only approach that logically must find a place for its critics. A voluntary and spontaneous pluralism would therefore be the best form for an intellectual community.[29]

A conventionalist might conceivably say that this vaunted pluralism is a sham, for if it has a point at all, it lies in its reflection of the realist understanding of moral and natural science: pluralism for the sake of (because rendered coherent only by the value of) self-critical striving for better theories of an elusive reality. Our conventionalist might charge that I'm describing a situation in which moral philosophy sneaks, somewhat Gyges-like, onto the public law throne. For although realism would rule invisibly and even inadvertently in the "pluralist" universe I describe, it would still rule. I might reluctantly concede that this is an admissible interpretation of my argument. Assuming arguendo that it is, my pluralism would be incoherent, for it would be a regime inconsis-

27. See Purcell, *Crisis of Democratic Theory*, chap. 11.

28. See Steven G. Salkever, "Aristotle's Social Science," *Political Theory* 9 (November 1981): 479–508.

29. See NEH Liaison Committee, "Political Science and the Humanities: A Report of the American Political Science Association," *PS*, Spring 1985, 247–49.

tent with its own justification. I have already shown why I can't make a realist case for realism's hegemony. Is there no satisfying the yen for unity, then, save by means that banish or downgrade some of us without compelling reasons?

Perhaps. But before we give up the quest for unity here, we might turn for help to those who need unity most and therefore understand sovereignty best. Maybe our conventionalist can make a case for realism's hegemony. If so, then Smith may yet discover a way to unify all approaches, as he says he wants to do. Maybe, in other words, a conventionalist like Smith can prove that unity in pluralism is (really) good. Let's see.

Ironically, conventionalism may well provide an argument for the hegemony of realism. If reason can't rise above our conventions, and if all is convention, then we'd seem to be stuck with the conventional distinction between nature and convention. The argument for realism would begin by exhorting us to theory that accommodates what common experience attests. And common experience reveals the distinction between nature and convention to be an institution with us; whatever else it may be, the distinction between nature and convention is an aspect of our conventional makeup. So, for the moment at any rate, we're stuck with the distinction between nature and convention. We're also stuck with conventional institutions, like science and moral philosophy, that pursue various dimensions of "nature." Denying the conventional distinction between nature and convention and the presuppositions, aspirations, and institutions concomitant to that distinction—totally denying all these conventional things—would require rising above convention itself. But that's something the conventionalists tell us we cannot do. Maybe they're right. It's remarkable, for example, how difficult it is for Smith to rise above the conventional understanding that distinguishes between nature and convention. Thus he can tell us on the one hand that pragmatic conventionalism "simply seems" right, but on the other hand that we must preserve the possibility of criticizing convention on grounds of "what seems to us more lasting aspects of our condition" (105). If our theories of reality can be nothing more than interpretations of our conceptions of reality, then let us be faithful to the perspective— our common perspective—that just can't shake the feeling that there really is a world "out there" about which we can have better and worse opinions, and that along with our opinions about what to believe, we can have better and worse opinions about how to live. Conventionalism as a philosophic position can't be faithful to our conventional understanding. Conventionalism self-destructs; it is faithless to itself.

Philosophical realism, as I've described it, can be faithful to our conventional understanding. The general idea that giving and exchanging reasons can lead to progressively better theories about an elusive physical and moral reality unifies two unshakable beliefs that would otherwise be incompatible: that some answers about what to believe and how to live are better than others, and that no such answer is beyond doubt. Few will deny the latter belief. Many will try to deny the former. They cannot succeed, for the very denial of that proposition presents itself as a statement about the world whose truth warrants the conformity of our beliefs, conduct, and institutions. Thus despite Shapiro's talk about no better or worse answers to normative questions, his view of reality somehow manages to yield controversial advice for two social institutions whose impact on the way we live is incalculable. I refer, of course, to government and political science. Government ought to be procedural democracy, says Shapiro in effect. And public law scholars ought to conform their beliefs and their conduct to the tenets of positivism's view of reality, lest they justly be blamed for being "truly crazy," obsolescent, corruptors of the youth, or some such.

Therefore—and I ask the reader to recall that this is a conventionalist argument that I do not want to make for myself, an argument I make in behalf of conventionalists like Smith—therefore, I say, "it simply seems true" that moral philosophy and a "jurisprudence of values" ought to be sovereign in public law—and why not? All of us will survive, albeit in our proper and less than sovereign places, for realism's sovereignty means unity in pluralism. The only ones who could complain would be the real philosophers who live in some conceptual never-never land of "ideal theory," and those who really live there won't bother to complain to us. And the "philosophers" who live here with us will "rule" in theory only, not in what we conventionalists call the real world. So they won't really rule. Realistically, so to speak, no approach will be sovereign here except that which would have us live and let live, if not in sweet harmony.

TOWARD A BETTER AGENDA FOR PUBLIC LAW

Our conventionalist's quest for unity thus reaffirms a conclusion C. Herman Pritchett reached some two decades ago: "There are both traditionalists and behavioralists who think that the gate is strait and the way narrow into the public law kingdom, but a more sensible text for all to contemplate is the old Chinese saying, 'Let a hundred flowers bloom.' "[30]

The first and most important item on the agenda of a field so unified would be to protect the diversity we now enjoy in public law. This involves securing a place even for those scholars who actively seek to destroy that diversity. Methodological pluralists must yield at least some quarter to those who oppose pluralism for the same reason that liberals must tolerate some measure of illiberalism. Yet all should be ready to combat the substitution of assertion and assertiveness for argument. One way to do that is to challenge imperialists of all stripes to show a candid world just how anyone can demonstrate the truths of their position. Thus, one might ask Shapiro if obsolescing scholarship explains the recent decline of positivism in the philosophy of science and how, if values are mere matters of personal preference, he can justify his conception of "democracy" and his preference for it.

Rather than exclude any approach, a pluralist public law should consider adding new ones. And a new appreciation for the live aspirations of moral realism should encourage the development of approaches that can combine ideal theory and the empirical study of institutions.[31] Political scientists who share a long-standing aspiration to distinguish their work from that of lawyers

30. C. Herman Pritchett, "Public Law and Judicial Behavior," in Marian Irish, *Political Science: Advance of the Discipline* (Englewood Cliffs, N.J.: Prentice-Hall, 1968), 219.

31. This section borrows from Sotirios Barber and Jeffrey Tulis, "Toward a New Constitutionalism in Constitutional Studies and American Institutions" (paper delivered at APSA Annual Meeting, Chicago, 1987).

can do so simply by asking questions from the nonlitigational and preeminently "political" perspective of those who have some practical responsibility for establishing and maintaining political systems as a whole. Political scientists operating from such a perspective would try to assess institutions as better or worse, and if worse, reformable in light of articulate ideals, while continuing to debate the relative merits of conflicting ideals. Because this perspective would combine ideal with systemic and practical concerns, one could call such an approach *constitutionalist*. Its agenda would be vast, for it would aspire to all the theoretical knowledge one would need to establish, maintain, and reform constitutions as the institutional practices of preferred ways of life. For examples of such an approach, one could begin with Aristotle's Politics and go on to the writings of Roberto Unger, stopping at the Federalist-anti-Federalist and Lincoln-Douglas debates along the way. Prominent also in the literature of this approach would be the century's important constitutional reformers and students of constitutional reform, from Goodnow and Wilson to Sundquist, Dahl, Lowi, Mansfield, and Benjamin Barber, names not often associated with today's "public law."

Bearing in mind that I am talking about a constitutionalist approach *in* public law, not *to* the (properly pluralist) field of public law as a whole, the constitutionalist's agenda would be governed by the components of a constitutionalist perspective. And since the structure of that perspective is itself a theoretical problem, the agenda item that ought to follow the question of what to do next in the continuing contest with the forces of antipluralism is what the rest of the agenda should be. If works like *The Federalist* and Aristotle's *Politics* can serve as models, a constitutionalist approach needs to debate philosophic-psychological hypotheses of what constitutes individual and collective identity, normative theories of the proper ends of government, mixed normative and empirical theories of the potential for moral progress in given political cultures, and theories of human incentive and choice, leader-follower interaction, public opinion formation, institutional behavior, institutional change, the internal and external politics of institutional maintenance and reform, and the formal and empirical conditions for institutional integrity and stability. In brief, and as I've already indicated, constitutionalist theory would need a web of theories as complex as the breadth of its responsibilities and the complexity of the social material for which it would prescribe.

Since the material of the constitutionalist's art is nothing less than society at large, the agenda of a constitutionalist's approach can never be satisfied or even fully set. And this fact should enlarge our conception of an agenda to include, in addition to research projects, the attitudes of researchers. Crucial to the right attitude is a multifaceted openness. To approximate its responsibilities constitutionalist theory must be open to normative improvement at the level of substantive ends and institutional means. It must also be open to the potential importance of an indefinite variety of intellectual disciplines, for social, environmental, technological, and scientific change can alter our understanding of the human condition (if not human nature) as well as humanity's prospects.

In sum, the constitutionalist commitment to openness requires an attitude of self-critical striving and a dialectical tone that disfavors methodological and ideological assertiveness and exclusivity. Add this new constitutionalism to what Smith proposes and what we already have in public law, along with a loose rule about doing your job and letting others do theirs, and you'll have about the only kind of "unity" anyone can defend.

ROGERS M. SMITH
Yale University

The New Institutionalism and Normative Theory: Reply to Professor Barber

Nowhere in political science was the "behavioral revolution" of the fifties more pervasive than in public law. Normative debates on constitutional issues were left largely to lawyers or to the dwindling number of scholars in American political thought. Recently, as Professor Sotirios Barber observes, normative inquiries have undergone a resurgence in this section of the discipline, a resurgence within which the bulk of my ongoing work rests (quite impenitently). This resurgence has many sources, one of which is a wider recognition in contemporary political science that ideas can shape political conduct and that empirical inquiries find their ultimate justification in their contributions to normative reflection.

Yet we are far from resolving the difficult problems of the role ideas actually play in political life and of just how empirical inquiries can assist us in our normative judgments. My essay "Political Jurisprudence, the 'New Institutionalism,' and the Future of Public Law," represents an effort to explore some answers to those problems as they appear in public law scholarship.[1] But although he and I are both convinced of the importance of ideas, both concerned to promote better normative discourse, and both proponents of what might be termed "liberal rationalist" political values, Barber feels the approach I suggest would "eventually expel the most important normative concerns from public law."[2]

Barber is egregiously wrong. His critique rests on two fundamental misapprehensions. He first mistakes the basic argument of my essay. He portrays it as a "report" on the state of contemporary moral philosophy, a brief for some types of moral theories over others, and a plea for modes of descriptive work

1. R. M. Smith, "Political Jurisprudence, the 'New Institutionalism,' and the Future of Public Law," *American Political Science Review* 82 (March 1988): 89–108.

2. For the similarities in our substantive values, see S. A. Barber, *On What the Constitution Means* (Baltimore: Johns Hopkins University Press, 1984), vii, 169; R. M. Smith, *Liberalism and American Constitutional Law* (Cambridge: Harvard University Press, 1985), 5, 206–07, 259.

that would tacitly rule out the types of moral theory I allegedly dismiss. In fact, the essay focuses on empirical concerns, especially how to connect descriptions of the role of ideas in decision making with other sorts of descriptive accounts. It deals only briefly with normative inquiry; but its suggestions for descriptive and normative work in no way preclude the "moral realism" Barber defends. Indeed they are probably necessary to develop such a view persuasively.

Barber's mischaracterizations of my essay reflect his second, more long-standing, misapprehension. He misconstrues the approach to normative argument I favor, incorrectly dubbing it "pragmatic conventionalism." Although I endorse the attention to history, context, and empirical realities some pragmatists call for, nothing in my work has ever assigned any authoritative moral weight to social conventions per se. Instead, I have consistently argued that we should decide on our moral positions via reasoned judgments about the conceptions of the human self, its worth, and its enhancement that seem most persuasive, guided by, among other things, "fundamental characteristics of the human condition" and history's lessons about how different ideals have worked out in practice.[3]

What, then, are the real differences in the empirical and normative approaches Barber and I favor, and what is the significance of these differences for how scholars might best study American public law and American political development more broadly? In fact, when we move beyond labels to examine the concrete steps involved in empirical inquiry and its utilization in moral reasoning, the approach I recommend actually is not so very different from that favored by Barber's philosophic beau ideal, law professor Michael Moore. But there are, I will argue, two important contrasts.

First, in regard to the relationship of empirical and normative work, I do lay *more* stress on empirical research into the ways ideas actually influence political decisions, and into the consequences ideas have had historically, as descriptive inquiries relevant to moral deliberations. That is why my work engages in historical explorations much more extensively than either Barber or Moore, and why I emphasize that "new institutionalist" studies of America's political evolution are valuable for contemporary American normative debates.[4] Failure to engage in these inquiries seriously cripples anyone's claim to have discovered persuasive moral precepts, whether they are termed "realist" or "pragmatist."

Second, in regard to normative positions, I do think it wiser to describe the conclusions of able moral deliberation as "reasoned choices" or "judgments," instead of insisting that they represent approximations of "moral reality" or "natural law." On the question of the existence of such a reality, I am not

---

3. Smith, *Liberalism*, 5–6, 170–71, 211–12, 220; "Political Jurisprudence," 100, 105.

4. Compare, for example, Barber's *On What the Constitution Means*, with my own *Liberalism*. Both books advance theories of the American Constitution that present it as aspiring to create a community of rationally inquiring and self-governing citizens. But my argument rests in part on extensive analysis of the historic failures of other constitutional outlooks, while Barber indicates that he is not "particularly interested in the doctrinal history of the Supreme Court (i.e., the story of how one judicial version of the law follows another)" (8).

dismissive, simply agnostic. I am confident, however, that I can claim no sure grasp of it myself, and that contemporary scholars who imply such claims promise more than they have delivered, at least as yet. Hence I find most appropriate a moral language that calls attention to the uncertainties and the choices involved in our moral positions. It is this linguistic preference, more than anything else in my arguments, that vexes Barber, and I will return to the issue of its propriety in my conclusion.

CAN THE NEW INSTITUTIONALISM ENCOMPASS MORAL REALITY?

Barber's effort to depict my article as hostile to his moral realism is hampered by the fact that my essay does not criticize his view. It simply does not discuss that position. So Barber argues in terms of the alleged implications of my reasoning and phrasing; but his inferences are persistently flawed, and his characterizations are mistaken.[5] His most important misconception about the descriptive approach my article advocates is that it cannot encompass moral realist perspectives or arguments. If this were true, my article would suggest at worst that these perspectives should continue alongside the partial unification the essay proposes. But in fact, far from "banishing" moral realist inquiries or conclusions, my approach is well suited to aid convincing exploration and defense of "moral realist" positions.

The nub of my argument is that in our descriptive accounts of political life, we should explicitly conceive of all of our explanatory factors at once as structures that shape political decision making as they are at the same time themselves often reshaped by political choices. Instead of taking group be-

---

5. To catalog the more minor apprehensions: Barber indicates my essay professes "to report all the relevant views among modern philosophers" to "the behavioral mainstream" and proposes to "unify all approaches" in public law, thus implicitly "banishing some elements" of normative discourse. The essay in fact never purports to be a "report" on the state of moral philosophy. Its focus is on empirical, descriptive work, discussed on fifteen of the published essay's seventeen pages of text. When it speaks of "the fundamental methodological question," causing Barber consternation, it plainly refers to descriptive studies, not methods of normative argument, as he supposes. And it claims only to unify "many," not all, of public law's "longstanding descriptive and normative concerns." The final two pages of the essay do address normative approaches and they do single out the contextual and historical concerns of contemporary pragmatist theories as well suited to employ this empirical agenda. But they also criticize certain relativistic tendencies in pragmatist thought in favor of some aspects of "natural law" reasoning (Smith, "Political Jurisprudence," 105). These two pages necessarily deal briefly with normative issues, not because I see them as "less than rational," but simply because of limited space in an essay mainly devoted to other concerns. I consider methods of normative reasoning, and many rival positions, in other writings (for example, Smith, *Liberalism*, 175–97, dealing with truly "conventionalist" democratic positions, neo-Aristotelian and Thomistic natural law theories, and neo-Kantian views; "Don't Look Back, Something Might Be Gaining on You: The Dilemmas of Constitutional Neoconservatives," *American Bar Foundation Research Journal* 1987 [1987]: 281–309, on libertarian legal economists and proponents of a jurisprudence of original intent; "After Criticism: An Analysis of the Critical Legal Studies Movement," in M. McCann and G. Houseman, eds., *Judging the Constitution* [Boston: Little, Brown, 1989]).

havior or class conflict or social systems per se as the basic object of descriptive inquiries, we would focus on the interaction of structures and decisions, specifying the structures we think influential, the decisions we hope to account for, and the hypotheses about the decisions those structures suggest. Factors as apparently diverse as the structure of social relationships to the means of production, the organization of state institutions, the array of ethnic communities in society, or, I have emphasized, the prevailing traditions of reasoning and arguing about politics—all these could be cast as structures that may be partial determinants of political choices. After generating hypotheses about how those choices would go if one or another of these structures proved in fact most influential, we could begin to determine the relative influence of different structures or combinations of structures by seeing which hypotheses were best borne out in actual decisions.[6]

Barber states that no one could oppose such research "as far as it goes," and suggests that such research is adequately performed already and that in any case it has limited value for normative concerns. But although many political scientists may accept that structures of ideas affect political behavior, we do not have any widely agreed upon methods for showing this, or for considering how much they matter in comparison to other, usually interrelated influences.[7] Instead, our many sorts of descriptive accounts—focusing on economic factors, state agencies, ideologies, and myriad other social elements—frequently seem so alien to one another as to be incommensurate, rendering genuinely synthetic appraisals of different accounts rare. This problem is often compounded by the lack of a clear sense of just what political behavior the different accounts are trying to explain. Widespread adoption of structural/institutionalist approaches would help meet these difficulties. A common concern to define carefully relevant structures and decisions would facilitate comparison of the relative success of different models and stimulate consideration of how they might be combined or corrected.

Besides contending that such comparisons are largely irrelevant to normative concerns, Barber denigrates this desire to explore which structures are most important, calling it an expression of intolerance toward "open questions at the fundaments." This criticism is bizarre: surely we should not be so tolerant of fundamental questions that we attack an approach for trying to answer them. I can only assume that Barber has not really grasped what is at stake

---

6. Smith, 1988, "Political Jurisprudence," 101–05. For an effort to engage in such an analysis of judicial decisions on corporate "personhood," see M. Barzelay and R. M. Smith, "The One Best System? A Political Analysis of Neoclassical Institutionalist Perspectives on the Modern Corporation," in W. J. Samuels and A. S. Miller, eds., *Corporations and Society* (New York: Greenwood Press, 1987).

7. Barber endorses Austin Sarat's remark that under the current pluralism in public law, "questions of fact and value go together." I see them more often going in parallel than in real communication with one another. Sarat, moreover, explicitly endorses probing the problem of legitimacy via the sorts of studies of legal ideology I advocate (as well as via Martin Shapiro's comparative work in *Courts*) (Austin Sarat, "The Maturation of Political Jurisprudence," *Western Political Quarterly* 36 [1984]: 557).

here, and that is regrettable, because these inquiries are in fact vital to his own enterprise.

Michael Moore has acknowledged that if we are to grant credence to moral realism, to the claim that there are rationally ascertainable natural moral truths that can influence moral beliefs and moral conduct, we must assume that moral reality can have a causal relation to moral beliefs and that those beliefs can affect behavior.[8] Barber himself stresses his concern for the possibility that we can be "moved to act for the sake of some general value" like "justice itself." But if we are at times so moved, then we should be able to find some way to uncover these empirical relations in our descriptive explorations of political behavior. I suggest not only that my comparative structural approach can permit us to ascertain such relations, if they exist, but that we are unlikely to gain evidence for them without it.

Moral reality, after all, presumably exhibits some pattern, structure, or, in Michael Moore's phrase, "functional organization" of moral concepts, precepts, or ideas.[9] Nothing in my recommendations prevents that organization from being specified and used to generate hypotheses about the beliefs political actors will form and the decisions they will make. In some cases, presumably, hypotheses based on the structure of moral reality will differ in their predictions of political beliefs and choices from hypotheses based on the actors' economic interests, or governmental positions, or even their inherited religious or political ideologies. If we found that, say, key decisions of Lincoln were better accounted for by the hypothesis that he had ascertained a specific structure of moral reality, of "justice itself," and then acted on it rather than the assumption that he was acting in accordance with partisan, economic, or ideological influences, we would have a good reason to give weight to claims for the power and existence of moral reality.

Barber simply fails to see the importance of this sort of descriptive argument for his own contentions. What is worse, he never suggests any rival empirical means for buttressing the belief that moral reality may sometimes influence us more than other determinants. He presents this belief only as an "ineluctable presupposition," one that he rhetorically encourages us to question, but without any concrete suggestions as to how we might do so fruitfully. One then begins to wonder how concerned Barber is to explore, instead of merely to assert, the existence of such a moral reality.

My essay does stress ideologies, not moral reality. It does so because I expect that the ideas of most political actors, most of the time, are better explained in terms of their ideological inheritances than by any new perceptions of moral truths. Barber makes heavy weather of my remark to this effect (while skirting around the fact that I said this only seems "largely" to be the case). Yet it is not clear that Michael Moore, or even Barber himself, disagrees with me on this point. Moore concedes that persons "admittedly view the world through the

---

8. Michael Moore, "Moral Reality," *Wisconsin Law Review* 82 (1982): 1104, 1127–33.

9. Michael S. Moore, "A Natural Law Theory of Interpretation," *Southern California Law Review* 58 (1985): 30l*n*44. Moore is more willing to assume that moral things have such an "organization" than that they have any discernible *internal* "structure."

conventions of the society of which we are a part," and although he stresses that we can alter those conventions "to fit the real nature of the world better," he accepts that with the greatest labor we reach only what we regard as the "best theory" of moral reality so far, and that we "have less of an idea of the sort of nature that distributive justice . . . might have" than of "physical nature."[10] Barber goes further, arguing that "we can never fully grasp" moral realities. If theorists like these, who presumably work hard at it, still see moral reality through "conventions" or inherited traditions of belief, and rarely if ever go beyond these to grasp moral truths clearly and certainly, is it so wrong to anticipate that the ideas of most political actors are "largely" traceable to their constitutive "conventional" inheritances?[11]

I think not; but again, if one thinks the contrary, the descriptive inquiries I propose in the article provide good ways to make a persuasive case for that position. And Barber's failure to see this is not the only, nor perhaps the most important, way he does not recognize how the approach might assist the positions he wants to defend. To see what the other benefits might be, we must turn to the issue my article did not try to examine very fully, the question of how normative arguments should be made.

OF MORAL REASONING, MORAL CHOICES, AND MORAL REALITIES

Again it is first necessary to clear away some of Barber's misapprehensions of my position. He presents me as a "conventionalist" who attacks "ideal" theory (in which he thinks I include his moral realism) and rational debate over "ideals," in favor of relying "simply" on "one's own" moral theory. I purportedly believe one reaches this theory by "finding, reporting, and applying empirical generalizations about certain social conventions of particular communities." These conventions are to be adopted as matters of less than rational "faith," an approach that betrays the Socratic commitment to critical inquiry and makes us unable to ask, for example, whether *Dred Scott* was morally wrong. This highly inaccurate portrait of my views involves misunderstanding of various particular statements.[12] Fundamentally, however, it stems from

10. Moore, "Moral Reality," 1143, 1146, 1150.

11. And see another of Barber's sources, Austin Sarat: "an individual's sense of entitlement to enjoy certain experiences and be free from others as well as his or her response to injustice is shaped by the prevailing ideology" ("Maturation," 557).

12. To list some minor points that will be clarified sub silentio: my criticism of "ideal" theory was aimed not at "moral realism" but at reliance on hypothetical "ideal" situations, like John Rawls's original position, Bruce Ackerman's spaceship, and Jurgen Habermas's "ideal speech" situation (the term "ideal theory" is Rawls's; as noted below, I do find value in his distinguishable notion of "reflective equilibrium"). Some sorts of "realists" endorse similar criticisms of "ideal theory." See, for example, I. Shapiro, *The Evolution of Rights in Liberal Theory* (Cambridge: Cambridge University Press, 1986), chaps. 4–6. I said we should not "simply" do normative theory only to stress that we should do both normative and descriptive work. While I did refer to persons' moral theories as "their own" and to their principles as "commitments," so does Michael Moore (Moore, "Moral Reality," 1063–64, 1113, 1124, 1150, 1155n213; "Natural Law," 287). By terming moral beliefs matters of faith I did not imply they were

Barber's persistent failure to perceive the distinction between my arguments on how governing authorities should decide political and moral questions—essentially democratically—and my arguments on how persons should form judgments on such questions—essentially by reflective judgments based on history, experience, and analysis of alternative political visions. My case for democratic government is indeed derived from my conclusions about the moral and political principles reasonable persons should endorse, and it does limit the power of any particular persons or officials to expound and enforce those principles authoritatively for all. But I have argued only that political institutions, not persons, must grant authority to the "prevailing social standards," the shared judgments of their fellow citizens about what constitute fundamental liberties.[13]

Barber has objected to this endorsement of democracy, which he wrongly thinks leaves no space for judicial review.[14] But even if he were correct on this issue, he would still not have thereby established my alleged conventionalism. Other realists make it clear that one can profess Barber's moral realism and still support more judicial deference to legislatures than he does, and that one can be a conventionalist and support activism.[15] Thus Barber is quite unwarranted in making assertions about my philosophic foundations based on my endorsement of democratic government. He also fails to expound at all how he and Moore believe one should go about perceiving moral reality. By considering both these neglected matters in turn, I will show that our real differences are not over the moral weight we grant to convention. They are over whether we can make better moral judgments by looking to history rather than simply to

---

subrational, merely that they were not matters of certain knowledge, a point Moore and Barber concede. Barber's assertions on *Dred Scott* reflect again his inaccurate reading of my methodological comments on descriptive work as prescriptions for normative evaluations.

13. Smith, *Liberalism*, 213. Barber quotes the "social standards" phrase (albeit as "community standards") while omitting the reference to "political institutions." The original sentence reads, in full: "Thus, political institutions should, through democratic processes, elicit and enforce prevailing social standards of what constitutes minimally rational, deliberative conduct and of what preserves the ability to engage in it."

14. S. A. Barber, "Review," *Political Theory* 15 (1987). My "rational liberty" theory still permits meaningful judicial review because, if the question of whether conduct can be termed important to "rational liberty" is genuinely controversial in a given society, the legislature must accept a heavy burden of proof: it must give compelling reasons as to why restraints on that conduct preserve basic liberties more than they violate them (Smith, *Liberalism*, 213, 229–30, 236, 239, 250–51).

15. Michael Moore contends that his realism "weakens, but does not eliminate, the democratic arguments against a judge who ignores conventional morals. . . in adjudication." He also views Ronald Dworkin, whom Barber repeatedly cites to support his own position, as a "deep conventionalist"; unlike Barber, Moore thinks such "conventionalists" can support judicial activism with some "fancy footwork" (Moore, "Moral Reality," 1155n215; Moore, "Natural Law," 299n35, 179n181, 391–92, 395–96). Also see Stanley Brubaker's "realist" defense of judicial self-restraint in "Republican Government and Judicial Restraint," *Review of Politics* 49 (1987): 570–72, and Barber's reply at 573.

our presuppositions, and whether we should contend that our conclusions deserve to be viewed as accounts of moral reality.[16]

In Liberalism and American Constitutional Law, I devote over 160 pages to analysis of the historical versions of American political philosophy visible in evolving constitutional doctrines, and another 30-odd pages to influential recent theories of American constitutionalism. I do so because I take people to be largely constituted by society, so that their reflections necessarily begin with the ideas they inherit as the primary ingredients of their political consciousnesses. I am suspicious, moreover, of analyses of political ideas that proceed without any reference to the problems that prompted articulation of those ideas, the persons and purposes they favored and opposed, and their consequences in practice. One often discovers much about what these ideas have meant and can mean in our world, much even about their philosophic obscurities and contradictions, by exploring carefully their historical origins and tendencies. In all this I do not think my method differs dramatically from that of Plato, whose dialectic starts with common opinions, and who writes dialogues in part to indicate the persons and circumstances by which certain ideas are favored or neglected. Nor do I differ in this respect so greatly from Aristotle, who collected much empirical information on the constitutions and histories of different regimes and regularly employed it in evaluating political claims concerning, for example, justice. Indeed, even Michael Moore concedes that the meaning of moral words "depends heavily upon the context of the utterance," although neither he nor Barber engages in much exploration of the historical contexts of legal ideas, and Barber deprecates these inquiries.[17]

Nowhere, however, do I attempt to choose among the different political outlooks in America's constitutional heritage by estimating empirically which are most widely shared, most truly conventional. Instead, my analysis of the intrinsic persuasiveness of those outlooks, buttressed by the lessons of their historical manifestations, finds considerable weaknesses in all past views, along with certain features that appear normatively commendable. To respond to the perceived weaknesses, I then proceed to work out what I believe to be a better theory of American liberal constitutionalism, in an argument that in no way relies on conventions. Instead, my ultimate appeal is to a Lockean "core conception" of human selves as embodied consciousnesses, as "corporate rational" beings, and I suggest we should take our moral bearings from the "fundamental characteristics" of our condition that are involved in "our experience of ourselves" as such consciousnesses.[18]

Those characteristics include a recognition that our sense of identity and obligations are initially, and to some degree always, derived from our various

16. For appeals to our presuppositions, see in addition to Barber's essay, Moore, "Moral Reality," 1103; and discussion below.

17. Plato, *The Republic*, Bk. 1; Aristotle, *The Politics*, Bks. 3 and 4; Moore, "Moral Reality," 1139; Barber, *Constitution*, 8.

18. Smith, *Liberalism*, 205, 211, 220. Barber ignores this argument, the foundation of my position.

social memberships. Yet we also develop limited but meaningful capacities to comprehend, criticize, and alter our sense both of who we are and of what we want to be, and the external conditions that aid or impede us in doing so. These capacities, in turn, mean that the human condition is "inherently characterized by uneasiness and tension, which can best be moderated, never overcome"— uncertainty about the internal and external forces that shape us and about how we should best cope with them. In light of these characteristics, I argue that it is reasonable to take the preservation and enhancement of our capacities for reflective self-direction as a fundamental moral imperative (stressing that these capacities include some measure of control over our social and material worlds as well as psychological self-governance). Such activity, I suggest, gives some relief to the constitutive uneasiness of the human condition. It helps us fulfill our more particular aims, contributing to our happiness. It expresses a sense of ourselves as responsible moral agents, contributing to our belief in human dignity. It also points to a view of human flourishing that can and must to a considerable degree be pursued cooperatively, not conflictually, yet with extensive latitude for personal choices. For all these reasons the book urges that we take the promotion of such capacities, of "rational liberty" for all citizens, as the basic goal of American constitutionalism.[19]

Whatever its vulnerabilities, this argument clearly only begins by learning from diverse past traditions. It evaluates those traditions, and develops its principles, by relying on conceptions of the human self and human condition that are founded on experience and our consequent judgments of the best we can attain. There is no significant sense, then, in which it is conventionalist. Because I agree with Barber and Moore that conventionality is not a morally persuasive argument for a position, I ground my case on what I take to be more basic and enduring aspects of human existence, in precisely the manner I recommend in the normative section of my article (a proposal Barber wrongly thinks I "pull back" from).[20]

It is true that, unlike those who term themselves natural law theorists, such as Michael Moore,[21] I do not claim that this conception of the human self approximates humanity's moral "natural kind," nor that my arguments based upon it express, albeit imperfectly, timeless, objective moral truths. That may be the case, but I am not knowledgeable enough to claim it. I indicate in the book that it is logically possible to view the human condition as I do and yet draw different moral conclusions from it.[22] I think the preponderance of reasons are on my side, and I therefore expect that most reasonable persons would, on reflection, eventually agree; but that is all I contend.

This view of the limitations of what "rational liberty" can claim, along with my theory's substantive commitments, account for my endorsement of basically democratic processes of governance. I can and do appeal to my own reading of the lessons of the past to form judgments about the existence of significant

19. Ibid., 200, 206–07, 216, 220.
20. Smith, "Political Jurisprudence," 105.
21. Moore, "Natural Law," 333–34, 397.
22. Smith, *Liberalism*, 207–08, 211–12.

capacities for reflective self-determination and what promotes and damages them. I feel no obligation in my own thinking to defer to some social majority's outlook on these topics, and I feel entitled to challenge such a majority's judgments by referring to features of human selves, the human condition, and historic experience that I think they neglect or distort. Yet my best judgments still seem to me less than certainties; and although others' opinions also seem vulnerable, they are also speaking from experience of our common condition, and they are also capable of meaningful, reflective judgments and self-governance. Thus when it comes to how political decisions governing society as a whole should be made, I think it both prudent and morally appropriate to seek to have those decisions made largely through deliberative democratic institutions—hence the endorsement of political democracy that Barber finds so troubling. But it is an endorsement of democratic decision making on how political institutions can best advance this conception of liberal purposes, not democratic will expressed toward any end whatsoever.[23]

Precisely where would Moore and Barber differ from all this? To find out we must contrast the mode of moral reasoning I have just sketched with the modes they recommend. I will focus on Moore, to whom Barber defers. But while Moore's discussions are fuller than Barber's, it must be said that he never examines very elaborately just how one goes about perceiving moral realities. He does say more on the related question of how we *justify* moral beliefs. As noted previously, Moore agrees that we view the world through social "conventions," through "our own conceptual categories," while stressing our ability to alter them as we "progressively experience" its "real nature." He also agrees that our beliefs are "states that occur in history," with meanings that are linked "heavily" to their contexts, and emphasizes that they may nonetheless capture timeless truths.[24]

How, then, do we move our originally conventional, contextually dependent moral beliefs progressively toward what we can more confidently recognize as expressions of such truth? Not by relying on any fundamental first principles. Instead, Moore aligns himself with W. V. Quine and with John Rawls's "reflective equilibrium": we simultaneously improve and justify our beliefs by examining how each belief "coheres" with "everything else" we believe. We make adjustments to resolve tensions and contradictions in those beliefs until we reach the "best theory" we can muster on particular factual and moral matters and on our general view of the world.[25] Moore recognizes that people in the past who have engaged in such reflection have often encountered seemingly irresolvable conflicts on moral matters; but he is confident that over time these differences can be resolved, because we all will progressively see "how the world really is" and discover that it is a world in which "moral principles need not conflict."[26]

---

23. Smith, *Liberalism*, 212–13, 226. Recall, too, that even Socrates found it proper in all but the most exceptional cases to obey the laws of his democracy.

24. Moore, "Moral Reality," 1098n75; 1098 1131; "Natural Law," 312.

25. Moore, "Moral Reality," 1108, 1112–13, 1143, 1150; "Natural Law," 312.

26. Moore, "Moral Reality," 1090, 1090n61, 1151–52.

I have no objection in principle to the method of "reflective equilibrium," and although I am less sanguine that there are no irresolvable conflicts, that is still an open question, and I am happy to have us try to resolve all the conflicts we can.[27] Reflective equilibrium's great difficulty, however, is that we cannot really engage in it very extensively. Checking every belief against "everything else" we believe, in light of all our increasing learning and experience of the world, obviously cannot be done regularly in any comprehensive way. We must take some shortcuts. Moore gives us no suggestions as to what these might be, and no further guidance on what in particular we should emphasize in moral reasoning. I believe the explorations in my book, of different political outlooks, their historic consequences, and of more enduring aspects of our condition, indicate the most important elements to focus on in approximating a full reflective equilibrium, although, of course, much more could be done than I do there. At any rate, that model represents a more specific account of moral reasoning, and a more elaborate effort to implement it, than Moore provides; yet Barber simply endorses Moore and adds his own belief that historical and empirical inquiries should play a relatively minor role in normative reflection, while failing to indicate just what he does explore in reaching his reflective equilibrium, beyond his own convictions. Again, his criticisms of the inquiries I suggest, inquiries that Moore's statements would seem to necessitate, raise questions concerning how serious Barber really is about pursuing the normative approach he professes to endorse.

Furthermore, readers might also be wondering why these realists, who do not actually engage in the process of reflective equilibrium to any apparent extent, nonetheless feel justified in claiming that the moral beliefs we settle on by this means approximate objective moral reality. How can realists, in Moore's words, endorse Quine's holistic "coherence theory of justification" while remaining "implicit correspondence theorists" about the relationship of those beliefs to an alleged real moral world?[28] Moore's own defenses for this claim are quite mild; and when we reflect on them, we are led to wonder whether anything substantive hangs on the claim.

Moore contends only that, as we compare our beliefs in a Quinean manner, "it becomes more plausible to *assume*" that our moral beliefs correspond (imperfectly) to a moral reality. He concedes that it is "logically possible" that no such correspondence is ever really achieved, but he argues that we can just as easily doubt the correspondence of the ideas of natural science to any physical reality, since we form those beliefs in similar fashion. If we are willing to assume physical nature exists, it is reasonable to assume moral reality exists, even though we are not logically "forced" to do so. Moore does admit that there are differences, however, that moral "things" probably do not have "a hidden

27. Barber, seemingly unlike Moore, believes such aspirations express a suspicious affection for peace.

28. Moore, "Natural Law," 312. Quine, after all, leaves little room for confidence in any straightforward "correspondence" theory of truth. See W. V. O. Quine, *From a Logical Point of View* (Cambridge: Harvard University Press, 1961), 20, 37–46.

nature of a physical sort," and that "we know less about what kind" of things they may be.[29]

Those qualifications surely cut against making any strong presumptions in the matter. And at any rate, Moore's case is much more an argument for *assuming* some sort of moral reality exists, and that moral reflection can grasp it, than it is an argument showing that moral reality exists or *how* we might grasp it. Clearly, the latter demonstrations would more significantly fortify Moore's position. Instead, both Moore and Barber repeatedly anchor their case for the realist assumption in one basic argument: our ordinary moral language and usages seem necessarily to "presuppose" a "realist metaphysics about the hidden nature of natural kinds," including moral "kinds." Efforts to avoid expressing such presuppositions are alleged recurringly to fall into contradictions. Therefore, we should treat these presuppositions as correct.[30]

This claim about language is unconvincing in several ways. First, I am quite willing to agree that we discuss moral principles as if they exist and that it is reasonable to do so. The important question is, what is the nature of this presumed existence? Clearly moral "things" are, at a minimum, beliefs in our minds, related in some way to our perceptions of the world. But might they not be simply the reasoned conclusions human beings form and decide to grant moral authority to when they reflect on the world—judgments of appropriate choices, based on the sorts of considerations I have described, which are generally persuasive to reasonable people, although perhaps not to all? Must moral principles instead exist "objectively" in the "real" world, "independently" of any human mind, albeit discoverable by our minds through deliberation on that world?

There is no apparent reason why the latter must be the case. I accept that, when we ponder on ourselves, our circumstances, and our moral choices, we sometimes have the feeling that we have discovered an answer that simply makes sense, whereas at other times we are more conscious of making a choice—one based on identifiable, weighty, but not overwhelming reasons. Yet nothing in this experience, or in our language, requires us to assume that this sense of discovery reveals the existence of external moral things, rather than our considerable confidence in some of the choices we decide after reflection to make.[31] Both explanations can account equally well for the claims and convictions Moore and Barber emphasize: our beliefs that we have reached the best answers we could, answers that most reasonable people would choose.

Perhaps more important, even if we were to accept the claim that our language involves "ineluctable realist" presuppositions, it is hard to see what difference that would make in our processes of moral reasoning or in our

---

29. Moore, "Moral Reality," 1124–25 (emphasis added); 1145–46, 1152–53.

30. Moore, "Moral Reality," 1077, 1080n43, 1111; "Natural Law," 311, 334, 341, 397.

31. I agree, too, that without appeal to certain knowledge of timeless moral truths, it is hard to define just why we find a set of reasons compelling. But that problem equally plagues Moore's realism, since he disavows all claims to certain knowledge and similarly describes us as acting on the basis of principles that we judge to have the most persuasive reasons on their side.

substantive conclusions. Such presuppositions are not in themselves evidence of the existence of "moral reality," only of our inescapable but perhaps wholly erroneous tendencies to imply its existence. Nor do these presuppositions help us in any way to find what the content of moral reality actually is. On Moore's telling, after all, we are still to settle on moral beliefs through precisely the same reasoning processes that we would use if we viewed those beliefs as our own reasoned conclusions instead of objective entities wholly independent of our minds. Again, with Quine and Rawls, we are asked to compare some beliefs with others in the light of experience and form the best theories we can. But how do we know when, in doing so, we have gone beyond simply making our beliefs more coherent in reflective equilibrium and have actually grasped or mirrored moral reality, or even come a little closer to it? Moore and Barber give us no signpost. And how does the assumption that the results of such reflection correspond to moral reality help us decide *which* substantive beliefs to endorse, *which* views of liberty, of human worth, of justice? The argument from language, if it has any force at all, merely speaks to the ontological label we should pin on our substantive values. It offers no guidance whatsoever in discovering or judging what they should be. That is one reason we find both realists and conventionalists embracing virtually every substantive political and moral outlook that has ever won currency in human life, from the classical polis to feudal kingship to liberal democracy to fascism and communism.

What difference does it make, then, whether we call our moral theories approximations of objective moral reality or articulations of principles we choose to regard as morally authoritative, based on specifiable reasons? I do not think that it does make much difference. Hence I have been much more concerned in my work to make substantive moral arguments than to speculate on their ultimate metaphysical status. Moore and Barber think metaphysical labels matter, because they believe we can have passionate commitment to our ideals only if we believe they capture moral reality, and that otherwise we have no principled reason for holding our ideals superior to anyone else's.[32] But in fact those of us who view our moral beliefs as reasoned judgments, based on reflection much like that Moore endorses, are as confident about our moral commitments as those who view their conclusions as tentative estimations of moral reality. Both sides contend their substantive beliefs articulate the best theory they can now reach, but not necessarily the ultimate truth. Both sides can claim principled reasons for adhering to their beliefs, even while they are equally compelled by their own arguments to remain open to alternatives.

Having said this, I do believe there are costs in the routine deployment of the language of moral realism. Although I cannot estimate their exact magnitude, they seem to me to outweigh the benefits. The costs come not from what moral realism, as Moore describes it, should entail, but from what it seems to entail in practice. I have argued here that there is nothing in moral realism that should be hostile to the new institutionalist inquiries I favor. I believe realists could gain more confidence that moral realities actually do influence belief and behavior, and they could better reach reflective equilibrium on what their

32. Moore, "Moral Reality," 1064.

moral principles are, if among their examinations of "everything" they featured the historical and empirical research I have defended. Furthermore, I agree with both Moore and Barber that the realist is in principle obligated not to be dogmatic or absolute but to continue inquiring and to explore all plausible criticisms.[33]

Barber's critique is evidence that the call to grasp moral reality can foster disregard for the sometimes tedious and always difficult forms of concrete research that can help provide insight on these matters, in favor of the claim that one is using philosophic reason to discern external moral truths in a mysterious manner. The persistent inaccuracies of his analysis also reveal that someone strongly attached to "moral realism" can be too quick to place all other positions in the single rival camp of pure, antirational conventionalism, without carefully examining whether they really fit that mold. I believe, in any case, that open and continual inquiry are best promoted by a language that calls attention to the debatable character of our moral conclusions: hence my preference for labeling my principles "reasoned choices" or "deliberate judgments" rather than (imperfect) articulations of "real moral truths."

When all is said and done, however, I am much less concerned about the labels we attach to our moral conclusions in order to advertise our speculation on their ontological status than I am about encouraging both concrete research into the role ideas have played in politics and normative reflection that is better informed and wiser as a result of such inquiries. That is why I wrote the "new institutionalism" essay. Of this much I am sure: whether or not there is a sun outside the human cave, we can never hope to see it by closing our eyes tightly and fiercely proclaiming what we believe it looks like.

33. Ibid., 1149.

MARTIN SHAPIRO
School of Law
University of California, Berkeley

Political Jurisprudence, Public Law, and Post-Consequentialist Ethics: Comment on Professors Barber and Smith

At professional meetings of political scientists and in journals there have occurred discussions of the future of studies in the field of political science traditionally labeled public law. Now we have the further comments by Rogers Smith in the *American Political Science Review* and Sotirios Barber in this volume of *Studies*. The editors of *Studies* have asked me to join in the Smith-Barber dialogue.

Before beginning, some caveats are in order. First, the term *political jurisprudence* was not originally employed as a shorthand for "the study of law and courts that is done or ought to be done by political scientists." Indeed the universe out of which it sought to carve a subset was not political science but jurisprudence. The term was consciously adopted to echo the earlier usage of *sociological jurisprudence*, and the point was explicitly made that political jurisprudence was a school of jurisprudence in the sense that impressionism or the school of Paris was a school of art.[1] By such labels we denote a set of persons, each of whose work is distinctly individual, but who share certain commonalities of style that make it convenient to treat them together for some purposes. Certainly to claim that Picasso and Miro but not Klee are members of the school of Paris is not to deny that Klee is a painter. Miro and Klee and some of the work of Picasso can be joined in another school we label surrealism. To claim that a certain kind of work is not political jurisprudence is not to claim that the

---

1. The term first appears in Martin Shapiro, "Political Jurisprudence," *Kentucky Law Journal* 52 (1964) in a symposium on jurisprudence. This contribution to *Studies* was written in Paris under the gun of a very short deadline. As a result I have not been able to provide conventional footnotes, for the most part. Most of the text references are to works cited by Smith and/ or Barber and included in their notes or are to authors and works well known at least to public law specialists.

work is not a legitimate part of jurisprudence, or that the person doing it is not a legitimate political scientist.

Nor is political jurisprudence coterminus with "public law" in political science. Indeed, with absolute futility, I personally have been inveighing against the label "public law" for many years because I believe that political jurisprudence must be based on the study of private as well as public law. Political scientists cannot reach a valid understanding of courts as political institutions by looking at only a part of what courts do. Surely one can be a political jurisprud and not a student of public law and vice versa.

Finally a caveat about disciplinary boundaries. Later I am going to say that I think political scientists can be employed most profitably in doing certain kinds of work distinct from the kind of legal doctrinal argument purveyed by many academic lawyers. On the other hand, there is a long and honored tradition of doctrinal work in political science. Reasonable persons may and do differ about its place in political science. Some excellent work by political scientists lies just at the boundary I would draw between academic law and political science were I drawing such boundaries. We ought not to concern ourselves with taking away anybody's union card, the more especially so because no political scientist who has claimed the "public law" designation in recent years lies so far over any set of reasonable boundaries that the issue is worth worrying about.

With these caveats on record, I can go on to the rather unctuous position of agreeing with both Smith and Barber. The kind of institutional analysis proclaimed by March and Olsen is the kind of analysis that many of those engaged in political jurisprudence have been doing all along anyway. Employing Glendon Schubert's terminology, the March-Olsen message to "public law" may be seen as "Process analysis ought to be given a place of equal honor with behavioral analysis in the study of law and judges." More broadly the new vogue in institutional analysis acclaimed by Smith is a return in certain respects to a more or less traditional political science as even the briefest glance at the first two volumes of these *Studies* clearly shows. In the endless battle between tradition and avant-gardism, public choice has taken the place of behaviorism. If March, Olsen, and Smith wish to turn the game on its head by claiming the avant-garde position for the tradition, more power to them.

I do not mean to suggest by this rather offhand comment that those who maintained an institutionalist perspective during the behavioral era were (or are now) justified in rejecting behaviorism or thinking they had nothing to learn from it. There is a sense in which March and Olsen are merely discovering that some of us were writing prose all along, but they make an important contribution in looking toward a more fruitful combination of relatively static rational-choice, interest-maximization analysis with more diacronic analysis of the evolution of institutions, including intellectual ones.

"PRAGMATISM" AND THE NEW MORAL PHILOSOPHY

My own early essay entitled "Political Jurisprudence" took up the problem of values so urgently raised by Barber. It explicitly argued what he quite rightly argues now, that reducing values or norms to "variables" may well be seen as the final positivist rape of normative political inquiry. To treat the values held by various persons at various times as a significant aspect of the empirical world is not the same as seeking to discover true values. Barber contends that institutional analysis reserves no secure place for the doing of political philosophy, as opposed to the doing of the history of political thought.

The crux of the difference between Smith and Barber, and of the difference between Barber and myself, lies in what approach one takes to the new movements in ethics and political philosophy that Smith labels "pragmatic." Precisely because Smith sees them as pragmatic and because of the nature of pragmatism, Smith does not make himself entirely clear on the issue that is most important to Barber. Smith sees the new pragmatists such as Rorty and Walzer—and here I might add Charles Fried—as arguing that a contemporary ethics can be, can only be, and ought to be built up from our traditional values. Smith sees the new pragmatists as relevant to institutional analysis of the sort he proposes for public law. Does that mean that like the new pragmatists, the new public law scholars ought to study our normative traditions in order to understand how law got to be what it is today? Or does it mean that like the new pragmatists they ought to study our normative traditions in order to construct new moral and political philosophies that specify normatively what law ought to be today? Barber is certain that there must be room for the latter endeavor in public law, and he accuses Smith, and certainly me, of leaving room only for the former.

A brief sketch of some recent developments in ethics, moral philosophy, and political-legal philosophy to which Barber alludes may make the differences between us clearer. At the time of World War II, utilitarianism in one form or another dominated moral philosophy. Disillusion with that philosophy and the inability to replace it with any other led to a dearth of postwar ethical studies as philosophers turned almost exclusively to technical attempts, through symbolic logic and ordinary language analysis, to straighten out our thinking and communications processes. During this same period political theory became almost exclusively either the history of political thought or empirical political theory. There was little political philosophy because utilitarianism was in disarray and no one could think of anything to replace it.

Smith in his *ASPA* essay makes much of Posner at various points. Fundamentally, the law and economics movement is the last gasp of utilitarianism. Given that it exhibits all the ethical weaknesses of utilitarianism, its rapid dominance of academic law can be accounted for only by the almost complete innocence of philosophy exhibited until recently by academic lawyers. Completely positivistic, it reduces values to mere personal preferences and is dedicated to the ethically insensitive standard of the greatest good of the greatest number. Posner and others have appreciated this latter problem and have sought to employ the ethically superior concept of Pareto optimality, which describes a position in which no one can be made better off unless someone else is made worse off. Such a position is ethically superior only if the endowments with which the players began have their own ethical status. Because what each person had at the start is the major determinant of how much he will have at the point of Pareto optimality, behind law and economics lie Nozick and ultimately

Burke, and neither of them has persuaded us that prescriptively acquired rights, such as inherited wealth, are moral rights.

The revival of moral and political philosophy that has occurred in recent years is a reaction to utilitarianism and is often labeled post-consequentialism. It appears in several varieties. I am going to argue here that its central thrust is the recreation of a theory of moral sentiments in the style of the Scottish commonsense school, and that for this reason the categories of realism versus conventionalism that dominate Barber's analysis do not quite fit. For the same reason, Smith's evident sympathy for one of the varieties does not place him as firmly in the positivist camp as Barber would have him.

The variety of post-consequentialism most familiar to political scientists is probably that of Ronald Dworkin and is most tellingly exhibited in the constitutional law of Lawrence Tribe. Dworkin can be made out to be a pure conventionalist, a pure positivist, and indeed, even a pure Kelsonian. His basic argument is that legal rights are derived from legal principles and the legal principles of any particular society are derived from the political theory of that society. Yet in endowing this logical pyramid with ethical weight, Dworkin appeals constantly to the ethical sentiments of his readers. His trump card is always "would you rather believe that rights exist or that all is power and chaos?" And in practice his writing is so ethnocentric that no distinction really emerges between the principles or political theory of the English-speaking world and universal principles or universal political theory. In the final analysis, I think it will emerge that Dworkin's apparent conventionalism is of the same kind as that of the pragmatists whom I will discuss in a moment, a conventionalism that supports a more fundamental appeal to moral sentiments far deeper, more universal and truer than mere conventions.

My major point, however, is a different one. When Dworkin and Tribe assert that legal rights rest on values—"our" values or "constitutional values" or "American" values or "Western" values—it turns out with amazing regularity that these values dictate with astonishing precision the exact policy positions of the moderate left, including those which Dworkin and Tribe personally desire. At least in the absence of a clearer way of establishing what the basic values are, and of stating them in a way that is not so general as to authorize all policy positions and each of their opposites, the suspicion must arise that the philosopher has arrived at his or her policy positions first, in the same disorderly way that the rest of us do, and afterward discovered the appropriate value positions and interpretations to support them. Dworkin may have persuaded many people to take rights seriously, but has he persuaded anyone except the most devoted proponents of the ideology peddled by the *New York Review of Books* that he has discovered a way of determining just how seriously which rights of whom ought to be taken when? And has Tribe convinced us that the values he keeps discovering in the Constitution really dictate the outcomes that he prescribes in particular cases?

Next to Dworkin in current political science consciousness, and perhaps above him, lies John Rawls. Rawls is the central figure in the resurgence of ethical self-confidence among the philosophical advocates of liberalism. They are devoted to putting the Humpty Dumpty of natural law—social contract theory back together again after its destruction by Kant, Hume, and assorted others. It is not a coincidence that Rawls ends up roughly where the Fabians came down after James Mill. We may all be cheered that liberalism is alive and well again, but the new veil of ignorance is as artificial a construction as Locke's original. The attempt of Bruce Ackerman and others to replace contract with conversation could appeal only to professors—that is, professional talkers. The new liberals are already under thunderous attack from the new communitarians such as Michael Sandel. There is no reason to believe that Rawls has done better than all the king's horses.

Postwar attempts in the United States to revive natural law, with or without God, have not been successful. The one attempt with God, the neoscholasticism built around the journal, the *Natural Lawyer*, dwindled even during the time when the Nazi atrocities to which it was a response were still fresh in our minds. The one without God, Leo Strauss's, has, according to Barber, fallen on hard times. Barber pins his hopes on the more recent secular attempt by my valiant colleague, Michael Moore. The very sophistication and complexity of Moore's argument suggests that he is going to fail at the same point as every natural lawyer does: that is the point at which it is demanded that a code of natural laws be set down on paper and set down with sufficient specificity that it dictates single correct solutions to current policy problems. The appeal of natural law is never going to go away because all of us would like to believe that law is the realm of reason rather than will, or at least a realm in which reason and will can be allies. I am not prepared to assert that reason is dead, and there is no space here to reply to Nietzsche and his followers even if I were qualified to do so. But even if we could be persuaded that natural law exists, little in its history suggests it could reach a level of specificity that would be useful in the analysis of legal problems except where, as in Puffendorf, a great deal of customary law is smuggled in.

We come then to that movement in ethics which Smith and Barber call pragmatic and in which they include such figures as Rorty, MacIntyre and Walzer. The label "pragmatic" does not help very much because that word has connotations of instrumentalism or interest adjustment rather than moral quest, as in "they arrived at a pragmatic solution to their problem" or "the court acted pragmatically." If understood as expressing a link between John Dewey's claim that truth is arrived at by constantly acting out philosophy rather than building a static system, the term is properly applied to this group. That the term, as I could show, could be equally well applied to Barber himself, however, indicates that something is wrong or incomplete because Barber rejects the pragmatic school. As I have already suggested, what is wrong is Barber's attempt to sort all philosophers into mutually exclusive conventionalists and realist categories and his placement of these pragmatic philosophers into the conventionalist camp. For these pragmatists actually are seeking to get away from what they see as the false problem posed by the conventionalist versus realist categorization. Indeed, I would argue that the entire new movement in ethics, including the work of such disparate figures as Unger and Dworkin, centers on just this attempt to escape conventionalist-realist dilemmas and employs a common method for doing so.

The conventionalist-realist dyad is founded on an epistemology inherited from the Greeks and Romans, who divided all learning into logic and rhetoric. Some matters could be logically demonstrated, such as a theorem in geometry, and some could be directly observed. One could know the truth of such matters. All the rest were matters of opinion and fell in the realm of rhetoric, where the aim was not truth but persuasion. (And, of course, by convention we mean an opinion held by a number of persons over time.) As Barbara Shapiro's *Probability and Certainty in Seventeenth-Century England* shows, the seventeenth century broke out of this rigorous dyad, adding a third and intermediate category of probable knowledge. Not everything that could not be logically demonstrated need be consigned to the realm of mere opinion. The probable truth of many matters could be established by evidence and argument and various degrees of probability and certainty established. For instance, we could not logically prove the existence of God as the scholastics had thought to do, or directly observe God, but we could become morally certain of the existence of God through reasoning from evidence and testimony. That same level of certainty, by the way, was the one that came to be required for conviction in a criminal trial—the jury's belief in guilt "beyond a reasonable doubt and to a moral certainty" as the jury instruction still runs in many American jurisdictions.[2]

As Chaim Perelman in his *The New Rhetoric* has argued, the scientism of the early twentieth century (what Barber refers to as the positivism now rejected in philosophy of science) led us away from this advance in epistemology and, because ethical values could not be logically demonstrated or directly observed, assigned ethics to the realm of mere opinion or preference. But the core of the recent revival in ethical studies that Barber applauds is the new consensus among moral philosophers that careful moral argument can lead to ethical propositions that, if not absolutely true, are more true than other moral propositions, and that agreement that such propositions are more true is not merely a matter of the consensus of opinion. It follows, of course, that as philosophic argument continues, such propositions will be revised toward even greater truth although absolute truth will never be obtained. Barber is himself a participant in this movement, but he does not admit the pragmatists to his club.

In the context of the breakdown of faith in utilitarianism and the attacks of logical positivism, Freudianism, and the like, the new probabilistic ethics faced grave difficulties. In the 1930s an intuitionist school argued that individuals had sound moral intuitions even in the absence of an articulated and widely accepted ethics. Echoes of that movement are familiar to public law people in the "hunch" theory of judicial decision and Edmond Cahn's *Sense of Injustice* and *Moral Decision*. But the new probabilistic, post-consequentialist ethics advances careful philosophical analysis and discourse as the key to reaching better, if not perfect, ethical formulations. This emphasis on discourse is an attempt to defend against the charge that the new philosophers too are just intuitionists. Careful arguments exchanged among persons well trained to use

2. See Barbara Shapiro, "To a Moral Certainty," *Hasting Law Review* 38 (1986): 153–94.

precise language provide a critical rigor that purges ethics of the illogic and idiosyncrasy of intuitionism.

Now, finally we come to the aspect of the new ethics that leads Barber to label some of its practitioners conventionalists. Critics of the new philosophy say that when the new moral discourse actually unfolds, after language has been clarified and internal contradictions eliminated, the turning points in the argument always come down to "Isn't this proposition more morally satisfying than that one?" To an outsider, it may appear that the philosophers are, when all else has been said, resorting to their own moral intuitions. The philosophers respond that this is not intuitionism because of the careful and critical nature of the discourse in which they engage, each checking the responses of the others. The outsider then responds, "Why should I trust the collective moral intuitions of a Princeton philosophy seminar, even those confirmed at its last meeting of the semester, more than I trust any other intuition?" It is at this point that the philosophers refer to moral traditions. They say "Not only are our moral findings checked and revised on the testing ground of critical discourse, but, to the extent that any suspicion of idiosyncrasy remains, our current moral propositions are subjected to the further check of all past moral discourse—that is, to our moral traditions." Now, if someone were a pure conventionalist in Barber's terms, he or she would not be such a philosopher, but an anthropologist or intellectual historian. The new philosophers are not simply recording our traditions or seeking to apply those traditions, right or wrong, to current circumstances. The new ethics is essentially an attempt to do ethical thinking and arrive at *probabilistic* ethical truth. Precisely because it is probable rather than absolutely logically demonstrable it must be checked both by careful analysis and by reference to past moral findings. The ethical conclusions of the Princeton seminar are held to be more probably true if they correspond to a long ethical tradition than if they do not. The pragmatists are not saying that moral truth is only conventional. They are saying that moral truth is probable and convention is a major piece of evidence in establishing a high level of probability for some truths.

A related aspect of what is going on here is the attempt to depart from the 1930s-brand psychology of intuitions for the older (and newer) realm of moral sentiments. To the natural lawyer, old or new, natural law is to be known through the faculty of reason that is God-given or otherwise natural to every person. It is no accident that the secular natural law of Moore which Barber so admires is intimately entangled with Moore's writings on psychology and law. The new pragmatic discourse constantly returns to the question, "After looking at all sides and clearing up all contradictions, don't you find this moral proposition more satisfying to your moral sense than that one?" After Unger completes to his own satisfaction the work of destroying modern liberal industrial ideology, he moves on not only to a utopian communitarianism but to a major effort to reconstruct our vision of the human personality.

Although they take various guises and sometimes only are implied or assumed rather than stated, theories of moral sentiments are designed to bridge the gap between conventionalism and realism, opinion and logic, morality and science, value and fact, just as are theories of probabilistic moral truth. The existence of moral sentiments can be established, at a quite high level of probability, by introspection, by anthropological investigation, by the investigation of the long historical record of moral thought and endeavor, and perhaps even by experiment as in the new gaming work on altruism. If moral sentiments exist, then ethics are both conventional and real because they are derived from moral sentiments whose reality is proven in part by the existence of conventions.

Notions of probabilistic moral truth and moral sentiments unite all of the post-consequentialists, and they are certainly shared by Barber and many of those philosophers whom he rejects as outside of his natural law camp. What does distinguish the group that Smith and Barber call pragmatists is their emphasis on the complexity of real-world moral choices and, therefore, the need to exercise a moral prudence that recognizes ambiguity and employs many disparate tools of moral analysis. Rather than building a static moral system and applying it rigorously, they counsel a certain eclecticism responsive to particular situations and adapted to each new situation. I confess I cannot understand Rorty beyond the general drift and prefer Bernard Williams on all this not only because Williams writes more simply but because he presents the relation of this new philosophy to the breakdown of utilitarianism in a useful way. This approach is obviously related to Dewey's pragmatism, and also to the Scottish commonsense philosophers. It expresses a confidence in the existential capacity of humans to make moral judgments that are neither perfect nor arbitrary, but are pretty good. Like the other post-consequentialists, Rorty and company refer to Judeo-Christian ethical traditions as a check on their own moral analysis and sometimes argue that those traditions provide the materials and tools of moral inquiry. That is not the same thing, however, as arguing that moral truths are not truths but merely the artifacts of intellectual history. It seems to me that Barber can strengthen his own position and even wean Smith from his positivism by admitting the pragmatists Smith admires to the same post-consequentialist camp as the new natural lawyers, like Moore. They could then all join hands in assisting at the birth of a new normative public law.

When all is said, although of course it never is, the message of the pragmatists is that we should actively cultivate and exercise our moral sentiments as checked by critical discourse and tradition, rather than fooling ourselves into believing that moral judgments are either simple or unnecessary or should be made by naked preferences. I cannot bring myself to disagree, but even within the realm of ethics, the message is a very indeterminate one. When transposed to public law, it tells us nothing more than that moral evaluation of legal institutions, processes, and acts is legitimate if done very openly and carefully. To begin such evaluations from the premise that ethics are multiple, complex, particular to each situation, and drawn from the whole repertoire of past Western moral thought is likely, however, to lead mostly to seat-of-the-pants policy analysis dressed up in ethical language after the fact. That is pragmatism in the bad sense, and I believe that it is this bad pragmatism that is likely to be the result of applying the approach of new pragmatic philosophers to public law. I do not agree with Barber that these people are not doing real ethics, but I do agree with him that they are unlikely to provide clear enough moral rules that can be simply enough applied to real legal problems to do public law much good.[3]

POST-CONSEQUENTIALIST ETHICS, POSITIVIST JURISPRUDENCE, AND THE STUDY OF PUBLIC LAW

It would be presumptuous for someone who is not a philosopher or even a political theorist, and who is not an active participant in the work I have briefly surveyed, to conclude that it will all come to nothing. It seems to me that political scientists interested in political theory might well pursue post-consequentialist endeavors. It seems wrong that all political theorists should watch other people doing political philosophy instead of doing some of their own. And, of course, no political scientist is forbidden to do political theory just because he has somewhere along the line acquired a public law badge. There are, however, four reasons that I would prefer that the new ethics be pursued in political theory rather than public law.

First, the new ethics depends heavily on critical discourse to raise itself beyond intuitionism. The risk of idiosyncrasy endemic in appeals to moral sentiment is to be reduced by continuous dialogue among a large number of participants, each applying critical intelligence to the moral conclusions of others. If someone wishes to engage in the production of moral theories or conclusions, then it would appear best for them to join this dialogue where it is waged, in philosophy and political theory, rather than from the shelter of public law where professional criticism of the highest quality will be scarce.

Second, moral theory in public law runs the risk of all interdisciplinary work. There is always the danger that the political scientist who works on forestry will be considered a wonderful political scientist by foresters and a wonderful forester by political scientists. It is difficult enough for political theorists to meet the professional standards of philosophers, let alone for public law political scientists to do so. Interdisciplinary work ought to meet the standards of two or more disciplines rather than the standards of none. The new ethics is a particularly suspect and challenging endeavor among philosophers themselves. A public law political scientist is unlikely to become a worthy participant in the endeavor unless he or she takes the plunge of full-scale entry into the philosophy-political theory community rather than treating ethics as one among the many concerns of public law.

Third, and here I reach my most fundamental reason, I personally do not think the new ethics is going to work, or if it works, that it is going improve our capacities in public law. I have already said that it is hardly for me to decree that

3. Given that I promised a survey, some brief mention of critical legal studies is required. To the extent that it is Marxist, it promises no ethic that has not been found wanting already. To the extent that it is neo-Marxist, it could be anything. Although there is a good deal of neo-Marxist social science and empirical theory, it is extremely disparate and no one supposes that there is a clear, unified body of neo-Marxist ethics. To the extent that it is Unger, the ethics and the social program required by those ethics are now increasingly clear, but they leave no place for public law.

this work is foolish or should end. Yet my best guess is that it will not produce an ethical consensus anywhere near as powerful as the old utilitarian consensus, which itself never went unchallenged. Even the fairly precise ethical rule cum decision procedure of the greatest good of the greatest number required a level of empirical prediction beyond the capabilities of social science. In any given law case or legislative choice, even if everyone agreed on greatest good as the decision rule, the two or three or six sides split because they disagreed on which course of action would in fact ultimately lead to the greatest good.

It is not clear whether the new ethics will settle on deontology or teleology. If it settles on the latter, that is, on the notion that current ethical choices should depend on some ultimate vision of the good person in the good state, then it too is likely to produce a dead end in public law. Even if all of us could agree on some elaboration of utopia, we would be very unlikely to be able to evaluate current legal choices in its light, because we would have little confidence in our ability to predict which policy choice was most likely to lead there. Moreover, even if our ethical friends succeed in arriving at a set of firm deontological rules, it remains to be seen whether they will supply rules of sufficient specificity to lead to agreed ethical evaluations of particular legal policy choices. If there is one thing with which we in public law are familiar, it is the thou-shalt-not rule that does not really dictate the outcome even in cases that appear to fall within the rule's central meaning. The clearest example is, of course, the endlessly proliferating jurisprudence of the First Amendment.

My fourth reason for counseling public lawyers out of ethics is a prediction about where the new ethics will lead in the near term. With Smith I believe that Rorty and company will have the dominant influence, at least among lawyers and political scientists who are interested in policy choices in the real world rather than in abstract moral speculation. What will emerge is a theory of the "prudent decision maker," whether legislator, executive, administrative official or judge. The ethical demand on that decision maker will be that he or she do more than act the ring master in an arena where rival interest group claims are registered and Pareto-optimized. Instead the *politique*, the person of affairs, will be expected to attend to both deontological and teleological values and arrive at a prudent policy choice. A prudent policy choice is one consonant with our ethical traditions, the best of our current moral thinking, and visions of the ideal of the good person in the good state, as well as consonant with available resources, interests, and other factors determining the practicality of achieving any particular outcome.

If I am correct that prudence will be the message of the new ethics to politics, then public law may proceed without much more attention to the new ethics than a brief nod to its prudential message. Barber appears to be particularly struck by those aspects of philosophy of science that show that there can be no purely positivist, absolutely value-free social science. Once we all acknowledge that basic lesson, we must still go on to make certain choices. Recognizing that the very questions we ask about the human condition are influenced by the values we already hold about that condition, should we devote our resources to describing as precisely as we can the actions of others and the values that determine them? Or shall we devote ourselves to the construction of objectively correct values and the employment of such values to declare whether the actions of others are good or bad? If the message of ethics is going to be prudence, then the former task is an ethically worthy one. Prudent decision makers need the information that a more or less positivist social science can provide them. As Smith's call for institutionalism signals, even public lawyers bent solely on description are now aware that there are dangers in an extreme reductionism that atomizes and homogenizes all ethical traditions, moral positions, and hopes for the future into currently measurable units of attitude.

If we are so aware, and the indeterminate prescription of prudence is the most that ethics is going to be able to offer us, then public law political scientists may keep doing what we have been doing—describing what is going on, including the values at play, as accurately as we can. I believe, for instance, that no matter what their intentions, or how noble their goals, the actual work of Walter Murphy and friends on constitutional interpretation amounts to no more than this. To my mind, Lief Carter's call for jurisprudence as art is also the rose of prudence by another name. If I am right about prudence, then even the efforts of those most anxious to develop a normative public law will come to no more than a comparison of their own prudential judgments with those of the actors.

Although I am arguing here that the new movement in ethics ought not to raise false hopes for a normative public law and that public law political scientists would be better employed at a positivist political jurisprudence than at a jurisprudence of values, I certainly am not arguing that students of public law should ignore the new movement. Quite the contrary, post-consequentialist ethics is precisely the kind of intellectual institution that Smith quite rightly insists must be of interest to public law political scientists. Changes in the approach to ethics by professional philosophers will, I believe, have an important impact on legal doctrines and on the relation of courts to legislators and administrators. Indeed, I would hope that my most recent book, *Who Guards the Guardians: Judicial Control of Administrative Action* (Athens: University of Georgia Press, 1988), would pass muster with Smith as a piece of institutional analysis. In order to give proper weight to institutional factors, it tells the same story three times. The first traces the movements in ethics we have been looking at here. The second treats the administrative law doctrine built by lawyers and judges as a relatively autonomous institution with its own dynamic of development. The third traces general developments in politics from the New Deal through the deregulation movement. The book then seeks to combine the three in order to anticipate new doctrinal developments in administrative law, new normative visions of administrative action and the kinds of behavior of courts toward agencies that may be expected in the next decade. This work certainly will fall under Barber's strictures. It observes ethics, as a variable for positivist analysis, rather than doing ethics. It does contain modest and clearly labeled prescriptions about the judicial role vis-à-vis regulatory agencies, but these prescriptions accept as givens the instrumental and procedural values of efficiency, democratic control, and economic growth that I take to underlie contemporary regulatory efforts. In addition to my own work, I would cite the recent work by Shep Melnick on air pollution law and Robert Katzman on law of the handicapped as examples of institutional analysis in public law.

Earlier, I decried the excessive concentration of political scientists on public law and the excessive concentration of public law political scientists on constitutional law, and I shall do so again at the very end of this piece. Nevertheless, we must go hunting where the ducks are, and some attention to constitutional law as practiced by political scientists offers important lessons. In the 1930s, political scientists held a preeminent position in constitutional law. Edward S. Corwin, T. R. Powell, J. A. C. Grant, and Robert Cushman were among the most widely known constitutional scholars of their day—indeed, Corwin and Powell were clearly the top two stars. I would argue that this situation occurred because of their comparative advantage in bringing an outsider's nonadversarial perspective to the field.

All four of these men did do doctrinal work—but work with a plus and a minus. The plus was their concern for the role of constitutional law in shaping the political system as a whole and in being shaped by it; the minus was the lawyer's almost instinctive movement toward making the best arguments possible on behalf of a client in full confidence that someone else will make the best arguments on the other side. (Krislov, Stumpf, and a number of other political scientists have made this point before me.) One may argue that Corwin's work is, in fact, often fatally flawed by his tendency to take FDR as his client, but in all four, and particularly in Powell and Grant, the scientific ethic of truth telling rather than the advocacy ethic of making the best case for your side comes shining through. Political science lost this dominance in the postwar period essentially because of behaviorism. Late-blooming statistical legal realism did not contribute enough on the positive side to keep us ahead, and it reduced our skills in the kind of outsider's doctrinal analysis that had benefited the prewar generation.

Barber argues that public law political scientists might differentiate themselves from academic lawyers by developing their work in a nonlitigational setting and perspective. Yet in his comments on the Straussians, he himself shows how easily good, truth-seeking political theory turns into litigation oriented advocacy when it crosses the border into constitutional law. Constitutional law is simply too litigation-centered. Political scientists bent on doing ethics and then bent on doing ethics in constitutional law are willy-nilly going to find themselves submerged in litigation-oriented thinking and in the same spot as their fellow lawyer participants in the jurisprudence of values. Their ethical discourse will lead to conclusions about which parties should win. Those parties will become their clients. And soon no one, least of all the political scientists themselves, will know whether their ethics generate their clients or their clients their ethics.

The trick for political scientists is to strengthen our skills at doctrinal analysis while maintaining an outsider's perspective—that is, while maintaining the truth ethic rather than the advocacy ethic. (Lawyers will say that advocacy is a truth ethic, too. But it takes three lawyers to tell the truth, two advocates and a judge. It takes only one political scientist.) Perhaps not as a matter of logic, but certainly as a matter of real-world experience, such a perspective is far easier to maintain from a positivist than from a normative position. There are very strong affinities between ethical discourse and the traditional adversary discourse of constitutional law, if for no other reason than that the latter is always desperately pretending to be the former. It is for this reason that I made the remark about the craziness of political scientists worrying about the craftsmanship of the Burger Court that Barber quotes early in his piece. Whose craft? Judges are part of the lawyers' guild. Their craft is the craft of advocacy, of telling one side of the case convincingly. Political scientists who get exercised about craftsmanship are joining the advocacy guild. (Of course a political scientist might simply be arguing that by failing to be craftsmanlike a judge risks alienating important constituencies, but when political scientists talk craftsmanship, the overtones I catch are moral fervor, not hard-headed constituency politics.)

Political science has taught for a long time that the doctrinal law review article was itself a political act, a mode of lobbying lawmakers. Such "law reform" has always been an acknowledged part of the law professor's work, and the political scientist is likewise entitled to write law review or other articles lobbying courts. Certainly I confess to having done so. Perhaps as citizens doing politics they are even entitled to play the lawyers' game of pretending that what they want is really already the true law only waiting to be recognized by the court. If they are to keep doing political science, however, they ought to keep clear in their own minds and make clear to others when they are doing politics and when they are doing political science. More precisely, when political scientists write that the equal protection clause requires or forbids affirmative action or that there is or is not a right to abortion in the Constitution, I don't know what else to do than to say to them that they may practice academic law and do politics if they wish, but that there are more than enough lawyers to do so. And I must treat their work as part of the constitutional politics that I observe as a political scientist rather than part of the work I do as a political scientist.

In fact, Smith, Barber, and I seem to agree that the comparative advantage of political scientists lies in their not doing litigation-oriented scholarship traditionally done by academic lawyers. All of us agree that advice about this comparative advantage ought not to be turned into legislation excluding people from political science public law or constitutional law. Where we disagree is in our estimates of how likely it is that investment in the new ethical studies will lead to something different and better than doctrinal advocacy. I am the most pessimistic of the three, predicting that the positive contribution will be slight and the negative impact is likely to be great. I take a very Protestant view of the propensity of public law-constitutional law-political scientists to fall into the sin of doctrinal advocacy once they get involved in a jurisprudence of values and particularly in a period in the throes of reaction to behaviorism.

Protestant as I may be in this respect, I have not come to the point of believing in predestination. So just as Smith and Barber have done, I suppose I must propose an upward path as well as decry the fiery pit. In brief, I believe most public law political scientists would benefit more from doing more public law than from doing some moral philosophy. There are important expansions underway. With the disinterest in government regulation and public policy that flowed from behaviorism, plus the influence of Morgenthau's and others' theories of power in international relations during the era of bipolar cold war, public law shrank to constitutional law alone. But a tiny and oblique revival in international law is now occurring among political scientists because of their new involvement in international political economy.

Even at the time public law had reached its narrowest confines of constitutional law, urban politics specialists found that if you wander around cities with your eyes open you run into courts and into police, and, probably because some aspects of criminal procedure had already been constitutionalized by the Supreme Court, public law political science added criminal trial courts to its repertoire. A similar dynamic accounts for much of the renewed interest in administrative law. Some of that interest begins with those who do public administration and public law like Lief Carter (although it may well be his legal training that gave him the means and incentive to move beyond the constitutional law fetish). Much of the momentum, however, comes from policy studies by people like Melnick and Katzman that I noted earlier in connection with the new institutionalism. If you wander around public policy with your eyes open, you keep running into administrative agencies and the enormous incursion of courts like the D.C. circuit into agency affairs.

Policy studies should lead to an interest not only in more courts than the Supreme Court but in many new areas of public law as well. Labor law, tax law, environmental law, welfare law, utility regulation, and so on and on, are public law. They are bodies of law central to politics. They are major vehicles for making, announcing, implementing, and resisting the implementation of public policy. Before public law political scientists begin worrying about RORTY, they might begin worrying about NEPA and OSHA. Indeed, the recent concern of a number of political scientists to trace a particular policy-making process from beginning to end might lead to an even more astonishing result—some political scientists might even begin to read statutes. Given the incredibly detailed and sophisticated levels that congressional studies have reached in political science, the refusal to pay any attention at all to the substance of the laws that Congress makes seems almost willfully perverse. Aside from the tradition of doing legislative histories of single statutes, there are hardly any attempts at systematically relating what Congress actually produces to the demands made upon it and its own internal processes. If Congress specialists are so afraid of law that they will not read statutes, we might expect public law specialists to help them out. More seriously, it is the public law specialists who are supposed to give political science its theories of law, but theories of law emanating from public law specialists are built up almost entirely from their observations of judge-made constitutional law rather than all law. Given that the bulk of all law in all modern industrial nations, even in so-called common law countries, consists of statutes and regulations, the theories of law we develop are bound to be sadly mistaken and incomplete.

Finally a brief note on comparative public law. If Americans in political science know little about American law, they do, thanks to public law specialists, know a bit about American courts. With a very few exceptions, and most of them Europeans by birth and often with European legal educations, comparative politics specialists know nothing about either the law or the courts of the countries they study. Only a very few public law specialists do any comparative work.

Exterior events plus our own preoccupation with constitutional law combine to suggest the possibility of some advances. Germany and Italy now have constitutional courts exercising judicial review. The European Court of Human Rights has been exercising a modified form of judicial review. The high court of the European Community, the European Court of Justice, has asserted a sweeping power of judicial review quite successfully although a debate exists over whether it has or has not gone too far or too fast.[4] Some French scholars, in the time-honored fashion of lawyers, are trying to convince the French that they already enjoy constitutional judicial review although they have not realized that they had acquired it with their last constitution. Some young American scholars, whose background is French politics rather than public law, have been challenging this interpretation of the recent decisions of the Constitutional Council.[5] Work by American scholars of Japanese and Indian judicial review has begun to appear. The fact that all these nations always have been full of public law may not have tempted American public law specialists in the past, but now that they are also full of constitutional judicial review, voila—I hope. The new emphasis on institutional analysis will also probably help break down the American parochialism of the public law field because a lot of institutionalist study in other fields is already comparative.

The bottom line of all this is that although I believe that public law scholars must treat the new activity in ethics as an important institutional influence on law, I think that to the extent that we ask public law people to move beyond their current expertise, it would be best to do more public law itself. For most of us this would mean any public law other than constitutional law, any court other than the Supreme Court, any public lawmaker other than the judge, and any country other than the United States.

---

4. See Hjalte Rasmussen, *On Law and Policy in the European Court of Justice: A Comparative Study in Judicial Policymaking* (Dordrecht: Nijhoff, 1986); Mauro Cappelletti, "Is European Court of Justice 'Running Wild'?" *European Law Review* 12 (1987): 3–17.

5. Louis Favoreu, *La Politique Saisie par le Droit* (Paris and Aix-en-Provence: Economics and Presses Universitaires d'Aix-Marseilles, 1988); John Keeler and Alec Stone, "The Emergence of the Constitutional Council as a Major Actor in the Policy-making Process," in Stanley Hoffman and George Ross, eds., *The Mitterand Experiment* (New York: Oxford University Press, 1987); Alec Stone, "In the Shadow of the Constitutional Council: The 'Juridicisation' of the Legislative Process in France," *West European Politics*, September 1988.

ARTICLES

DAVID PLOTKE
Yale University

The Wagner Act, Again: Politics and Labor, 1935–37

Why write about the Wagner Act again? There is no shortage of commentary, yet disagreement persists on basic questions: Why did the measure pass? Did the Wagner Act make any difference. If so, how?

Here I argue that the Wagner Act was passed by Progressive liberals inside and outside the government, in alliance with a mass labor movement. The National Labor Relations Act (NLRA) played a major positive role in the emergence of new industrial unions.

Claims such as these are often asserted but seldom defended in full view of their implications or arguments to the contrary. To sustain such claims requires entering into sharp debates over how to understand the sources of the Wagner Act and its consequences. These debates involve not only historical accuracy but readings of contemporary political situations still significantly shaped by the conflicts of the 1930s, as well as theoretical differences about structure and political change.

An explicit evaluation of contending views seems especially appropriate given the contested status of almost every assertion about the Wagner Act. We need a narrative—but the most important arguments often come down to choices about how this narrative should be constructed and how its actors are named. Differences about "what happened" are linked to and sometimes determined by analytical differences. As the issues at stake matter not just for our understanding of the Wagner Act but for our views of how major political changes occur in the United States, I have tried to sharpen choices in areas of reasonable contention rather than use narrative devices to settle issues. I hope this will be a persuasive way to engage alternative views; at least it will allow those who are unpersuaded to see where they disagree.

For helpful comments on an earlier version of this article, thanks are due to the editors of *Studies in American Political Development* and a reviewer. This article was written at the Institute for Advanced Study, where my stay in 1987–88 was made possible by a grant from the National Endowment for the Humanities. Thanks to Lucille Allsen at the Institute for crucial technical assistance.

My argument concerning the NLRA derives from a broader argument about the crucial position of the conflicts of 1935–37 in establishing a new political order in the United States.[1] Both that argument and the present account assign a major role to political processes, both discursive and institutional, in shaping political outcomes. Thus what follows has a double aim: to show how the Wagner Act originated and what it meant, and to advance theoretical claims for the causal importance of politics.

This article starts from a framework defined by the intersection of those neo-Weberian and neo-Marxist approaches that accord a significant causal role to politics. Yet my account sits uneasily within that framework. I want not only to make strong claims about the substantive and causal importance of politics but to argue that this importance crucially concerns political discourses and practices as well as institutions. In other words, "politics" is not just another way of naming social classes or state institutions. To defend this view is one of the aims of what follows. Because even using the term *discourse* is often enough to raise fears of hopeless indeterminacy. I will stay close to the actual processes of the mid-1930s in specifying how political processes shape political and other outcomes.

For some liberals and neoconservatives, the 1930s recalls a politics when parties properly aggregated interests and selected candidates. For some left-liberals and socialists, a special opportunity was lost to construct a more consistently liberal or perhaps social democratic party and program.[2] The labor movement remains near the center of debate—in relation to economic crisis, to legislative and judicial action, and to the expanded unions.[3] Questions about the Wagner Act are questions about how the labor movement emerged, what sort of movement it became, and whether basically different courses were real possibilities.

1. The full argument is developed in a book manuscript, "The Democratic Political Order, 1932–72."

2. The first view colors recent works on contemporary parties which contain little direct discussion of the 1930s or 1940s, such as Nelson Polsby's *Consequences of Party Reform* (New York: Oxford University Press, 1983). For different versions of the second argument, see James MacGregor Burns, *Roosevelt: The Lion and the Fox* (New York: Harcourt, Brace and World, 1956); Michael Davis, *Prisoners of the American Dream* (London: Verso, 1986); and Theda Skocpol, "Legacies of New Deal Liberalism," *Dissent* (Winter 1983): 33–44.

3. Relevant works published in the last decade include: G. William Domhoff, "The Wagner Act and Theories of the State: A New Analysis Based on Class-Segment Theory," *Political Power and Social Theory* 6 (1987): 159–85; P. K. Edwards, *Strikes in the United States, 1881–1974* (Oxford: Basil Blackwell, 1981); Ruth Milkman, ed., *Women, Work and Protest: A Century of U.S. Women's Labor History* (Boston: Routledge & Kegan Paul, 1985); Theda Skocpol, "Political Response to Capitalist Crisis: Neo-Marxist Theories of the State and the Case of the New Deal," *Politics and Society* 10, no. 2 (1980): 155–201; Christopher L. Tomlins, *The State and the Unions: Labor Relations, Law, and the Organized Labor Movement in America, 1880–1960* (Cambridge: Cambridge University Press, 1985); Stanley Vittoz, *New Deal Labor Policy and the American Industrial Economy* (Chapel Hill: University of North Carolina Press, 1987); and a volume of articles on labor in the 1930s, Maurice Zeitlin, ed., *Political Power and Social Theory* 4 (1984).

In assigning the key role in the Wagner Act's passage to Progressive liberals in conjunction with the labor movement, I argue for the importance of political action in facilitating and shaping the labor movement, and reject views of unionization as a reflex of socioeconomic development. Getting the Wagner Act right means understanding what happened in one important case when a high level of working-class mobilization accompanied sharp political conflict over labor relations. The contemporary decline of American trade unions directs further attention to how labor relations were reshaped in the 1930s. What were the conditions in which a major growth of unions occurred? Are basic features of the institutions and understandings created at that time responsible for the contemporary decay of the labor movement?[4]

The view of the Wagner Act proposed here has implications for other controversies about the 1930s as well. Conflicts persist about the meaning of popular political movements.[5] New Deal agricultural policies are debated, as are its racial practices.[6] The origins of Social Security legislation are still controversial.[7] Although I focus on the Wagner Act, insofar as my reading can be sustained it underlines the need to conceive changes in these other areas more as a consequence of political processes than as an adaptation to social and

4. Efforts to explain the contemporary decline of the unions are crucial not only for accounts of the labor movement, but for overall views of recent developments in American politics. Recent works in which these connections are clear include: Thomas Ferguson and Joel Rogers, *Right Turn: The Decline of the Democrats and the Future of American Politics* (New York: Hill and Wang, 1986); Richard B. Freeman and James L. Medoff, *What Do Unions Do* (New York: Basic Books, 1984); Michael Goldfield, *The Decline of Organized Labor in the United States* (Chicago: University of Chicago Press, 1987); and Michael J. Piore and Charles F. Sabel, *The Second Industrial Divide* (New York: Basic Books, 1984).

5. Alan Brinkley's *Voices of Protest: Huey Long, Father Coughlin, and the Great Depression* (New York: Alfred Knopf, 1982) offers a sympathetic view of 1930s populism. For treatments of the Communist experience, from critical to antagonistic, see Richard H. Pells, *Radical Visions and American Dreams: Culture and Social Thought in the Depression Years* (New York: Harper and Row, 1973); and Harvey Klehr, *The Heyday of American Communism: The Depression Decade* (New York: Basic Books, 1984).

6. On race relations, see Doug McAdam, *Political Process and the Development of Black Insurgency, 1930–1970* (Chicago: University of Chicago Press, 1982); Harvard Sitkoff, *A New Deal for Blacks: The Emergence of Civil Rights as a National Issue* (New York: Oxford University Press, 1978); and Nancy J. Weiss, *Farewell to the Party of Lincoln* (Princeton: Princeton University Press, 1983).

7. For the recent debate on the Social Security Act, see Jerry R. Cates, *Insuring Inequality: Administrative Leadership in Social Security, 1935–54* (Ann Arbor: University of Michigan Press, 1983); G. William Domhoff, "Corporate-Liberal Theory and the Social Security Act: A Chapter in the Sociology of Knowledge," *Politics and Society* 15, no. 3 (1986–87): 297–330; G. John Ikenberry and Theda Skocpol, "Expanding Social Benefits: The Role of Social Security," *Political Science Quarterly* 102, no. 3 (Fall 1987): 389–416; Jill Quadagno, "Welfare Capitalism and the Social Security Act of 1935," *American Sociological Review* 49 (1984): 632–47; and Theda Skocpol and John Ikenberry, "The Political Formation of the American Welfare State in Historical and Comparative Perspective," in *Comparative Social Research*, vol. 5, *The Welfare State, 1883–1983*, ed. Richard F. Tomasson (Greenwich, Conn.: JAI Press, 1983), 87–148.

economic crises. And we need to take seriously the political discourses in which the struggles were fought out.

I will develop my argument in two parts, both of which treat events in 1935–37. The first tries to explain the Wagner Act—why it was written and passed as it was. The second part mainly assesses its effects. There is some overlap between the two parts. First, in accounting for the Wagner Act's passage, some issues are clarified by looking at how it was implemented. Moreover, to highlight the analytical issues, I have had to crisscross over the same ground several times to adjudicate among competing views.

WHY DID THE NLRA PASS?

The Wagner Act—the National Labor Relations Act—was passed in 1935 amidst economic and political crises. It helped resolve both. Support for the Wagner Act was strong in the House and Senate in June 1935; it was signed by Roosevelt early in July.[8] This apparently sweeping approval is misleading, as once passage seemed assured, some who would have preferred a different bill or no bill at all supported it. In 1934 a similar bill failed to pass, and received little support from the administration.[9]

Aspects of the Wagner Act were prefigured in prior New Deal legislation, mainly Section 7(a) of the National Industrial Recovery Act (NIRA) passed in 1933:

> Every code of fair competition, agreement, and license approved, prescribed, or issued under this title shall contain the following conditions: (1) That employees shall have the right to organize and bargain collectively through representatives of their own choosing, and shall be free from the interference, restraint, or coercion of employers of labor, or their agents, in the designation of such representatives or in self-organization or in other concerted activities for the purpose of collective bargaining or other mutual aid or protection; (2) that no employee and no one seeking employment shall be required as a condition of employment to join any company union or to refrain from join-

---

8. The initial vote in the Senate was 63–12; efforts to modify the pro-union emphasis of the bill in the House were voted down. The House then approved the bill without a record vote (Harry A. Millis and Emily Clark Brown, *From the Wagner Act to Taft-Hartley: A Study of National Labor Policy and Labor Relations* [Chicago: University of Chicago Press, 1950], 28). Also see the House Conference Report (No. 1371 on S.1958) in *Legislative History of the National Labor Relations Act*, vol. 2 (Washington: U.S. Government Printing Office, 1935), 3252–67.

9. In 1934, Roosevelt expressed no great urgency about changing labor law. He suggested a radically simplified version of the bill, locating any new agencies within the Labor Department, and restating Section 7(a) of the NIRA. He was inclined to recommend further study (Memo, "President's Conference with Senators," April 14, 1934, Folder "U.S. Senate 1933–36," President's Secretary's File 188, Franklin D. Roosevelt Papers as President, FDR Library). Also see Irving Bernstein, *New Deal Collective Bargaining Policy* (Berkeley: University of California Press, 1950), 63–70; Daniel Albert Sipe, "A Moment of the State: The Enactment of the National Labor Relations Act, 1935" (Ph.D. diss., University of Pennsylvania, 1981), 147–49.

ing, organizing, or assisting a labor organization of his own choosing; and (3) that employers shall comply with the maximum hours of labor, minimum rates of pay, and other conditions of employment, approved or prescribed by the President.[10]

The NIRA, however, lacked means of enforcing these provisions, and efforts to use 7(a) to force employers to recognize unions were thwarted.[11] When the Supreme Court overturned the NIRA in May 1935, the vacuum in labor legislation provided a favorable opportunity for advocates of the NLRA.

The Wagner Act affirmed a right for workers to form unions and bargain with employers:

> It is hereby declared to be the policy of the United States to eliminate the causes of certain substantial obstructions to the free flow of commerce and to mitigate and eliminate those obstructions when they have occurred by encouraging the practice and procedure of collective bargaining and by protecting the exercise by workers of full freedom of association, self-organization, and designation of representatives of their own choosing, for the purpose of negotiating the terms and conditions of their employment or other mutual aid or protection.

The act further stipulated that none of its sections should be construed as interfering with the right to strike.[12] A potentially powerful National Labor Relations Board (NLRB) was authorized to organize representation elections and to investigate unfair labor practices, including employers' efforts to avoid recognizing or dealing with unions. Through the NLRB and the courts, the Wagner Act could compel employer recognition of unions.[13]

The right to unions had been acknowledged before, but the Wagner Act strongly asserted a right to organize, stressed unfair labor practices by management, and provided significant means of enforcement. All this broke sharply with the prior "equality" which matched labor's right to organize with management's right to try to block unionization. The NLRA collected themes that had

10. National Industrial Recovery Act, H.R. 5755, June 16, 1933, in *Public Laws of the U.S.A.—Passed by the Seventy-Third Congress, 1933–34* (Washington: U.S. Government Printing Office, 1934), 195–200.

11. Complaints about the inability of the labor relations machinery to secure compliance and thus to protect efforts to achieve unions began in 1933 and persisted. Many reports of these problems were made to Roosevelt (Letter, William Connery to Roosevelt, 11/26/33, Folder 1933–34, Official File 407—Labor, Franklin D. Roosevelt Papers as President, FDR Library).

12. National Labor Relations Act, July 5, 1935, *Public Laws of the U.S.A.—Passed by the Seventy-Fourth Congress, 1935–36* (Washington: U.S. Government Printing Office, 1936), 449–57.

13. Legal conflict was a central process for the contending parties. It concerned the legitimate uses of government power, including physical force, in industrial relations. Employers' willingness to accept legal outcomes they opposed was due to a combination of commitment to legal practices and lack of realistic political alternatives. The centrality of legal conflict in the decade is one of the main points of Peter Irons, *New Deal Lawyers* (Princeton: Princeton University Press, 1983).

been current on the left of Progressive liberal policy circles for several decades and formulated them in a manner clearly favorable to the formation of unions. At the national level, the Wagner Act as a whole was sharply discontinuous with prior practices, though elements of its approach were prefigured in Woodrow Wilson's wartime administration and in the NRA.[14]

Alternative Paths to the NLRA

This sketch of the NLRA's context and content raises as many questions as it answers. The questions cluster around a central problem: in a country so often hostile to unionization, why did the Wagner Act pass? To answer this question, I have outlined different conceptions of the path to the Wagner Act, selecting those for which a serious argument can be made. All these conceptions address two problems: identifying the main forces that yielded the NLRA, and specifying how these forces interacted. To treat these problems requires treating causality not simply as a binary choice but as relations of varying form and intensity. The most significant causal forces included the economic crisis, the labor movement, state elites, reformist capitalists, the Democratic party, and liberal reformers. To start I will combine state elites, the Democratic party, and liberal reformers into a single term—political reformers.

These sketches downplay a causal relation that is rarely part of persuasive accounts of the period—full determination (see 4 in the diagram), in which a single variable sufficiently influences others to produce all the variation in question. "Reflects" (1 in the diagram) means that causal pressures originating elsewhere are transmitted by an agent or institution, without basically changing the direction or intensity of the pressures. "Selects" (2 in the diagram) means that an agent or process significantly influences an outcome mainly within terms set by another, analytically prior variable—for example, that liberal Democrats made choices about the Wagner Act, but their choices were given by economic crisis problems and working-class pressure. "Shapes" (3 in the diagram) is a claim both that the causal relation is stronger than selection (that more variation is explained) and that it operates via an external and internal logic—for example that the logic of the labor movement's own development shaped the range of choices of political actors so that major labor law reform was required.

Given these alternative paths to the Wagner Act, it is possible to look again at the course of events to find patterns or moments that adjudicate among claims about causal relations.

The Economic Crisis. Almost everything about the mid-1930s was unusual. That everything seems to have been changing at once makes it difficult to fix analytical points of departure. There was, first of all, an extraordinarily severe

14. See Bernstein, *New Deal Collective Bargaining*; Joseph P. Goldberg, "The Law and Practice of Collective Bargaining," in Goldberg, ed., *Federal Policies and Worker Status since the Thirties* (Madison: University of Wisconsin, Industrial Relations Research Association, 1976), 13–19; J. Joseph Huthmacher, *Senator Robert F. Wagner and the Rise of Urban Liberalism* (New York: Atheneum, 1948), 103–45.

Paths to the Wagner Act

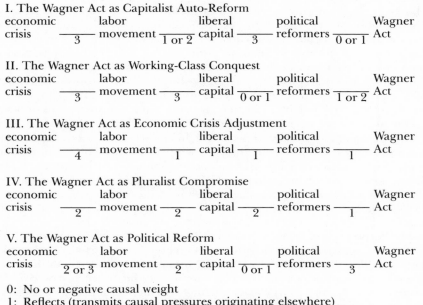

I. The Wagner Act as Capitalist Auto-Reform

economic crisis $\dfrac{}{3}$ labor movement $\dfrac{}{1 \text{ or } 2}$ liberal capital $\dfrac{}{3}$ political reformers $\dfrac{}{0 \text{ or } 1}$ Wagner Act

II. The Wagner Act as Working-Class Conquest

economic crisis $\dfrac{}{3}$ labor movement $\dfrac{}{3}$ liberal capital $\dfrac{}{0 \text{ or } 1}$ political reformers $\dfrac{}{1 \text{ or } 2}$ Wagner Act

III. The Wagner Act as Economic Crisis Adjustment

economic crisis $\dfrac{}{4}$ labor movement $\dfrac{}{1}$ liberal capital $\dfrac{}{1}$ political reformers $\dfrac{}{1}$ Wagner Act

IV. The Wagner Act as Pluralist Compromise

economic crisis $\dfrac{}{2}$ labor movement $\dfrac{}{2}$ liberal capital $\dfrac{}{2}$ political reformers $\dfrac{}{1}$ Wagner Act

V. The Wagner Act as Political Reform

economic crisis $\dfrac{}{2 \text{ or } 3}$ labor movement $\dfrac{}{2}$ liberal capital $\dfrac{}{0 \text{ or } 1}$ political reformers $\dfrac{}{3}$ Wagner Act

0: No or negative causal weight
1: Reflects (transmits causal pressures originating elsewhere)
2: Selects (exerts causal influence, mainly within exogenous limits)
3: Shapes (exerts strong causal influences, within endogenous and exogenous limits)
4: Determines (sufficient cause)

depression. Its origins involved both international and domestic factors. Among the latter, flawed financial markets were crucial in detonating the collapse, turning it into a prolonged, deep slide well into the middle of the decade. Underconsumption tendencies were particularly acute in the 1920s and 1930s, given the growth of mass production industries which spawned enormous productivity increases while the capacity to absorb the new products was limited.

All views of the path to the Wagner Act sketched in this diagram treat the Great Depression as causally significant. To show that this was not the case, one would have to prove that pressures to pass such a measure were mounting in the 1920s and would have intensified into an imaginary period of continued growth in the next decade, so that the Wagner Act would have resulted. It is much more likely that without a depression, the coercive factory regime of the 1920s would have persisted, and reforms would have been slower and more limited.[15]

15. The authoritarianism of the 1920s factory regime is clear in accounts both of welfare capitalism and of conditions early in the depression. While the mass production industries

A more serious claim would be that the Wagner Act represented a necessary process of adaptation in efforts to escape the crisis. This is implied in some Marxist accounts of the decade.[16] This view recognizes the empirical reality of political struggle over the Wagner Act, but claims that an overarching logic of crisis resolution so constrained choices as to limit other variables to reflecting deep economic pressures. Such an argument (as a functionalist version of economic determinism) claims much more precision and closure for the causal influence of the crisis process than can be shown. The key functional require-ments posited are an industrial relations system within which production would be reasonably stable, and an expansion of mass consumption sufficient to provide a broad basis for the stable expansion of mass production industries. Because numerous arrangements might have met these needs, one cannot claim that only the Wagner Act formula (which addressed both through state-supported collective bargaining by independent unions) was appropriate. If we distinguish between helping to shape reform and determining its outcome, we can rule out one of the paths sketched above—the Wagner Act as Economic Crisis Adjustment (path III)—even before reaching the Act's immediate con-text.

The turbulence of that context went beyond the economic crisis itself. In 1934, widespread labor action sometimes emerged in massive citywide strikes with a political dimension.[17] In 1935, the number of such strikes declined, yet overall strike activity persisted at a high level, and the turbulence of 1934 was easy to recall.[18] This upsurge made a strong statement of working-class discon-tent and of the potential for further efforts. Populist movements were growing rapidly.[19] The failure of the NIRA seemed to create a dangerous vacuum. A sweeping Democratic victory in the 1934 midterm elections expanded con-gressional reform forces and widened their field of maneuver. There was polarization between the national administration and business.

---

provided an eventually favorable setting for new types of collective action, the fullest account of welfare capitalism in the 1920s argues only for the unhappiness of workers with the package of wages, working conditions, and benefits it supplied, not that rebellion was immi-nent prior to the depression. The unions had been defeated, and employers had the economic and political resources to limit reform efforts, given a continued growth in wages and produc-tivity. See Stuart D. Brandes, *American Welfare Capitalism: 1880–1940* (Chicago: University of Chicago Press, 1976), 136–48.

16. For example, see Michel Aglietta, *A Theory of Capitalist Regulation* (London: New Left Books, 1979).

17. Irving Bernstein provides a graphic account of the upsurges of 1934–35 in *The Tur-bulent Years* (Boston: Houghton Mifflin, 1970). Dramatic press accounts are collected in Melvyn Dubofsky, ed., *American Labor since the New Deal* (Chicago: Quadrangle Books, 1971).

18. In 1934, 1,856 strikes resulted in 19.6 million "man-days" idle; in 1935, 2,014 strikes resulted in 15.5 million lost days (Bureau of the Census, *Historical Statistics of the United States— Colonial Times to 1970* [Washington: Bureau of the Census, 1975], D 970–985, "Work Stop-pages, Workers Involved, Man-Days Idle, Major Issues, and Average Duration: 1881–1970").

19. Arthur Schlesinger, *The Politics of Upheaval* (Boston: Houghton Mifflin, 1960), 242–54; Brinkley, *Voices of Protest*.

Political Forces for and against the NLRA. In this setting, how were the main political actors aligned? Political interest groups representing business opposed the Wagner Act, whether or not they were willing to support other New Deal initiatives or had supported parts of the early New Deal. In 1935 business antagonism to the Roosevelt administration was sharp and mounting.[20] There is certainly not enough evidence of business support for the NLRA to support an interpretation in which business elites collectively initiated the reform to head off more radical measures.[21] Most of business preferred that the law not pass and favored company unions or no unions.[22]

Labor's political representatives supported the Wagner Act. The AFL lobbied hard for it in 1935, although voluntarist traditions remained strong within the AFL, and its leaders were cautious about supporting state intervention.[23] The forces that would develop into the CIO had a less voluntarist view than the AFL unions and unhesitatingly advocated the NLRA. Yet the industrial unions were only taking shape in 1934–35 and could not play a major direct political role.

The Communist party criticized the Wagner Act, as it did most New Deal measures well into 1935. Still burdened by its Third Period militancy, the CP combined an ultramilitant rejection of the act with a quasi-voluntarist rationale for doing so.[24] The CP did not help pass the Wagner Act, but indirectly, its

20. In addition to Schlesinger's account in *Politics of Upheaval*, 270–320, see Burns, *Roosevelt*, 205–40, and Ellis Hawley, *The New Deal and the Problem of Monopoly* (Princeton: Princeton University Press, 1966), 154–55, for statements of business opposition to the administration.

21. Not surprisingly, one of the most extended analyses of the New Deal from a perspective that emphasizes the role of business self-organization and the state's alliance with business projects contains no discussion of the Wagner Act. See Gabriel Kolko, *Main Currents in Modern American History* (New York: Harper and Row, 1976), 100–56.

22. This view is argued in Bernstein, *Turbulent Years*, 336–51, and more recently in Stanley Vittoz, *New Deal Labor Policy*, 149–53. Efforts to demonstrate substantial business support for the Wagner Act have been unsuccessful. Thomas Ferguson tries to show that business groups were important, but there are two major problems. First, his evidence is very weak, amounting to little more than meetings of Gerard Swope with Wagner. He seems not really to want to claim that these meetings determined the course of events. Second, even if broader contact between the Progressive liberals and business could be found than seems to have occurred in the course of the writing and passage of the act, it would be necessary to show that this represented a business initiative rather than a response to a Progressive effort to cope with an emerging political and economic crisis. See Thomas Ferguson, "From Normalcy to New Deal: Industrial Structure, Party Competition, and American Public Policy in the Great Depression," *International Organization* 38 (Winter 1984): 88.

23. Ruth Horowitz, *Political Ideologies of Organized Labor: The New Deal Era* (New Brunswick: Transaction, 1978), 110–27, 131.

24. See Bert Cochran, *Labor and Communism* (Princeton: Princeton University Press, 1977), 78, and Bernstein, *New Deal Collective Bargaining*, 108–09. Sympathetic accounts of the role of the Communists in the labor movement often pay little attention to the CP's early opposition to the NLRA. A good example of this delicacy is Roger Keeran's *The Communist Party and the Auto Workers* (Bloomington: Indiana University Press, 1980), 121–47. In 1935, testimony for the Communist party against the NLRA was given by a writer for the *Daily Worker*, William Dunne. See "Statement of William Dunne," Hearings before the Senate Committee on Education and Labor, in *Legislative History of the National Labor Relations Act*, vol. 2 (Washington: U.S. Government Printing Office, 1949), 1966–73.

contribution to mobilizing the industrial working class provided pressure for it.

Populist movements feared the potential organized power of the working-class movement; they also acknowledged the injustice of employers' antiunion militancy. Although these movements favored labor law reform, especially when their leaders were trying to outflank Roosevelt from the left, the Wagner Act was certainly not a priority, and they were not a major direct determinant of the result.[25]

The Republican party had nothing good to say about the NLRA in 1935 or 1936. Closely tied to business elites who opposed it—or representing rural districts suspicious of unions—Republicans made their opposition clear in the code words of the time: "We pledge ourselves to: Protect the right of labor to organize and to bargain collectively through representatives of its own choosing without interference from any source."[26] By the mid-1930s the Progressive Republicanism which was important in the post-1896 political order was marginal to the Republican party, though it could furnish support for the New Deal in alliance with Democratic liberals.

Republican opposition is no surprise. But there was little enthusiasm for a prolabor measure from the organized Democratic party. The 1932 platform made no reference to passing any such measure, or even to unions.[27] Nor was labor law a central Democratic issue in the 1934 campaign, though the labor upsurge of that year influenced the campaign debate.[28] The Democratic forces represented by James Farley, head of the Democratic National Committee, and by conservative Democrats in the cabinet offered at most qualified support.[29]

Nor was there more than lukewarm support from President Roosevelt.[30] He was uninterested in a 1934 labor bill proposed by Wagner and did not actively support the NLRA early in 1935. When the Supreme Court nullification of the NIRA (May 27, 1935) created a void in labor relations procedures, his interest grew rapidly.[31] Roosevelt's eventual support for the measure was crucial (both

25. Brinkley, *Voices of Protest*, 246–48.

26. "Republican Platform of 1936," in Donald Bruce Johnson, comp., *National Party Platforms* (Chicago: University of Illinois Press, 1978), 367.

27. Johnson, *National Party Platforms*, 331–32.

28. Obviously Roosevelt was aware of the year's labor conflict, and if somehow it had escaped his attention, he received many reminders from within the administration. For example, see Memo, Isador Lubin (Bureau of Labor Statistics) to Roosevelt, n.d., Official File 407B—Strikes, Roosevelt Papers, FDR Library. He received many letters complaining about disorder and urging action against the strikes, as in 1934 Folder, 1935 Folder, Official File 407B—Strikes, Roosevelt Papers, FDR Library.

29. Thus the secretary of commerce advised the inclusion of language very similar to that in the Republican platform (Letter, Daniel Roper to Roosevelt, June 20, 1935, Official File 300, Roosevelt Papers, FDR Library).

30. See R. W. Fleming, "The Significance of the Wagner Act," in Milton Derber and Edwin Young, eds., *Labor and the New Deal* (Madison: University of Wisconsin Press, 1957), 128. Also see Frances Perkins, *The Roosevelt I Knew* (New York: Harper & Row, 1964), 239.

31. In 1934 and 1935, participants in the labor boards criticized the lack of mechanisms for securing compliance in decisions. Compliance with decisions that required employers to make concessions seems to have occurred at most one-third of the time, probably a good deal less

in guaranteeing that it would not be vetoed and in signaling allies about the stance they should adopt), but he never took the initiative.

What does this quick inventory of actors' stances and behavior suggest about how to account for the passage of the Wagner Act? What has been reported to this point rules out one view: portraying the Wagner Act as a working-class conquest (path II) overstates the power of the labor movement vis-à-vis other political actors in 1935.[32] Although there was a growing labor movement, its limits were apparent in the difficulties it had in winning strikes in 1934–35. It was a militant but fragile minority movement within the working class. To attribute the Wagner Act to the labor movement's choices, expressed politically by reform forces, would require a demonstration of the direct power of labor that no one has come close to providing. Labor representatives (AFL lawyers) were consulted in drafting the legislation, for example, but did not dictate its forms.[33] The main institutional expression of the labor movement, still the AFL, reacted as much as acted vis-à-vis the NLRA.

Simple views of the Wagner Act as capitalist autoreform (path I) must also be dismissed. The Wagner Act was not the fruit of a self-conscious effort by capitalists in general to reorder labor relations. If "capitalist reform" means a classwide, generalized consensus, or even a large, public pro-Wagner faction, this approach has to be rejected entirely. I will turn to a more complex version of this view later.

Opposition Weaknesses, Labor Action, and Progressive Reformers. If capital was not reforming itself, if the unions were too weak to claim a direct leading role, if the organized Democratic party was divided, and if Roosevelt himself was disinterested or ambivalent, how can one explain the passage of the NLRA? The explanation involves three elements. The first—the weakening of normally opposing forces—operated substantially through the effects of the economic crisis.

The NLRA's passage hinged on the conjunctural weakness of political forces who normally would have blocked it. The Republican party had lost two major

---

(Letter, J. W. R. Maguire to Roosevelt, 5/9/35, and Memo, Hopkins to Roosevelt, 2/12/35, both in Folder Labor 1935, Official File 407—Labor, Roosevelt Papers, FDR Library). Roosevelt's disinterest is clear in the lack of attention given to the NLRA in his main statements and speeches in 1935, and in the modest tone of his statement upon signing the act. See Roosevelt, *The Public Papers and Addresses of Franklin D. Roosevelt*, vol. 4, *The Court Disapproves—1935* (New York: Random House, 1938), 294–95. Also see William E. Leuchtenburg, *Franklin D. Roosevelt and the New Deal* (New York: Harper and Row, 1963), 145.

32. The main way of making such a case seriously is to focus on the mass action of 1934. Although they are not enthusiastic about the Wagner Act, Frances Fox Piven and Richard Cloward attribute its passage mainly to the actual and prospective disruption caused by the working-class mobilization. They overstate its (substantial) extent and thus see political mediation as mainly conservative. See Piven and Cloward, *Poor People's Movements* (New York: Vintage, 1979), 120–33.

33. In addition to Bernstein, *The New Deal Collective Bargaining Policy*, 88, and Vittoz, *New Deal Labor Policy*, see James A. Gross, *The Making of the National Labor Relations Board*, vol. 1, 1933–1937 (Albany: State University of New York Press, 1974), 130–33.

national electoral contests. Its grip on the national state had been ended; its position in Congress was dramatically weakened. The political representatives of business, within and outside the party organizations, shared the burden of the Republican defeats.

A crucial power of business elites—to withhold investment—was limited by the already deep economic difficulties, for which business was widely blamed. Business groups could not threaten to disrupt an already devastated economy with anything close to their normal power. How could conventional claims that unions would prevent orderly production be taken seriously, when business leadership had yielded social and economic disasters?[34]

For the pre-NLRA New Deal state, the problem was both incapacity with respect to labor conflicts and the existence of strong divisions (even within the cabinet) about labor legislation.[35] This weakness hindered government forces who might otherwise have been able to block the NLRA in favor of a less strongly prolabor bill.

Potential opposition from voluntarist tendencies in organized labor was also weakened. For the AFL, the economic and social hardships suffered by its members compelled a more positive attitude toward state intervention, both in providing relief and helping unions establish themselves. The threat from emergent industrial union forces put additional pressure on those who might have wished to retain a purely voluntarist position.[36] In sum, the economic crisis was a major source of the NLRA as it weakened likely opponents of labor law reform.

The second key element in the NLRA's passage was popular pressure, mainly from the working class. This pressure, as expressed in the strikes of 1934 and 1935, threatened public order and industrial stability—at a moment when simply settling disputes on the employers' terms was not politically feasible. This mobilization was also an electoral threat, one that seemed to have materialized in 1934.[37]

Labor action strengthened opposition to the Republicans and business interest groups. And it enhanced the position of prolabor forces in the emergent Democratic coalition, who could more credibly argue that only strong measures would restore stability. The strikes in 1934 were not sufficient to pass the measure, nor did they give shape to an organized movement that in 1935 directly secured passage of the NLRA. The preparation of the legislation was

---

34. Fred Block argues that such crises offer opportunities for reformist coalitions between state managers and subordinate social groups, expanding the power and freedom of maneuver of the first group while reducing the power of business elites to prevent reform (Block, "The Ruling Class Does Not Rule: Notes on the Marxist Theory of the State," *Socialist Review* 7. no. 3 [May–June 1977]: 6–28).

35. Many examples of the federal government's incapacity are reported to Roosevelt in Official File 716—NLRB; a good collection of them appears in Hermann Kebrunk, "Report to the National Labor Relations Board," 2/26/36, Official File 716—NLRB, Roosevelt Papers, FDR Library.

36. The persistence of AFL voluntarism is a major theme in Tomlins, *The State and the Unions*, as well as in Horowitz, *Political Ideologies of Organized Labor*, 73, 121.

37. Leuchtenburg, *Roosevelt and the New Deal*, 114–17.

directed by Robert Wagner and Leon Keyserling, his aide.[38] But if working-class pressure was mediated within the administration, it was mediated by officials who presented reports such as this in 1934:

> When I was in Detroit in December automobile manufacturers told me frankly that section 7a was a mistake and they did not intend to live up to it. This statement was made at a meeting of the Regional Labor Board and representatives of employees heard it. The sentiment aroused by this attitude is largely responsible for the growth of union membership in Detroit in recent months, and the cases were brought to the National Labor Board primarily to get the Government to inform the automobile industry that it could not pursue such a lawless course.
>
> The employees were confident that the National Labor Board and the Administration would make a decision that section 7a cannot be violated by the automobile companies or anyone else. They have been disappointed in that, and the attempt to compromise and conciliate without making a clear-cut decision on the charges of law violation is, I think, a very serious mistake in policy, that will forfeit confidence of working people in the Administration.[39]

Labor's mobilization was crucial. It is unlikely that the NLRA would have been passed without the labor upsurge of 1934 and 1935. Accounts that downplay the role of labor claim that those directly responsible for the NLRA were interested in order. Yet it would seem to follow that major reform legislation would not occur if secure order already existed. Thus such accounts become incoherent if they go beyond a reasonable claim—that the labor movement was not the directly leading agent in shaping the Wagner Act—to argue that it reflected only reform impulses originating elsewhere. The labor movement was a major causal influence: it helped to select outcomes within boundaries imposed both by its own limited capacities (prior weakness, lack of direct access to political power at the national level, ideological uncertainty) and the other political forces on the scene.

The third and most immediate element in the passage of the Wagner Act was the efforts of political reformers, the Progressive liberals.

Progressivism before World War I had spanned both parties, but its reformist heirs in the 1920s were mainly in the Democratic party (although Republican Progressives from the West and Upper Midwest played a major role in the New Deal). In the Republican order, Democratic Progressivism was usually a subordinate current within the national party, but persisted in state and local admin-

38. Huthmacher describes the preparation of the bill, in *Robert F. Wagner*, 187–97. A recently published interview with Leon Keyserling underlines the role of Progressive liberal policy intellectuals (mainly lawyers and economists) in the discussions that led to the framing of the NLRA. Keyserling and others were in contact with labor leaders, mainly through the lawyers for labor organizations. See Kenneth M. Casebeer, "Holder of the Pen: An Interview with Leon Keyserling on Drafting the Wagner Act," *University of Miami Law Review* 42, no. 2 (November 1987): 285–363.

39. Letter, William M. Leiserson to Frances Perkins, April 11, 1934, Official File 407B—Strikes, Roosevelt Papers, FDR Library.

istrations as well as in academic and intellectual life. Democratic Progressive liberalism had developed a substantial reform agenda over several decades. Roosevelt was involved with this movement, which in the 1920s fought to reorient the national Democratic party. Although this fight failed to win its full objectives, a substantial reform current developed within the party.[40]

The main proponents of Democratic Progressivism, usually middle class in their social positions, were characteristically drawn from newer strata of professionals—lawyers, academics, social workers, health care professionals, and members of new planning professions.[41] By no means anticapitalist, Democratic Progressivism was serious about reforms aimed at a fairer and more regulated social order.[42] Where pre-World War I Progressivism was ambivalent toward labor, New Deal reformism was more sympathetic, even if often paternalistic.[43] With the depression, Progressivism became more critical of the political and economic leadership of business elites.

By the mid-1930s, this political force was significant in Congress. It was also a major source of those being hired to direct and staff new state agencies. Its activists had experience in professional life, sometimes also in policy formation and politics at the state and local levels. (At the outset of the New Deal, most such people were not employed by the federal government.)[44] Democratic

40. David Burner stresses Roosevelt's role in the modernizing efforts of the 1920s; his own candidacy was crucial to continuing that direction (Burner, *The Politics of Provincialism* [New York: W. W. Norton 1975], 142–57). Also see Kenneth S. Davis, *FDR: The New York Years, 1928–1933* (New York: Random House, 1985).

41. This social portrait emerges clearly in general accounts of the decade and in treatments of particular legislative and judicial conflicts. See Huthmacher, *Robert F. Wagner*, 118–30; Irons, *New Deal Lawyers*, 3–10; and Marion Clawson, *New Deal Planning—The National Resources Planning Board* (Baltimore: Johns Hopkins University Press, 1981).

42. A recent study convincingly shows that much of pre-World War I Progressivism had reformist aims. See James T. Kloppenberg, *Uncertain Victory: Social Democracy and Progressivism in European and American Social Thought* (New York: Oxford University Press, 1986), esp. 349–84. By the early 1930s, even Progressive intellectuals who contemplated a major extension of planning did not conceive their egalitarian and centralizing projects as anticapitalist. See Bernard Sternsher, *Rexford Tugwell and the New Deal* (New Brunswick: Rutgers University Press, 1964), as well as Rexford Tugwell, *The Brains Trust* (New York: Viking, 1968).

43. Here, Kloppenberg's argument for the convergence of American Progressivism with European social democracy in the first two decades of the century is dubious. In Europe, even conservative tendencies within social democracy were often in dialogue with organized working-class political and social movements that presented themselves as the central agents of overall reform. European social democrats were located in a different field of assumptions than American Progressives, whose intermittent support for labor issues was much more paternalistic. There is a difference between viewing the labor movement as a major force for democratic reform and viewing the extension of citizenship as requiring reforms in working conditions. During the 1930s, some Progressives became willing to view labor as a genuine ally in a process of democratic reform and reorganization. This development originated both in state and local experiences and in disillusionment with the variants of Progressivism represented in the Hoover administration. See Sipe, "Moment of the State," 73–80.

44. In addition to Huthmacher, *Robert F. Wagner*, 103–15, and Tugwell, *The Brains Trust*, see Davis, *FDR: The New York Years*, 269, and Jerold S. Auerbach, "Lawyers and Social Change in the Depression Decade," in John Braeman, Robert H. Bremmer, and David Brody, eds., *The*

Progressives were relatively free of obligations to national political structures or to the main public interest groups of capital or labor. The Wagner Act was passed—developed, proposed, and fought through Congress—by Democratic Progressive liberals. Sen. Robert Wagner was both the actual leader and a representative figure. He directed the legislation, knowing a substantial group in Congress shared his views.[45]

The success of the NLRA, then, signaled the maturation of sections of a new political elite. These groups made the New Deal prolabor in a more adamant and less paternalist way than in 1933–34. But especially among the leaders, few Progressive liberals saw themselves primarily as representing labor in politics. Rather they represented a broad collection of social groups whose interests intersected their own vision of a more democratic and better ordered polity. This Progressive liberalism was a key element in (and on the left of) the array of tendencies that converged in the New Deal.[46]

Specifying the Progressive Liberal Path

Perhaps one could stop here. I have ruled out two paths and much of a third way of thinking about the origins of the Wagner Act: as the immediate result of economic crisis, as the direct victory of the labor movement, and as the effect of a reform project that actively engaged a majority or even a large minority of capital. And I have identified the forces who directly passed the act. Why not simply declare a winner—that the Wagner Act resulted from Progressive reform?

We need to continue because what has been said so far does not decide among several reasonable views of the Wagner Act's passage. The views that remain have been (or might be) argued strongly. Thus the problem is to find ways of choosing among credible approaches to a complex historical process of political change, one whose outcome still shapes the contemporary scene.

Three views deserve further attention. First, while assigning direct responsibility to Progressive liberals who were not themselves capitalists, one might try to rescue a more complex view of the process as capitalist autoreform. Second, one might allow everything said so far and claim that it ratifies pluralist insights into the multisided nature of political conflict in the United States.

I will return to these views after making a case for the third view, which sees the Wagner Act mainly as political reform—in my terms, as Progressive reform. Even naming this view makes clear that further choices are required. The most direct agents of the passage of the Wagner Act were Progressives, but they

---

New Deal: The National Level (Columbus: Ohio State University Press, 1975), 132–69. Auerbach's account is one of several to note that anti-Semitism in elite private legal circles helped make public service an attractive choice for young Jewish lawyers.

45. See Murray Edelman, "New Deal Sensitivity to Labor Interests," in Milton Derber and Edward Young, eds., *Labor and the New Deal* (Madison: University of Wisconsin Press, 1957), 186–88.

46. Progressive liberalism was a vehicle for linking a range of reform tendencies—such as social feminism—to New Deal political-economic projects. See Susan Ware, *Partner and I: Molly Dewson, Feminism, and New Deal Politics* (New Haven: Yale University Press, 1987), 167–243.

were also Democrats, at least in their voting. They were members of the new middle classes in their social origins, and they often would become state managers. To use any of these terms invokes not only an account of events but a view of political change.

Who Were the Progressive Liberals? As the key reformers were simultaneously Progressives, Democrats, professionals, and (at least prospective) state managers, we might suppose that these identities went together in the mid-1930s. Indeed, it is easy to treat them as essentially related. But doing so obscures a political process of building complex identities, whose elements had to be connected meaningfully through political efforts. That two referents—to class/occupation and to sector—seem mainly social, whereas the other two seem primarily political, does not establish an essential relation such that the political identities are the necessary result of the social identities. If the reformers who initiated the Wagner Act articulated complex identities that engaged all these terms, was it their social identification as professionals that was crucial or their political identity as Democrats? When advocating the Wagner Act, how were professional identities related to Progressive arguments?

These questions—which necessarily refer to meanings and to discourses— are important for distinguishing among reasonable causal accounts of the Wagner Act, as pluralist competition, reform by liberal capital, and Progressive reform. When identities—as durable sets of preferences, normatively interrelated—are complex and contain multiple elements, a causal claim must also be a claim about how political actors interpreted structural situations in formulating their strategies. To treat the Wagner Act as Progressive reform, reference to political discourses is essential. Without it, it is very difficult to adjudicate among accounts that survive the mainly structural and behavioral arguments made above for ruling out several views of the path to the Wagner Act.

The earlier discussion does provide grounds for one further judgment: although the reformers who passed the Wagner Act were mainly Democrats, it is misleading to use this aspect of their political identity as the starting point for an explanation of what occurred. The Democratic party was not the central agent of reform; both at the national and state levels, it was divided.[47] Given Democratic weakness and fragmentation, the labor law reform process cannot be explained by designating the party as the main protagonist. Perhaps one could salvage such a view by claiming that reform was the work of a Progressive faction of the Democratic party. Descriptively, this has merit, but analytically it

47. The conservative impulses of large parts of the Democratic Party are clear in the accounts of Schlesinger, *The Politics of Upheaval*, and Leuchtenberg, *Roosevelt and the New Deal*. Internal conflict between pro- and anti-New Deal factions was rampant, coloring letters outlining local political situations sent in response to a 1936 form letter by DNC Chair James Farley soliciting judgments of Roosevelt's reelection prospects. The questionnaire is in Folder Farley's Forms for Campaign Correspondence, Miscellaneous Democratic Papers 1932–38, Papers of the Democratic National Committee, FDR Library. Among the many accounts of conflict are Letter, Charles H. Deuel to Farley, September 3, 1936; Letter, Eds. C. Purpus to Farley, October 2, 1934; Letter, James Meeks to Farley, August 17, 1936—all in Correspondence of James Farley, Papers of the Democratic National Committee, FDR Library.

ascribes a centrality to Democratic identification in the political practices of reformers that was not there.

Saying the reformers were middle class is also true, and arguably more important. Everywhere one looks in the New Deal, there are lawyers. Where there aren't lawyers, there are economists, planners, and social workers.[48] The key question (which invokes a vast literature on social structure and politics) is how much explanatory weight this identification can be made to bear. One boundary can be drawn easily: it is certainly not a sufficient explanation. If so, why weren't all politically active members of the professional middle classes Progressive reformers in the 1930s? Some were Communists and Socialists, whose aims overlapped with the New Deal at points, but whose outlook and actions were distinct.[49] Others were direct agents of capital—for example, lawyers for the corporations who bitterly fought the Wagner Act. Others were traditional Republicans or conservative Democrats. Thus to explain New Deal reform, referring to the "interests" of new middle strata is not enough, as these groups were politically multivalent.

At the other boundary, if we imagine a United States without the processes of social and economic change that encouraged the elaboration of new middle strata, we are in a different society than the one that existed. And if we imagine a middle class in which professionalism played less of an ideological and organizational role, we miss key aspects of how those strata were formed. Thus we can say that their social emergence was a condition of Progressive reform, but that does not make a class label a sufficient explanation, nor provide an account of the process involved.

What about stressing the identity of reformers as state managers, who whatever their class origins or party identification were led toward labor law reform out of their interest in order and in securing resources necessary for the state's existence? This appealing view encounters empirical and analytical problems.

Democratic Progressivism had a rationalizing thrust, and it expanded the state. And the story cannot be told without reference to state institutions, their

48. Evidence of the middle-class social character of the leading liberal reformers permeates accounts of particular governmental institutions and reform and reorganization projects, such as Irons, *New Deal Lawyers*; Gross, *The Making of the National Labor Relations Board*; and Richard Polenberg, *Reorganizing Roosevelt's Government* (Cambridge: Harvard University Press, 1966).

49. The Communist and Socialist parties remained small; their middle-class membership numbered in the tens rather than the hundreds of thousands. But their reality shows the limits of reducing political choices to the alleged social interests of the agents involved. Just as this approach is not adequate for explaining Progressive liberalism, it will not work with the Communists. The increase in membership of the Communist party in the mid-thirties occurred during and after the turn from United Front to Popular Front policies. The latter formulation was explicitly multiclass; the new membership was disproportionately middle class, compared with the prior composition of the party. Yet the CP's Popular Front turn was not caused by its changing class composition; instead, that major strategic shift was caused by judgments regarding the shape of American politics and pressures from the international Communist movement. See Cochran, *Labor and Communism*, as well as Al Richmond, *A Long View from the Left: Memoirs of an American Revolutionary* (Boston: Houghton Mifflin, 1972).

prior weakness in ordering labor relations and perceived needs for stability. Yet the rationalistic elements of many "state-centered" accounts can subtly confuse outcomes with causes. The Wagner Act did not result from an effort to take greater power by a preformed state; it was not mainly the self-serving initiative of state managers seeking to expand their power.[50] Rather, it was a *political* initiative by forces within and outside the state, which had the *effect* of reshaping and extending the state.

Part of the problem lies in defining the state, a difficult task at moments of political flux in the United States. If one adopts a restrictive definition, as the national bureaucracy plus the presidential administration, empirical evidence precludes attributing passage of the NLRA primarily to this entity. Within this core state, there was ambivalence about the measure, extending into the Labor Department and dividing Roosevelt's advisers.[51] Many key actors in passing the Wagner Act were not already in positions of power within this state—they were in Congress, and in universities and professional associations.

A broad definition of the state—to include Congress, state and local government, elites of the government party, professionals employed by state universities or in consultative relations with government bodies—opens the way toward conceiving the NLRA as a rationalizing measure by state elites. Casting the net this widely does catch most of the main political actors other than the unions. The analytical cost, however, is high, because such a definition is usually unaccompanied by any statement of what unifies this disparate state, or

50. The efforts of state managers to secure a stable environment, obtain resources, and expand the state itself are central to the arguments of Block, in "The Ruling Class Does Not Rule"; the articles on social and economic policy in the United States by Theda Skocpol and her colleagues cited above; and Margaret Weir and Theda Skocpol, "State Structures and the Possibilities for 'Keynesian' Responses to the Great Depression in Sweden, Britain, and the United States," in Peter Evans, Dietrich Roeschemeyer, and Theda Skocpol, eds., *Bringing the State Back In* (Cambridge: Cambridge University Press, 1985), 107–63. State building is conceived as the process resulting from such maximizing efforts. Thus given known and roughly constant objectives by state managers (economic resources and order), variation in outcomes hinge on variation in the capacities of state institutions to achieve those objectives. This fruitful approach tends toward a rationalistic conception of political action; what disappears is the political framework within which state building is or is not attempted. Bureaucracies expand in some directions and not others, with some aims and not others. The forms of expansion chosen depend partly on the substantive political aims of "state managers," as needs for order and resources almost always require specification.

51. In 1935, substantial forces within the administration sought to modify the pro-union and pro-labor force of the NLRA. Suggestions for changes were made in a long memo from Attorney General Cummings to Senator Wagner, summarizing a White House conference of May 24 on the bill. A letter from Secretary of Commerce Roper argued for including clauses to protect employees from "union intimidation," implying a defense of their right to join company unions. Other administration figures who generally supported the bill, including Frances Perkins, wanted to put the NLRB in the Labor Department, a step that would have limited its power (Memo, Homer Cummings to Roosevelt, 5/28/35; Letter, Harold Stephens to Robert Wagner, 5/27/35; Memo, Daniel Roper to Roosevelt, 6/20/35; Letter, Frances Perkins to Mr. McIntyre, 6/18/35—all in Folder Labor 1935, Official File 407—Labor, Roosevelt Papers, FDR Library).

what logic guarantees optimal (or even tolerable) results. The way is then open to the same sort of loose claims about (state) "interests" which have been too often made by Marxists about the capitalist class.[52] When one finds, as in 1935, that key roles were played by Progressives outside the core state, one is then left either with functionalist arguments about the state needing to cause its own expansion or with mainly descriptive inventories of what individuals and agencies did. The early New Deal state was not a unified instrument in the hands of ambitious state managers; state managers were often divided, and expanding the state in any substantive direction required alliances with nonstate actors. The state-in-construction was shaped via political conflicts within and around it.

Analogously, rather than treating Progressive reform in the Wagner Act as an "expression" of new middle-class interests, it makes more sense to see the process as one of constructing a new class-linked political force. Without denying the middle-class or state-linked nature of reform, what appears crucial is both the separation of the political sphere from socioeconomic classes as such and its irreducibility to state institutions. Only within that political space, cutting across state and nonstate institutions, could individuals "from" a social group of such still modest numbers and weight achieve what they did. Democratic Progressivism did not "represent" this social class—or "the state"—so much as articulate an overall political conception of how American society could be more fairly organized and more actively regulated.

Debating the NLRA

Seizing an opportunity provided by business and Republican weakness, Progressive liberals in Congress, the administration, and professional networks passed a radically prolabor measure, for which strong pressure from the working class was essential.[53] To go further in specifying causal relations it is necessary to examine not only the alignment of forces in 1935 but the logic of the political conflicts. Without attention to the substance of the debates, the

---

52. The combination of structuralism and rationalism that characterizes the approach of such Marxist analysts as Nicos Poulantzas—for whom structural forces virtually dictate what the state and political forces must do to reproduce capitalism—is not improved if one substitutes "state" for "capital" and assumes "rational" state managers. For a very good critique of the Poulantzian approach to politics, see Theda Skocpol, "Political Response to Capitalist Crisis: Neo-Marxist Theories of the State and the Case of the New Deal," *Politics and Society* 10, no. 2 (1980): 179–81. In a more recent account, Skocpol recognizes that focusing on the state does not solve the problem of accounting for the actions of state managers. Her response is mainly to stress the immediate interests of state managers as a group in their positions and privileges. This concern clearly motivates some state officials at some points, but as a general formulation it leaves far too little space open for politics. See Skocpol, "Bringing the State Back In: Strategies of Analysis in Current Research," in Evans et al., eds., *Bringing the State Back In*, 14–15.

53. Vittoz offers a similar account of the act's passage. But when he concludes that though capitalists failed to realize their immediate preferences, the overall experience is best understood as "interest brokering" within the confines of American capitalism, he undermines his own account by downplaying the scope of the political and social change that occurred (Vittoz, *New Deal Labor Policy*, 7, 171).

way is open to a rationalistic attribution of interests to actors that risks missing key determinants of the process. In the fluid, conflictual moment at which the NLRA was passed, groups were not solidly fixed, and the terms of debate mattered both for their own development and for the shape and consequences of the bill.

The Wagner Act's substantive origins were in several decades of Progressive reform experience and in emergent policy networks, most of which were formally nonstate at the national level. These networks intersected governmental institutions, universities, and professional associations. The more immediate origins of the act's formulations were the experiences of the labor boards in the early New Deal, whose failures to regulate labor relations were clear by 1935, and the perceived need to draft a law that might have a chance of withstanding judicial review.[54]

Vigorous debate over the Wagner Act occurred before and after it passed. Much of the press opposed it, and there was a steady stream of criticism, especially but not only from business circles.[55] Critics stressed that the unions protected by the NLRA would unfairly restrict the rights of owners and managers.[56] Many "legitimate" company unions would be destroyed (some had grown considerably under the NIRA). It was repeatedly argued that the new unions' efforts to gain power would produce coercion against workers. Unions were portrayed as self-interested organizations with little regard for anyone outside their membership, and only an instrumental view of their members.[57] State assistance for unionization would produce powerful bureaucracies more concerned with their own strength than workers' needs. In any case, the act was an unconstitutional intervention into essentially private matters. This last judg-

54. See Huthmacher, *Robert F. Wagner*, 153–63, and the account of the bill's preparation in Irons, *New Deal Lawyers*, 227–31.

55. In 1935 there was extensive testimony on the NLRA before the Senate Education and Labor Committee. The following relies on the records of those hearings and the 1935 congressional debates, as well as Bernstein, *New Deal Collective Bargaining* and *Turbulent Years*; Horowitz, *Political Ideologies of Organized Labor*; Irons, *New Deal Lawyers*; Sipe, "Moment of the State"; and Tomlins, *The State and the Unions*.

56. Employers insisted that the unions envisaged by the Wagner Act would be unable to avoid committing endless crimes against their property rights. The volume of such testimony—and the virtual absence of major employers taking opposed positions in public—is impressive, although its shrillness and unoriginality doubtless helped limit its persuasiveness in a situation where a simple reaffirmation of faith was not politically sufficient. A livelier than usual sample is the testimony of James Emery, general counsel of the National Association of Manufacturers, before the Senate Education and Labor Committee on March 21, 1935, in *Legislative History of the National Labor Relations Act*, 1935, vol. 2, (Washington: U.S. Government Printing Office, 1949), 1626–50.

57. Christopher Tomlins's account of labor law in the 1920s and 1930s seems to offer a brief on behalf of the AFL's voluntarist conception of unions as autonomous private organizations engaged in supplying labor. His account of the adaptation of voluntarism to organizational pressures for individualism and against republican themes early in the century is compelling. But as he moves toward the 1930s he loses sight of the overall political and ideological context and he fails, for example, even to note the great vulnerability of a conception of unions as private entities supplying labor to a conservative/populist critique of them as privileged interests (Tomlins, *The State and the Unions*, 103–60).

ment may have tempered the nonetheless strong expression of business opposition in 1935, as employers anticipated a favorable judicial outcome.[58]

The lack of novelty in these arguments may have been partly responsible for
their failure, as they could be criticized as abstract professions of faith irrelevant to the nation's crises. The clear hostility of most critics of the NLRA to
genuinely independent unions also ruled out a coalition with forces in the AFL
uncertain about the statist potential of the NLRA prior to its passage (and later
opposed to the NLRB's encouragement of industrial unionism and sympathy for
the CIO).[59]

What of the arguments for the Wagner Act? A central defense claimed it
would counteract underconsumption tendencies:

> The inequality of bargaining power between employees who do not possess
> full freedom of association or actual liberty of contract, and employers who are
> organized in the corporate or other forms of ownership association substan-
> tially burdens and affects the flow of commerce, and tends to aggravate recur-
> rent business depressions, by depressing wage rates and the purchasing power
> of wage earners in industry and by preventing the stabilization of competitive
> wage rates and working conditions within and between industries.[60]

Thus the NLRA would permit workers to gain a larger share of national income;
this would expand demand and mitigate against new downturns. Wagner and
others knew this argument might make the act more appealing to those uneasy
about unions and that such a defense increased the likelihood of the NLRA
surviving judicial review via the commerce clause of the Constitution. Yet
stressing the positive economic functions of the act expressed a strong belief,
not a ploy.

A second theme articulated the rationalizing side of the Progressive tradition. Wagner and others argued that the arbitrary character of employers'
power in labor relations was producing disorder.[61] The Wagner Act would
stabilize a crucial sphere of social activity, whose irrationalities were dangerous.
This argument was made at the intersection of mass working-class pressure
with Progressive concerns about stable administration and economic growth.

Without strikes and related actions, "order" would not require labor law
reform at all, and the underconsumption argument would stand alone. Both
the scope and dramatic public effects of the labor mobilization and the Progres-

58. Bernstein, *New Deal Collective Bargaining*, 106–10; Irons, *New Deal Lawyers*, 247.

59. The AFL support for the NLRA was also encouraged by the argument that a voluntaristic
approach, whatever its previous virtues, was not adequate to the challenges it faced. When the
NLRB appeared to favor the CIO, the AFL was compelled to fight on a new terrain regarding the
forms and extent of state intervention in labor relations. In addition to the accounts of
Tomlins and Bernstein, see Walter Galenson, *The CIO Challenge to the AFL* (Cambridge:
Harvard University Press, 1960).

60. National Labor Relations Act, July 5, 1935, in *Public Laws of the U.S.A, 1935–36*, 449.

61. The underconsumption argument for the Wagner Act was often intertwined with
notions of the desirable economic consequences of industrial order (Letter, H. A. Millis to
Roosevelt, 6/21/35, Folder NLRB July–October 1935, Official File 716—National Labor
Relations Board, Roosevelt Papers, FDR Library). Also see Bernstein, *New Deal Collective
Bargaining*, 112; Fleming, "Significance of the Wagner Act," 129.

sive concern with order mitigated against conceiving labor relations in purely private terms. Thus pressures from "below" and "above" converged to encourage a view of unions as agents representing workers as a group in a setting whose proper functioning was a legitimate object of public concern.

A third argument appeared: the Wagner Act would bring about greater fairness among competing social groups. The lack of unions was an unfair obstacle to a free play of interests; the state's intervention would allow fairer contests and (by implication) better outcomes.[62] Equality of bargaining power would sustain the possibility of genuine freedom of contract in a large-scale economy.[63]

The first two arguments were stressed by economists, other professionals who supported the NLRA, and the handful of capitalists willing to countenance it. The theme of fairness was emphasized by the act's most strongly prolabor supporters.[64] There is little record of liberal capital speaking up on behalf of the Wagner Act. If one could find more energetic defenses of the act by capital, or if the fairness theme were marginal to the overall enterprise, one might claim that the first two arguments were coordinated with capital's views (even if their expression were infrequent in public). Neither move is defensible.

Labor and Class in the Debates. The debates on the act and the subsequent public arguments are also revealing about the orientation of the labor movement. When the fairness argument was stressed by labor groups, claims in class terms rarely appear; the emphasis is on the right of groups of individuals to seek political and economic benefits.

The labor arguments for the NLRA were not well developed in the prepassage debates, and took shape slowly thereafter. Partly this was because labor was lobbying for an initiative that came from outside its ranks. The unions were also still influenced by voluntarism and stamped by their defensive position. They had trouble articulating a clear public position that went beyond demanding recognition. In practice the Progressive defense of unions was taken up by the unions themselves. Independent and strong unions would create a reasonable balance between employers and workers, in which each group had its rights and obligations. This vision was almost bland, with little substantive account of the political and social outcomes that might result from the new balance.[65]

Newer labor voices and some of the NLRA's congressional supporters sometimes made a fourth argument, more often in 1936–37 than during the de-

62. Fairness could be conceived either in organizational terms, as a form of counterplanning with respect to the power of monopoly and oligopoly forms, or as meeting the needs of the downtrodden for respect and dignity. See Hawley, *The New Deal and the Problem of Monopoly,* 195, 276; and Burns, *Roosevelt,* 218–19.

63. This fusion of rationalizing and egalitarian arguments marks "Senate Report No. 573 on S. 1958," in *Legislative History of the NLRA,* 2302–03.

64. In 1935, Roosevelt was deluged with fairness arguments from union forces; they appear in Official File 407—Labor, Roosevelt Papers, FDR Library.

65. Horowitz, *Political Ideologies of Organized Labor,* 127–30; Tomlins, *The State and the Unions,* 149.

bates over the NLRA's passage. They claimed that the NLRA would encourage "industrial democracy."[66] This term did not mean "workers' control" in a form that would overturn property relations. It had a negative element—to remove the routinely humiliating forms of domination workers experienced in the prior factory regime. And it had a positive side—to create a less arbitrary framework for decision making about hours, job assignments, and the pace of work, within which workers and their organizations would have a voice.

Most of what supporters of the NLRA had in mind in references to "industrial democracy" could be said as well in terms of the aim of achieving a more equitable order in labor relations. And using the term risked antagonizing those who needed to be persuaded that employers' charges that the Wagner Act was a guaranteed route to massive state intervention against established property rights were hyperbolic. Nonetheless, given that "democracy" was a crucial ideological stake of the political conflicts of the day, linking it—via images of "fairness"—to a particular reformation of labor relations was a powerful discursive strategy.

When Roosevelt entered the field of labor relations, his own notion of fairness meant a duty to save the poor and oppressed from utter degradation, as well as a willingness to support efforts by the newly organized to participate in American political and social life. His vision was, of course, selective; nonetheless, the concepts of democracy and fairness linked his paternalistic orientation with the more participatory conceptions of some Progressive liberals and parts of the CIO. Thus, "democracy," "fairness," and "order" were linked in defenses of the Wagner Act. For these links to be persuasive, labor relations had to be conceived as significantly more public than had previously been typical. Given this shift, unions could be conceived as playing a representative democratic role.[67]

The Wagner Act was not defended in 1935–37 as a measure whose merit was in redistributing power toward the working class. Class terms were not dominant in the main discourses of the labor movement, certainly not among AFL unions nor within the CIO.[68] That such a crucial measure regarding relations in production was advocated in nonclass terms is striking. What about treating the debates as "ideology" floating above the "real" world of class struggle? There were real struggles, among socioeconomic groups linked to class positions, but they were not prediscursive and were always intertwined with political efforts to make sense out of "objective" structures of class positions. The debates over the

66. Huthmacher, *Robert F. Wagner*, 192; Horowitz, *Political Ideologies of Organized Labor*, 175–77.

67. Tomlins criticizes this shift toward the public—and the state—but neglects the ways in which, on the actual political field, antistatism was fused with employers' rights. Thus "democracy" was a powerful stake of conflicts that the AFL's voluntarism could barely even engage (Tomlins, *The State and the Unions*, 239, 243).

68. That the unions rarely made claims in class terms is clear not only in "traditional" labor histories, such as Bernstein, *Turbulent Years*. Oral histories also show that explicit class terms were marginal in popular discourse, beyond leftist groups for which such language verged on being a private code. See Staughton and Alice Lynd, *Rank and File: Personal Histories by Working Class Organizers* (Boston: Beacon Press, 1973). Also see Vittoz, *New Deal Labor Policy*, 164–66.

Wagner Act were partially constitutive of the economic and political identities and the actions of the labor movement, not a distraction.

The NLRA was debated in terms of its economic contribution, the role of the state, the rights of unorganized groups to compete for power, and the limits of employers' rights in their property.[69] Unions were regarded as (potentially) representative institutions in a new political and social order. They would encourage social stability and economic growth as well as embody democratic norms. Alternatively, they were attacked as self-interested attempts to interfere with property rights, threatening economic ruin and social chaos. Posing the issue this way disadvantaged conventional AFL voluntarism and made it vulnerable to antiunion arguments. There were also major conceptual problems in relating notions of unions as private organizations that supply labor to the new mass industrial settings. In these settings, an enormous semiskilled production force was already present and wholly dependent on the factory setting in order to work; workers were *in* production, not simply contracting with employers to perform specified projects.

If an explicit discourse on class was mainly absent, passing the Wagner Act and fighting to implement it nonetheless meant replacing one political common sense with another regarding the range of groups whose political and social claims should be taken seriously. In context, this change meant a major shift of power toward subordinate groups. That it was not framed as a means of producing further radical shifts (for example, "workers' control") is no surprise unless one simply refuses to listen to its protagonists and their opponents.[70]

From Passage to Implementation. The debate over the Wagner Act continued for several years after its passage, as opposing forces met in judicial, political, and economic settings. The arguments and actions of groups after passage allow us to infer some of what they intended to achieve, which can help us sort out alternative accounts of why the NLRA passed.

The NLRA's encouragement of unions was fiercely resisted by most employers in both large enterprises and small companies. Strikes multiplied in 1935–37. From an already high level, they increased slightly in 1936, although the

69. In an important article, Karl Klare stresses the extent to which the Wagner Act meant sharply limiting employers' rights. In context, however, this assault emphasized efficiency, order, and fairness. See Klare, "Judicial Deradicalization of the Wagner Act and the Origins of Modern Legal Consciousness," *Minnesota Law Review*, 62, no. 3 (March 1978): 277–90.

70. That even militant sections of the labor movement were generally not calling for "workers' control," much less socialism, is such an obvious point that it is almost embarrassing to have to make it. But doing so is still necessary. Sometimes anecdotal evidence is cited to show a burgeoning labor radicalism, without a serious effort to weigh the strength of different currents. In some leftist accounts, there is a striking absence where one might expect some discussion of what workers really wanted; thus the notion of a frustrated radical upsurge is sustained less with reference to frustrated radicals than via an implicit notion of the forms of political consciousness appropriate to the working class in capitalist societies, or via a notion of social movements as constituted by disruptive forces demanding more. See Davis, *Prisoners of the American Dream*, and Piven and Cloward, *Poor People's Movements*, 96–180.

number of workers involved declined. Then in 1937 strikes more than doubled to 4,740, the highest figure to that point in the twentieth century.[71]

A massive working-class mobilization, through the 1937 sit-down strikes, was crucial in implementing the act. To imagine the post-Wagner years without this mobilization is to envision unions as much smaller and weaker. Yet support for the act did not come only from below. Both the NLRB and the broader administration, as well as Progressive liberals in Congress, made political, legal, and administrative decisions on behalf of implementing the act. One can claim that these decisions were not crucial for what happened to the labor movement—a claim I will consider later—but they certainly imply a prior support for the Wagner Act, pointing again to a crucial dynamic between labor and Progressives.

For the view that the NLRA was a sophisticated effort at capitalist autoreform, the strike pattern presents a major problem. Why would capitalists who wanted unions face such a high level of strike activity? Perhaps the strikes were not about unions. But in 1935–37, the proportion of strikes over union recognition was much higher than in 1929–33; here the peak occurred also in 1937, when almost twice as many strikes were mainly over recognition as over wages and hours.[72] Thus workers aimed at establishing unions capable of bargaining effectively with employers over wages and mitigating the factory despotism that was increasingly experienced as intolerable.

Although its defenders had urged the NLRA as a means of providing industrial stability, that was not the immediate result, mainly because employers were unwilling to cooperate with the new unions.[73] Even employers who made flexible public statements often fought unions bitterly in their own firms. This sequence strongly suggests that the idea that employers initiated the NLRA or even accepted it as a way to coopt an existing labor movement badly misjudges the context. They fought the implementation of the Wagner Act and hoped not to incorporate the new unions but to avoid them.[74] Employers resisted the

71. Bureau of the Census, *Historical Statistics*, D 970–985, "Work Stoppages, Workers Involved, Man-Days Idle, Major Issues, and Average Duration: 1881–1970."

72. It is hard to establish this quantitative relation with certainty, given the unreliability of the categories and data on strikes in periods of great turmoil, but the prevalence of recognition strikes is beyond dispute. The next question, of course, is what was meant by union recognition. It was both an aim and a symbol of other aims. Working conditions—the pace of work, the abusive power of foremen, the lack of any seniority protection—were at least as powerful as and probably more urgent than immediate wage issues in the labor upsurge of 1935–37. David Montgomery argues this view in *Workers' Control in America* (Cambridge: Cambridge University Press, 1980), 140–49.

73. The NLRB was deluged with cases where employers refused to bargain and discriminated against employees because of their union affiliations. This pattern is apparent in reports sent to Roosevelt from the NLRB, such as Letter and Memo, J. Warren Madden to Roosevelt, January 28, 1936, Folder NLRB 1936, Official Folder 716—NLRB, Roosevelt Papers, FDR Library. Also see Harry A. Millis and Emily Clark Brown, *From the Wagner Act to Taft-Hartley* (Chicago: University of Chicago Press, 1950).

74. Comparison with the Social Security Act is useful here. In that case, one can find some empirical support for the view that business initiated and sustained the reform process,

NLRA legally and illegally, acquiescing only when they seemed to have no better choice. Interpreting this final acquiescence as clever cooptation reverses the sequence.

The resistance of employers largely failed, but it was based on reasonable judgments about how things might evolve. Within production, employers had ample recent evidence of their own strength and of the weakness and conservatism of both the AFL and much of the working class. Resistance had worked in the decade before the depression, when a combination of welfare capitalism and brutal antiunionism undermined the union strength achieved by the end of World War I. And if unions could not be wholly avoided, experience under the NRA suggested that company unions might work. Employers were confident of their strength against labor within production, and their confidence encouraged a broad strategy of resistance.

Business opposition was also based on reasonable political judgments. The Supreme Court had ruled against the NIRA and other New Deal measures, and the Wagner Act seemed vulnerable to similar objections.[75] Why comply with a law that would be overturned? There were also good grounds for thinking that support for the Wagner Act might pass. There was, after all, a recent forty-year period of Republican domination when popular support for trade unions was modest and politically weak.

Thus in 1935–37, most sections of capital initially judged that the New Deal labor program should be opposed, not accommodated. The Wagner Act helped polarize political forces and was a major source of the continual attacks made on Roosevelt by Republicans and conservative Democrats.[76] Employer resistance meant that passage of the NLRA was not enough to create a new industrial relations system.

Capitalist Reform?

The fierce conflicts over the implementation of the Wagner Act, in conjunction with what we know of its passage, make it very difficult to treat the act as capitalist autoreform. It is not possible to do so if this means a conscious, public, political choice by a large section of capital. And from the prepassage debates

---

though in the end such an interpretation is problematic. With the NLRA, the difficulty of even getting such an argument off the ground at the empirical level drives those who try toward vague functionalist claims about the ultimately conservative nature of the new unions. On Social Security, see, for example, Edward Berkowitz and Kim McQuaid, *Creating the Welfare State: The Political Economy of Twentieth Century Reform* (New York: Praeger, 1980), 113, 165–67.

75. The decision to uphold the NLRA was a surprise. Its departure from the logic of most Supreme Court decisions in 1935–36 required several years of intense legal and political pressure. Many of the restraint of commerce objections to the NIRA might have been made against the NLRA. See Irons, *New Deal Lawyers*, 260–90.

76. Often starting with tax and spending issues, many of the attacks on Roosevelt and the New Deal featured the Wagner Act and the subsequent labor upsurge as examples of what had gone wrong. See Leuchtenburg, *Roosevelt and the New Deal*, 177–79; Schlesinger, *Politics of Upheaval*, 515–47; James T. Patterson, *Congressional Conservatism and the New Deal* (Lexington: University of Kentucky Press, 1967), 71–75; and James Holt, "The New Deal and the American Anti-Statist Tradition," in Braeman et al., *The New Deal*, 27–49.

and postpassage fights it is hard to assemble enough material to make a serious case for viewing the act as the work of a small but crucial group of capitalists.

Nonetheless, it is worth noting several ways in which such an interpretation might be defended. For one thing, views of major reform efforts that are rooted in variants of elite or neo-Marxist theory are sometimes correct; if they are not adequate here, it is worth knowing why. Such views, as well, tend to gain credibility from a contemporary perspective. We now know that the fierce struggles of the 1930s did not lead to anything like the dire outcome predicted and feared by business and that the new industrial relations system was capable of combining a dominant position for employers with sustained economic growth. Given that the long-term outcomes seem to have been favorable enough for capital, it is reasonable to believe that sophisticated employers might have been aware of this possibility at the time. And given their power, such perceptions might have been decisive for shaping new realities. For these reasons we should at least examine the possibility that the Wagner Act was a process of capitalist autoreform before rejecting it.

There are three ways such an argument could be made. The least promising approach grants that although the number of capitalists who supported the act was very small—more a handful than a faction—this small group was distinctively powerful as the key force on behalf of the act. But simply showing that a few capitalists, such as Gerard Swope, approved the act does not come close. Swope was an important figure in American business, but so were dozens of bitter opponents of the Wagner Act. No persuasive argument about the special status of the NLRA's few capitalist supporters has been made, and one can only note that all individuals with a given class position are never unanimous in politics.[77]

A second approach would designate liberal capital as Roosevelt himself and certain of his advisers and associates from capitalist backgrounds.[78] Yet Roose-

77. An argument about the causal role of a handful of capitalists could be made by showing that a small group had a privileged position by virtue of its economic location. This is the type of argument Thomas Ferguson wants to make about business support for the New Deal as a whole in "From Normalcy to New Deal—Industrial Structure, Party Competition, and American Public Policy in the Great Depression," *International Organization* no. 38, 1 (Winter 1984): 41–94. His key claim is that the more capital-intensive and internationally oriented a sector was, the more likely its support for the New Deal. Ferguson has so far made modest progress toward showing that the predicted support for the New Deal actually existed, but much less in showing that it was causally important. Regarding labor law in particular, his evidence on business involvement is very unpersuasive. A second approach might fare better by reducing its claims dramatically. In this view, the function of a Swope would be mainly to mark left boundaries. Those engaged in reform activity could test its limits by inquiring about Swope's response, and inferring that if he were strongly opposed to a given measure, its prospects would be limited. This might permit one to claim a role for (a fraction of) capital in helping bound the reform process. The fact of meetings with Swope or others does not demonstrate even this modest causal relation, however, without attention to what was said and evidence that reformers needed restraining.

78. See G. William Domhoff, "The Wagner Act and Theories of the State—A New Analysis Based on Class-Segment Theory," *Political Power and Social Theory* 6 (1987): 178–80. Domhoff arrives at this argument when he finds that of the three main groups of capitalists he

velt was not an early or energetic proponent of the NLRA. Even if he had been, this claim simply assumes what it needs to demonstrate—that the proper way to explain Roosevelt's political behavior is by reference to his class origins. The latter are relevant for his actions, but by 1935, he had for two decades been engaged in a political career with its own logic. Of course, Roosevelt was not anticapitalist, and he repeatedly affirmed his intent to "save" and "reform" capitalism. Yet such claims cannot explain the "true class nature" of the New Deal without a hyperfunctionalist notion of what was required to save capitalism.

A third approach is more promising. It claims that political reformers (crucially lawyers and economists) were agents of capitalist autoreform, rather than mainly state managers or Democrats or class actors in their own right—or political reformers. This approach requires linking the NLRA's course with both a sociological analysis of the new middle classes after World War I and an account of the substance of Progressive and other reform discourses. Unfortunately, much debate has not taken us very far in this regard and the prospects are not promising. William Domhoff and others have focused on institutional and personal connections between capital and middle-class intellectuals and managers. Without a textured account of political discourses and the ways they were shaped and articulated by intellectuals, the connections prove little.[79] Given a capitalist society, such connections are certain to exist. As Block and Skocpol insist, to infer an objective logic of political determination from them is untenable. Yet their rejoinders also have problems. They insist that middle class intellectuals cannot be arbitrarily designated as capital's agents.[80] This is true, but the actual identities are what is in question.

Both approaches argue as though actors must be defined as directly interest-seeking agents of a class (capitalist or middle class) or of state institutions; there is little space open for political discourse. In Domhoff's account, the only way an intellectual could fail to be a bourgeois intellectual would be by failing to have a university affiliation, by attaining no funding from the usual sources, or by becoming the employee of another class's organization, such as the unions. For Block or Skocpol, it seems hard for an intellectual to be a bourgeois intellectual other than by opening a factory or hiring on as a corporate manager, given that such individuals typically have middle class-social positions and/or work for the state.

To reject in principle the possibility of using class labels to describe political

identifies—southern capital, oligopoly/international capital, and competitive/national capital—the last two were opposed to the NLRA, and the first was willing to go along only if much of the South were excluded.

79. Domhoff asserts that Robert Wagner should be treated as an agent of capitalist autoreform on the basis of a definition of "reformers, politicians, and experts who started by accepting the existence of the emerging framework of corporate capitalism and then attempted to incorporate other groups into that framework." Given the structure of American political discourse, this definition includes just about everyone, and with only slight work on the notion of "accepting," Popular Front Communist intellectuals could be added (Domhoff, "The Wagner Act," 172).

80. Theda Skocpol, "A Brief Response," *Politics and Society* 15, no. 3 (1986–87): 331–32; Block, *Revising State Theory* (Philadelphia: Temple University Press, 1987), 14–15.

and intellectual forces turns a necessary caution into an indefensible rigidity. It misses the possibility of building durable relations between social forces and political actors; when this happens, we can use a class label to designate this political outcome. But using such labels requires more than citing personal backgrounds or institutional locations, as both are almost always politically multivalent.

To use a class designation to explain the course of the NLRA as capitalist autoreform means claiming that the relevant policy intellectuals functioned as bourgeois intellectuals, closely linked to capital. It means claiming that they took as their problem the defense and consequently the reform of capitalist relations of production and engaged in political conflict with that aim. To affix this term as more than rhetoric requires assessing both the process of forma-tion of these intellectuals and the substance of their aims and practices. To make this argument about the Wagner Act—conceiving its proponents as new bourgeois intellectuals—requires a real engagement with the intellectual and political substance of Progressivism from before World War I into the 1930s.[81]

Does this approach offer a good account of the political formation and orientation of those who fought for the NLRA? On balance, no. One problem is that the mass of intellectuals in and around the New Deal was not homoge-neous. Can we imagine a conceptualization of "bourgeois" (or "middle-class") intellectuals with much richness which would apply to Raymond Moley, Wil-liam Leiserson, Rexford Tugwell, Frances Perkins, Robert Wagner, Leon Key-serling, and Nathan Witt?

The narrowness and condensation of the left side of the American political spectrum opens the way to an indiscriminate expansion of the notion of "bourgeois intellectuals" if the latter includes everyone not explicitly and ener-getically opposed to capitalism—that is, almost everyone. The concept needs boundaries: on the left, a line can be drawn. On one side, there were intellec-tuals for whom Progressive reform was an instrumental commitment in the service of an energetic defense of a capitalist social order, whether they viewed this order in mainly individualistic or corporate terms. On the other side, there were those for whom democratic and egalitarian reform was the primary substantive goal.

This line between strategic and principled reformers makes a political dis-tinction in a setting where global opposition to capitalism was marginal and the subordinate classes articulated Progressive and populist discourses. Applied to the Wagner Act, it distinguishes between the most active supporters of the

---

81. The danger of applying class labels to explain political choices is as great with "middle class" as with the others. By the 1930s, so many different currents had a "middle-class" social element—from the more flexible strains of Republican thought about association and cooper-ation through the center of the New Deal to Popular Front Communism—that the term is little more than a marker. For example, when Martin Shefter depicts efforts to enlarge state agencies and build issue-oriented "responsible" parties as an expression of the "class interests" of the middle class, he has made an interesting connection, but given the multivalent nature of middle-class "interests" and ideologies, it is not clear what is being explained (Shefter, "Party, Bureaucracy, and Political Change in the United States," in Louis Maisel and Joseph Cooper, eds., *Political Parties: Development and Decay* [Beverly Hills: Sage Publications, 1978], 241–43).

measure and those who came around reluctantly—between the Wagners and Keyserlings, and center-right New Deal currents.

Reformers who fought for what they understood as noncoerced order, expanded democracy, and a more egalitarian distribution of income were "bourgeois" in that they did not presume the incompatibility of their aims with some form of capitalism. But to apply this designation, beyond reiterating the lack of anticapitalism, simply imports all the explanatory problems into a new, expanded notion of "bourgeois intellectuals." Since within that group, some passed the Wagner Act, others fought it bitterly, and many were ambivalent, it is not clear what the term explains in this context.

Distinguishing between principled and strategic reformers shows that conceiving the NLRA as capitalist autoreform cannot be sustained unless one broadens the notion of "bourgeois intellectual" far enough to hollow it out. Those Progressive intellectuals most responsible for passing the Wagner Act escape any reasonably rigorous use of the category. Reform Progressivism can be clearly distinguished both from the Hooverite association-minded reformers of the 1920s and from intellectuals (from lawyers to economists to academics) who adamantly expressed antistatist and antiunion positions throughout the 1930s. A class designation that includes the theoretical and practical efforts of all these groups is not useful.

Specifying the Wagner Act as a radical reform opposed to capital's articulated preferences does not necessarily rule out a Gramscian approach to the New Deal reform process as a whole. Whether such an approach—as the best way to formulate a Marxist analysis of the decade—is adequate needs a broader discussion than is appropriate here. One does not have to decide about the New Deal as a whole to see that accounting for the Wagner Act requires acknowledging that it registered a clear defeat for capital and many groups of explicitly bourgeois intellectuals.

The Limits of Pluralist Accounts

To rule out viewing the Wagner Act as capitalist autoreform leaves a choice between a pluralist reading of the process and a view of it as political reform. Enough has been said so far to rule out most pluralist accounts.

In a weakly descriptive sense, it is easy to find pluralism where no single social or political force can impose its will on all others without compromise. This condition was specified earlier; yet such pluralism is nothing more than a loose-fitting description of conflicts among powerful actors. In a stronger form, pluralism makes claims about the properties of government institutions with respect to social and political actors. Two major claims are relevant to, and not supported by the NLRA's story. The first is that government institutions play at most a secondary role in determining political outcomes; in the pluralist path to the Wagner Act, political reform, conceived as including such institutions, mainly reflects causal pressures originating elsewhere.[82] Yet in a situation in

82. It is unfair to burden all pluralist analysis with an extreme denial of the relevance of concepts of the state or even government institutions. Nonetheless, most pluralist formulations link claims about the political efficacy of socially based interest organizations with an

which capital opposed the Wagner Act and labor did not have enough strength to impose it, both the formulation and implementation of the measure were significantly dependent on what occurred within governmental institutions and political discourses.

The second relevant claim is that the overall political process is relatively permeable to various actors—if not equally open to all at a given moment, then open in principle. "Democratic countries are distinguished by a general freedom to form and join organizations—religious, cultural, intellectual, labor, agricultural, commercial, professional."[83] For this claim to have any analytic bite, one needs to be able to say what counts as access to the political process and what counts as regular means of obtaining it. This can be done partly by defining the routine procedures available for entry for new agents, and then looking at what does and does not happen through them. In this light, what is striking is how hard it was for the labor movement to gain entry. If the mass action of the mid-1930s was key to the passage and enforcement of the Wagner Act, the implication is that routine points of entry would not admit a reform process. Doubtless in the 1930s most people would have preferred not going on strike to going on strike, not engaging in illegal takeovers of factories to risking them.[84] Reform, it would seem, required extraordinary economic and political action—a forced entry. Thus the process was pluralist only in the weak sense that diverse forces fought hard and were differentially successful.

THE WAGNER ACT AS POLITICAL REFORM: BUILDING A NEW LABOR MOVEMENT

I have argued for viewing the Wagner Act as a process of political reform, led by Progressive liberals in coalition with the labor movement. My aim in this part of this article is to complete the answer to my first question—how do we explain the passage of the NLRA?—and to respond to the second—what difference did it make? I argue that the Wagner Act was a crucial part of the political process of constructing a new labor movement. What follows examines how this occurred in 1935–37, and in doing so elaborates my account of why the NLRA was passed.

At this point our five possible paths to the Wagner Act outlined earlier have been reduced to a single model. What remains uncertain is how to decide

---

argument that outcomes can be treated as the result of interacting decisions about deploying resources, given a varying intensity of preferences.

83. Robert A. Dahl, *Dilemmas of Pluralist Democracy* (New Haven: Yale University Press, 1982), 38.

84. This is only a claim that labor action had objectives and aimed reasonably to achieve them. An alternative view, in which labor action could be discounted as an index of the real structure of political and social opportunities, would treat it as a nonrational response to suffering. To make this latter argument stick, one would have to show both a strong relation between immiseration and labor action in the decade, and the presence of real opportunities to form independent organizations before the mass action of 1936–37, which workers failed to exercise. But through 1935, unionization faced bitter opposition; and labor action was not at its highest when social and economic conditions were at their worst, in the early 1930s.

between two versions of it: are political reformers better understood as state managers or as Progressive liberals? It is worth displaying this path again.

The Wagner Act as Political Reform

economic crisis	$\xrightarrow{\text{2 or 3}}$ labor movement	$\xrightarrow{\text{2}}$ liberal capital	$\xrightarrow{\text{0 or 1}}$ political reformers	$\xrightarrow{\text{3}}$ Wagner Act

0: No or negative causal weight
1: Reflects (transmits causal pressures originating elsewhere)
2: Selects (exerts causal influence, mainly within exogenous limits)
3: Shapes (exerts strong causal influences, within endogenous and exogenous limits)

Again, "political reformers" includes varied social and political referents—middle class, state manager, Democratic, Progressive liberal. I have argued that central importance cannot be attached to the partisan affiliation of the Wagner Act's proponents. As for their middle-class status, no necessary relation caused middle class intellectuals and politicians to be Progressives; thus the connection that did exist has to be regarded as a process of political construction. But should we emphasize the institutional location or the political commitments of these reformers? What is at stake is how one thinks about the relationship between the state and politics in processes of political change. Thus, defining the identity of these political actors—how its multiple elements were related—also means designating a causal logic.

For the Wagner Act, the political process was primary. In this respect, New Deal "state building" was a political project not reducible to the immediate interests of those who already had positions in the state. As accounts of state building and of Progressive reform can each claim real referents—the state did expand, reform did occur—we need to explore how the process unfolded after the NLRA was passed in order to make distinctions. One could treat the Wagner Act's effects in many areas; I will focus on government and the labor movement.

Who Expanded the State?

There is little debate on one point: the Wagner Act meant an expansion of government institutions.[85] The NLRA expanded presidential power, as the executive gained control of a new and important agency. The accompanying polarization of political forces outside of governmental institutions opened space into which the latter could expand.[86] The number of new positions

85. Tomlins is right to stress the NLRA's role in this regard, though he downplays prior intervention in labor relations, *against* unions and labor action (Tomlins, *The State and the Unions*, 146, 150–60, 185, 221).

86. The form of this expansion matched Roosevelt's preference, which was to govern by encouraging alternative views and competing powers before choosing among them. Thus the NLRB was both under presidential control and an alternative source of perspectives on labor relations to the Labor Department. Burns calls this a "broker leadership" in making clear his preference for a more disciplined, centralizing approach (Burns, *Roosevelt*, 191–200).

created immediately was small. In its first year of operation, the NLRB had roughly 180 employees.[87] Yet the agency immediately entered a large number of industrial conflicts, widening the scope of government regulation. This raised the possibility of a later expansion of employees and activities.

Obviously the NLRA in itself did not cause the overall growth of government. Rather, its passage and implementation exemplified a state expansion which occurred along many fronts. And the state did grow, in both its responsibilities and staff. From 1933 to 1937, executive branch employment exclusive of defense and the postal service increased from roughly 200,000 to over 400,000, while federal expenditures for items other than military spending, veterans benefits, and interest increased by roughly 80 percent.[88] In labor relations, it is hard to see how this sort of expansion would have occurred without the NRLA. Perhaps emergency measures could have been taken to expand governmental action, but they would have been precarious and unlikely to produce stable forms of regulating labor relations.

The key question here is: can one treat the passage and implementation of the NLRA mainly as a project of internally directed state building? Was the Wagner Act mainly an effect of efforts by those managing the state, given an interest in ordering their environment, to initiate a new approach to labor law? In fact, the main actors within core governmental institutions in 1934–35 were by no means unified on behalf of the Wagner Act. There was a general belief that some form of labor regulation was necessary, but for many, the appropriate forms were much less prolabor than what emerged. For others, labor law reform was simply not a priority.

It is not possible to assign the primary role to any clearly specified group of state managers in formulating, passing, and implementing the NLRA. Promising places to look for candidates are the Labor Department and the prior labor boards. Regarding the former, Secretary of Labor Frances Perkins engaged in a losing fight to put the new NLRB in her department and was ambivalent about the creation of an independent agency (despite her commitment to labor law reform). Regarding the latter, there was some overlap in personnel.[89] And

87. See the first Annual Report of the National Labor Relations Board, submitted January 4, 1937, for the fiscal year ending June 30, 1936 (Letter, J. Warren Madden to Roosevelt, January 4, 1937, plus "Appendix 1—Names, Salaries, and Duties of All Employees and Officers in the Employ or under the Supervision of the Board," Official File 716—NLRB, Roosevelt Papers, FDR Library).

88. During the Hoover administration, federal expenditures increased significantly, especially in 1932, but executive branch employment grew only from 169,000 in 1928 to 196,000 in 1932. Those who stress the continuities between Hoover and Roosevelt can make a modest case regarding emergency expenditures, but badly miss the dramatic growth of the permanent administrative apparatus under Roosevelt (Bureau of the Census, *Historical Statistics*, Y 308–317, "Paid Civilian Employment of the Federal Government: 1816 to 1970," Y466–471, "Outlays of the Federal Government by Major Function: 1900 to 1939").

89. In heading the new National Labor Relations Board, there was no rush by prominent state managers to seek nomination. When the nominations were made in 1935, one member, John Carmody, was a member of the National Mediation Board when appointed. The new chair, J. Warren Madden, was a law professor. The third member was a holdover from the 1934 NLRB, Edwin S. Smith, a former personnel manager who came quickly to be targeted by

some individuals, including Wagner, were active both on the old boards and in writing and implementing the NLRA.

But these continuities do not reveal the driving force in the process of passing or implementing the act. Those who framed the new legislation were connected to previous labor relations efforts; their response was to recognize, and try to compensate for, their failures. These failures opened space for a political effort to create a new agency, one that would break sharply with past practices by virtue of its capacity to go beyond mediation in helping constitute bargaining units, enforce election results, and adjudicate complaints. At the agency level, discontinuity was an important element of the NLRB's relative success.

The primary aspect of those engaged in passing the Wagner Act was their identity as Progressive liberal reformers aiming to commit the state to a new type of social and economic regulation. This political effort included many individuals within Congress, universities, and professions, in addition to people who already occupied governmental positions. The *result* was state building—but this term is misleading if taken as a means of explaining what happened with reference to a notion of the ("rational") self-aggrandizing action of the managers of an already existing state.

A simple way of putting this—yet one that resists many structuralist or rationalistic accounts of political development—is that states are mainly built for political purposes. The NLRA was about defining a new state, working on previous institutional and discursive materials. In this political project, the Wagner Act, the judicial defenses of it, and the practice of implementing it combined not only to assert governmental responsibility but to shift the content of policy. Previous state efforts responded to threats to public order; especially through the courts, state intervention protected employers against unions and much less often defended unions' right to exist. The new intervention was directed by a new Progressive institution effectively allied with much of the labor movement and opposed by employers.

Once the Wagner Act passed, the NLRB was built not by empire-building long-term "state managers" but by the hiring of large numbers of relatively young lawyers who were disproportionately Jewish and politically on the left. They were mostly people who had modest prior experience in New Deal agencies or none at all. They chose to become state managers—one might better call them political cadres of the New Deal—mainly because of political commitment.

Most influential employees of the early NLRB strongly supported unionization, especially regarding the mass production industries. They understood their legal charge to be encouraging it, and they were supported in this view by Progressive liberals in Congress and the administration.[90]

---

business as adamantly prolabor (and pro-CIO). See Gross, *The Making of the National Labor Relations Board*, 149–56.

90. They conducted the board's affairs competently under the new law in ways that limited the number of early NLRB decisions overturned by the courts, although business condemned the NLRB from the start, and the AFL soon came to view it as hopelessly biased in favor of the CIO. See Millis and Brown, *From the Wagner Act to Taft-Hartley*, 235–43.

The early NLRB implemented the aims of the Wagner Act. It responded to conflicts in production and helped reshape relations there in the service both of economic aims and of a concept of ordered fairness. For New Deal progressivism, the expansion of state power was necessary for such ends and could thus be conceived as either an essential means or a positive virtue.

The passage and implementation of the NLRA exemplify the crucial political accomplishments of Roosevelt's first terms. Active efforts to attenuate the economic crisis and limit social disorder underlined a new political direction. There was a new commitment to maintaining social and economic order, even after the demise of the NRA and the shift away from global planning themes, through a growth in state responsibilities. There was also an expanded state economic commitment, with forays into deficit spending. Spending increases helped prevent further deterioration, and aided those who received government jobs and relief.[91]

The state expanded as new agencies were created within the executive branch—first the relief agencies and the NRA, and then in 1935–37 new agencies to administer the major reform legislation. A new conception of government responsibilities encouraged further federal intervention, as in housing and urban policy, where political forces won recognition of the need for policies and established new programs.[92] The results of the new policies depended on economic obstacles, political feasibility, and the availability of competent managers. Despite their problems, the new agencies delivered services to often desperate recipients, and legitimate government intervention was broadened. This intervention fell short of its promises, but was nonetheless central to resolving the political crises that Hooverism had opened.

By the end of 1937, a functioning new institution (the NLRB) had emerged as the result of political initiatives which expressed and helped institutionalize a new political identity, a Progressive liberal conception of government regulation for the purpose of achieving social and political fairness. "Fairness" now meant a much-expanded notion of popular participation, through unions and other organizations. The dynamic between prior forms of Progressivism and the mass action of the labor movement opened the way to include and reshape other elements: Democratic, middle class, public-spirited (willing to work for the government).

Politics and the Course of the Labor Movement

Progressive reform initiatives expanded the state, as in the process following the passage of the NLRA. How did the Wagner Act influence the course of the labor movement? Two main views exist. The first is that the Wagner Act was much more an expression of social and economic conflict and development than a means of shaping it. The second view is that the Wagner Act played a

---

91. Federal, state, and local expenditures on public welfare more than doubled between 1932 and 1936, from $445 million to $997 million (Bureau of the Census, *Historical Statistics*, Y 533–655, "Federal, State, and Local Government Expenditure, by Function: 1902 to 1970").

92. Efforts at urban policy, which at the national level only began as such after 1932, illustrate the process. See Mark Gelfand, *A Nation of Cities: The Federal Government and Urban America, 1933–65* (New York: Oxford University Press, 1975).

major role in reshaping labor relations. My claim is that the causal importance of the Wagner Act (that is, of the political conflicts and initiatives that resulted in its passage and extended from 1935–37) was substantial and direct in shaping a new labor movement, both at the political and economic levels.

A stark choice between syndicalism and paternalism still frames much of the argument about the Wagner Act's effects: either the act meant little, as the real dynamic was in the factories and communities where workers fought employers and built unions; or it meant everything, as a generous government extended its hand to a needy and grateful working class.

In the simplest version of a syndicalist argument, workers were building their power in any event, through their increasingly militant conflicts with capital. Thus the economic crisis eventually discredited both welfare capitalism and AFL lethargy, and opened the way toward a release of explosive working-class energies. For this view there is an overwhelming problem: labor action was not particularly dynamic in 1929–31, and not very successful as of 1934 or even 1935. The NLRA was passed after the massive strikes of 1934 had often failed to win their objectives, and unions were not growing dramatically.

It would seem, then, that some type of political intervention was required beyond the economic crisis and its delegitimating consequences. The Wagner Act promised a new type of support, both symbolic and practical. Earlier, the passage of the NIRA had been used by union organizers, citing Section 7A, to claim that Roosevelt wanted them to unionize.[93] With the NLRA in hand, such claims may have been more persuasive. This would be irrelevant if workers had already shown themselves strong enough to force employers to accept independent unions without state intervention. Yet decades of failure to do this— and the recent bitter experience of the 1920s—were a clear referent.

Recall the sequence again. By the last years of the Republican order the labor movement was small and weak.[94] In 1930, unions organized little more than 10 percent of the nonagricultural labor force in the United States.[95] Labor was closer to the Democratic party than to the Republican party, but its influence within the Democratic party was not substantial, as many party factions mistrusted or even opposed the unions.[96] The labor movement in the late 1920s

93. Similar approaches persisted. Dorothy Healey reports that at the end of the decade, union organizers were still using the claim that Roosevelt wanted workers to unionize as a central argument for unionization. Naturally, many employers, and a number of Democrats, objected (Interview, Dorothy Healey, Washington, D.C., October 24, 1984).

94. The story of its weakness is told in David Brody, *Steelworkers in America: The Nonunion Era* (Cambridge: Harvard University Press, 1960); David Montgomery, *The Fall of the House of Labor* (New York: Cambridge University Press, 1988); and Melvyn Dubofsky, "Abortive Reform: The Wilson Administration and Organized Labor, 1913–1920," in James E. Cronin and Carmen Sirianni, eds., *Work, Community, and Power: The Experience of Labor in Europe and America, 1900–1925* (Philadelphia: Temple University Press, 1983), 197–220.

95. Bureau of the Census, *Historical Statistics*, D952–69, "Labor Union Membership, by Industry: 1897 to 1934."

96. Both Bernstein and Brody emphasize the unions' weakness by 1930 (Bernstein, *The Lean Years*, 334–57; Brody, *Workers in Industrial America* [New York: Oxford University Press], 44–45, 82).

and early 1930s was mainly the AFL, with a small number of independent unions outside it. In 1930, roughly 3 million of 3.6 million unionized workers were enrolled in AFL unions.[97] While the AFL often allied locally with Democratic machines, divisions within the unions limited their power. A number of important AFL unionists were Republican even after the onset of the depression, as was a significant part of the rank and file.[98]

In the 1932 election, then, labor's support for Roosevelt was not crucial, but the next few years saw remarkable change. After the passage of the NLRA, both the AFL and the emergent CIO rallied to Roosevelt's support in 1936. Much of this support was channeled through an independent organization, Labor's Non-Partisan League, which claimed to represent both the AFL and CIO, but was dominated by the latter.[99] Through this medium, the CIO made large organizational and financial contributions to Roosevelt's campaign. The AFL acted through the labor division of the national campaign committee and through its ties with local Democratic organizations. The labor movement could take substantial credit for Roosevelt's victory in 1936. It was now linked to a single party, within which its power grew, although it required the entire decade for voluntarist traditions to be subordinated to political action initiatives.[100]

In this narrative, did labor's political and economic emergence result directly from the dire economic and social circumstances workers faced? Were the unions themselves a reasonably faithful expression of the aims of the mass insurgencies or a drastic narrowing of the initial aspirations?[101]

Labor's Weakness. The disruption and suffering caused by the depression helped spur workers to attempt to unionize, and the militant and creative efforts of unorganized workers were central to building the new unions. Yet respect for the dignity and frequent heroism of these popular efforts should not mean overstating their effects: by 1935, unionization was limited and the labor movement fragile.

This weakness had several recent sources. Rapid structural changes in industry from World War I through the 1920s, including the widespread adoption of assembly-line production and the partial adoption of Taylorist techniques of organizing labor, created a new industrial setting to which the unions and

97. Bureau of the Census, *Historical Statistics*, D940–45, "Labor Union Membership, by Affiliation: 1897 to 1934."

98. For a strong claim about Republican strength among urban workers, see James Sundquist, *Dynamics of the Party System*, 200.

99. On 1932, see Leuchtenburg, *Roosevelt and the New Deal*, 10–17. On 1936, see Schlesinger, *Politics of Upheaval*, 592–95.

100. American labor law's hostility to union organization and the voluntarism of the AFL had long reinforced each other. As Horowitz notes, this voluntarism allowed an interpretation of positive acts of state intervention, such as the Norris-La Guardia Act, as enabling acts within which voluntarist relations might flourish. And voluntarism persisted in the AFL (Horowitz, *Political Ideologies of Organized Labor*, 55, 73, 80, 219, 241).

101. Bernstein's work exemplifies the first view; the second is put sharply in Piven and Cloward, *Poor People's Movements*, 155–75.

unorganized workers were unable to respond immediately.[102] Part of the unions' growth in the 1930s was due to greater familiarity with the new setting of mass production.[103]

A second source of weakness was the success of employer strategies in the 1920s, which aimed at avoiding independent unions through a combination of coercion and selective distribution of benefits. Although workers were dissatisfied with this system, it was not about to burst prior to the depression.[104] Benefits could be provided, given a low wage base and rising productivity; coercion was omnipresent, both in the factory (given managers' power over hiring and job assignment) and in the promanagement stance of most of the courts.

In the short term, labor was further weakened by the disorganizing power of the depression. While it eroded welfare capitalist arrangements, the depression also weakened existing unions and blocked the formation of others because of high unemployment and massive residential dislocation. Vulnerable unions could not easily take advantage of popular discontent with Hoover's policies or support for Roosevelt's.

Thus it is hard to imagine that widespread unionization could have taken place without major political efforts. Still, the lag between the depression's onset and deepening and the spread of unions might be explained as the effect of a cycle of working-class disorganization and organization: when economic conditions began to improve, the working class grew more capable of effective collective action.[105] Thus the growth of unions might have registered the economic recovery.

102. Harry Braverman's account of Taylorism overstates its spread but identifies its main themes. Gordon, Reich, and Edwards treat both the assembly line and Taylorism as part of what they term the "homogenization" of labor. Empirical indexes of these shifts in the 1920s include growth in the size of establishments, the number of production workers, capital per production worker, and value added per worker (Braverman, *Labor and Monopoly Capital: The Degradation of Work in the Twentieth Century* [New York: Monthly Review Press, 1974]; Gordon et al., *Segmented Work, Divided Workers*, 130–35).

103. Bernstein's *Lean Years* and *Turbulent Years* provide information about these learning processes, as do memoirs and ethnographies, such as Peter Friedlander, *The Emergence of a UAW Local, 1936–39: A Study in Class and Culture* (Pittsburgh: University of Pittsburgh Press, 1975).

104. For employers, the aim of avoiding independent unions was conceptually linked with an image of a harmonious, integrated factory system. This view recognized the reality of social relations in the factory and the need to organize them positively, allowing welfare capitalist efforts to take root. Brody argues that the depression was required to destroy relatively successful efforts at welfare capitalism; Piore and Sabel offer an even more positive view of the system, in which it prefigures contemporary efforts to reorganize work in more cooperative ways. The latter account downplays the extent of coercion required to hold welfare capitalism together inside and outside the factory (Brody, *Workers in Industrial America*, 20–78; Michael J. Piore and Charles F. Sabel, *The Second Industrial Divide* [New York: Basic Books, 1984], 125–30).

105. Some degree of industrial stability was important in providing a framework for union insurgency. With the major exception of the mineworkers, when unions started to grow, they developed most quickly in larger metropolitan areas, owing to the more liberal political

Karen Orren offers such an account, without syndicalist political illusions: "most of the activity, as well as its ebb, can be explained by the strategically favorable business upturn of 1935 and the recession of 1937. . . . the delaying tactics of business—refusal to bargain, refusal to sign a written contract—were effectively eliminated only after 1938 when the most dramatic gains had already been registered." She argues that at the turn of the century, unionization occurred in another phase of economic improvement following a severe depression—but without a friendly government. This suggests that developments in 1933–38 were economically determined.[106] Orren's analogy has merit in capturing an underlying pattern in American labor relations: significant union growth occurs within periods of a few years, during extraordinary times such as wars or economic crisis. But her account is dubious regarding the causes of union growth in the 1930s. Differences in the type of unions built, given the much higher proportion of semiskilled and unskilled labor in mass production settings in the 1930s, helped make unionization dependent on political support in the later period.

The limits of an economic account are suggested by these figures on the percentage rates of increase of union membership and gross national product:

Year	GNP Growth	Union Membership Growth
1934	9.1%	14.8%
1935	9.9	16.1
1936	13.9	11.3
1937	5.3	75.5
1938	−5.0	14.8
1939	8.6	9.1
1940	8.5	−5.2

Variance in economic conditions is not nearly enough to explain variance in union membership. Unions grew more rapidly in 1934 and 1935 than in 1936, when economic conditions were improving most rapidly. Then the poor economic year of 1937 saw a huge increase in union membership. The real slump of 1938 was accompanied by further strong union growth, exceeded only by that of 1935 and 1937. If one took union growth as a function of the prior year's economic course, giving an interval for the process of organizing collective action, the dramatic union growth of 1937 could be linked to the strong economic growth of 1936. But what purely economic dynamic could explain

culture of some of those areas and the greater institutional resources available to unions there. See Milton Derber, "Growth and Expansion," in Derber and Young, *Labor and the New Deal*, 38–42.

106. Karen Orren, "Liberalism, Money, and the Situation of Organized Labor," in J. David Greenstone, ed., *Public Values and Private Power in American Politics* (Chicago: University of Chicago Press, 1982), 183–84.

how a modest increase in GNP growth between 1935 and 1936 (from 9.9 to 13.9 percent) caused a massive increase in union growth (from 11.3 to 75.5 percent) between 1936 and 1937, whereas a much greater GNP increase between 1938 and 1939 (− 5.0 to 8.6 percent) accompanied a sharp decline in union growth between 1939 and 1940 (from 9.1 to −5.2 percent)?[107]

Economic circumstances cannot be accorded the central, direct role in accounting for union growth. They were important: had conditions remained as terrible as they were in 1930–33, unionization prospects would have been significantly worse throughout the decade; without the recovery of 1935–37, collective action would have been more difficult; and the recession of 1937–38 had a negative effect. The point is not that there was no relation between economic circumstances and union growth but that the fit is so loose that additional major sources of union growth must have been at work—especially in 1937, when a qualitative change in unions' size and scope occurred.

Does insisting that the Wagner Act helped produce outcomes that would otherwise not have occurred require that we replace syndicalism with paternalism? This is not necessary, given the significant role of the labor movement in passing the Wagner Act itself.

Labor's Political Formation. The positive dynamic between emergent labor forces and Progressive liberalism is crucially about the political construction of a new labor movement. Of what sort? Against what alternatives?

The first key moment in this process was the legitimation of union organization, begun with the NIRA in Roosevelt's first term. The next major political event was the government response to the citywide strikes of 1934. Although hardly supportive, the response of local and federal authorities did differ from prior practices, as serious efforts at compromise occurred along with the usual defense of order. The result of these uprisings was not immediately to produce unions but to pressure national political forces to take the labor movement more seriously. Next came the midterm election in 1934. At a minimum, those elected were more open to political compromise with labor than those they replaced. The Democratic triumph also emboldened Progressive liberals within the party, the supporters of the New Deal most open to cooperation with labor.[108] Yet the ensuing union victories remained modest.

The next major event was the passage of the NLRA in 1935. Passed with an eye on the turbulence of 1934 and the prospect of more ahead at a time when union activism was linked to wide strata among the urban working class and

107. Bureau of the Census, *Historical Statistics*, D 946–51, "Labor Union Membership and Membership as Percent of Total Labor Force and of Nonagricultural Employment: 1930 to 1970"; F 31, "Gross National Product, Total and Per Capita, in Current and 1958 Prices: 1869–1970."

108. Sinclair's analysis indicates that incoming congressional Democrats in 1932 and 1934 were somewhat less supportive of New Deal programs than were veterans. But the differences are not dramatic, as Democratic newcomers were a source of support for the New Deal (Barbara Deckard Sinclair, *Congressional Realignment, 1925–1978* [Austin: University of Texas Press, 1982], 31–33).

poor, the Wagner Act per se did not immediately empower the labor movement enough to establish unions that could negotiate wages and working conditions, especially in the mass production industries. It was not accepted by employers. Further political conflicts were required to register major increases in union membership.

One front of political conflict was opened in 1936 with the La Follette Committee hearings in the Senate on employers' violations of workers' civil rights—now violations of labor law. These hearings had two aims: to create a body of evidence that would assist in litigating the Wagner Act and to create political support both for the labor movement and for the administration.[109] They were perceived as successful in both respects, although it is hard to be certain how much importance they had for a 1936 election result that affirmed popular approval of the New Deal and the Roosevelt administration. Given the obduracy of employers, however, especially in mass production industries, even the Roosevelt landslide did not simply create unions. But it did make clear how different the balance of political forces was from that to which capital was accustomed and drastically narrowed the political space open for resisting unions altogether.

Very soon after the 1936 election, the next crucial political event was the sit-down strike wave and the government response to it in 1937. Why treat this as a political event at all, rather than an economic process which shows the limits of political action in creating unions? There are two reasons. First, the pattern of sit-down strikes in the 1930s suggests that these strikes were a strategic response to an overall political situation, one informed by a realistic appreciation of a more favorable context. If the sit-downs were only part of a socioeconomic conflict unfolding on its own, we would expect a much less concentrated pattern than what took shape: the great bulk of all such strikes occurred in 1937.[110] Second, because of the extent of the disorder and the explicitness of the illegality involved, they necessarily became matters of public political concern. In this setting, the reluctance of Roosevelt and Governor Frank Murphy of Michigan to use force against the occupiers of the automobile factories in early 1937 was a sharp break with past policy and was widely understood as

---

109. The La Follette Committee's work played a major role in discrediting company unions. See Gross, *The Making of the National Labor Relations Board*, 214–23; Derber, "The New Deal and Labor," 114.

110. In 1936–39, 82 percent of all sit-down strikes, involving 77 percent of all the workers involved in such strikes, occurred in 1937. And after that year, such actions declined precipitously, from 477 in 1937 to 52 the next year and only 6 in 1939 before the wartime clampdown on labor action (Monthly Labor Review [1939], 1130; [1940], 1105, cited in P. K. Edwards, *Strikes in the United States, 1881–1974* [Oxford: Basil Blackwell, 1981]). On the sit-down strikes, see Bernstein, *Turbulent Years*, 499–501; Cochran, *Labor and Communism*, 114, 122; and Sidney Fine, *Sit Down: The General Motors Strike of 1936–1937* (Ann Arbor: University of Michigan Press, 1969). The sit-down strikes are better understood as an explosion of working-class anger focused on the aim of securing recognition of unions, for the purposes noted above, than as a tactic congruent with an essential radicalism of the new labor movement.

such. A torrent of letters and cables arrived at the White House demanding that Roosevelt deal harshly with the strikes:

> Your apparent unwillingness to advise the Nation [of] your attitude toward the high handed, brutal and lawless display of power exhibited by labor union leaders as expressed in the prevailing epidemic of "sit-downs" leaves many of us bewildered and apprehensive. Your silence can only be construed as politically inspired and as unmindful of the evil effects of such lawlessness upon the entire population.[111]

Roosevelt's resistance to pressure to use force against the strikes amounted to encouraging the right to organize—even tolerating extralegal measures when management refused to accept unions. Later, introducing his 1937 public statements, he wrote:

> Enemies of labor were quick to condemn in 1937. From familiar circles came the old cry of the Tories: "Something drastic must be done to curb labor; it is getting too powerful." Of course what these people really want and strive for is to return to the good old days when labor was unorganized and weak, and starving for jobs. . . . You could always reason with a starving applicant for a job. But it is so inconvenient to bargain with a strong, united group of employees who know that they are entitled to a fair share of the profits of an industry. . . .
> From a few hysterical sources came even the demand that Federal troops be called out to put down the strikers. I consider the calling out of Federal troops during a strike, except in a national emergency, one of the most dangerous things that can happen in a democracy.[112]

Finally, the Supreme Court decisions upholding the NLRA promised legal force on behalf of unions. In its key decision of April 12, 1937, NLRB v. *Jones & Laughlin Steel Corp.*, the court insisted on the right to organize:

> Thus in its present application, the statute goes no further than to safeguard the right of employees to self-organization and to select representatives of their own choosing for collective bargaining or other mutual protection without restraint or coercion by their employer.
> *That is a fundamental right.* Employees have as clear a right to organize and select their representatives for lawful purposes as the [company] has to organize its business and select its own officers and agents. Discrimination and coercion to prevent the free exercise of the right of employees to self-organiza-

---

111. Letter, R. D. Small to Roosevelt, 4/8/37, Folder 1937, January–May, Official Folder 407B—Strikes, Roosevelt Papers, FDR Library. Roosevelt was deluged with complaints about administration "weakness" in not forcing workers to abandon their sit-down in the automobile strike. Murphy and Roosevelt were also pressured by the AFL not to encourage a settlement of the auto situation that would benefit the CIO and weaken AFL units (Telegram, William Green to Franklin Murphy, 2/6/37, Summary of Franklin Murphy telephone call to White House, 2/8/37, Folder Auto Strike 1937, Official Folder 407B—Strikes, Roosevelt Papers, FDR Library).

112. Roosevelt, *The Public Papers and Addresses of Franklin D. Roosevelt,* 1937 volume, *The Constitution Prevails* (New York: Macmillan, 1941), 7, 20, 23, 274.

tion and representation is a proper subject for condemnation by competent legislative authority.[113]

The Wagner Act and the Supreme Court decisions regulated union behavior in the context of a massive political shift toward a recognition of the rights of unions as public representative entities. The legal shift helped provide necessary political conditions for their existence.[114] Sustaining the NLRA communicated two key messages: the state's power would not support legal action against union efforts within the NLRA framework; and state violence was not routinely available against unionizing efforts.[115] Following Jones & Laughlin, employer noncompliance persisted, but often with mainly tactical aims in local fights rather than as part of an overall strategy to prevent the appearance of unions.[116]

This pattern of union building meant expanded legal intervention in labor relations. But a strong claim is appropriate: without such political intervention, the likelihood is that the labor movement, even after the extraordinary wave of sit-down strikes, would still have been unable to establish durable unions with anything close to the success achieved when union membership surged from 4 million members in 1936 to 8 million in 1938.[117] Union growth accompanied critical political victories for prounion forces in 1936 and 1937.

To isolate the effects of a new political alignment in 1937, imagine the sit-down strikes, but a basically hostile federal and state government. What might have ensued? It would have been perfectly in keeping with American political traditions for increasing force to be deployed against strikers, including federal troops, until the strikes were broken and further efforts blocked by intimidation. Force might not have settled all the disputes on capital's terms, but, had it been appealing to the administration, the outcome surely would have been

113. Chief Justice Hughes, decision in NLRB v. *Jones & Laughlin Steel Corp,* 301 U.S. 1, April 12, 1937, in *Court Decisions Relating to the National Labor Relations Act,* vol. 1 (Washington: U.S. Government Printing Office, 1944), 323.

114. This shift was a political aim of New Deal forces. In 1936, the question of how to force Court acquiescence in New Deal legislation was discussed widely in administration circles, and the election was perceived partly as a choice between the Court and the administration's view of the Constitution. Attorney General Cummings proposed a platform plank calling for an amendment to affirm social and economic regulation as a governmental responsibility. Felix Frankfurter made similar proposals (Letter, Homer Cummings to Roosevelt, 6/20/36, Folder Justice Department 1933–37, President's Secretary's File, Roosevelt Papers, FDR Library; Letter, Frankfurter to Roosevelt, 5/29/35, Folder Frankfurter 1933–35, President's Secretary's File, Roosevelt Papers, FDR Library). It was later argued within the administration that despite the debacle of the "Court-packing" bill, its introduction encouraged the Court to rethink its position.

115. The key role of the Supreme Court's decision is emphasized in accounts written by those involved in the NLRB's work, such as J. Warren Madden, "Birth of the Board," in Louis G. Silverberg, ed., *The Wagner Act after Ten Years* (Washington: Bureau of National Affairs, 1945), 34–42.

116. Vittoz, *New Deal Labor Policy,* 171.

117. Bureau of the Census, *Historical Statistics,* D946–51, "Labor Union Membership."

very different.[118] That this did not occur hinged on the choices of Roosevelt and many state and local officials. In these choices, such officials behaved as Progressive liberals who were state managers, interested not just in "order" but in shaping a *new* order against the stark backdrop of an overall political context in which capital had temporarily lost the ability to define what forms of disorder were legitimate and illegitimate.

The critical year of 1937 was one of political force—of workers' illegal occupation of factories, of employers' often illegal actions, of choices by elected officials and police about how to use force.[119] Political and economic conflict became an immediate and explicit physical matter: Who would be permitted to go where, in factories, under what conditions? When would force be used to stop one course of action, or not be used and thus permit another? Answering these questions was the practical role of a state in formation, not just as a diffuse collection of administrative agencies and elected officials, but as a factor of political unification amidst conflicting forces. This New Deal state, reshaped through Progressive liberal initiatives, reestablished control over legitimate violence on a terrain in which violence had often been deployed by employers against workers. The centralization of violence and the refusal to use it indiscriminately or as a matter of first resort against workers was a radical shift. It is entirely missed by analysts who berate Roosevelt's occasional castigation of labor, or by cheerful arguments that the eventual outcomes once again demonstrate the flexibility and openness of American politics.

Employers recognized in 1937 that although the politics of labor relations required an ultimate resort to physical force, they could no longer rely on state violence to buttress their refusal to admit independent unions into their factories. That order could be restored once unions were recognized—and workers subjected to the discipline of a new factory regime—did not seem like a small price to capital at the time. They paid it grudgingly, often angrily, usually hoping to subvert what they regarded as an illegitimate imposition.[120] After

118. It isn't necessary to go far for relevant examples. In sectors where federal support for unionization was nonexistent or weak, employers' violence and that of local authorities could be frequent, brutal, and generally effective. Perhaps the best example is agriculture, where workers were particularly vulnerable both before and after passage of the NLRA, which did not cover them. See Jerold S. Auerbach, *Labor and Liberty: The La Follette Committee and the New Deal* (New York: Bobbs-Merrill, 1966); and Cletus Daniel, *Bitter Harvest: A History of California Farmworkers, 1870–1941* (Berkeley: University of California Press, 1982), 204–05, 225.

119. Although there was an explicit use of considerable force by workers in the sit-downs, and the threat of more, the amount of physical violence to individuals in these strikes was less than in some of the turbulent strikes fought by more conventional means, such as the Little Steel strike.

120. The grudging quality of employers' eventual acceptance of unions is very clear. Howell John Harris divides management into four groups regarding unions in the 1930s: sophisticated and belligerent antiunionists, "realists," and "progressives." Yet not only did the first two groups fight unions energetically; almost all of the third group and a good portion of the fourth did so, differing mainly in how soon they came to view unions as unavoidable. Given the small size of his fourth group, that makes the number of major employers who put no serious obstacles in the way of unions (much less encouraging them!) a very modest one. See

they failed either to break the sitdown strikes or to win judicial relief via the Supreme Court, employers in 1937 admitted their defeat and proceeded to negotiate. Thus an abrupt increase in unionization occurred that year. But almost immediately thereafter, in 1938–39 and then after World War II, employers began to chip away at the bargain they had accepted under duress.[121]

Thus the process of "state building" in labor relations that began with the NIRA and the early labor boards was realized in the achievement of both a new political-administrative framework and a practical capacity to deploy force in its defense. In 1937 this emergent state was certainly a capitalist state, aiming not to expropriate employers but to reform and stabilize factory relations. If this side of the state had ever been in question in the decade, capital might have breathed a sigh of relief. The infrequency of such responses in 1937 testifies to the marginality of anticapitalist political projects in these years, such that employers never felt the need to be grateful for much of anything in what they perceived as a long process of governmental abuse and industrial disorder.

In sum, the Wagner Act mattered a great deal as a critical point in a political sequence: NRA, 1934 election, NLRA, La Follette Committee, 1936 election, sitdown strikes, NLRB v. *Jones & Laughlin*. This sequence marks a process of establishing unions. Its protagonists were Progressive liberals within and outside Congress and the administration, and a new labor movement. Without working-class mobilization the pressures would have been so much less intense that Progressive liberals would not have created unions as a sort of gift to workers. *Yet the key political measures did not recognize a de facto state of affairs in production.* Rather, these measures were crucial in constituting the unions.[122]

Cooptation? If the Wagner Act and ensuing political conflicts were crucial in causing labor relations to take a new direction, how should one assess the course taken? One might admit that the labor movement was weak early in the

Harris, *The Right to Manage: Industrial Relations Policies of American Business in the 1940s* (Madison: University of Wisconsin Press, 1982), 23–37.

121. The story of the employers' counterattack is recounted in James Patterson, *Congressional Conservatism and the New Deal*; Tomlins, *The State and the Unions*; and Millis and Clark, *From the Wagner Act to Taft-Hartley.*

122. Stressing the political side of the formation of the unions opens the way toward analyzing where unions took shape and where they did not. Clearly the perception that the formation of mass unions in modern industrial sectors was key is well founded. But some such sectors were organized more rapidly than others; and in other areas unions were not uniformly unsuccessful. The prior history of unionization efforts, the character of relations among firms, the geographic location of sectors, and the gender and racial composition of workers all entered into the determination of rates of unionization. Thus, arguing for the crucial role of politics in forming the unions does not stop at the national level, but also concerns political processes at other levels. A systematic examination of these processes is beyond the scope of this article, however. Stanley Vittoz offers a useful discussion of unionization by sector in *New Deal Labor Policy*, 34–46, 65, 119, 126; so do several articles in Ruth Milkman, ed., *Women, Work and Protest: A Century of U.S. Women's Labor History* (Boston: Routledge & Kegan Paul, 1985).

decade and political action was required to assist it, but maintain that the actual process of political intervention was conservative.

This view can provide a way to claim that the defeats of the labor movement in the last two decades are linked to the character of the agreements reached among conflicting forces in the 1930s. Yet this connection should be put carefully. Elements of the New Deal labor relations system may eventually have become obstacles to the growth of the labor movement—given many intervening developments. Yet to make this claim does not show either that this result was inevitable or that the new system was a significantly more conservative outcome than others that were realistically possible at the time.[123]

To make the latter argument returns us to ideology, the discourses of the labor movement and of sections of the working class that remained outside of it. Just as calling intellectuals of middle-class social origins and positions "bourgeois intellectuals" makes sense only if one can prove it, claiming cooptation is reasonable only if one can show it happened. This is not equivalent to showing that some sections of the labor movement were more radical than was reflected in the settlements that occurred. One can find such tendencies. A generous estimate would gauge their size as roughly equal to that of the CIO unions in which Communist party members played a major role as more than individual organizers. This current, between one-quarter and one-third of the CIO, understood itself as being to the left of—while allied with—the mainstream of Progressive liberalism in the New Deal.[124]

Given the substantial size of these forces, it is not hard to compile oral histories that, if put in a single stack, imply a predominant popular radicalism

123. For discussions of the contemporary weakness of the labor movement with substantial reference to the nature of the labor relations framework built in the 1930s and 1940s, see Davis, *Prisoners of the American Dream*; Goldfield, *The Decline of Organized Labor in the United States*; and Tomlins, *The State and the Unions*. Raising this issue would be pedantic if it were not so often the case that analysts of the labor movement treat long-term conservative consequences as cooptation. Even leaving aside the crucial question of whether such consequences are necessary, showing cooptation requires showing that a real force actually was coopted. Thus when David Montgomery claims cooptation on the grounds that "the government's intervention also opened a new avenue through which the rank and file could in time be tamed and the newly powerful unions be subjected to tight legal and political control," he simply assumes a mass radical movement for direct workers' control which he has not come close to showing existed (Montgomery, *Workers' Control in America*, 165).

124. The claim is obviously not that one-third of the members of the early CIO (as of 1938, 700,000–800,000) identified with the Communist party. Rather, a section of the overall labor movement roughly equivalent to that figure was composed of diverse political forces who conceived their aims in terms significantly to the left of the center of the labor movement and the New Deal. Within this radical current the number of members of Socialist or Communist political organizations was a small fraction, considerably less than 10 percent—Communist party membership (at a time when the class composition of the party was quite varied) reached no more than 70,000, and other socialist organizations were much smaller. For an account of Communist influence in the early CIO, see Joseph R. Starobin, *American Communism in Crisis, 1934–57* (Berkeley: University of California Press, 1975), 38.

which was betrayed. This current was populist and radical-democratic in its discourses, with programmatic elements that in European terms would be called social democratic. It was not socialist, nor on the verge of becoming so; nor was it committed to a vision of workers' control of production.

These last points may seem so obvious as not to require mention. It is necessary to do so, however, because the presence of a substantial working-class radicalism—unusual enough in American political history—seems so often to lead analysts to overstate both its size and the transformative dimension of aims. This popular radicalism was also constrained by an overall political context within the working class which is rarely mentioned in accounts of cooptation. Beyond the substantial current on the left of the CIO which supported the New Deal but wanted it to go further in democratic and egalitarian directions, what about the other two-thirds of the CIO, the AFL, and the majority of the working class which by 1937 remained nonunionized? How might these forces have responded to a practical effort to implement a sharp break with Progressive liberal policies in 1936–37? What would this have meant in factories and offices? Would workers have been attracted by the boldness of a rejection of contractualism, snapped into awareness of the limits of their previous practices? To make the cooptation argument persuasive, it would be necessary to show that the above estimate of working-class radicalism is too low and that much larger sections of the working class and other groups were clearly to the left of the New Deal. No one has done so. If there is an error here, it is probably in claiming too much for radicalism.

Alternatively, one could claim that working class attachments to other political and social views were so fragile that things could have been dramatically altered amidst the turbulence of the mid-1930s. Although popular views during the decade shifted well to the left of what they had been, it is a different matter to claim that the shift could have continued past populist and radical democratic discourses. The lack of credible evidence for such a prospect forces its proponents to rely on a recitation of villainy to explain why actual efforts to break sharply with Progressive liberalism were not successful, whether conducted by Third Period Communists early in the depression, or by Trotskyists later on, and why Popular Front Communism was a betrayal.

The objectives of the labor movement's upsurge focused not only on gaining securely increased wages but on establishing a factory regime in which workers had greatly increased protection against managerial abuses, both in hiring and firing and in the day-to-day organization of work. Unions were recognized as an instrument through which such goals might be won. That this would imply an institutionalization of seniority, grievance procedures, and wage determination was for most of the labor movement not an unfortunate stopping point in a dynamic whose essential nature would have led toward more and more radical initiatives. Instead, the institutionalized rejection of conventional practices was precisely the point. The real aims of the mass labor upsurge were understood to entail drastic changes in the prior industrial regime; that some of them were actually won testifies to the political skill as well as the courage of the labor movement.

CONCLUSION: A NEW LABOR MOVEMENT
AND A NEW POLITICAL ORDER

The passage of the Wagner Act was primarily the result of political initiatives undertaken by Progressive liberals, in alliance with the labor movement. These initiatives occurred amidst economic crisis, but were not determined by it; they resulted in expanding the state, but their origins do not lie mainly in maximizing efforts by state managers. The Wagner Act and ensuing political conflicts played a central role in building a new state and in shaping new labor relations with large industrial unions independent of management control.

These answers to the two questions with which I began—why was the Wagner Act passed? what difference did it make?—can be recast as claims about the political construction of a new order. States—and labor relations systems—are built for political purposes, not via an automatic logic of economic or organizational development. The leaders of the reform process operated in the first instance as Progressive liberals, political agents with commitments to reordering labor relations. These commitments drew on, and were consistent with, the prior social and political experiences of those involved, both in class and occupational terms and in terms of the history of prior efforts at Progressive reform. An elaboration of state capacities and a broadening of state functions were means of attaining what was conceived as a further and more democratic order. "Order" was an aim, but stability was conceived as entailing particular social and political objectives.

In concluding, let me briefly sketch labor's political role in 1936–37: that is, its role in the dynamic through which both politics and industrial relations were reshaped, and labor gained considerable political power without the creation of a labor party.

In 1936, the labor movement made a major financial contribution (about $750,000) to Roosevelt's campaign. This aid was all the more important because some sources of campaign funding that might normally have been available to a Democratic nominee were not, given depression difficulties and the hostility of most of business.[125] Labor also helped organize and mobilize, urging its membership and supporters to vote Democratic or for Roosevelt on a labor line.[126] Labor actively recruited new political supporters and educated them about the policies of the Roosevelt administration and the New Deal.

Yet if the labor movement was a powerful political force, it was still fragile. In this fluid political moment, the labor movement was trying to create a new institutional position through its political intervention. In 1936, those in the labor movement could help deliver voters, but they had not achieved a secure

125. In 1932, bankers and brokers alone contributed 24 percent of all sums of $1,000 or more; in 1936 that figure fell to 4 percent (Louise Overacker, "Labor's Political Contributions," *Political Science Quarterly* [1939]: 60).

126. Leuchtenburg credits the labor movement with carrying Ohio, Illinois, Pennsylvania, and Indiana for Roosevelt, and for swinging a number of previously Republican cities into the Democratic column (Leuchtenburg, *Roosevelt and the New Deal*, 189). Lubell's classic account also stresses the effects of the unions' mobilization (Lubell, *The Future of American Politics* [New York: Harper, 1951], 46–55).

establishment of unions. They worried about their lack of growth, interunion conflicts, and the course of upcoming industrial struggles. There was no guarantee of a continuing favorable political climate. Even for the emergent CIO in 1936, the elections mattered as much as new organizing because the fate of the labor movement was understood to depend on the political outcome.[127]

Labor acted politically in local and national Democratic efforts (and less often, in quasi-independent efforts), through voter mobilization efforts, and in political dialogues with Roosevelt and other Democratic leaders.[128] Its social and economic goals required political action; such action also built its own political credibility. The labor movement's political fight for unions was not a dilution of movement radicalism; union leaders were also movement leaders and were often to the left of the movement as a whole.[129]

The labor movement helped elect Roosevelt, while the campaign helped create a new political labor movement. How was the movement related to the Democratic party? The new labor movement lacked direct power in the national party organization. Few members of the national committee or other leading figures in the national party emerged from the labor movement or were primarily identified with it. Of Democrats in Congress even after 1936, very few came directly from the labor movement.[130]

One reason for the absence of labor representatives at the top of the party and Congress was the political character of the organized Democratic party. Much of the party at the state and local levels was to the right of the labor movement, especially the industrial unions, and was not interested in turning

127. See Greenstone, *Labor in American Politics*, 49–50. In contrast, Piven and Cloward's stress on economic disruption in forming the unions leads them to downplay the importance of the 1936 election, in *Poor People's Movements*, 160–61.

128. In 1936, Roosevelt wrote to a meeting of Labor's Non-Partisan League state chairmen: "I should like to have you know that I am sincerely proud that you are gathering in support of my candidacy. This could not be the case if you did not know, out of the experience of the past three years, that the present Administration has endeavored to promote the ideal of justice for the great masses of America's wage earners and to make that ideal a reality" (Letter, Roosevelt to George L. Berry, August 3, 1936, Official File 407, Roosevelt Papers, FDR Library). Also see Burns, *Roosevelt*, 276–77.

129. Those who insist on treating unionization as cooptation have so little persuasive evidence of this in terms of mass political consciousness that they are forced to adopt other explanatory strategies: to conceive the dynamic of the labor movement mainly in terms of militance and disruption, and avoid the issue of political or economic consciousness; to posit that a potentially radical mass orientation was blocked by the emergent union leadership; or to focus attention in a highly unrepresentative fashion on socialists and communists within the left of the labor movement.

130. Although many representatives considered that they owed their election partly to labor's efforts, the recruitment of political elites was not changed so dramatically as to include a large number of individuals from subordinate social classes. The fragmentary archival evidence, including the state folders in the DNC records and Farley's correspondence, is that Democratic elites in 1936 were first of all lawyers, then other professionals and career politicians, and much less prominently, businessmen. See state files (esp. California, Georgia, Iowa, Illinois, New York), Papers of the Democratic National Committee, 1928–48, FDR Library.

over major leadership positions to individuals from the unions. At the 1936 Democratic convention labor organizations did not play a major public role, and the labor division of the campaign committee that year was small and poorly funded, with little direct power.[131] At the national level, most union political influence went through the AFL or Labor's Non-Partisan League directly to the administration and the campaign. In some local cases unions were more directly powerful, mainly in eastern and midwestern cities. The form of intervention varied according to several factors, notably the strength of new union forces with respect to the AFL, the prior character of the local Democratic organization, and the size of the state or city.[132] In general, the stronger the new unions, and the more influential the pro-New Deal Democratic forces, the greater the political power of the unions in the party.

In exceptional cities where the labor movement was very powerful relative to other political forces, party forms briefly emerged resembling those of European mass parties, integrating labor and party constituent organizations and activities.[133] Even then the unions were less likely to rebuild the Democratic Party than to coexist with its prior forms. And there were still limits, such as reluctance to run union officials even for municipal offices, much less major

131. On the convention, see the *Official Report of the Proccedings of the Democratic National Convention—1936*. In 1936, the Republicans tried to win labor votes by attacking Roosevelt's relationship with Lewis, hoping that this would win over AFL members and unaffiliated workers. The head of the labor committee, Daniel Tobin, often found himself trying to persuade AFL leaders that Roosevelt's closeness to the LNPL did not signify a choice for the CIO (Letter, Tobin to James Farley, August 20, 1936, Folder 8/14–21, 1936, Official Folder 300—Democratic National Committee, Roosevelt Papers, FDR Library).

132. The head of Labor's Non-Partisan League claimed his group had organized in every state and most congressional districts, but it is hard to know how much this "organizing" meant. Although direct labor intervention sometimes influenced the behavior of officials and shifted electoral outcomes, the image of a coherent, mass, disciplined force turning out masses of voters everywhere would greatly overstate labor's political reach and coherence (Letter, George L. Berry to Steven Early, 9/9/36, and Memo, "Notations for the President," Official File 2251—Labor's Non-Partisan League, Roosevelt Papers, FDR Library).

133. It is hard to make a quantitative estimate of the scope of "mass party" forms. Much of the literature on labor in the decade makes no effort to describe the organizational forms of local political involvement; the line between them and active interest group mobilization of a fairly conventional type is hard to draw. The modest scope of such forms is indicated by the small set of places that met their apparent preconditions: that the area be Democratic; that the CIO be at least as strong as the AFL; that there not exist a powerful Democratic machine capable of blocking new organizational efforts. Mass party forms were the exception rather than the rule and probably emerged with force in less than a third of major cities. An indirect method of guessing the extent of interest group and mass party organization is to review the early voting studies of the mid-to-late 1940s and monographs on labor's political involvement in that period. This survey suggests either a very narrow scope for mass forms in earlier years or a great fragility, inasmuch as they seem so weak by the 1940s. Michigan is an exception, but apparently an exception built after 1935–37 rather than at that time. See Paul F. Lazarsfeld et al., *The People's Choice* (New York: Columbia University Press, 1948); Fay Calkins, *The CIO and the Democratic Party* (Chicago: University of Chicago Press, 1952).

state or national positions.[134] Direct public political leadership by labor was uncommon in city and state politics, as even the struggles of 1935–36 left many localities without major unionization.

Nor was a top-down route to a labor party open, as the Democratic party had no interest in becoming one. Even Progressive currents in the Democratic party who agreed programmatically with labor had little interest in transforming relations of organizational power at the national level. The labor movement's key political linkages were with parts of the administration and trusted congressional allies. In these relations, the labor movement had considerable influence and little direct decision-making power. It had access to Roosevelt and top administration officials, but never had veto power over major administration choices.[135]

Nonetheless, the political power of the labor movement grew as the state expanded. Prolabor forces built new state agencies in order to realize a Progressive political vision. Thus in 1936 and 1937, Progressive liberals on the NLRB and the La Follette Civil Liberties Committee worked closely with the CIO and parts of the AFL, encouraging the organization of new unions and making a political and legal case for their legitimacy.[136] In these efforts, which gained support from broader circles within the administration and Congress and among liberal professionals, a powerful political identity was both constructed and articulated. This identity fused Progressive commitments with a new (partisan) political choice and linked notions of effective state management and responsible performance of professional obligation to a substantive reform vision.

At the same time, the substantial political power of the labor movement made it a pillar of the new order in 1936–37—even before the new unions were firmly established. The formation of this movement required sustained popular mobilization and a split among prior union leaders. With a leadership bloc drawn from parts of the AFL, the political left, and previously unorganized industrial groups, the new labor movement had as a primary political objective the securing of state intervention to compel unwilling employers to recognize unions. When the labor movement fought for this aim, it signified a fight to

134. Local and especially state administrations were often unsympathetic to labor after 1936, even in places where labor's political efforts had been very important for the presidential campaign. National-level arrangements were crucial in shielding labor from local administrations. See James T. Patterson, *The New Deal and the States: Federalism in Transition* (Princeton: Princeton University Press, 1969), 125.

135. When Lewis and others pressed Roosevelt on patronage issues after the 1936 election, expecting something in return for their support, they were generally disappointed by the result (Report of meeting, Lewis et al. with Roosevelt, n.d., 1937, Official Folder 2251—Labor's Non-Partisan League, Roosevelt Papers, FDR Library).

136. This cooperation is discussed in Auerbach, *Labor and Liberty*, 75–120. It is also apparent in the first yearly reports of the NLRB which read, at great length, like energetic briefs against employers for obstructing unionization. See especially the sections entitled "Principles Established," in Second Annual Report of the National Labor Relations Board (Washington: U.S. Government Printing Office, 1937), 58–156; and Third Annual Report of the National Labor Relations Board (Washington: U.S. Government Printing Office, 1938), 51–215.

extend effective citizenship rights to wide sections of the working class. This entailed important political shifts as well as major changes in how production was organized and carried out. The secure establishment of unions required a massive redeployment of coercion away from conventional antiunion and antipopular practices, aimed at achieving an equity whose future was uncertain. As labor helped build a new political order, it was in turn constructed as a powerful political force.

ANDREW J. POLSKY
Hunter College, CUNY

The Odyssey of the Juvenile Court: Policy Failure and Institutional Persistence in the Therapeutic State

The human services have come to occupy a vital position in the modern welfare state, penetrating nearly all its activities and institutions. Beyond providing a minimum level of support, these services seek to restructure the behavior of their clients so they can better cope with the demands and challenges of modern life. To realize this goal social personnel employ an approach that can most accurately be defined as therapeutic: the situation of the client is viewed as a condition that must be diagnosed; the caseworker establishes a helping relationship; a suitable treatment plan is designed and implemented. Although the middle class voluntarily avails itself of therapeutic services, public intervention by social personnel has a distinctly lower-class bias and an authoritarian character. The middle class purchases therapeutic services from private providers. The state focuses on marginal populations and its subjects usually have no choice about assuming a client status.

As an object of analysis, the therapeutic state sector remains elusive. Its programmatic strongholds are easy enough to list: the juvenile courts, public assistance to families with dependent children, veterans' services, drug treatment centers, community mental health clinics, and child abuse agencies. But these organizations do not constitute a visibly integrated system. Just as important, no common dialogue binds together all the practitioners of the therapeu-

This article began as a paper presented at the 1986 meeting of the American Political Science Association. I would like to thank Theda Skocpol, Francis Fox Piven, George Curtis, and John Drew for their comments on that paper. Stephen Skowronek and Karen Orren guided me through the revision process, and I was further aided by the suggestions of an anonymous referee who reviewed an earlier draft. I was ably assisted in my research by three Hunter College students, Jenelline Connors, Lionel Francois, and Andrea Lewis. I received a grant from the Professional Staff Congress-City University Faculty Research Award Program to help support the writing of this article.

tic approach. Juvenile justice, for example, forms a discrete policy field, and those who participate in the ongoing debates about court-sponsored treatment rarely communicate with those outside their own narrow circle. With programs so fragmented and policy analysis so specialized, we readily lose sight of the whole.

The problem of identifying the therapeutic sector has not prevented us from recognizing that something has gone drastically awry in the human services. Social personnel find themselves everywhere on the defensive, and their dismal record cannot be explained away entirely by pointing to insufficient resources. A lack of funds does not account for the client opposition to tutelary oversight, the movement to restore clients' formal legal rights, the bungled cases of probation and child abuse prevention, or the inability of social agencies to reliably predict or modify behavior. Clearly the therapeutic approach has not yet delivered on its promise.

The central question raised by the therapeutic state sector is why its institutions persist, even thrive, in the face of manifest policy failure. For all the disappointments, the therapeutic apparatus has not only endured but proliferated. Instead of a dismantling of agencies and programs, policy failure has produced more therapeutic institutions. When social personnel have grown disenchanted with a particular line of therapeutic activity or when a given set of institutions no longer suits their purposes, they have embarked upon a relentless quest for new casework techniques and for the creation of new institutions in which to apply their basic techniques afresh. The therapeutic sector has expanded in the face of failure, adding incoherence to ineffectiveness.

OVERVIEW: DISCOURSE AND POLITICS IN THE JUVENILE COURT

To explore the peculiar development of the therapeutic state, I will examine historically one of its pivotal institutions, the juvenile court. The court was the first innovation in public tutelage, and it has proven an enduring experiment. Durability notwithstanding, the court has had a troubled history and has been vilified by social personnel themselves as one of their outstanding disappointments. We do not want for critical historical treatments of the court. The studies by Sanford Fox, David Rothman, Ellen Ryerson, Anthony Platt, and Steven Schlossman are important to any understanding of the institution's development.[1] These accounts, however, prove inadequate when we confront the puzzle posed above. They capture the mix of bold promise and acute failure that infuses the court's history, but by focusing their attention on the

---

1. See Sanford J. Fox, "Juvenile Justice Reform: An Historical Perspective," *Stanford Law Review* 22 (June 1970): 1187–1239; David J. Rothman, *Conscience and Convenience: The Asylum and its Alternatives in Progressive America* (Boston: Little, Brown, 1980); Ellen Ryerson, *The Best-Laid Plans: America's Juvenile Court Experiment* (New York: Hill and Wang, 1978); Anthony M. Platt, *The Child Savers: The Invention of Delinquency*, 2d ed. (Chicago: University of Chicago Press, 1977); Steven L. Schlossman, *Love and the American Delinquent: The Theory and Practice of "Progressive" Juvenile Justice, 1825–1920* (Chicago: University of Chicago Press, 1977).

relationship between the court and certain legal and correctional antecedents, they fail to situate the court in the broader context of the growth of the therapeutic apparatus. More important, the historians take the survival of the court as a given. They move from its founding era to the most recent reforms, with precious little to say about the forces that keep alive a notoriously ineffective institution. To understand the history of the juvenile court as but one aspect of the development of the human services in the American state and to penetrate the mystery of its persistence, we need an analytic framework that is wider and more fully articulated than those now available to us.

The work of Michel Foucault and Jacques Donzelot on the role of "discursive movements" provides a useful point of departure. Foucault argues that new ways of perceiving social conditions often give rise to new forms of knowledge and then to various small-scale efforts to put that knowledge to use. Although the practitioners of an emerging discipline are but loosely organized, they share a preoccupation with their technique and an imperial conception of their role in society. In this sense they constitute a movement. These discursive movements, determined to realize the instrumental potential implicit in their new knowledge base, seek ultimately to refashion the public exercise of power to reflect their specific methods and objectives.[2] Building upon this formulation, Donzelot has shown how the evolution of modern family life reflects the impact of various lines of discursive activity. Discursive movements have implicated the family in a new sphere of services that embraces all classes and transcends public-private distinctions, a sphere he calls the "social." Public human services can best be understood, he says, as the form of therapeutic intervention designed to normalize certain population groups: here current bourgeois standards of well-adjusted family life are imposed by social personnel upon working-class and other marginal subjects.[3]

Unfortunately, the practical value of the discursive approach has been lessened by the failure to distinguish the particular role that the state plays in shaping the impact of discursive forces. Donzelot exemplifies the problem of emphasizing discursive influences without attention to the independent significance of political factors. With his sweeping notion of the social, he can suggest ways in which the normalizing enterprise of therapeutic intervention has penetrated the whole of society. But by erasing the line between private and public, he loses any sense of the state as an autonomous arena with its own history, a past that will condition the exercise of its normalizing powers.

My approach draws upon the insights of Foucault and Donzelot, but also considers the role of politics in creating a new state sector. Recent studies of the politics of state building argue that new forms of state organization emerge from the friction between political entrepreneurs who want to promote innova-

2. See especially Michel Foucault, *Power/Knowledge: Selected Interviews and Other Writings, 1972–1977*, edited by Colin Gordon (New York: Pantheon, 1980).

3. Jacques Donzelot, *The Policing of Families* (New York: Pantheon, 1979), esp. pp. xxv–xxvi. Donzelot is the one historian who has situated the juvenile court in the larger therapeutic apparatus.

tions in response to external pressures and established public structures that resist and contain change.[4] Pursuing this line of analysis for the therapeutic state means treating the introduction of normalizing human services as another exercise in state building within an established political system. Governing institutions had to be bent under pressure from policy entrepreneurs to accommodate an additional functional responsibility—assisting those on the margin of the political order to achieve a well adjusted life-style. The results were unforeseen and profoundly disappointing.

In focusing upon both discursive and political forces, we need to distinguish carefully between them. Discursive movements define policy approaches and also seek to shape institutions. With power and legitimacy at stake, friction between these movements seems inevitable. Where such a collision occurs within a particular institutional setting, I treat it under the heading of a "discursive conflict" rather than a political one. This usage, I suggest, keeps our gaze fixed upon the true basis of the battle over institutional development, which lies in contrary intellectual orientations toward the constitution of power, its exercise, and the goals for which it ought to be employed. I use the term politics to refer to the extra-institutional circumstances with which a given therapeutic agency must reckon. Political factors condition the strategic resources available to discursive movements over time.

This two-pronged approach will allow us to examine several propositions about the emergence and persistence of the therapeutic state. To put the evolution of public human services in broad terms, public tutelage was inspired by a new discursive enthusiasm and then buffeted by discursive and political conflicts that worked both to sustain the therapeutic apparatus and to subvert its coherence. We can best grasp the logic behind the invention and later elaboration of the tutelary state if we direct our attention first to the discursive movement that defined for public social personnel their distinct mission and method. We shall see that when their method has faltered in practice, especially in the face of opposition within their own institutions or because their approach worked poorly, they have looked again and again to their discursive foundations for the solution. Their intellectual commitment therefore helps explain the tenacity of the therapeutic apparatus. At the same time, the fate of public tutelage as a discursive enterprise always has reflected the pervasive impact of politics. Although human services brought the state into a new field, the therapeutic apparatus was laid atop a functioning political order. Hence, the design for a normalizing state set forth by discursive actors has had to pass through an external terrain defined by established public institutions, policy entrepreneurs with their own agendas, partisan politicians, fickle public opinion, and the press. As discursive actors came to appreciate that they must function in a broader political environment, they learned to use their institutional positions strategically. The interaction of discursive and political conflict fostered the expansion of public tutelage and explain its tenacity.

4. See, for example, Stephen Skowronek, *Building a New American State: The Expansion of National Administrative Capacities, 1877–1920* (New York: Cambridge University Press, 1982); John Mollenkopf, *The Contested City* (Princeton: Princeton University Press, 1983).

The juvenile court provides a concrete case through which we can elaborate this line of analysis. Because the court stands at the border of the therapeutic sector, with close links to the legal system, discursive conflict was inevitable. The court's particular clientele and the fragmented political system in which the institution is situated also made it a center of political conflict.

I make three claims about the place of the juvenile court in the therapeutic sector and about the institution's durability. First, the invention of the court reflected the influence of a discursive movement composed of philanthropic cadre, social scientists, and reformers. Entrepreneurial judges made an important contribution to the progress of the court, but the institution took its distinctive shape from tutelary doctrine rather than juridical or penal forerunners. The discursive movement set tasks for itself that required a union with the state. As the embodiment of that union, the juvenile court presumed, in its very conception, that therapeutic means and public authority could reinforce each other to normalize marginal children and their families.

Second, the presence of an alternative discourse within the new institution set the stage for internal conflict and led ultimately to the political disputes that fragmented child protection efforts. With the juvenile court's other participants oriented toward the discursive tradition of the law, the new institution proved unable to commit itself unequivocally to the therapeutic approach. To establish their hegemony over this inhospitable setting, social personnel first pursued a discursive strategy—they sought to improve their knowledge base. When that effort failed, they adopted a political strategy and created competing agencies that might normalize children and circumvent judicial intervention. The results ultimately destroyed the possibility of policy coherence in the field of child protection.

Third, the juvenile court, through the discursive and political adaptability of its leading players, has withstood all attempts to dislodge it from its position in handling problem juveniles. Although social personnel had abandoned the court as ill suited to their purposes, they had bestowed upon its judges a justification for the institution's existence and procedures. Judges have learned to use that justification to ward off calls for reform or dissolution emanating from the legal profession. A new discursive conflict has swept over the institution since the 1950s, as judges and their legal critics have differed over the place of formal legal rights within the courtroom. Ironically, the therapeutic logic that the court consistently failed to put into practice now has been transmuted into a rhetorical resource that permits the institution to deflect the due process challenge: in this dispute the judges have harked back to Progressive therapeutic discourse for principles that justify their broad discretion in juvenile court proceedings. Meanwhile, on the external front, the court has generated resources that bolster its position in contemporary politics. As social personnel have established new normalizing agencies outside the court, it has been compelled to negotiate a path through a cluttered and confused policy field. Yet much to the frustration of its opponents, the court has succeeded in developing the political resources to remain the focal point of services for children in trouble or in need. Amid a fragmented array of child protection groups the juvenile court prospers—a tutelary instrument that no one believes can adjust its clients, yet one so dominant in its field that further innovation has been effectively inhibited.

PHILANTHROPY AND THE DEVELOPMENT OF THE THERAPEUTIC AGENDA

Philanthropy emerged during the nineteenth century as a class-based response to the changes in American society. Bourgeois social reformers and charity operatives voiced alarm over the social dislocations caused by rapid capitalist development. The spread of urban-capitalist social forms, it was held, led to instability in working-class families, weakened individual morality, and prompted working people to form dangerous labor and political organizations. Of particular concern was the fact that contact between elites and lower social ranks had been reduced. This gap drew close attention because community notables still subscribed to a preindustrial ideal of a moral economy in which elites were to exercise stewardship over the behavior and values of the entire community. By overseeing the conduct and welfare of their inferiors, reformers believed they could forge social bonds that would bridge any class divisions.[5] The "social question" emerged out of this vision of the moral economy and the threat that urban slums and factories posed to it: in the face of social conditions that eroded the traditional sources of order, how might the moral decay of the urban working class be stemmed and class conflict thus be averted? The working-class family was identified as the point of contagion, and philanthropists determined to make it the vehicle for the regeneration of morals.

In the second half of the nineteenth century, they devised a strategy to erect moral barriers around this family unit. On one side, since the family plainly had been weakened by its surroundings—dense slums and overcrowded tenements—its environment had to be sanitized. Dangerous urban conditions prompted a series of philanthropic efforts that might be grouped together under the heading "social hygiene." These included sanitation improvements, the promotion of urban parks, and private initiatives to construct model tenements.[6] But moral decay could not be arrested, philanthropists maintained, unless the victims themselves became the direct target of moralizing influence. Thus, on the other side, the autonomy of the working-class family was chal-

5. See Paul D. Boyer, *Urban Masses and Moral Order in America, 1820–1920* (Cambridge: Harvard University Press, 1978). For a vivid and influential contemporary statement, see Charles Loring Brace, *The Dangerous Classes of New York and Twenty Years Work among Them* (New York: Wynkoop and Hallenbeck, 1872).

6. On sanitation, see Robert H. Bremner, *The Public Good: Philanthropy and Welfare in the Civil War Era* (New York: Alfred A. Knopf, 1980), 34; Sam Bass Warner, *The Private City: Philadelphia in Three Periods of Its Growth* (Philadelphia: University of Pennsylvania Press, 1968, 1971). On public parks. see Frederick Law Olmsted, "Public Parks and the Enlargement of Towns," *Journal of Social Science* 3 (1871): 17, 20; Thomas Bender, *Toward an Urban Vision: Ideas and Institutions in Nineteenth Century America* (Lexington: University Press of Kentucky, 1975), 169, 172, 176–77. On social housing, see Roy Lubove, "The New York Association for Improving the Condition of the Poor: The Formative Years," *New York Historical Society Quarterly* 43 (July 1959): 321–22.

lenged and its members were exposed to genteel intervention designed to teach them to conform to bourgeois norms. Because the children appeared most vulnerable, this line of philanthropic activity took as one of its objectives child protection. Groups like the children's aid societies tried to shield children from urban street life by placing them out in rural communities or by creating industrial training schools. Later, private organizations waged campaigns against juvenile vagrancy and street begging.[7] At the same time, philanthropy tried to correct what it saw as the indifferent attitude of working-class adults toward wage labor and thrift. Private charity organization societies sent women volunteers, "friendly visitors," into the homes of relief applicants to investigate the circumstances that lay beneath their poverty and to instill the resolve needed to overcome it. Philanthropic relief thereby tried to project itself deeply into the working-class family so as to moralize it from within.[8]

As each of these lines of activity intersected with public authority, philanthropy generated its own ideal of the state. Preservation of the working-class family, especially its moral integrity in bourgeois terms, became the standard by which to judge the appropriateness of public intervention. Where the threat to the family could be neutralized only by authoritative action, philanthropy did not hesitate to seek state support. Many social hygiene measures, for example, depended upon the exercise of eminent domain. By contrast, where public involvement was seen to imperil both the working-class family and the liberal social constitution, philanthropy fought to circumscribe public responsibility.[9] We find this position best expressed in the struggle that philanthropy waged in the 1870s against public outdoor relief. In the view of philanthropic relief leaders, the distribution of aid by a public department dominated by a local political machine threatened a chain of disasters: if the working-class family received relief as a political inducement, it would lose sight of the flaws within itself that reduced it to poverty; the heavy burden of poverty could bankrupt the public treasury; and the easy availability of relief could compromise the integrity of the system of wage labor. Philanthropic groups therefore joined with antimachine political elements to contain the public relief menace, a drive that succeeded in New York and several other eastern cities in the late 1870s. Control over relief activities was returned in part to private hands.[10] In Gilded Age philanthropic discourse, therefore, the state emerged with a new combination of duties and limits. Degrading conditions called for the most vigorous

7. Brace, *Dangerous Classes of New York*, 90–93, 234–35; Bender, *Toward an Urban Vision*, 133–35, 143–44, 147–48; Joseph M. Hawes, *Children in Urban Society: Juvenile Delinquency in Nineteenth Century America* (New York: Oxford University Press, 1971), chap. 8.

8. Walter I. Trattner, *From Poor Law to Welfare State: A History of Social Welfare in America*, 2d ed. (New York: Free Press, 1979), 80–85; Roy Lubove, *The Professional Altruist: The Emergence of Social Work as a Profession, 1880–1930* (1965; reprint, New York: Atheneum, 1980), chap. 3; Boyer, *Urban Masses and Moral Order*, 144–52; Robert H. Bremner, *From the Depths: The Discovery of Poverty in the United States* (New York: New York University Press, 1956, 1972), 17, 51–52; Donzelot, *Policing of Families*, 55, 64–65, 69.

9. See Donzelot, *Policing of Families*, 55.

10. Blanche D. Coll, *Perspectives in Public Welfare: A History* (Washington, D.C.: U.S. Department of Health, Education, and Welfare, 1969), 43–44; Bremner, *Public Good*, 200–01.

public measures, even at the risk of conflict with those required to bear the financial cost. But direct subsidies to the working-class family were prohibited, lest the market economy and its system of wage labor be fatally compromised.

This philanthropic conception of the state invited an expansion of public efforts on behalf of working-class children. Hoping to shield children from a destructive urban-industrial environment, philanthropic organizations reached across class lines to form an alliance with labor on behalf of child labor laws and compulsory school laws. While pressing for some legislation, however, child protection groups developed much more sustained ties with the judiciary. They often found themselves in conflict with the family and learned early the value of public authority as a wedge against obstructive parents. The courts were called upon by child-placing agencies that wished to secure guardianship of a minor placed at risk through parental neglect or exploitation. When societies to prevent cruelty to children appeared in the 1880s, they also used the judiciary to press charges against the parents of youngsters found begging.[11] Still, a note of caution characterized these philanthropic appeals to the courts; judicial intervention followed only a clear demonstration of degraded behavior by the child or his parents.

Despite the practical achievements of nineteenth-century philanthropy, the premises upon which it rested were called into question by its Progressive heirs. Philanthropic ideology had linked most social problems to the moral unfitness of the working-class family. But in the 1890s, amidst a serious economic depression, the charity organization field staff and the residents of the new settlement houses discovered that the mass of unemployed workers were generally of sound character.[12] Poverty was now traced to the instabilities of the industrial economy. Even the pathologies of working-class life, still a philanthropic concern, were seen to be a product of destructive social arrangements.[13] With attention fixed on the social roots of poverty, the condition of its victims raised for Progressive philanthropy a matter of justice rather than charity. That society denied many of its members the bare minimum they needed for an adequate standard of living was seen as a violation of their fundamental democratic rights.[14]

11. Fox, "Juvenile Justice Reform," 1226–27; Hawes, *Children in Urban Society*, 132–33, 139.

12. Boyer, *Urban Masses and Moral Order*, 154–55; Jane Addams, *Twenty Years at Hull House* (1910; reprint, New York: New American Library, 1961), 162; John Graham Brooks, "The Future Problem of Charity and the Unemployed," *Annals of the American Academy of Political and Social Science* (cited hereafter as *Annals*) 5 (1894): 11–12.

13. Edward T. Devine, *Misery and Its Causes* (New York: Macmillan, 1909), 11, 13–14; Lee K. Frankel, "The Relation between Standards of Living and Standards of Compensation," New York State Conference on Charities and Corrections (cited hereafter as NYSCCC), *Proceedings* 7 (1906), 23, 30; Mary Kingsbury Simkhovitch, "Friendship and Politics," *Political Science Quarterly* 17 (June 1902).

14. John A. Ryan, "The Standard of Living and the Problem of Dependency," National Conference of Charities and Corrections (cited hereafter as NCCC), *Proceedings* 34 (1907), 343; Mary Kingsbury Simkhovitch, *The City Worker's World in America* (1917; reprint, New York: Arno, 1971), 20, 48–49, 170–71, 176.

Just the same, while Progressive philanthropy rejected the earlier moralizing posture, the problems it defined for itself bore a familiar imprint. The social question was not forgotten, of course, but merely rephrased in the new jargon of social science: how could the elements of an interdependent society be brought into functional harmony, how could individuals be protected from unseen social forces, and how could class antagonisms be contained? And, as before, philanthropy situated the working-class family at the center of its analysis. The family suffered from maladjustment; it coped poorly with the conditions in which it found itself, from poor housing to low wages. It was entitled therefore to make a claim for support upon the larger community.[15]

The strategic approach that followed also drew upon previous philanthropic endeavors. First, to reshape the destructive slum environment, social hygiene was revived and expanded. Joining with organized labor and the public administration movement, philanthropic elements pressed for broad-gauged laws like strict building codes and social programs that would benefit all working people.[16] Measures to create a secure space for children, off the streets and outside the factories, drew strong support.[17] But the social hygiene effort operated on a level too general to reverse the pathologies that infected a given family unit—its demoralization, low values, and inability to cope with the demands placed upon it. The working-class family, long regarded as unfit, was now deemed incompetent and therefore still in need of close philanthropic attention. Hence the second item on Progressive philanthropy's agenda became direct intervention in the family to repair its internal workings and give it the capacity to sustain its burdens.

Charity workers, settlement house residents, and other philanthropic cadre refined the casework techniques inherited from private relief to develop a rigorous model for family rehabilitation. The condition of the working-class family was viewed as something akin to a disease, requiring intervention patterned after that employed by modern medicine. As the critical first step, an outside agent established a personal relationship with the members of the family. This allowed her to prepare a specific diagnosis of their condition, to devise a suitable remedial plan, and to gain their support for the therapeutic program of domestic tutelage that she next introduced.[18] (Use of the female

15. On the new version of the social question, see especially works in the social gospel tradition such as Washington Gladden, *Social Salvation* (Boston and New York: Houghton, Mifflin, 1902). On society's obligation to aid the working-class family, see Edward T. Devine, *The Principles of Relief* (New York: Macmillan, 1904), 21; Jane Addams, "Charity and Social Justice," President's Address, NCCC, *Proceedings* 33 (1906, 2d ed.), 2–3; Mary E. Richmond, *Friendly Visiting among the Poor: A Handbook for Charity Workers* (1899; reprint, Montclair, N.J.: Patterson Smith, 1969), 141.

16. On the reform coalition, see Martin J. Schiesel, *The Politics of Efficiency: Municipal Administration and Reform in America, 1880–1920* (Berkeley: University of California Press, 1977). On philanthropy's commitment to social hygiene measures, see Devine, *Principles of Relief*, 36–39, 42, 46, 69.

17. See Platt, *Child Savers*, 99; Donzelot, *Policing of Families*, 82–83.

18. Jane Addams, "The Objective Value of a Social Settlement" (1892), in Christopher Lasch, ed., *The Social Thought of Jane Addams* (Indianapolis: Bobbs-Merrill, 1965) (cited hereafter as *Social Thought*), pp. 57, 61; Richmond, *Friendly Visiting among the Poor*, chap. 11.

pronoun is apt here, given that most of the first caseworkers were women from bourgeois backgrounds who were drawn to this activity as an acceptable alternative to domesticity.) If family mores and behavior seemed "functional"—that is, they contributed to the adjustment process—she reinforced them. But tutelage also served to discredit customs rendered obsolete by modern living conditions and to implant the latest bourgeois household management techniques.[19] Furthermore, to prevent any relapse into the old ways, the caseworker tried to link the family permanently to outside agencies.[20]

Although charity practices had provided some basis for therapeutic intervention, the model formulated by Progressive philanthropy represented an extraordinary accomplishment. The therapeutic design—contact, diagnosis, normalizing measures, and continued oversight—went far beyond anything previously attempted. In this ambitious design Progressive philanthropy established the pattern for modern human services. More than that, the therapeutic approach suggested the possibility of vast power, at once subversive and constitutive. The caseworker selectively destroyed the family's behavioral patterns, even its cultural heritage, and then provided the substitute skills her clients needed to cope with their surroundings. She particularly sought to make use of the gender bond between her and the mother to overcome any resistance grounded in the breadwinner's determination to assert his sovereignty over the family. If all went as planned, the working-class family emerged from the program with a thoroughly reordered life style. Educative measures might give the father a more positive attitude toward his job or employment prospects, modernize the mother's practice of the domestic arts and household budgeting, and prepare the children for their future role in the work force or the home.[21]

In her project of family rehabilitation, the therapeutic caseworker made far greater use of scientific knowledge than had her charity predecessor. The working-class family could master its situation only by calling on the intellectual tools appropriate to a complex society. Problems of everyday life no longer lent themselves to solution by folk wisdom; they instead required the application of domestic science, child psychology, and other new disciplines.[22] Since the family lacked scientific information, the caseworker had to function as a social technician, applying the latest findings in a practical setting. By giving her the means to raise the quality of family relations or to enhance an individual's

19. Robert A. Woods, "Social Work: A New Profession" (1906), in Woods, *The Neighborhood in Nation-Building* (1923; reprint, New York: Arno Press, 1970) (cited hereafter as *NNB*), 93–94; Robert A. Woods and Albert J. Kennedy, *The Settlement Horizon: A National Estimate* (New York: Russell Sage Foundation, 1922), 143–50; Ellen H. Richards, *Euthenics: The Science of Controllable Environment* (1910; reprint, New York: Arno Press, 1977), chap. 2.

20. Woods and Kennedy, *Settlement Horizon*, 311; Jane Addams, *The Spirit of Youth and the City Streets* (1909; reprint, Urbana: University of Illinois Press, 1972), 47.

21. Addams, *Twenty Years at Hull House*, 208–09; Lilian D. Wald, *The House on Henry Street* (New York: Henry Holt, 1915), 55–58; Woods and Kennedy, *Settlement Horizon*, 241, 250–51, 256; Simkhovitch, *City Worker's World*, 157.

22. Sheila M. Rothman, *Woman's Proper Place: A History of Changing Ideals and Practices, 1870 to the Present* (New York: Basic Books, 1978), chap. 3.

capacity to function in the modern world, expertise became a crucial power resource.[23] It also served to ease her path into the home. Unlike the friendly visitor, the caseworker rejected moral judgments in favor of neutral diagnoses and offered advice based upon demonstrable scientific propositions that clients could readily see to be in their own interest.[24]

To legitimize its growing commitment to normalizing technology, philanthropy expanded upon its definition of the social living standard. Charity personnel and domestic science experts asserted that an adequate standard should include not just material goods but also a well-ordered domestic life.[25] Only a program of tutelage could enhance the family's capacity to meet the full range of its members' psychic needs. Over time, casework intervention created a basis upon which might be realized a decent standard of living, in the modern bourgeois understanding.[26] And since the living standard was treated as a matter of right rather than charity, therapeutic services became a basic component in the philanthropic conception of civic duty. The working-class family was entitled to be free of domestic pathologies, and if it was unable to master its own deficiencies, the community was obligated to provide the appropriate adjustment support.[27]

A further implication of the living standard principle did not escape philanthropy's notice: if aid and tutelage failed to normalize the marginal family, disciplinary steps were entirely justified. With enhanced social rights for the impoverished and incompetent came reciprocal obligations. A community that offered many benefits to the working-class family could insist that the recipients uphold conventional behavioral norms.[28] If the family refused to conform, it should be subject to sanctions. Those who did not attain the behavioral standard set by the community, it was suggested, ought to be placed under restrictive control.[29] Thus in the hands of philanthropy the living standard principle proved to be highly versatile: first a liberating vision of society's material obligation to the laboring masses, then an argument for an elaborate therapeutic program, and finally the basis for coercive measures against any family that defied normalization.

Pursuit of the tutelary agenda quickly revealed the inadequacy of voluntary methods and forced philanthropists to seek a broader base of support. To begin with, in an era before rationalized fund-raising through community

23. Foucault, *Power/Knowledge*, 52, 119.

24. Lubove, *Professional Altruist*, 34–35; Donzelot, *Policing of Families*, 167.

25. Devine, *Principles of Relief*, 10–11; Edward T. Devine, "Remedies for Too Low a Standard of Living," NYSCCC, *Proceedings* 9 (1908), 63; Samuel G. Smith, "Social Standards," President's Address, NCCC, *Proceedings* 32 (1905), 8.

26. Thomas J. Riley, "A Sociological View of Poverty," NYSCCC, *Proceedings* 14 (1913), 187; Samuel H. Bishop, "The New Movement in Charity," NYSCCC, *Proceedings* 2 (1901), 91; Richmond, *Friendly Visiting among the Poor*, 6, 8–9, 191–93.

27. Simkhovitch, *City Worker's World*, 19–20.

28. Devine, *Principles of Relief*, 19, 22–23.

29. Frank A. Fetter in "Discussion of 'Ethics of Too Low a Standard of Living,'" NYSCCC, *Proceedings* 9 (1908), 62. See also Brooks, "Future Problem of Charity and the Unemployed," 24, 27.

chests, private agencies obtained only meager subsidies from middle-class and corporate donors. Therefore only a small fraction of those in distress could be reached, especially in times of economic crisis.[30] Experience with hostile or suspicious families also persuaded field staff of the need for some greater enforcement power to back the caseworker's approach to the home. Visiting nurses, for example, found that, lacking official status, they could not gain entry to many tenement apartments.[31] And despite the proliferation of service agencies like settlement houses, many marginal families still eluded the reach of the normalizing apparatus or kept it at arm's length.[32] Philanthropy soon recognized that its mission required the cooperation of the state. For only the public sector commanded sufficient fiscal resources and possessed the potent legal tools needed to embrace all marginal families in the therapeutic project.[33]

The methodological innovations of this discursive movement and its determination to put its new kind of knowledge to work on a large scale had set the stage for development of a therapeutic state sector. But before the state might be so employed, the limits that philanthropy itself had been trying to impose upon public action would have to be transcended. In the name of family preservation, philanthropy had struggled to confine state involvement on such matters as outdoor relief. Public officials, it had long been argued, showed no aptitude for casework methods and were indifferent to the consequences of government subsidies. Even in the Progressive Era philanthropists worried that the state lacked the capacity to do effective casework.[34] Only as an adjunct to child protection work had public authority been enlisted constructively in philanthropic remedial efforts.

It was necessary, therefore, to equip the state for effective therapeutic service. Philanthropic methods and principles would have to be made the basis for new or remodeled public organizations. To these organizations philanthropy would transfer the normalizing technology it had so carefully developed in its own field laboratories. Moreover, since public agencies had no competent social personnel of their own, experienced philanthropic cadre would themselves function as the first public caseworkers. Their direct participation best ensured that the state would understand its expanded mission—to sustain the standard of adjustment for the working-class family.[35]

---

30. Robert A. Woods, ed., *Americans in Process: A Settlement Study* (Boston: Houghton, Mifflin, 1902), 7; Addams, *Twenty Years at Hull House*, 219; Mrs. William [Hannah B.] Einstein, "Pensions for Widowed Mothers as a Means of Securing for Dependent Children the Benefits of Home Training and Influence," NYSCCC, *Proceedings* 11 (1910), 225.

31. Wald, *House on Henry Street*, 44; Addams, *Twenty Years at Hull House*, 146, 211–212.

32. William I. Cole, *Motives and Results of the Social Settlement Movement* (Cambridge: Harvard University Department of Social Ethics, 1908), 16; Simkhovitch, *City Worker's World*, 67.

33. Robert A. Woods, ed., *The City Wilderness* (Boston: Houghton, Mifflin, 1899), 290–304; Robert A. Woods, "Settlement Houses and City Politics" (1900) *NNB*, 68; Addams, *Twenty Years at Hull House*, 238.

34. Mary Conyngton, *How to Help: A Manual of Practical Charity* (New York: Macmillan, 1909), 192–93; Frederic Almy in "Discussion of 'Pensions to Widowed Mothers as a Means,'" NYSCCC, *Proceedings* 11 (1910), 232, 234.

35. Wald, *House on Henry Street*, 60, 261; Jane Addams, "A Function of the Social Settlement" (1899) *Social Thought*, 197; Einstein, "Pensions for Widowed Mothers as a Means," 231.

JUDICIAL TUTELAGE: THE IDEAL AND EARLY
PRACTICE OF THE JUVENILE COURT

The first attempt to join the normalizing technology developed by philanthropy to public authority came with the invention of the juvenile court. Most historical studies of the court properly stress that it was a radical departure in jurisprudence, intended to alter fundamentally the terms of judicial intervention in the life of problem juveniles. But the point should be pushed further. The new institution occupied a shadowy ground between legal tribunal and social agency. In its scope, proponents hoped, the court would reach beyond offenders to any child who might be deemed maladjusted. It would then treat the child and his family with the most advanced therapeutic methods. Normalizing intervention backed by the court promised results far superior to those attained by private child-protection groups. Beyond this striking reconfiguration of the judicial role, we also find the court at the center of an emerging therapeutic sector. As other public human services soon began to appear, court proponents saw that judicial tutelage would be able to enlist a range of adjustment tools to surround its clients with corrective influences. Court enthusiasts imagined that the results would amount to a fundamental reordering of the tie between the state and its most marginal citizens.

The campaign to reorient juvenile justice to the therapeutic approach began in the early 1890s, well before any other philanthropic efforts to enlist the state in a tutelary alliance. For two decades or more, as we have observed, philanthropic groups and courts had cooperated closely in child protection. Probation experiments in Massachusetts made use of philanthropic volunteers, private field agents in several cities reported to the judge on a child's background prior to disposition, and sectarian child-placing agencies relied heavily on judicial authority.[36] Amidst the Progressive agitation on behalf of children exposed to slum conditions, it was only natural to build upon the working relationship that already linked philanthropy with some courts. A coalition of reform-minded judges, women's clubs, and sectarian placement agencies formed to redefine the judicial processing of cases that involved children.[37]

Through this court-philanthropy axis, the juvenile court emerged in 1899 to join judicial intervention to the therapeutic model. Jurists strained to find a coherent legal basis for the new institution, but the court clearly owed more to the discourse of the human services than to traditional jurisprudence.[38] Although the court incorporated earlier judicial innovations, its proponents

36. Ryerson, *Best-Laid Plans*, 19–20; Thomas D. Eliot, *The Juvenile Court and the Community* (New York: Macmillan, 1914), 122–24.

37. The dynamics of this coalition were explored some years later by its participants. See the various essays in Jane Addams et al., *The Child, the Clinic and the Court* (1925; reprint, New York: Johnson Reprint Corp., 1970). Fox overstates the role of sectarian child protection organizations in producing the 1899 Illinois Juvenile Court Act and misunderstands its emphasis when he claims it was primarily intended to upgrade institutional conditions. See Fox, "Juvenile Justice Reform," 1222–23, 1226–27. For a more balanced account based on the Wisconsin experience, see Schlossman, *Love and the American Delinquent*, 133–37.

38. On the legal rationales for the court, see Schlossman, *Love and the American Delinquent*, chap. 1; Bernard Flexner, "The Juvenile Court—Its Legal Aspects," *Annals* 36 (1910): 51–52.

correctly understood that it was not merely an incremental step to unify judicial child protection. Linking a court apparatus to philanthropy's larger tutelary project represented a great leap beyond the established judicial role into the exercise of the new therapeutic power under state auspices.[39]

That a therapeutic commitment guided the juvenile court movement can be seen first in its ideal conception of the institution's jurisdiction. The new court claimed an open-ended mandate. All dangerous or endangered minors were to be brought by the juvenile court within reach of child-protection agencies. It thus would become an essential point of support for the social technicians determined to excise the pathologies of working-class family life.[40] By including in the court's domain conduct that would not be criminal if committed by an adult, social personnel would be able to address a situation in its earliest stages and thereby prevent more serious damage to the child.[41]

The therapeutic orientation, according to the movement model, similarly ran through the court's entire operating procedure. Each child called to official notice was to become an object of inquiry for diagnostic specialists. By means of this initial evaluation the court would identify the family context and social setting that had precipitated deviant behavior or placed the minor at risk.[42] A hearing would follow that was supposed to more closely resemble a physician's examination than a criminal trial. The judge would use the diagnostic profile as well as other testimony to choose for the child a mode of treatment tailored to his individual needs.[43] Whenever possible the juvenile court would order a program of follow-up staff visits to the child in his own surroundings to address his maladjustment at its source. This aftercare, known as probation, necessarily focused on the family as the unit of treatment. With the child serving as the point of entry, the court would extend its tutelage over the entire household. Parents would be accused and admonished, other siblings would be given advice, and domestic behavior would come under official surveillance. Not until both the minor and his family had been rehabilitated was the court to relax its attention.[44]

---

39. For a vivid early account of the therapeutic orientation of the court, see Harvey H. Baker, "Procedure of the Boston Juvenile Court," *Survey* 23 (February 5, 1910): 643–52. Fox asserts that the juvenile court should be seen as merely an incremental reform because it continued a pattern of procedural informality in juvenile justice. See Fox, "Juvenile Justice Reform," 1221–22. It is clear from court movement writings, however, that informality was but an adjunct to the full therapeutic revolution that proponents intended.

40. On the scope of juvenile court jurisdiction and its connection to philanthropic strategy, see Donzelot, *Policing of Families*, 109–10, 87–88. Fox also stresses the value of the court for philanthropic intervention. See Fox, "Juvenile Justice Reform," 1227.

41. Ryerson, *Best-Laid Plans*, 43–47.

42. Donzelot, *Policing of Families*, 119–20, 122–24; Rothman, *Conscience and Convenience*, 215, 218; Annie Ramsey, "Work of the Probation Officer Preliminary to the Trial," NCCC, *Proceedings* 33 (1906, 2d ed.), 132–35; Bernard Flexner, "The Juvenile Court as a Social Institution," *Survey* 23 (February 5, 1910): 628.

43. Baker, "Procedure of Boston Juvenile Court," 646–49; Donzelot, *Policing of Families*, 99–102, 107–08.

44. Frederic Almy, "Juvenile Courts and Juvenile Probation," NYSCCC, *Proceedings* 2 (1901), 284; Sophonisba P. Breckinridge and Edith Abbott, *The Delinquent Child and the Home* (New

To justify tutelage by the juvenile court, proponents had to characterize its adjudication as noncriminal and its dispositions as benign. The model procedures plainly disregarded a child's claim to formal legal rights and left few procedural safeguards. Yet though rhetoric about the right of a community to impose discipline might satisfy social personnel, it would not satisfy the legal establishment, which needed to know what benefit the minor derived for surrendering his rights.[45] It seemed useful, then, to depict the relationship between the court and the child as a kind of bargain. The child gave up recourse to ordinary judicial safeguards while the new institution promised not to affix blame on him for his acts. Further, rather than punish him as it might a criminal, the court pledged to care for him as a unique individual.[46]

For the child to triumph over his maladjustment, it was soon realized, the court would need to apply the most advanced scientific knowledge. Only science, with its ability to grasp fully the plight of the troubled child, could restore the delinquent to a normal status.[47] Since no reliable science of delinquency yet existed, one had to be generated. Accordingly, the juvenile court was to join forces with social and behavioral scientists, the former providing cases so that the latter might test the latest theories. Within a decade the first juvenile psychopathic clinic was established to help the judge diagnose the child's condition.[48] The addition of social experts and clinicians also broadened the base of the original court movement.

But if the court hoped to adjust clients through the use of science, the movement appreciated that judicial tutelage also entailed the possibility of coercion. In its probation system the juvenile court would demonstrate that judicial authority could reinforce therapeutic technique. While a probation officer was to try to gain the confidence of the minor and his family, the judge would reserve disciplinary sanctions that he could invoke at any time. As one put it, "The discomfort of punishment affords in some cases an indispensable

York: Russell Sage Foundation, Charities Publication Committee, 1912), 170; Donzelot, *Policing of Families*, 103–04; Ryerson, *Best-Laid Plans*, 50–52.

45. For a penetrating legal critique from this period see Edward Lindsey, "The Juvenile Court Movement from a Lawyer's Standpoint," *Annals* 52 (1914): 141–44. Even within the court movement questions arose over the procedural latitude granted the institution. See Flexner, "Juvenile Court as a Social Institution," 637–38.

46. These views were frequently expressed by Julian Mack, the second Chicago juvenile court judge. See Mack, "The Juvenile Court: The Judge and the Probation Officer," NCCC, *Proceedings* 33 (1906, 2d ed.), 123–31; Mack, "Juvenile Courts as Part of the School System of the Country," NCCC, *Proceedings* 35 (1908), 369–83; Mack, "The Law and the Child," *Survey* 23 (February 5, 1910): 638–43. See also Ryerson, *Best-Laid Plans*, 76–77.

47. Carl Kelsey, "The Juvenile Court of Chicago and Its Work," *Annals* 17 (1901): 299; Charles T. Walker, "The Work of the Juvenile Protective Association," Child Conference for Research and Welfare, *Proceedings* 1 (1909), 60. Ryerson contends that the need to put the court's work on a scientific footing was recognized only later, but these early statements demonstrate that a scientific foundation was sought from the outset. See Ryerson, *Best-Laid Plans*, 100ff.

48. "Testimony of Judge Merritt W. Pinckney," in Breckinridge and Abbott, *Delinquent Child and the Home*, 234–35. See also the essays in Addams et al., *Child, the Clinic and the Court*.

stimulus or moral tonic which cannot be supplied in any other way."[49] In effect the judge would suspend more severe measures, as Donzelot says, to create an opening in which educative remedies might take hold.[50] The child was to be given his chance, so to speak, as the court maintained an ongoing surveillance. If either he or his family balked at the probation officer's instructions, harsher measures might be taken, including removal of the minor from the home or incarceration in an industrial school. Hence the critical value of probation: in place of a definitive judgment to resolve a case, the juvenile court would implicate child and family in a process of perpetual evaluation.[51]

Besides relying on the power of the court itself, the probation officer would call on other agencies to accomplish his adjustment tasks. Here we must consider what court historians have not—the position that proponents expected the court to occupy in a web of normalizing services. The probation officer was to forge connections between the family and the other normalizing agencies serving the neighborhood.[52] Public schools, municipal hospitals, and free clinics were beginning to incorporate the tutelary approach as an adjunct to their other operations. And several new public institutions like school and neighborhood centers were founded upon normalizing methods. Social personnel from these agencies also sought to renovate the "irregular" family—to reorder its responsibilities, reduce its pernicious autonomy, and impose new functions so that it more closely resembled its bourgeois counterpart. Through a cooperative effort, the court and the emerging tutelary apparatus would penetrate the walls around the family. It would be seen as adjusted when it accepted permanent intervention by the human service network.[53]

The court's first advocates saw their invention, then, as but part of a broad effort intended to reshape the relationship between the state and a segment of civil society. Previously the liberal state had encountered the working-class family only sporadically. Even the attempts by nineteenth-century philanthropy to push public agencies into an active role in family preservation had at most a modest impact. Public authority rarely crossed the threshold of the home or challenged parental sovereignty. Now, by contrast, those families brought into the juvenile court or introduced to another therapeutic agency would find their most intimate behavior a matter of official concern and regula-

49. Baker, "Procedure of Boston Juvenile Court," 650; Thomas Murphy, "The Juvenile Court of Buffalo," NYSCCC, *Proceedings* 3 (1902), 137–38; Mrs. Helen W. Rogers, "The Probation System of the Juvenile Court of Indianapolis," NCCC, *Proceedings* 31 (1904), 376.

50. Donzelot, *Policing of Families*, 108–09.

51. Almy, "Juvenile Courts and Juvenile Probation," 288–89; Donzelot, *Policing of Families*, 110–11.

52. Mabel Carter Rhoades, "A Case Study of Delinquent Boys in the Juvenile Court of Chicago," *American Journal of Sociology* (cited hereafter as *AJS*) 13 (1907): 77; Henry Thurston, "Some Phases of the Probation Work of the Juvenile Court," NCCC, *Proceedings* 32 (1905), 180–82; Flexner, "Juvenile Court as a Social Institution," 630, 632.

53. George W. Kirchway, "Social Work and the Law: Forms of Cooperation between Law and Social Work," National Conference of Social Work (cited hereafter as NCSW), *Proceedings* 53 (1926), 182; Bernard Flexner and Roger N. Baldwin, *Juvenile Courts and Probation* (New York: Century, 1914, 1916), 80–81; Donzelot, *Policing of Families*.

tion. Client status would impose on family members an obligation to reveal their frailties to social personnel. Here the court stood out above all other agencies, with its thorough investigation of the minor's condition and its relentless observation of his progress under treatment. Moreover, clients of public normalizing agencies would be bound to meet officially established standards of conduct. Again no institution exemplified this compulsory power so well as the juvenile court; if the child failed to remodel his behavior as instructed, he faced removal from his home and a loss of his liberty.

First Lessons

The juvenile court drew support from a broad movement during the first decade of the twentieth century. Middle-class women's groups, settlement house residents, and social scientists gave the court idea their enthusiastic backing. To further expand the new institution's appeal, a well-orchestrated promotional campaign was mounted. Judges like Ben Lindsay in Denver and other movement leaders vigorously promoted the court. Moreover, in a striking triumph of the therapeutic ideal, treatment-oriented jurisprudence earned the endorsement of Progressive legal theorists like Roscoe Pound. They praised the court for its twin commitment to "socialized" and "individualized" justice. The new institution pledged in the abstract to consider the environmental influences on its clients' behavior, while at the same time treating each child as a unique individual requiring carefully differentiated treatment.[54]

Idealism was not the only force working for the court; it gained a stamp of approval from powerful institutions. In the legislative arena, mundane fiscal considerations worked to the short-run advantage of court proponents. State legislatures appear to have welcomed the court not on its own merits but for the "economies" it promised. By shifting juveniles out of institutions, probation promised to save the state a significant cost.[55] In the judicial arena outside the juvenile court, the legal principles upon which the new institution was established were found to be consistent with constitutional standards. When the first appeals challenging the jurisdiction and approach of the new court reached the higher state courts, they quickly affirmed the validity of judicial intervention premised upon a condition rather than an act.[56]

As the juvenile court spread and entrenched itself, it contributed to the elaboration of a new state sector devoted to therapeutic intervention. Its first judges seem to have looked for inspiration to philanthropic circles rather than to the legal profession. They attempted to realize through their own efforts the therapeutic ideal of a comprehensive set of adjustment agencies. Wherever

54. See, for example, Edward F. Waite, "The Outlook for the Juvenile Court," *Annals* 105 (January 1923): 234; Roscoe Pound, Foreword, to Pauline V. Young, *Social Treatment in Probation and Delinquency* (New York: McGraw-Hill, 1937), xxv, xxviii.

55. Schlossman, *Love and the American Delinquent*, 62–63, 66; Fox, "Juvenile Justice Reform," 1224.

56. Julian W. Mack, "Legal Problems Involved in the Establishment of the Juvenile Court," in Breckinridge and Abbott, *Delinquent Child and the Home*, 190–91; Ryerson, *Best-Laid Plans*, 67–68.

they discovered a gap in the local service apparatus, they simply created a substitute under the court's own direct control.[57] Similarly, they agitated for new programs to augment the court's resources. Juvenile court judges in Illinois, for example, played an important role in the campaign to establish mothers' aid programs.[58] In many states the court then assumed responsibility for administering the aid allowances.[59] At the same time, other agencies appeared with philanthropic support to assist the court, and the principles that guided the juvenile court movement became the basis for further judicial innovations. Courts of domestic relations and family courts sought to extend the therapeutic approach to an even broader clientele.[60]

Such surface measures of progress, however, did not deceive those close to the juvenile court. It was certainly true that a new population of minors accused of lesser infractions or "status offenses"—conduct deemed improper in a juvenile that would not be illegal if committed by an adult—had been brought under legal discipline.[61] Further, family maladjustment came to the attention of other official bodies. The juvenile court, its allied agencies, and the other new treatment-oriented courts had extended the reach of the state over the working-class family and secured an important opening into the family for social personnel. Nevertheless, the juvenile court performed at a level far below what proponents had anticipated. The initial claims of astonishing results proved misleading. The court was not a panacea for many forms of social maladjustment. Within fifteen years the juvenile court movement began to assume a defensive posture and to reveal severe internal strains.

In practice, courts for children rarely adhered to the model procedures defined by the movement. Every step in the process, from intake to disposition, fell far short of expectations. Rather than provide a complete diagnostic tool, the preliminary investigation amounted to nothing more than a disjointed compilation of hearsay, gossip, and trivia. Few courts could call on the services of a clinic, for only about a dozen had been established by 1918.[62] Further,

57. Eliot, *Juvenile Court and the Community*, 13–14, 16; Pound, Foreword, xxviii–xxix; Alice Scott Nutt, "The Future of the Juvenile Court as a Case-Work Agency," NCSW, *Proceedings* 66 (1939), 371.

58. For example, Chicago judge Merritt W. Pinckney argued for mothers' aid in an important charity conference debate. See Pinckney, "Public Pensions to Widows: Experiences and Observations Which Lead Me to Favor Such a Law," NCCC, *Proceedings* 39 (1912).

59. Emma O. Lundberg, *Public Aid to Mothers With Dependent Children: Extent and Fundamental Principles*, Children's Bureau Publication no. 162, U.S. Department of Labor (Washington, D.C.: U.S. Government Printing Office, 1926), 9–10.

60. Waite, "Outlook for the Juvenile Court," 240; Charles N. Goodnow, "The Chicago Court of Domestic Relations," in Sophonisba P. Breckinridge, ed., *The Child in the City* (Chicago: Department of Social Investigation, Chicago School of Civics and Philanthropy, 1912), 330–40.

61. By the Second World War over 65,000 children each year were placed on probation (Lowell Julliard Carr, *Delinquency Control* [New York: Harper, 1941], 135).

62. Roger Baldwin, "The Presentation of the Case," in Breckinridge, ed., *Child in the City*, 341–44, 347; Flexner and Baldwin, *Juvenile Courts and Probation*, 44–45, 51; Katherine F. Lenroot and Emma O. Lundberg, *Juvenile Courts at Work: A Study of the Organization and Methods of Ten Courts*, Children's Bureau Publication no. 141, U.S. Department of Labor

when most judges conducted hearings, they ignored the child's condition and instead let the nature of his infraction determine the disposition. They thus repudiated the movement's assumption that the offense was a poor guide to a juvenile's needs.[63] Just as unsatisfactory was the handling of the child by the court after it had adjudicated the case. Probation did not extend meaningful tutelage into his everyday life. Probation departments were poorly administered and caseloads in most courts averaged over a hundred per officer. Under such circumstances a probation officer found it necessary to reduce "treatment" to an occasional office visit.[64]

Court proponents were disturbed, too, by the behavior of the institution's clients. Most came from working-class backgrounds.[65] Viewing the court as the coercive instrument of an alien culture, they did all they could to keep it at arm's length. Juveniles and their parents quickly discovered that court officials were strongly influenced by a pretense of cooperation, and the court had no capacity to get beneath appearances.[66] It followed that the institution could have little impact on delinquency. Early claims that juveniles seen once by the court rarely returned gave way to the frank recognition that rates of recidivism remained as high as before its invention.[67] More children had been brought into contact with the normalizing apparatus, but the court failed to adjust them or invest their families with bourgeois values.

To explain the court's shortcomings advocates pointed first to the debilitating impact of established political arrangements. Juvenile courts caught on because they seemed a cheap alternative to state institutions, but they soon became fiscal orphans. State legislatures permitted communities to introduce probation without providing funds to cover the cost; local governments in turn refused to allocate resources for professional staff or therapeutic facilities. Clearly the political weight of therapeutic discourse was limited. Permissive state statutes also allowed each county to adopt its own approach to juvenile justice. A wide variety of court organization and practice emerged, with especially pronounced differences between urban and rural counties.[68] Moreover,

---

(Washington, D.C.: U.S. Government Printing Office, 1925), 94, 100–01; Douglas P. Falconer, "Making the Child Safe for the Community," NCSW, *Proceedings* 53 (1926), 165.

63. Bernard Flexner, "The Juvenile Court — Its Legal Aspects," *Annals* 36 (1910): 53, 55; Mack, "Law and the Child," 640; Flexner and Baldwin, *Juvenile Courts and Probation*, 75, 77.

64. Flexner, "Juvenile Court as a Social Institution," 614–15, 620–21, 636–37; "Testimony of Judge Merritt W. Pinckney," 207–08; Thurston, "Some Phases of the Probation Work of the Juvenile Court," 178–79.

65. Breckinridge and Abbott, *Delinquent Child and the Home*, 56–57, 61, 70, 160.

66. Ibid., 170–71, 173–74; Nutt, "Future of Juvenile Court as a Case-Work Agency," 373; Lenroot and Lundberg, *Juvenile Courts at Work*, 111, 195.

67. For contemporary discussions of the early findings on recidivism, see Carr, *Delinquency Control*, 173–80; Grace Abbott, "The Juvenile Court and a Community Program for Treating and Preventing Delinquency," *Social Service Review* (cited hereafter as *SSR*) 10 (1936): 233–34.

68. Emma O. Lundberg, "The Juvenile Court as a Constructive Social Agency," NCSW, *Proceedings* 49 (1922), 155; *Dependent and Delinquent Children in North Dakota and South Dakota*, Children's Bureau Publication no. 160, U.S. Department of Labor (Washington, D.C.: U.S. Government Printing Office, 1926).

even in the urban centers where the movement was strongest, politics intruded on the court. Party politicians, determined to pursue the usual calculations of partisan advantage, backed the creation of public probation services as an opening for patronage.[69]

The court was further hampered, its supporters realized, by the narrow base of the discursive movement on which judicial tutelage depended. Philanthropic groups and trained social technicians were clustered in cities in the East and Midwest. In rural areas, with no representation of the philanthropic viewpoint, the juvenile justice system had neither models nor personnel upon which to draw. Therefore rural courts did not incorporate the adjustment rationale into their operations.[70] Even in the cities the philanthropic-public network of human services was plagued by many gaps. Juvenile courts acquired their own service apparatus not simply because of their enterprising judges but also because other agencies did not step forward to meet the needs of problem youngsters. Worse yet, courts without such support services made a managerial decision to overlook a child's symptomatic behavior because no resources were available to address it.[71]

If many disappointments could be attributed to external political constraints, however, practice also revealed a serious division within the court itself. The early alliance between philanthropy and the judiciary that made the court the logical starting point for a therapeutic state masked the underlying difference between two discursive traditions.[72] Social personnel soon learned that aside from a few celebrities, juvenile court magistrates did not share the therapeutic orientation. Instead the typical judge remained wedded to the conventions of the criminal court bench. This accounted for his preoccupation with the question of the child's guilt rather than with his condition.

To explain why old judicial values persisted, one only needed to look at the juvenile court judges' background and their broader affiliation. Rapid institutional expansion—more than two thousand courts identified themselves as having special juvenile jurisdiction by the early 1920s—precluded careful selection of judicial personnel. Far from the ideal jurist-therapist embodied by the first judicial entrepreneurs, the average judge hearing children's cases came to the task with no special qualifications. As a lawyer and a judge, he had acquired experience in criminal law. Nothing in his past fitted him for the role of diagnostician and therapist. Equally important, the juvenile court often was carved out of the county criminal court, which retained control over the selection of the magistrate for its offshoot. The position typically was filled by rotation. This secured a judge who continued to view himself as a member of

---

69. Eliot, *Juvenile Court and the Community*, 22, 25; Pound, Foreword, xxx; Rothman, *Conscience and Convenience*, 244.

70. Nutt, "Future of Juvenile Court as a Case-Work Agency," 378; Carr, *Delinquency Control*, 161–62.

71. Lenroot and Lundberg, *Juvenile Courts at Work*, 122, 225, 228, 245.

72. Herbert M. Baker, "The Court and the Delinquent Child," *AJS* 26 (1920): 178; Pound, Foreword, xxviii, xxxiii; Ryerson, *Best-Laid Plans*, 139.

the criminal court bench and thus failed to appreciate the juvenile court's unique approach.[73]

Judges wedded to conventional legal values posed a grave threat to the movement because they tended to rely on punishment rather than treatment to reform behavior. Enthusiasts boasted that the genius of the institution lay in its combination of coercive authority, compassion, and therapeutic techniques. Left in the hands of a judge who knew only criminal law, however, the court absorbed his orientation and belied its ideals.[74] Court procedure degenerated into a repressive exercise, with the judge insisting upon a confession as the first step in rehabilitation and his probation officer seeking through blunt threats to render the minor docile.[75]

When a juvenile court behaved in this manner, proponents recognized, it compromised its legitimacy as an institution. Rather than using therapy and judicial power to reinforce each other, the court corrupted both elements. On one side, law enforcement values pervaded the court and its human service mechanisms. Neither the family subjected to a police-style investigation nor the child confined in a "diagnostic" detention center as a warning would ever accept such court intervention as benign.[76] Conversely, therapeutic logic cost the court its reputation as an instrument through which even the most humble could secure justice. The court continued as a matter of convenience to subscribe to the movement claim that due process formalities would hinder efforts to help the child. Yet once all procedural safeguards were discarded, the court could no longer persuade its clients of its commitment to fairness.[77] In sum, treatment and justice stood together or not at all.

Underlying these criticisms was a conviction among certain social personnel that the court had failed to take advantage of their expertise. Important advances in the study of juvenile behavior had been made in the psychopathic institutes and clinics. Yet the ordinary judge lacked sufficient vision to introduce science into his courtroom. Common sense or folk insight guided his work instead. Even the exceptional judge committed to a therapeutic approach

73. Eliot, *Juvenile Court and the Community*, pp. 23–24; Francis H. Hiller, "The Juvenile Court as a Case Working Agency: Its Limitations and Its Possibilities," NCSW, *Proceedings* 53 (1926), 142–43; Pound, Foreword, xxvi; Ryerson, *Best-Laid Plans*, 85–86.

74. Nutt, "Future of Juvenile Court as a Case-Work Agency," 374.

75. Baldwin, "Presentation of the Case," 347–48; Eliot, *Juvenile Court and the Community*, 32–33; Willard E. Hotchkiss, "The Juvenile Court as It Is Today," NCCC, *Proceedings* 39 (1912), 456–57; Bernard Flexner, "A Decade of the Juvenile Court," NCCC, *Proceedings* 37 (1910), 108, 110–11; Young, *Social Treatment in Probation and Delinquency*, 14–15; Nutt, "Future of Juvenile Court as a Case-Work Agency," 374. This aspect of juvenile court development has been much discussed by historians. See, for example, Rothman, *Conscience and Convenience*, 261–63.

76. Kirchway, "Social Work and Law," 182; Abbott, "Juvenile Court and a Community Program," 237; William Healy and Augusta F. Bronner, *New Light on Delinquency and Its Treatment* (New Haven: Yale University Press, 1936, 1950), 147, 205, 222; Young, *Social Treatment in Probation and Delinquency*, 163, 166; Nutt, "Future of Juvenile Court as a Case-Work Agency," 373–74.

77. Baker, "Court and the Delinquent Child," 178; Flexner, "Juvenile Court as a Social Institution," 637; Pound, Foreword, xxvii.

blundered forward on his own, seeking to accomplish by sheer entrepreneurial spirit what required the highest level of professional skill.[78]

If some social personnel felt slighted, however, others took a more sober view and conceded that responsibility lay as much with themselves. Here and there a judge enlisted the aid of social workers and behavioral scientists and tried to follow closely their advice. But the specialists produced simplistic diagnoses and arrived at only general or obvious prescriptions. The fact that recidivism among juvenile offenders subject to expert handling showed no appreciable decline[79] indicated that, though the court had been vested with major therapeutic functions, social personnel could not support it with the behavioral knowledge that normalization required. As one social worker concluded, "The social and biological sciences have not progressed sufficiently to aid us in understanding adequately human personality, motivation, social life, mental conflicts, and the interplay between the social situation and the genetic constitution of the individual."[80] If the experts' recommendations yielded results no better than the judge's own intuition, the latter surely had little reason to accept the guidance of the former. The court's repressive and amateurish practices would continue, it was asserted, so long as the human sciences remained in their primitive state.[81]

By the late 1920s the court movement was in a precarious position. The public attitude toward delinquency took a conservative turn, and the institution faced intense external pressure to make even greater use of its disciplinary resources.[82] To withstand this pressure the court urgently needed to demonstrate the essential validity of its therapeutic credo. Making matters worse, politicians starved the juvenile court of funds for normalizing services. Inside the court, meanwhile, control rested with judges who were at best overmatched by their therapeutic task. More often than not, they brought along the intellectual baggage accumulated during a career in the criminal court. Support from the legal elite counted for little when the everyday administration of the court rested in such hands. Plainly social personnel had failed to establish the hegemony of the therapeutic approach over established political arrangements or retributive values.

78. William Healy, "The Psychology of the Situation: A Fundamental for Understanding and Treatment of Delinquency," in Addams et al., *Child, the Clinic and the Court*, 48; Henry S. Hulbert, "Probation," in Addams et al., *Child, the Clinic and the Court*, 239, 241, 243–44; Young, *Social Treatment in Probation and Delinquency*, 605; Carr, *Delinquency Control*, 4, 18–19, 158. For a contrasting view see A. L. Jacoby, "The New Approach to the Problem of Delinquency: Punishment versus Treatment," NCSW, *Proceedings* 53 (1926), 180.

79. Sheldon Glueck and Eleanor T. Glueck, *One Thousand Juvenile Delinquents: Their Treatment by Court and Clinic* (Cambridge: Harvard University Press, 1934); Rothman, *Conscience and Convenience*, 245–48; Abbott, "Juvenile Court and a Community Program," pp. 233–34.

80. Young, *Social Treatment in Probation and Delinquency*, 25–6, 126, 132, 292.

81. Ibid., 603–04; Baker, "Court and Delinquent Child," 177; Carr, *Delinquency Control*, 198–99.

82. Eliot, *Juvenile Court and the Community*, ix; Justin Miller, "Introduction," to Young, *Social Treatment in Probation and Delinquency*, xxxiv; Ryerson, *Best-Laid Plans*, 78–79.

Strategies for Redemption

When a discursive movement encounters obstacles, it responds forcefully with the weapons at its disposal—its techniques and knowledge. Far too much has been invested to permit a graceful retreat or withdrawal. And the participants in the movement remain inspired by the potential for the effective exercise of power that they still believe their discursive methods can tap. The first approach by a frustrated discursive movement, then, is a more rigorous assertion of its founding principles and the further amplification of its distinctive techniques.

Proponents of the juvenile court pursued just such an aggressive campaign from the 1920s to the New Deal period. Determined to master their adversaries both outside and within the institution, and thereby to overcome manifest failures, enthusiasts initiated a number of organizational reforms and embarked upon a new quest to strengthen the court's scientific foundation. No thought was given to abandoning the court experiment; many improvements appeared within reach. Court leaders and their allies in new public bureaucratic structures began by generating pressure on children's courts to live up to the model of judicial tutelage. But with resistance entrenched inside the court in the person of the judge, court proponents recognized that their social agency ideal would triumph only through direct confrontation at the point of discursive contact. Therefore social personnel in this period sought to elevate the role of behavioral knowledge in juvenile justice practice. By removing treatment from the judge's hands or dictating his choices, behavioral technicians would reorder the court's priorities. This new hope fueled a search for better scientific tools to interpret juvenile deviance and its causes.

Even those in the movement who doubted that a court was competent to administer normalizing services had no wish to see juveniles returned unaided to their environment.[83] Beyond the fear that working-class neighborhoods and family life, left unchecked, would place the child at grave risk, lay the fact that other human services had begun to depend on the court to sustain their normalizing program. If a family refused to submit to treatment recommended by social workers or specialists, the court stood ready to order compliance.[84] Judicial support also had brought managerial economy to the field of human services. In the juvenile court social agencies found a place to discard clients who responded poorly to voluntary therapeutic measures. Thus unburdened, the agencies conserved their resources for more suitable cases.[85] Whether one took a "humane" or pragmatic view, then, therapeutic child protection demanded that problems be addressed within the judicial framework.

83. Ruth I. Workum, "The Relationship between the Functions of the Juvenile Court and Those of the General Child-Caring Agencies," NCSW, *Proceedings* 49 (1922), 142; Hotchkiss, "Juvenile Court as It Is Today," 450, 455; Lindsey, "Juvenile Court from a Lawyer's Standpoint," 147–48. See also Donzelot, *Policing of Families*, 98.

84. Eliot, *Juvenile Court and the Community*, 151–52.

85. Young, *Social Treatment in Probation and Delinquency*, 28; Rothman, *Conscience and Convenience*, 247; Donzelot, *Policing of Families*, 112, 124–25.

Proponents knew they needed to maneuver around difficult fiscal obstacles if they hoped to overcome the shortcomings in the court's therapeutic performance. Time and again the movement called for more resources.[86] But in the post-Progressive Era, when the human services faced external threats to their very survival, realists appreciated that the court for the moment had to protect what it had already gained. Other means to advance the therapeutic agenda within the juvenile court would have to be found.

For a start court supporters tried to increase the influence of the movement's leadership over the daily operations of the disparate children's courts. Those who campaigned most vigorously for the court shared a passionate commitment to the therapeutic ideology, but their impact on the institution's everyday workings had been minimal. Just after the First World War the leaders convened to define standards for juvenile court organization and procedure. They sought to eradicate the lingering traces of criminal jurisprudence, enshrine casework norms, and promote a high degree of professionalism among court staff.[87] With the strong support of the women in the U.S. Children's Bureau, at the time an enthusiastic force for the social-agency conception of the court, the movement leadership disseminated its standards widely to court officials and philanthropic groups. The Children's Bureau sponsored follow-up studies by social workers to publicize successful operations in a number of courts.[88]

To impose standards upon an institution that bore the scars of a fragmented and permissive political system, moreover, it seemed vital to counter with a more centralized political vehicle. Court proponents in the 1920s urged the creation of a state-level agency to oversee local court operations. It was hoped that such an instrument would promote merit selection and professionalism in probation departments, and so neutralize both partisanship and judicial mishandling.[89]

Neither the drive to promote therapeutic standards for the court nor the introduction of state bureaucracy produced the kind of results that court leaders desired. On the one hand, against the limitless variety in court forms that resulted from local politics and judicial discretion, even a determined effort to promote a unified vision had but a modest impact. On the other hand, with the court movement concentrated in a handful of heavily urbanized states,

86. Lundberg, "Juvenile Court as a Constructive Social Agency," 157–58; Hiller, "Juvenile Court as a Case Working Agency," 144; Rothman, *Conscience and Convenience*, 286–88.

87. See *Juvenile-Court Standards*, Children's Bureau Publication no. 121, U.S. Department of Labor (Washington, D.C.: Government Printing Office, 1923). For a discussion of this work, see Marguerite Rosenthal, "The Children's Bureau and the Juvenile Court: Delinquency Policy, 1912–1940," *SSR* 60 (June 1986): 306–07.

88. On the role of the Children's Bureau in promoting the social agency model, see H. Warren Dunham, "The Juvenile Court: Contradictory Orientations in Processing Offenders," *Law and Contemporary Problems* 23 (1958): 513–14; Rosenthal, "Children's Bureau and the Juvenile Court," 307. For an example of a promotional (but still critical) follow-up study, see Lenroot and Lundberg, *Juvenile Courts at Work*.

89. Lundberg, "Juvenile Court as a Constructive Social Agency," 159–60; Katherine F. Lenroot, "The Evolution of the Juvenile Court," *Annals* 105 (January 1923): 221; Hiller, "Juvenile Court as a Case Working Agency," 146–48.

few state agencies were established. And these could do little to elevate court practice in rural areas that lacked indigenous therapeutic cadre.[90]

Alas, as some court advocates cautioned, so long as a criminal justice mentality prevailed in the juvenile court, little could be achieved through external pressure alone. It was necessary to confront the reality of a judge who lacked either the capacity or the will to turn his court into an instrument of adjustment. Naked compulsion had dislodged therapy, and behavioral experts and social workers needed to restore the latter to its rightful role at the helm.[91] Court supporters redoubled their efforts to capitalize on what they saw as the social technician's strongest weapon—expert knowledge.

At first it was thought that a hierarchy of expertise could be created in the court simply by making scientific knowledge more accessible. The philanthropic Commonwealth Fund in the early 1920s sponsored the creation of child guidance clinics to work closely with judges and probation staffs.[92] Psychiatrists and other specialists took this as an opportunity to translate their arcane research findings into a language court officials could understand. They believed that once these officials were confronted with sound and comprehensible advice, they would feel compelled to follow it. As we have noted, however, the actual results obtained through these early clinical applications did not cause a judge to bow before the social technicians. Diagnoses became more sophisticated, yet behavioral specialists still lacked the tools that would permit them to adjust deviant behavior through nonpunitive treatment.[93]

Only when their intervention rested upon a stronger base of knowledge could social personnel hope to alter the equation of forces in the juvenile court. A reliable science of human behavior held the promise of a strategic reversal. As one clinician asserted, "Scientific findings should become guides to treatment; they should find their greatest function, not in classifying and labeling, but in determining details of therapy."[94] Where the experts had chafed beneath the judge's peremptory style, henceforth they could demand that the court take note of their recommendations for a child's treatment. The incipient scientific regime thus would tame the court's repressive tendencies.[95]

Seeking a scientific discipline to meet these practical needs, social personnel fastened upon a succession of possibilities in the 1920s and 1930s. Social psychology and psychiatry developed followings, especially in the child guidance clinics. But though these approaches suited the individual orientation

90. Nutt, "Future of Juvenile Court as a Case-Work Agency," 377–78.

91. Healy, "Psychology of the Situation," 47–48; Healy and Bronner, New Light on Delinquency, 141, 146–47, 220–22; Carr, Delinquency Control, 283.

92. Barry C. Smith, "The Commonwealth Fund Program for the Prevention of Delinquency," NCSW, Proceedings 49 (1922), 168–74; Herbert H. Lou, Juvenile Courts in the United States (Chapel Hill: University of North Carolina Press, 1927), 200.

93. Healy and Bronner, New Light on Delinquency, 16.

94. Augusta F. Bronner, "The Contribution of Science to a Program for Treatment of Juvenile Delinquency," in Addams et al., Child, the Clinic and the Court, 79.

95. Healy and Bronner, New Light on Delinquency, 223; Young, Social Treatment in Probation and Delinquency, 622; Donzelot, Policing of Families, 97, 116, 118–19.

favored in social casework, treatment results under court auspices were discouraging.[96] When psychoanalytic theory began to circulate in American intellectual circles in the late 1920s, then, social personnel were singularly receptive. Like other psychiatric approaches, Freudian doctrine lent itself to the individualized treatment that the court provided. But psychoanalysis also spoke directly to the conviction among clinicians and social workers that a science of human behavior ought not to rest on overly rationalistic assumptions—assumptions contradicted by the record of casework interventions.[97]

Through the use of psychoanalytic methods social personnel believed they would finally realize the constructive power of judicial tutelage. Freudian techniques allowed a skilled practitioner to open up a child's inner mental universe, revealing the peculiar source of his disturbances. After analysis disclosed the basis for a minor's maladjustment, he would be aided in reconciling himself to his situation.[98] The approach would disarm the child and win him over. He would learn that psychoanalysis disdained blunt judgments of his condition and his needs that other court officials so casually formed. Above all, when he came to appreciate his true needs through therapy, he would recognize that analysis would be put to use only on his own behalf.[99]

Psychoanalytic techniques also would allow social personnel to gain the upper hand in the struggle for hegemony over the juvenile court. Using these techniques the behavioral specialist would be best able to penetrate appearances and generate positive conduct. For the first time it would be possible to determine the true significance of a trivial offense: was it just youthful excess, as the judge guessed, or the first manifestation of serious unresolved family conflicts? Faced with such clearly superior understanding, the juvenile court judge would be outmatched. Social personnel would claim victory in the discursive struggle that had sabotaged the early court.[100]

DISCURSIVE DISPLACEMENT AND INSTITUTIONAL TENACITY

If we review the major historical accounts of the juvenile court, its survival in the wake of its early failures remains a mystery. The historians leap directly from the court's initial shortcomings to the recent due process "correctives." But the court did not stand still from the 1930s through the 1960s. Much

96. Kirchway, "Social Work and the Law," 185–86; Lubove, *Professional Altruist*, 45, 55–56, 63–66, 76–77, 83, 88–89; Rothman, *Conscience and Convenience*, 247–48; Ryerson, *Best-Laid Plans*, 105–06, 110.

97. Bronner, "Contribution of Science to a Program for Treatment of Juvenile Delinquency," 82–83; Ryerson, *Best-Laid Plans*, 113–14; John H. Ehrenreich, *The Altruistic Imagination: A History of Social Work and Social Policy in the United States* (Ithaca, N.Y.: Cornell University Press, 1985), 52.

98. Healy and Bronner, *New Light on Delinquency*, 141–42; Young, *Social Treatment in Probation and Delinquency*, 289–90; Ryerson, *Best-Laid Plans*, 110; Lubove, *Professional Altruist*, 89, 91–102, 108–10, 114, 119–21.

99. Young, *Social Treatment in Probation and Delinquency*, 320, 324–28, 330–31; Donzelot, *Policing of Families*, 170; Ehrenreich, *Professional Altruist*, 117–18.

100. Ryerson, *Best-Laid Plans*, 110–11; Donzelot, *Policing of Families*, chap. 5.

happened during that interval to alter the institution and its position within the larger therapeutic sector. Social workers and behavioral experts abandoned the court and sought new settings in which to apply the therapeutic approach; the juvenile court became the scene of a new discursive conflict between judges wielding the rhetoric of therapeutic justice and lawyers committed to a strict ideal of due process; and juvenile court judges, confronted by the institutional rivals that social personnel created, fought to keep the court at the center of the therapeutic sector. These parallel currents reveal a process of discursive displacement and at the same time explain the court's remarkable tenacity.

Scientific Disenchantment

Social personnel did not succeed in their quest to establish a hierarchy of expertise in the court, and the problems they had identified in the 1920s continued to fester. Despite their best efforts, clinicians still occupied an awkward position in the judicial process. A few optimistic social workers castigated judges and probation staff for not knowing how to use science and contended that additional expert resources had to be introduced to the court.[101] Yet, as before, judges and probation officers showed little affinity for behavioral knowledge.[102] Relations between the behavioral specialists and the court's other set of participants—the juvenile and his family—also proved discouraging. By the 1950s the refusal of clients to embrace a treatment ideology had to be acknowledged. They grasped, even as the social technician might not, the cold fact that they were subject to legal discipline. Rather than accept the clinician as a partner, juvenile offenders treated him as an annoyance or sought to manipulate him to secure lenient treatment.[103]

The continued weakness of social personnel within the institution reflected an enduring discursive failure—the inability to make any real progress against recidivism. For all that had been expected of psychoanalysis, the Freudian approach quickly had come under attack from some of its own influential practitioners. Competing schools arose to challenge its dominance within the medico-psychiatric community. The court could extract little clear guidance from such intellectual turmoil. All that clinicians could do was to superimpose one approach atop another.[104] They were left unable to penetrate appear-

101. See Alfred J. Kahn, *A Court for Children: A Study of the New York City Children's Court* (New York: Columbia University Press, 1953), 4–5, 230, 294–95, 308–09, 312. Note that even Kahn expresses doubts about what clinical services can achieve; see pp. 10–11.

102. Paul W. Tappan, "Children and Youth in the Criminal Court," *Annals* 261 (January 1949): 129; Frederick W. Killian, "The Juvenile Court as an Institution," *Annals* 261 (January 1949): 92–93, 95; Kahn, *Court for Children*, pp. 104, 106, 114–15, 117–19, 140, 147, 155, 157, 161, 164–65, 169–70, 174, 177–79, 269; Bernard C. Fisher, "Juvenile Court: Purpose, Promise, and Problems," *SSR* 34 (1960): 80.

103. Harris B. Peck, "Resistance in Delinquency," *Social Work in the Current Scene* (NCSW Selected Papers) 77 (1950): 379–81; Dunham, "Juvenile Court: Contradictory Orientations in Processing Offenders," 523–24; Elliot Studt, "The Client's Image of the Juvenile Court," in Margaret Keeny Rosenheim, ed., *Justice for the Child: The Juvenile Court in Transition* (New York, Free Press, 1962), pp. 209–10.

104. Advocates of this approach before the Second World War expected comprehensiveness alone to yield results. See Carr, *Delinquency Control*, 382–83.

ances, groping for answers to the complexities of personality and situation.[105] Clinical intervention in the juvenile court, it was acknowledged, did not obtain any better results than would be anticipated through an adolescent's natural maturation process.[106]

The contentious state of behavioral sciences exposed judicial tutelage as a real danger to the court's clients. Clinicians willingly participated in an enterprise designed to remold personality and behavior. But since their theories were unproven, their efforts were not so much treatments as experiments. The court, as some critics suggested, needed a new metaphorical image: it was less a hospital than a laboratory, with all the uncertainty that entailed.[107] They were quick to point out that, as the clinicians went stumbling about in the dark, their subjects were clients who had not been asked whether they wished to participate.[108] The doubtful science being practiced in the juvenile court made its inadequate treatment facilities appear a blessing in disguise.

Social personnel also came to appreciate that a fundamental tension existed between therapeutic discourse and the juvenile court as an institution. As we have seen, they had realized early on that the judge represented another discursive tradition, but that difficulty seemed to be a narrow matter focused on a single (if dominant) personality. Soon it became clear that the problem ran much deeper. To begin with, a legalistic outlook warped the court's understanding of its clients: science might disdain rigid categories and simple labels, but a judicial institution found them indispensable. Only if clients fit under the behavioral headings set forth in the statutes could the juvenile court establish proper jurisdiction, and only if a child's life story were neatly condensed into a package that a judge could appraise in a few moments could the court process its enormous volume of problem juveniles. Furthermore, though the clinician might seek to aid each maladjusted client, a court did not command the necessary resources to treat most of those adjudicated delinquent. Clinics survived in the court apparatus despite their poor treatment performance because they helped the judge rationalize his institution. When the behavioral specialists determined that a particular child had a poor prognosis, the judge conserved his scarce resources for other cases.[109]

105. Francis A. Allen, "The Borderland of the Criminal Law: Problems of 'Socializing' Criminal Justice," *SSR* 32 (1958): 113, 115; Dunham, "Juvenile Court: Contradictory Orientations in Processing Offenders," 516; Eileen L. Younghusband, "The Dilemma of the Juvenile Court," *SSR* 33 (1959): 11, 18, 20; Robert G. Caldwell, "Juvenile Court: Its Development and Some Major Problems," *Journal of Criminal Law, Criminology, and Police Science* (cited hereafter as *JCL*) 51 (1961): 502, 508.

106. Paul W. Tappan, "Judicial and Administrative Approaches to Children with Problems," in Rosenheim, ed., *Justice for the Child*, 148–49; Dunham, "Juvenile Court: Contradictory Orientations in Processing Offenders," 522, 526.

107. Ibid., 521; Younghusband, "Dilemma of the Juvenile Court," 11.

108. Allen, "Borderland of the Criminal Law," 114; Younghusband, "Dilemma of the Juvenile Court," 12; Caldwell, "Juvenile Court: Its Development and Some Major Problems," 509.

109. Karl Birnbaum, "A Court Psychiatrist's View of Juvenile Delinquents," *Annals* 261 (January 1949): 57–58; Kahn, *Court for Children*, 129–30. For an earlier statement of these concerns, see Healy and Bronner, *New Light on Delinquency*, 6, 169–71.

As the court demonstrated a continuing inability to normalize its clients, leading social workers denounced the very notion of therapy in authoritative settings. They pointed out that according to the therapeutic ideal a client had to participate voluntarily in the treatment relationship. And casework along Freudian lines—the model during the 1940s and 1950s—demanded close contact over a prolonged period. Contrary to all sound therapeutic principles, the juvenile court dealt with clients who had not consented to its intervention, and it expected change after superficial and abbreviated adjustment efforts.[110] It was vital, then, to find some alternative to judicial tutelage.

Social personnel did not need to look hard for such a model. From the early days of the court a few Progressive reformers had steadfastly recommended that therapeutic tasks be shifted to other agencies. Most notable among these critics was Thomas Eliot, who devoted a career to promoting nonjudicial forms of therapeutic intervention. Eliot had argued repeatedly that when the court assumed various child protection functions, it exceeded its proper boundaries. As a court it was suited for adjudication, nothing more. Accordingly, it needed to be given a more modest role, and the burden of therapeutic work should be transferred to noncoercive agencies like schools, clinics, and family service agencies. Rather than encourage the service network to refer all problem juveniles to its care at the start, the juvenile court should urge voluntary tutelage as a first resort.[111]

During the 1930s these views gained greater support, especially in that segment of the court movement linked historically to environmentalism and social action. Grace Abbott and her colleagues at the Children's Bureau, who had promoted a social agency ideal of the court in the previous decade, now concluded that the institution simply could not overcome its casework liabilities. For the Children's Bureau leadership, delinquency was but one aspect of a broader problem of child welfare. Local administrative units organized to provide various social services for children thus appeared to be a more suitable instrument than the juvenile court for realizing the therapeutic ideal of a comprehensive and rational human service network.[112]

An opportunity to put this alternative to the test presented itself with the drafting of the 1935 Social Security Act. At the behest of Katherine Lenroot, Abbott's successor as chief of the Children's Bureau, the legislation included a provision under which the federal government agreed to subsidize child welfare departments in rural counties.[113] We will consider later some of the

110. Alice Scott Nutt, "The Juvenile Court in Relation to the Community — An Evaluation," *SSR* 17 (March 1943): 3–4; Dunham, "Juvenile Court: Contradictory Orientations in Processing Offenders," 523; Tappan, "Judicial and Administrative Approaches to Children with Problems," 152.

111. Eliot, *Juvenile Court and the Community*. See, similarly, Baker, "Court and the Delinquent Child," 181.

112. On the shifting views of the Children's Bureau, see Rosenthal, "Children's Bureau and the Juvenile Court," 308–11. For a statement by a bureau official supporting child welfare departments as an alternative to the court, see Nutt, "Future of Juvenile Court as a Case-Work Agency," 377–78.

113. Rosenthal, "Children's Bureau and Juvenile Court," 312–13.

limitations that attended this attempt to use federal power to spread the therapeutic gospel. For the moment we need only observe that social personnel had created a vehicle outside the juvenile court that they hoped would preempt its intervention in all but the most serious cases of delinquency.

Social work leaders like Abbott also stepped outside the therapeutic tradition, returning to their early experiences in the settlement houses, in their search for a way around the court. During the 1930s the Children's Bureau gave its support to a Chicago pilot program organized by community activists that sought to draw in neighborhood groups to combat delinquency. Abbott hoped such neighborhood ventures might offer another alternative to the overgrown court apparatus.[114]

Another determined push by social personnel and community activists to reduce court intervention in adolescents' lives began in the 1960s. Social personnel, arguing that the court justifies its intervention by inflating a child's problem and then bungles his treatment, have advocated "diversion" to keep status offenders and first-time law violators out of the juvenile justice system.[115] The technique can be seen as but the latest effort to realize Thomas Eliot's vision of a juvenile justice apparatus in which the court acts only as an absolute last resort. Meanwhile, echoes of the grass-roots approach that Abbott urged also were heard. In many cities community-based programs sought to provide troubled adolescents with recreational outlets and employment training.[116]

Aside from its concrete programmatic consequences, the disenchantment of reform-minded social personnel during the 1930s had a significant impact upon the intellectual character of the juvenile court movement. In the previous decade the circle of participants in the discourse about delinquency had already begun to narrow. Where once the voice of the settlement worker or charity volunteer could be clearly heard in open conferences on the court, these events had given way by the late 1920s to meetings of the professional associations of judges and probation officials. (This transition entailed, too, a change in the gender complexion of the movement: where women had been well represented among the social reformers, the judges and probation leaders were overwhelmingly male.) Similarly, as environmental prescriptions for delinquency had lost credibility among behavioral specialists, their journals had confined themselves to discussion of personality-oriented approaches. With the alienation of the Children's Bureau leadership and others from the court movement, its ongoing inquiry into delinquency and its treatment fell under the grip of a set of actors with very limited imagination. The result over time was a notable loss of intellectual vitality.

Despite the dismal record of judicial tutelage, the professionals and academics still clustered around the court have remained fixed in their outlook. Alternative conceptions of delinquency control not based on differential case-

114. Abbott, "Juvenile Court and a Community Program," 227, 238–39. On the neighborhood strategy see Young, *Social Treatment in Probation and Delinquency*, 583–85.

115. Platt, *Child Savers*, 189; Ryerson, *Best-Laid Plans*, 158–59.

116. On these community programs, see Platt, *Child Savers*, 183–84.

work attracted little notice. The early Chicago neighborhood experiments inspired scant curiosity among behavioral specialists and few calls for imitation.[117] Delinquency was to be addressed solely as a personality problem, on the terms established and sanctioned by psycho-medical practitioners. Later, as social personnel on the outside concluded that there was no knowledge solution to juvenile maladjustment, the clinicians still associated with the court continued to pursue casework innovations and to grasp eagerly at each new technique.[118] Even today the hope remains among the court's dwindling core of behavioral specialists that new knowledge will emerge to allow them to redeem the promise of therapeutic intervention.[119]

No more extreme example of the intellectual bankruptcy of the court's behavioral personnel can be found than that of their attempt after the Second World War to defend themselves against peer criticism. When influential social workers and behavioral specialists started to question whether any therapeutic relationship could be established in a coercive setting, the social technicians connected to the juvenile court defended their practice in the best Orwellian double-speak: discipline is freedom. All casework, it was argued, entailed a measure of control over the client, for he needed to reconcile himself to the social limits on his behavior. The minor in the juvenile court simply required a greater degree of restraint than clients in other agencies. Because he still had to choose whether to accept the limits being urged by the court, he preserved that measure of autonomy necessary for successful therapeutic change.[120]

Such labored attempts at self-justification have earned steadily less support among even the specialists in personality therapy. Psychiatrists and psychoanalysts were, each in their turn, forced to admit that maladjustment could not be addressed through the juvenile court. They joined the sociologists and community activists in the 1960s in a search for some approach that could transcend the limits of judicial tutelage.

With the disenchantment of the last therapeutic cadre, a process substantially complete by the late 1950s, no intellectual strings tied the court to the discursive forces from which it arose. We might accurately say that at that moment the juvenile court movement ceased to exist. But we must hasten to add that the institution itself lost none of its potency. While normalizing discourse was essential to the birth of judicial tutelage, the court subsequently learned to derive strength from various sources. Important among these, ironically enough, was the rhetoric of tutelage itself, which having been adopted by juvenile court judges now took on a life of its own.

117. Carr, *Delinquency Control,* 149, 249–56.

118. Younghusband, "Dilemma of the Juvenile Court," 20. For an example of this enthusiasm for new techniques, see Michael M. Miller, "Psychodrama in the Treatment Program of a Juvenile Court," *JCL* 50 (1960): 453–59.

119. See, for example, August Aichorn Center for Adolescent Residential Care, Inc., *Plan for Residence No. 1* (New York, 1981).

120. Kenneth L. M. Pray, "The Place of Social Case Work in the Treatment of Delinquency," *SSR* 19 (1945): 235–44; John Otto Reinemann, "Probation and the Juvenile Delinquent," *Annals* 261 (January 1949): 118; Kahn, *Court for Children,* 231–32; Gerald A. Tracey, "A Social Worker's Perspective on Social Work in Probation," *Crime and Delinquency* 7 (1961): 131–36.

Counterrevolution in the Law

If social personnel after the New Deal turned their back on the juvenile court, the legal profession moved in just the opposite direction. During the two decades after the Second World War the court was drawn out of the shadows of the legal system. State legislatures and higher courts, responding to the concerns raised by the legal profession, imposed certain due process requirements during the 1960s. By bringing more lawyers into the juvenile court, these reforms have precipitated a new discursive tension. The practice of judicial tutelage now is a matter of debate among participants who share a common schooling in the law, but they still talk past each other. Current discursive conflict revolves around contrary notions of justice—whether help for a maladjusted minor can best be secured, as judges insist when they invoke Progressive catchphrases, by the exercise of judicial discretion or, as defense attorneys claim, by a strong commitment to formal rights.

Through the first fifty years of the juvenile court's existence, it had attracted much less notice from lawyers than from social personnel. It is true that an occasional protest from the bar had been advanced against the notion that the promise of treatment was a fair exchange for the surrender of procedural protections. But, as we have seen, early appellate decisions supporting the movement's claim that a juvenile court was not engaged in criminal proceeding defused resistance among lawyers. Just as crucial, for many years the court escaped scrutiny because of its low visibility and lack of prestige. The legal profession regarded the court as a career dead-end. Once the early judicial entrepreneurs had carved out their empires, leading jurists avoided serving on the juvenile court bench. For their part, successful attorneys declined to practice in a setting where they were made to feel superfluous and clients could not afford their fees.[121]

In the 1950s, however, lawyers finally were provoked to take notice of the juvenile court both by the spread of some of its principles and by their own evolving norms. Therapeutic ideology had initially taken root only in courts dealing with family matters, but by mid-century it began to influence criminal justice institutions as well. In one important example, an influential bar association group during the 1940s promoted the idea of a youth correctional authority to raise the age of criminal responsibility and extend to young adults the principle of treatment instead of punishment. As the juvenile court exerted wider influence, it could no longer be ignored.[122] Moreover, the legal profession by this time was imposing a more demanding standard of due process on nonfederal courts. When the juvenile court was established, its procedural latitude differed only in small degree from other local courts, but by the 1950s it appeared to be as primitive in its attention to due process as a star cham-

121. Killian, "Juvenile Court as an Institution," 93; Lewis Yablonsky, "The Role of Law and Social Science in the Juvenile Court," *JCL* 53 (December 1962): 427, 429.

122. John Forbes Perkins, "Indeterminate Control of Offenders: Arbitrary and Discriminatory," *Law and Contemporary Problems* 9 (1942): 624–34; Yablonsky, "Role of Law and Social Science in Juvenile Court," 435.

ber.[123] In yet another vein, the notion that the law should express a community's moral strictures regained a strong following among legal scholars at about this time. This idea had fallen from fashion in the Progressive jurisprudence that accompanied the rise of the juvenile court, a discourse that spoke only of what society owed the offender. Now the legal moralists asserted that it was proper for society to penalize those who refused to conform to its limits.[124] Together, all of these value shifts prompted lawyers to scrutinize the court much more carefully than they had before.

The lawyers were most alarmed by the court's disregard for juvenile rights. In exchange for treatment, court movement theory had held, the minor agreed to surrender his due process safeguards. Yet it was clear that the court did not assure him real adjustment services. Rather, it engaged in a linguistic subterfuge: any disposition, no matter how punitive its effects, was labeled treatment. Meanwhile, the judge conducted his courtroom according to his whims, the minor faced adjudication and disposition without legal representation, and no record was kept that might give a basis for appeal.[125] Reiterating a charge some court proponents had made in the 1920s, the lawyers asserted that the court's indifference to common judicial safeguards left a deep negative mark on its clients. Both the juvenile and his family felt wronged, and they questioned the legitimacy of the juvenile court and the law in general.[126]

Legal observers swiftly concluded that it was necessary, as in other courts, to place checks on judicial discretion and arbitrary power. Since the court had not delivered on its part of the rights-for-treatment bargain, the juvenile ought to have his full constitutional protections restored. This should include the right to counsel, time to prepare a defense, the opportunity to question witnesses against him, recorded hearings and rationales for dispositions so that he would have a basis for appeal, and more. Of particular interest, the lawyers rejected a favorite Progressive argument still advanced by judges that a confession was a vital first step in treatment and insisted that no minor be pressured to incriminate himself.[127]

123. Ryerson, *Best-Laid Plans*, 57–59, 61. The comparison with the star chamber was first advanced by Roscoe Pound in the 1930s. See Pound, Foreword, xxvii.

124. Platt, *Child Savers*, 152–155.

125. Allen, "Borderland of the Criminal Law," 116; Dunham, "Juvenile Court: Contradictory Orientations in Processing Offenders," 516–17, 519; Tappan, "Judicial and Administrative Approaches to Children with Problems," 149, 159; Caldwell, "Juvenile Court: Its Development and Some Major Problems," 504–06; Yablonsky, "Role of Law and Social Science in Juvenile Court," 431–33.

126. John F. Perkins, "Common Sense and Bad Boys," *Atlantic Monthly* 173 (May 1944): 47; Allen, "Borderland of the Criminal Law," 117; Younghusband, "Dilemma of the Juvenile Court," 15–17; Studt, "Client's Image of the Juvenile Court," 204; Ryerson, *Best-Laid Plans*, 132–35.

127. Caldwell, "Juvenile Court: Its Development and Some Major Problems," 507; Yablonsky, "Role of Law and Social Science in Juvenile Court," 431. See also Allen, "Borderland of the Criminal Law," 118–19; Fisher, "Juvenile Court," 78–79; Howard E. Fradkin, "Disposition Dilemmas of American Juvenile Courts," in Rosenheim, ed., *Justice for the Child*, 121.

As some members of the legal profession probed the status of the juvenile's rights in the court, others considered what might be termed the community's rights. According to these legal moralists, any court must stand ready to validate the behavioral limits established by the community. One vital function of the judicial system, in short, was to declare clearly that an act was wrong. The social agency ideal of the juvenile court completely overlooked this essential judicial responsibility. To make matters worse, social personnel in the court had urged the judge to base his decision not on what the child had done but rather on what he was. If the court followed the direction favored by its social personnel, it abdicated its duty to utter the public's condemnation of the minor's act.[128] Interestingly enough, studies suggested that juvenile offenders and their families shared the moralist view that antisocial behavior ought to be censured. Adolescents knew full well that they had done wrong, and they voiced contempt for adults in the court who sought only to "explain" such behavior. Clients, too, wanted the juvenile court to act more like a court and less like a social agency.[129]

To ward off challenges from the legal profession, many judges fell back upon the social agency rationale of the court. They needed extraordinary discretion if they were to aid the child, and any procedural checks that interfered with their flexibility threatened not only the institution but the child himself. Moreover, in a return to the language of their Progressive counterparts, these judges asserted that a child's social rights ought to rank above mere formal legal protections.[130]

These invocations of the court's founding principles faced hard going among skeptical professional peers. State courts, rejecting the contention that the juvenile court only treated and did not punish, began to rule in the late 1950s that a child was entitled to full procedural safeguards. These decisions often were overturned on appeal, however, indicating that a segment of the judiciary remained convinced by the old movement ideology. But within a few years legislatures in New York, California, and other states passed statutes that made counsel available to some indigent juveniles.[131] Here policy entrepreneurship counted heavily again, for the legislative campaigns depended upon

128. Caldwell, "Juvenile Court: Its Development and Some Major Problems," 507–09; Tappan, "Judicial and Administrative Approaches to Children with Problems," 147–48, 151, 154–55. For an early statement of this position, see John H. Wigmore, "Juvenile Court vs. Criminal Court," *Illinois Law Review* 21 (1926): 375–77.

129. Dunham, "Juvenile Court: Contradictory Orientations in Processing Offenders," 520–21; Younghusband, "Dilemma of the Juvenile Court," 17; Studt, "Client's Image of the Juvenile Court," 209–10.

130. Gustav L. Schramm, "Philosophy of the Juvenile Court," *Annals* 261 (January 1949): 102–03; Orman W. Ketcham, "The Unfulfilled Promise of the Juvenile Court," in Rosenheim, ed., *Justice for the Child*, 25–28; Paul W. Alexander, "Constitutional Rights in the Juvenile Court," in Rosenheim, ed., *Justice for the Child*, 84–85, 87–90, 92.

131. Alexander, "Constitutional Rights in Juvenile Court," 83–84, 92; Fox, "Juvenile Justice Reform," 1235; Peter S. Prescott, *The Child Savers: Juvenile Justice Observed* (New York: Alfred A. Knopf, 1981), 7, 63–64.

the initiative of a few legal aid attorneys.[132] The U. S. Supreme Court also began to erode the constitutional foundation of the juvenile court, particularly in the 1967 Gault decision that affirmed a minor's due process rights.[133]

Legislative mandates and court rulings have threatened the judge's monopoly over proceedings, and with that, much that has distinguished the juvenile court from most other judicial institutions. Defense lawyers have been grafted onto the court apparatus, expanding the circle of actors dealing with the juvenile offender. The "client" now has a representative who, at least in theory, will speak on behalf of his constitutional rights and, if he is adjudicated delinquent, demand the treatment he needs. Since the child has an attorney, the state also requires one. Frequently the case against the juvenile offender is argued today by a prosecutor rather than a probation officer.[134] By extension, with a legal presence established in the court, the institution's impulse to cast itself as a social agency has been formally neutralized. The new legal agents can speak for both public safety and formal due process.

But, alas, if the civil libertarians hoped to secure the procedural rights of the child, they too have had reason to be disappointed. During the late 1950s and the 1960s, before the addition of defense counsel to the court, the more conscientious judges became sensitive to the due process issue and felt obliged to look after the juvenile's formal rights. Now it is assumed that the lawyer representing the minor will protect him.[135] Some attorneys do work diligently to defend their young clients. But the court continues to attract low-caliber lawyers who feel more at ease taking the side of the court staff against their client. Since the juvenile himself regards his attorney as a part of the system, mutual hostility quickly surfaces.[136] Representation in court therefore has not achieved what its legal advocates desired.

When defense lawyers take seriously their client's due process rights, moreover, the juvenile court finds itself once again beset with a polarizing discursive conflict. On one side, many judges continue to insist that discretionary power remains the best means to help a child and advance other social values. They try to run their courtroom much as before. On the other side, conscientious defense lawyers, who think that the child can best be aided by an institution that attends to formal rights, also want the court to base its dispositions on a full understanding of the child's needs and to let itself be guided in these dispositions by a commitment to do the "least harm" to its clients. The defense agenda, then, brings together Progressive ideas and revisionist skepticism in an awkward fit—the minor is owed both the safeguards due any accused person and the solicitude due any innocent victim.

This discursive antagonism plays itself out in the courtroom in a way that mocks the Progressive ideal of judicial tutelage. Although judges, prosecutors,

132. Ibid., 51, 59–61.
133. *In re Gault*, 387 U.S. 1 (1967). For a discussion of the Court's reasoning and determination, see Ryerson, *Best-Laid Plans*, 147ff.
134. Prescott, *Child Savers*, 65, 219.
135. Fox, "Juvenile Justice Reform," 1237.
136. Platt, *Child Savers*, 164–69; Prescott, *Child Savers*, 5, 18–19, 102.

and defense attorneys all still pay homage to "the best interests of the child," the process they have created leaves no possibility that his interests will be considered. His representative fights to keep information about him out of the court, the prosecutor presents the worst picture possible, and the judge ignores exculpatory evidence. Defense lawyers object when the judge in disposing of a case fixes upon the gravity of the offense and slights their client's condition and treatment needs. Judges retort that for all the defense attorneys' rhetoric about doing what is best for the minor, they merely seek to do for him what they would do for an adult criminal defendant—to beat the charge through any procedural device available or, failing that, to persuade the court to accept whatever disposition their client wants. Even if strong evidence comes to light that the youngster is severely troubled, his lawyer first strives for a dismissal and then seeks to bargain for the least restrictive placement. Moreover, if the minor is found delinquent, there is no one left who is concerned with treatment. The disposition options available to the court, ranging from probation to placement in a secure facility, are seen by the judge and the attorneys as gradations of punishment, not instruments of therapy. In reality, the court's final determination depends not on scientific recommendations but on such factors as the minor's record and the availability of space in detention homes or training schools.[137]

Political Survival in a Patchwork State

Although the juvenile court has faced an increasingly complicated political environment since the New Deal, the institution has demonstrated extraordinary resilience. The disenchantment of social personnel left the court without an organized political constituency and also gave rise to institutional competitors. But much to the frustration of social personnel, their new agencies, rather than circumvent the court, merely have contributed to the fragmentation and redundancy that plague the field of child protection. As for the court itself, the judges stood fast, cultivated new allies, and became a potent political force in their own right.

The external conditions that influenced the court at the beginning have continued, of course, to shape it in the modern era. Rampant localism, for example, has characterized court operations to the present day, so that court practices remain as diverse as judges' personalities. There has never been a single entity that we can properly call "the juvenile court," but instead a cluster of judicial organs grouped for convenience under that heading. Only autonomous big-city courts with historic ties to philanthropy seem to have aspired to the social agency ideal.[138] By contrast, where the court has been but a branch of the criminal court system, the criminal justice mentality has persisted.[139] Even the so-called socialized courts have demonstrated no uniformity in such practices as the use of unofficial dispositions.

137. Ibid.
138. Caldwell, "Juvenile Court: Its Development and Some Major Problems," 497–98, 506.
139. Tappan, "Children and Youth in Criminal Court," 128, 132; Dunham, "Juvenile Court: Contradictory Orientations in Processing Offenders," 513, 521.

At first, the defection of reform-minded social personnel left the juvenile court without outside allies in its efforts to cope with this political environment. The court had depended upon settlement houses and women's organizations to encourage political support in the wider circle of Progressive politics. These actors had helped in the legislative battles and the contests with local political machines, and they had led the campaign for centralized oversight to raise the standards of court practice. As the juvenile court disappeared from reform agendas, it could count on the support only of the organizations formed by its in-house professionals, the judges and the probation officers. This narrowing of the institution's political base came at a time when, with the dissemination of the costly psychoanalytic approach, the court's fiscal needs rose.[140]

Moreover, since social personnel sought to circumvent judicial intervention with a separate child welfare apparatus, their disenchantment produced concrete institutional rivals to the court. Recall that leading figures in the Children's Bureau incorporated provisions in the Social Security Act to establish in rural counties child welfare departments outside the court's orbit. By working with an autonomous administrative structure, it was hoped, the federal government could make services available to *children*, not to the *court*. By the early 1940s nearly every state had passed legislation to take advantage of the new federal money. It appeared that in rural areas a therapeutic instrument would be put in place that would remain beyond the reach of the juvenile court judge with his traditional legalistic outlook.[141]

Yet rather than generate an institutional counterweight to judicial tutelage, the strategy pursued by social personnel at times strengthened the court's hand. It was one thing for Children's Bureau planners to envision a service structure growing up entirely apart from the court and quite another to impress this conception upon social workers cast adrift in isolated places. Again localism shaped the implementation of reform. The staff of the new county child welfare program frequently chose to cooperate with the juvenile court judge, converting the agency into his probation arm.[142] With more resources at its disposal in such instances, the court actually found its reach extended.

At the same time the timidity of the attempt to sidestep the court made complete success impossible. Social personnel at first hoped to promote child welfare departments in urban as well as rural counties. But certain philanthropic interests, notably the Catholic child protection groups, objected, fearing that they would be displaced by public organizations. Rather than risk losing a confrontation with such interests, the architects of the legislation chose not to try to impose on cities the same coordinated, nonjudicial control of child welfare.[143] The federal government during the New Deal therefore left undisturbed the central position of the urban juvenile court.

However necessary this political accommodation was, it has had far-reaching consequences. The court at that time was especially vulnerable, with its reform

---

140. Ryerson, *Best-Laid Plans*, 104–05.
141. Rosenthal, "Children's Bureau and the Juvenile Court," 313.
142. Ibid.; Nutt, "Future of Juvenile Court as a Case-Work Agency," 378.
143. Rosenthal, "Children's Bureau and the Juvenile Court," 317*n*40.

allies gone and the public, under the impact of the depression, for once tolerant of many forms of delinquency.[144] Just as significant, social personnel failed to pursue the opportunity to rationalize the child protection field. They knew that services for children in cities had suffered not only because of court mismanagement but also because of a lack of coordination among all service agencies. The disjointed efforts of private, judicial, local, and state actors already had resulted in a service labyrinth.[145] When social personnel acquiesced in these arrangements, they made certain that duplication, waste, and omission would continue to define urban child welfare activity. At various times since the New Deal, particularly during the 1960s and early 1970s, the federal government has invested heavily in urban delinquency control measures outside the juvenile court. But the chance to dislodge the court has passed. And even if federal programs in cities have helped belatedly to create alternatives to judicial tutelage, their larger impact has been to further distend the sprawling system of child protection services.

Despite major reform initiatives during the New Deal and the Great Society, then, social personnel since mid-century have found the child protection situation a source of continuing dismay. They have promoted important institutional rivals to the court, it is true, and thus have redirected the efforts of therapeutic cadre toward Thomas Eliot's vision of normalization by noncoercive human services. But this has not masked their defeat. Far from the integrated tutelary apparatus long imagined by therapeutic discourse, a patchwork state sector that still depends on parochial philanthropic groups has administered child protection. More services for the child have been made available, yet there is no assurance he will receive those he needs. Because many agencies accept only promising cases, a minor who has committed no offense might be "dumped" on the court.[146] Moreover, as child protection has remained fragmented and inefficient, expansion has failed to plug important gaps in the service network. For example, urban child welfare agencies and juvenile courts have long reported particular difficulties in arranging foster care placements for the minority children who have made up a growing percentage of the caseload.[147]

Through all this, the juvenile court itself has retained its pivotal role in the processing of problem youngsters. To the frustration of social personnel, who felt it was taking far too many cases that belonged elsewhere, the volume of court business expanded relentlessly after the Second World War. More juveniles than ever before passed through children's courts, with an annual total of some 500,000 cases by 1959. In that year the Children's Bureau estimated that some 12 percent of all American youth would encounter the court at least once, with an even higher percentage in cities and among certain groups, notably

144. Carr, *Delinquency Control*, 56–57.
145. Nutt, "Juvenile Court in Relation to the Community," 5–6.
146. Tappan, "Judicial and Administrative Approaches to Children with Problems," 155.
147. Nutt, "Juvenile Court in Relation to the Community," 6–7; Kahn, *Court for Children*, 243; Alfred J. Kahn, "Court and Community," in Rosenheim, ed., *Justice for the Child*, 231–32; Fox, "Juvenile Justice Reform," 1232.

black males.[148] Recent policy reforms, like the celebrated diversion efforts of the 1970s, have scarcely altered the pattern of heavy reliance on judicial intervention.

Whatever might be said about the vulnerability of the court in the 1940s, the window of opportunity for the institution's critics closed tightly as public attitudes began to shift. Public reaction to delinquency during the past forty years has been conditioned by certain demographic trends. First and foremost, the nation has experienced a broad cultural upheaval—the emergence of adolescence as a distinct life phase—that adults have not known how to manage. After the Second World War a combination of factors (including delayed entry into the labor force, extended schooling, and rising family incomes) created a large population group that soon adopted its own values and behavioral mores. Succeeding decades have brought an elaboration of this youth culture. Much adolescent conduct has perturbed adult society, and the court has found itself called upon to address new activities the community regards as deviant.[149] In addition, many urban communities have been through a wrenching process of racial succession that has focused public fears on the behavior of minority youth.

Public alarm over delinquency has expressed itself in the form of legislative and electoral pressure upon the juvenile court. On several occasions, especially when delinquent conduct has assumed a more violent form and lurid accounts have appeared in the press, the public has demanded a "get tough" posture toward problem juveniles.[150] Then state legislatures have responded by adopting a stricter approach to youth crime.[151] Public pressure can also make itself felt more directly: in many communities the juvenile court judge has held his post through either election or periodic popular reaffirmation. He therefore has had to remain sensitive to public sentiments about delinquency and to claims in the local press that his institution can do nothing to stem the tide.[152]

Far from a burden, this external pressure has been a valuable asset to juvenile court judges. They have used the public craving for punishment to fend off any incursions into their domain by child welfare agencies. When social personnel associated with competing agencies have complained that the court panders to the worst popular instincts, judges have cited public opinion as support for their effort to reaffirm the community's moral values. They also have accused the social workers and behavioral specialists of being indifferent to the community's legitimate demand for safety. Meanwhile, even though lawyers have established a principle of representation for juvenile offenders,

---

148. Figures given in Yablonsky, "Role of Law and Social Science in Juvenile Court," 433; Charles Shireman, Foreword to Rosenheim, ed., *Justice for the Child*, v–vi.

149. Studt, "Client's Image of the Juvenile Court," 207–09; Ryerson, *Best-Laid Plans*, 127–31.

150. Tappan, "Judicial and Administrative Approaches to Children with Problems," 145; Fisher, "Juvenile Court," 78; Angel Castillo, "Juvenile Offenders in Court: The Debate over Treatment," *New York Times*, July 24, 1981, B4.

151. Prescott, *Child Savers*, 29–30, 219–20.

152. Alexander, "Constitutional Rights in Juvenile Court," 86.

judges can exploit public opinion to thwart from yet another direction the drive to protect juvenile rights in the court. Just as judges use Progressive rhetoric to neutralize defense counsel in court, public sentiment ensures that the due process movement will falter in the political arena. Fox observes that formal legal rights are expensive because the public has to pay the salaries of defense lawyers, expand programs to train them, and add court staff and trial rooms.[153] With public anger over violent youth crime running high, state legislatures have not been any more eager to pay for juvenile rights than juvenile treatment. As a result defense lawyers have to manage excessive caseloads, and the low remuneration draws the least distinguished legal talent.

Even where public sentiment has not made itself felt, the judges have shown an ability to look after their institutional position. Social personnel in the 1940s and 1950s established an array of new therapeutic agencies only to find that the court, as first player on the scene, had situated itself as the gatekeeper for all child welfare services. Often a juvenile had to be adjudicated delinquent or in need of supervision in order to receive care from any agency.[154] More recently juvenile court judges have undermined the diversion approach. Social personnel, as we have noted, see diversion as a way to steer children who have not committed serious offenses away from the court. Many lawyers have backed the idea and encouraged the American Bar Association to pursue such a change.[155] But the judges have resisted strongly. And because they sit atop the established institution defining the field of juvenile justice, their views command significant support within the legal profession. They have defeated a proposal that the ABA recommend stripping the court of its responsibility for status offenses.[156] Thus the court in many communities has checked this latest initiative by the service professionals to reduce its scope of operations.

CONCLUSION: INNOVATION AND DRIFT IN THE THERAPEUTIC STATE

The fate of the juvenile court has rested upon the play of discursive forces and political influences. From its origins in Progressive philanthropy through its latest internal conflicts, the court has been inspired and sustained by discursive currents in social work and law. At the same time, the broader political environment, often acting as a constraint that compromised discursive principles and altered the court movement's expectations, ultimately worked to insulate the institution from discursive challenges.

Similar combinations of discursive and political factors best account for the development of the therapeutic sector as a whole. The therapeutic apparatus emerged from a discursive movement, and normalizing public agencies have endured because that discourse institutionalized itself. But the component pieces have been uncoupled by political pressures.

The programs for distributing mothers' aid (or "widows' pensions"), for

153. Fox, "Juvenile Justice Reform," 1238.

154. Nutt, "Responsibility of Juvenile Court and Public Agency," 315–16; Yablonsky, "Role of Law and Social Science in Juvenile Court," 433.

155. Prescott, *Child Savers*, 120, 239.

156. Ibid., 238–40.

instance, not only offered a public relief allowance but also brought a case-worker into contact with the working-class family and paved the way for contact with other therapeutic services.[157] Here, as in the court, the client was bound to meet an officially established standard of conduct, and failure by a mother to remodel her behavior as directed might cost her public support.[158] Experienced charity caseworkers joined the public pension departments to ensure the therapeutic content of the new program.[159]

Widely adaptable, the therapeutic approach quickly became the reigning ideology of the human services, and it has continued to set the terms for policy discussion in the field. A cadre flowed out of social work schools in the 1920s to help staff public agencies and carry forward the tutelary banner in future policy debates.[160] The vision of an all-embracing, multisided tutelary apparatus continues today to hold a fascination for social personnel teaching about or engaged in the practice of the human services. When normalizing intervention fails, moreover, behavioral science is still seen to hold the solution.

As a result, even where the therapeutic approach has encountered significant discursive opposition, this opposition has failed to dislodge it. Rarely did the therapeutic approach command anything like universal assent. Nevertheless, therapeutic practitioners in other tutelary agencies have not felt compelled to abandon their position as they did in the juvenile court. In these agencies senior personnel have received formal training in casework techniques, and organizational norms leave no room for alternative policy approaches.

However influential therapeutic discourse has been in human service agencies, political constraints have always checked their therapeutic ambition. This pattern became clear with the first experiments in public tutelage. Supporters prevailed initially because they presented programs as inexpensive and because organized opposition was rare.[161] But because the size of the potential constituency and the cost of serving it had been minimized to secure legislative approval, the new normalizing programs were systematically underfunded.[162] Moreover, although permissive legislation avoided conflict with foes at the

157. Richard M. Neustadt, "Home Conservation—A Step in Social Conservation," *Report of the New York State Commission on Relief for Widowed Mothers* (Albany, 1914); Florence Nesbitt, *Standards of Public Aid to Children in Their Own Homes*, Children's Bureau Publication no. 118, U.S. Department of Labor (Washington, D.C.: U.S. Government Printing Office, 1923), 31–35.

158. Edith Abbott and Sophonisba P. Breckinridge, *The Administration of the Aid-to-Mothers Law in Illinois*, Children's Bureau Legal Series no. 7, U.S. Department of Labor (Washington, D.C.: U.S. Government Printing Office, 1921), 38–40, 41–42.

159. Einstein, "Pensions for Widowed Mothers as a Means," p. 231; Hace Sorel Tishler, *Self-Reliance and Social Security, 1870–1917* (Port Washington, N.Y.: Kennikat Press, National University Publications, 1971), 153–54.

160. Lubove, *Professional Altruist*, chap. 5.

161. Edith Abbott, "The Experimental Period of Widow's Pension Legislation," NCSW, *Proceedings* 44 (1917), 154–55.

162. See especially Mary F. Bogue, *Administration of Mothers' Aid in Ten Localities*, Children's Bureau Publication no. 184, U.S. Department of Labor (Washington, D.C.: U.S. Government Printing Office, 1928).

start, resistance could not be avoided indefinitely. The struggle to establish programs like pensions had to be waged in each county, to be determined by the local balance of discursive and political forces. Fragmentation, that bane of the juvenile court, recurred in each Progressive tutelary program.

To overcome these political obstacles, program administrators and supporters after the First World War redoubled their political efforts. Organizational reform was put forward as one answer to localism in service administration.[163] Meanwhile, administrators and social work leaders pursued incremental legislation to expand the tutelary apparatus.[164] By virtue of these political strategies, therapeutic actors ensured the survival of public human services. Despite the atmosphere of reaction, programs did not disappear, and they even enlisted new clients. Wherever public authority and tutelary methods had been joined, the union endured the decline of Progressivism.

Just the same, therapeutic forces have never tamed the political environment in which they operate. To consider only the most ironic political complication, the accumulated triumphs of the therapeutic sector gradually destroyed the possibility of policy coherence. Therapeutic entrepreneurs seeking to expand the reach of adjustment services have encouraged the multiplication of normalizing agencies. Each new wave of policy innovation has deposited another layer of service organizations upon a sediment formed by earlier ventures. Agencies have inevitably learned to see each other not as partners in a common enterprise but as competitors for resources and patrons of rival tutelary doctrines.

Thus has arisen the obscurity of the therapeutic sector in the modern American state. On one side, since social personnel first made their techniques the basis for normalizing agencies, their discourse has not invited lay participation. On the other side, the attempt to create a comprehensive tutelary apparatus to surround the marginal family ran afoul of established political structures and other political forces. Localism, institutional jealousy, and political maneuvering have gnawed away at the organic unity of the human services. But we should not mistake the dispersion of the therapeutic state for its destruction. As clients would attest and advocates of alternative social policies have learned, even this attenuated Leviathan can be formidable when provoked.

---

163. Abbott, "Experimental Period of Widow's Pension Legislation," 162–63; Lundberg, *Public Aid to Mothers with Dependent Children*, 4.

164. Abbott and Breckinridge, *Administration of Aid-to-Mothers Law in Illinois*, 114; Bogue, *Administration of Mothers' Aid in Ten Localities*, 1n.

ROBERT MEISTER
University of California, Santa Cruz

The Logic and Legacy of
Dred Scott: Marshall, Taney,
and the Sublimation
of Republican Thought

The continuing repression by jurists and scholars of the role of *Dred Scott* in our constitutional history has given that case a pervasive influence that is rarely, if ever, acknowledged. The following discussion will abstract from the moral embarrassment of *Dred Scott* in order to treat its jurisprudence as the missing link that connects the underlying framework of Marshallian constitutionalism with later struggles over the meaning of the Fourteenth Amendment. Without such a link the Civil War is left as a constitutional silence, perhaps a second American Revolution, separating two discontinuous systems of government. That silence can be filled only by acknowledging the fundamental continuities between our present conceptions of constitutional equality and the system of government that could permit the existence of slavery.

My thesis is that the logic of Taney's opinion in *Dred Scott*, hinging on the status of free Negroes, set the terms in which slavery would be constitutionally abolished within a framework of federalism, and in which individual rights would and would not be constitutionally protected by the federal courts against the actions of state governments. For this reason *Dred Scott* is the negative template on which the logic of the Fourteenth Amendment and its subsequent judicial interpretation have been based. I shall argue that whatever the defects in Taney's reasoning on particular points, at the level of constitutional jurisprudence the structural innovations of *Dred Scott* are still with us.

Early research on this paper was supported by fellowships from the Rockefeller Foundation and the Harvard Law School. The preparation of the manuscript was funded by grants from the Academic Senate of the University of California, Santa Cruz, and from the Law, Society, and Ethics research group on the Santa Cruz campus. I am grateful to Karen Orren, Stephen Skowronek, Ann McConnell, Jerome Neu, Grant McConnell, Joel Yellin, and an anonymous reviewer for helpful comments on an earlier draft. Douglas Reed and Melody Rose provided able research assistance.

AMERICAN CONSTITUTIONALISM AND THE
FAILURE OF REPUBLICAN THEORY

Dred Scott and the Forms of Constitutional Argument

The case of *Dred Scott* began as a simple suit for freedom brought by a slave against his master and ended as a test of the constitutional power of Congress to forbid slavery in the territories (and, ultimately, to abolish it in the newly admitted states). The evidence that this progression may have been avoidable, both legally and practically, has led some commentators to speculate on the obscure motivations of the parties, the gratuitous racism of the justices, and the political agendas of those who wished to force a constitutional confrontation. Most modern commentators properly characterize the case as a moral abomination and a legal travesty—illustrating one or another "lesson" about the pitfalls of judicial intrusions into politics—without ever confronting the forms of constitutional reasoning that underlay the Taney Court's decision.

This neglect is unfortunate because *Dred Scott* is in many ways a sustained reflection on two constitutional issues that have been with us since the beginning: When do the legal rights that individuals can claim against each other place constitutional restraints on the legislative powers of government? When do the constitutional rights of individuals against their government affect the rights that they can claim against each other?[1] Even if there had been no slavery in this country and no territorial expansion, these questions would have been fundamental to our constitutional scheme. In an era concerned with reconciling the perpetuation of slavery with the expansion of federalism into the territories, these questions were explosive.[2]

Chief Justice Taney's opinion in *Dred Scott*[3] was driven by the recognition that the institution of slavery raised both of these questions, assuming without apology that slavery is a paradigm case for defining the relationship between private and public law under our Constitution, and for showing how each effectively limits the other. Taney does not consider the possibility that the private law of slavery is unconstitutional because the means necessary to enforce it would violate the rights of Negro citizens. Rather, his approach to *Dred Scott* presupposes a legal point that is at once obvious and, to our modern

1. The works of Edward Corwin are seminal in all discussions of the continuing significance of pre–Civil War constitutional jurisprudence. See Corwin, *The Doctrine of Judicial Review* (Princeton: Princeton University Press, 1914). That collection reprints his important article "The Dred Scott Decision in the Light of Contemporary Legal Doctrines," *American Historical Review* 17 (October 1911): 52–69. For the foundation of the analysis attempted in this essay, see Corwin, "The Basic Doctrine of American Constitutional Law," *Michigan Law Review* 12, no. 4 (1914): 247–76; "The Doctrine of Due Process of Law before the Civil War," *Harvard Law Review* 24 (1911): 366–485, 460–79.

2. I rely on Arthur Bestor, "State Sovereignty and Slavery: A Reinterpretation of Proslavery Constitutional Doctrine, 1846–1860," *Illinois State Historical Society Journal* 54 (Summer 1961): 117–80; and, "The Civil War as a Constitutional Crisis," *American Historical Review* 69, no. 2 (January 1964): 327–52. A less persuasive effort to deal with the same area is Robert R. Russel, "Constitutional Doctrines with Regard to Slavery in Territories," *Journal of Southern History* 32, no.4 (November 1966): 466–86.

3. *Dred Scott* v. *Sandford* 19 Howard 393 (1857).

sensibilities, shocking: the meaning of freedom under the private law of slavery is not the same as the meaning of political freedom under the Constitution. In the first sense freedom is essentially defensive—a specific legal response to the claims of an individual who would otherwise be entitled to hold one in slavery; in the second it is an affirmative right to equal citizenship and hence to membership in the sovereign "people." Taney argued that under the private law of slavery Negroes were eligible for freedom only in the first, more limited, sense, and that no change in the private law of slavery (up to and including abolition) could implicitly confer upon them freedom in the second sense.

Dred Scott is an outrageous opinion regarding the problem of slavery, but it does not deviate from the broad tradition of constitutional thought about the relation of public and private law. Rather, Taney's jurisprudence reflects the pull of two basic models that underlie most serious thinking about constitutional law. One expresses the notion that the Constitution functions as *law*. The other expresses the notion that this body of law is *constitutional*.

(1) The first model derives from the adjudication of private lawsuits between *individual and individual*. In the private law model rights are effectively limited by the remedies available to others, and a justiciable issue arises whenever the rights claimed by one party to the pleadings are incompatible with the remedy claimed by another. In such circumstances courts of appropriate jurisdiction have the duty to resolve the underlying dispute between the parties by deciding which assertion of rights will prevail.

The legal history of *Dred Scott* began with a case of this kind. Dred Scott originally sued a Mrs. Emerson in Missouri courts for assault and false imprisonment—which is what enslavement would be if he were legally free. She responded that he had no remedy because she acted within her rights as his lawful owner (presumably in her capacity as trustee of the estate of her deceased husband, who had once been Dred Scott's undisputed owner.) Thus was the issue joined.[4] Dred Scott won his case in trial court on the grounds that the relevant Missouri precedents freed slaves who had been held for a time in free states, even if their masters had been on military assignment, as Dr. Emerson was. The Missouri Supreme Court, however, reversed in a split decision directly overruling the key precedent on which the lower court decision had been based.[5] When Mrs. Emerson subsequently remarried, she was legally barred

4. See Don E. Fehrenbacher, *The Dred Scott Case: Its Significance in American Law and Politics* (New York: Oxford University Press, 1978), chap. 10; Walter Ehrlich, *They Have No Rights: Dred Scott's Struggle for Freedom* (Westport, Conn.: Greenwood Press, 1979), pt. 2. These are the best recent historical sources on Dred Scott. In general I rely on Fehrenbacher, who provides a broader and more nuanced account of the case.

5. *Scott (a man of color)* v. *Emerson*, 15 Mo. 576 (1852). This case, and the precedent case, *Rachel* v. *Walker*, 4 Mo. 350 (1836), are summarized in Helen Tunnicliff Caterall, *Judicial Cases concerning American Slavery and the Negro*, 5 vols. (Washington D.C.: Carnegie Institute, 1926–37), 5:148, 185, and discussed in Fehrenbacher, ch. 10. In overturning *Rachel* v. *Walker*, the *Emerson* court said, "Times now are not as they were when the former decisions on this subject were made. Since then not only individuals but States have been possessed with a dark and fell spirit in relation to slavery, . . . whose inevitable consequence must be the overthrow and destruction of our government" (Caterall, 5: 185).

from administering her deceased husband's estate in Missouri, and her brother, John Sanford (the name is misspelled in the opinion), could arguably be considered the owner of Dred Scott in Missouri under the terms of Dr. Emerson's estate. The possibility, never contested, that Sanford, by then a citizen of New York, had become Scott's nominal owner allowed Scott to bring a new suit under the diversity jurisdiction of the federal courts on the theory that Scott, if free, could sue as a citizen of Missouri.[6] In arguing that he was no longer legally a slave in Missouri Dred Scott pleaded the same facts and law against Sanford on which he had lost in state courts in his case against Mrs. Emerson.[7] The federal case, however, raised not only the original issue of whether Dred Scott remained a slave under Missouri law but also the new issue of whether, even if he was not a slave, he could be considered a citizen of Missouri for purposes of federal diversity jurisdiction which, under Article III, authorizes federal courts to decide cases and controversies between citizens of different states.

(2) The second model derives from the adjudication of conflicts between *government and individual*. In the public law model, individual rights are effectively limited by the legitimate power of the state to promote the public good, and vice versa. A justiciable issue arises whenever the state invokes a power to enforce a law that arguably conflicts with an immunity claimed by an individual. In such circumstances courts of appropriate jurisdiction have a duty to resolve such disputes in a manner that is articulately consistent with the best available theories that justify governmental power and individual rights in that political system.

Dred Scott's case had a public law dimension because he claimed to have become free in Missouri through the direct effect of either Illinois or federal law rather than through a transaction performed by his owner. His claim assumed, moreover, that, if he were free in Missouri and a citizen of no other state or country, he would have standing to sue in federal court as a citizen of Missouri. Chief Justice Taney rejected Dred Scott's claim that the effect of Illinois law had made Scott free in Missouri. This, Taney said, was a matter of Missouri law which had been definitively decided by the Missouri courts.[8] Taney did not directly address the parallel issue of whether the Missouri Compromise, an act of Congress regulating slavery in the territories, had the effect of freeing slaves who returned to Missouri under Missouri law. Instead,

6. The issue of ownership is clouded by the fact that after the Supreme Court decision, and Sanford's death, Emerson's widow, now Mrs. Chaffee, sold Dred Scott in Missouri. The buyers were members of the Blow family, which had originally sold Dred Scott to Emerson between 1830 and 1833. Since this family had apparently financed his freedom suit for over a decade, and since they eventually freed him, it remains a puzzle why they did not purchase his freedom to begin with. The ownership issue may not, however, be legally relevant since, under Missouri law, freedom suits could be brought against persons who did not claim to be the legal owners of the slaves under their control.

7. This prompted Taney to suggest that the case should have come before the Supreme Court, if at all, on direct appeal from the state court decision, rather than as a new case based on issues already adjudicated (*Dred Scott* v. *Sandford* 19 Howard 393, [1857] at 453).

8. *Dred Scott* v. *Sandford* 19 Howard 393 (1857) at 452–53.

Taney chose to address a different issue. Under the U.S. Constitution, he ruled, descendants of slaves could never have a general immunity against having state power invoked to enforce attempts to enslave them as long as slavery legitimately existed in any single state of the Union. This meant that the Missouri Compromise was unconstitutional, even as it applied to federally administered territory. Taney concluded that any freedom that was available to Dred Scott would not be a basis of public law rights of citizenship that could be asserted against the state, but merely a private law defense allowed in the property law of certain jurisdictions against claims of ownership brought by a particular party.

The *Dred Scott* case illustrates how both the public and private law models figure into our thinking about constitutional questions, and how neither can be wholly eliminated. Many constitutional arguments, including the most powerful arguments in this decision, are based on three sorts of claims about the relation of the public and private law models.

The first type of claim implicitly treats the public and private law models as defining two distinct levels of the case which can be directly compared. By this I mean that the private law question of whether Scott is a slave under Missouri law can exactly parallel the public law question of whether he can sue in federal court as though he were a citizen of Missouri to challenge the Missouri Supreme Court's view of the matter. If the two levels are clearly distinguishable and are also presumed to be mutually consistent, then a clear answer to the issues that arise on one level could be invoked to resolve the knotty problems of the other.[9]

The second type of legal argument in *Dred Scott* implicitly treats the public and private law models as interpenetrating. By this I mean that the remedial power of government in private disputes is identical with the power of enforcement that the government could invoke on its own initiative in the public law model.[10] In *Dred Scott* some of the justices argue that the governmental protection that Dred Scott invokes in his private suit against Sanford implicates the public power of government to divest Sanford of property without compensation. Taney himself fears that if the ownership of slaves could be divested by

9. Several justices concur with Taney that the State Supreme Court decision that Scott was still Mrs. Emerson's slave under Missouri law (*Scott v. Emerson* 15 Mo. 576 [1852]) would require that his federal case be dismissed on the grounds that no slave under Missouri law could sue in federal court as a citizen of Missouri. This would preclude a federal test of whether the Missouri Supreme Court had the discretion under the U.S. Constitution to reverse itself on the effects of Illinois or federal law on Missouri slaveholders. Taney relies here on his prior decision in *Strader* v. *Graham* 10 Howard 82. See *Dred Scott* v. *Sandford* 19 Howard 393 at 452, and especially, the concurring opinion of Nelson beginning at 457. For a critique of Taney's use of *Strader*, see Fehrenbacher, pp. 385–87.

10. The essential continuity between the two analogous models of law can be put more broadly. On the one hand, we often justify the remedial powers that individuals seek in court by invoking the public interest. From this perspective individual right-holders have been delegated the ability to bring public power to bear on other individuals. On the other hand, we often justify public interest legislation on remedial grounds. From this perspective public law is largely an effort to shift the burden of harm from some social groups to others.

federal legislation, then Negroes would have a statutory basis for claiming the protection of the federal courts against summary operation of the Fugitive Slave Law—a possibility that the Supreme Court was anxious to deny.[11] Because of the interpenetration of Dred Scott's suit against his putative master and his implicit public law right of standing to assert his freedom in federal court against all non-Missourians who would attempt to treat him as a slave under color of law, Chief Justice Taney finds it necessary to deny *both* Dred Scott's claim to freedom and his claim about what such freedom would mean for purposes of public law rights. The Court thus holds that any freedom available to Dred Scott as a descendant of slaves is not comparable to the freedom possessed by citizens who make up the sovereign "people" of the United States. The "freedom" of Negroes in Taney's pre–Civil War America could amount to little more than a legal defense against a particular master and his successors in interest—not political freedom, a public law immunity of citizens against all claims of subjection based on private right.

The third type of legal claim in *Dred Scott*, potentially the most interesting, implicitly recognizes that the public and private law model can *conflict*. Whenever the possibility of such conflict is perceived, we cannot say, as a rule of thumb, "to know what remedy you have against another individual, ask what coercive powers the state would be able to invoke on its own behalf; to know what power the state has over you, ask what it could do on behalf of another individual." In order to avoid a potential conflict between the two models Chief Justice Taney found it necessary to place wholly novel constraints on both the state law of slavery and the federal law of citizenship— judicial inventions that outraged Justice Curtis and generations of subsequent scholars. In the face of contrary historical practice Taney found that as long as slavery is permitted in any state, no state could subsequently confer citizenship on former slaves in a way that would be legally recognizable in other states. This, he said, would require naturalization, which could be done only by an act of Congress.[12] But, again in the face of contrary historical practice (especially regarding American Indians), Taney argued that Congress had no power to naturalize persons who were not born as citizens of some other nation.[13] Even if state law conferred state citizenship on free Negroes, in Taney's view U.S. citizenship would not follow. If *Dred Scott* had remained good law, there would be two classes of state citizens—those who were also citizens of the United States and those who were not.

11. It had already done so in *Prigg* v. *Pennsylvania*, and would do so again in *Ableman* v. *Booth*, as we shall see below.

12. *Dred Scott* v. *Sandford* 19 Howard 393 (1857) at 405–07. In his twelfth edition of Kent's *Commentaries* (1873) Oliver Wendell Holmes approvingly cites both *Dred Scott* and the Fourteenth Amendment on this point. My reference comes from James Kent, *Commentaries on American Law*, 13th ed. (Boston: Little, Brown, 1884), vol. 1, Lec. XIX, *424—which incorporates Holmes's note. For the previously established view of naturalization, see Joseph Story, *Commentaries on the Constitution of the United States*, 3 vols. (Boston: Hilliard and Gray, 1833), 3: 1–15.

13. See *Dred Scott* v. *Sandford* 19 Howard 393 at 419, along with Curtis's factual refutation of Taney's claims at 581, 586.

Taney's most outrageous conclusions in *Dred Scott* are largely an effort, as we have seen, to avoid a potential contradiction between the private law model, based on the rights of property, and the public law model, based on the rights of citizens, by asserting that freeing persons under the private law model does not create citizens. The implication of Taney's legal argument is that without a federal constitutional amendment "free" Negroes and their descendants were not politically free but merely "wild"—no longer capable of being legally owned but legally subject to capture and detention at the behest of any private party wishing to claim ownership or of any public authority concerned with the safety and welfare of citizens. This view reflected the fear of free Negroes which, by the 1840s, had led to the gradual removal from the laws of slavery of elements that favored manumission and the introduction of new elements denying free Negroes the protection of state law. At the federal level, Taney's view reflected the widespread conclusion that the Constitution could not be neutral on the question of slavery and that if slaves were to become free there would need to be some other legal basis for the repression of Negroes as a race. Justice Curtis of Massachusetts, a dissenter in *Dred Scott*, shares this general conclusion. He rejects Taney's argument that citizenship is constitutionally denied to free Negroes largely on the ground that states would be free to discriminate against Negroes on the basis of race, even if free Negroes were considered to be citizens of the United States.[14] The debate between Taney and Curtis in *Dred Scott* is the moment in our constitutional history that transposes the contradiction between the private and public law models, between civil and political rights, from the rhetoric of slave versus free to the rhetoric of black versus white.[15] Taney's approach in *Dred Scott* would have confirmed the legal status of the free American Negro as a special category, "domestic alien,"[16]

14. *Dred Scott v. Sandford* 19 Howard 393 at 583–84.

15. For a postwar literary reenactment of that transition see Mark Twain's *Pudd'nhead Wilson*. For an appreciative, but critical, contemporary discussion of the various opinions in *Dred Scott* on these points, see John Codman Hurd, *The Law of Freedom and Bondage in the United States*, 2 vols. (Boston: Little, Brown, 1858, 1862), chaps. 16, 23, 24. For a discussion of the legal treatment of fugitives see chaps. 25–26. Hurd points out, for example, that the novel step of considering slaves as federal common law property under the Fifth Amendment was unneccessary in view of Taney's earlier assumption that the liberty of freed slaves—who were clearly not property—could not be protected under the due process clause (para. 507). The legal disabilities of freedmen and their descendants before the Civil War are extensively discussed in Ira Berlin, *Slaves without Masters* (New York: Pantheon Books, 1974).

16. The legal framework for this technique of racial domination was largely in place by the time of the Civil War. Hurd adapts the concept of "domestic alienage" in private international law in order to explain the American law of slavery from its origins in the British Empire to its place in the antebellum Constitution. His treatise expounds the theory that the British Empire developed a form of "quasi-international" private law, allowing British subjects basing legal claims on positive law elsewhere in the empire to be treated as "domestic aliens" in all courts under the Crown. The clear implication of Hurd's view is that under the federal supervention of imperial law the descendants of chattel slaves within the empire would, as a class of domestic alien, become "subjects" in American law, without thereby being citizens of the United States. (See *Law of Freedom and Bondage*, vol. 1, chaps. 2–9; vol. 2, pp. 222ff.).

denied the rights of citizens—a technique of racial domination that would later become the legal rationale for South African apartheid.[17]

Law and Politics in the American Republican Tradition

I suggested above that the tension between the public and private law models of adjudication is a driving force behind much of constitutional law, including the reasoning in *Dred Scott*. This is so despite (or perhaps because of) the fact that our dominant political culture commits us to either denying that such a tension exists or denouncing the tension, whenever it appears, as evidence of a deep corruption. In order to understand the constitutional issues in *Dred Scott* we must first articulate the assumptions about law and politics in our dominant political culture which tend to obscure the potential conflicts between the two models of adjudication.

For the purpose of this essay I shall call this dominant political culture "American republicanism" and distinguish it from Marshallian constitutional jurisprudence. In doing so, however, I wish to sidestep the current historical debate about whether American political ideology is characterized by a consensus on the values of liberal individualism or by a continuing conflict between a dominant culture based on Lockean liberalism and a counterculture based on classical republican ideas of civic virtue and community.[18] I agree with those who argue that this debate is largely at cross-purposes[19] insofar as both sides fundamentally agree in their descriptions of the "constitutional" ideology of the American Revolution: a form of Whig legalism that eventually led to a rejection of the sovereignty of king and parliament in the name of a sovereign "people."[20] In using the term *republicanism* to evoke the antimonarchical ideology of the American Revolution I do not wish to deny that the revolutionaries were also deeply "liberal" in their respect for legalism and their belief in the natural rights of individuals. My purpose is, rather, to evoke the elements common to most historical accounts of the American revolutionary creed and still resonant in popular political rhetoric. I shall then argue that the Marshallian framework of constitutional analysis is a structural response to the

17. See, for example, George Frederickson, *White Supremacy* (New York: Oxford University Press, 1981), chaps. 4, 6.

18. Louis Hartz is the leading proponent of the view that American political culture is based on a Lockean consensus. See *The Liberal Tradition in America* (New York: Harcourt, Brace, 1955). For expressions of the revisionist view that the American Revolution was based on classical republican ideas, see Bernard Bailyn, *Ideological Origins of the American Revolution* (Cambridge: Harvard University Press, 1967); J. G. A. Pocock, *The Machiavellian Moment* (Princeton: Princeton University Press, 1975); and Gordon S. Wood, *The Creation of the American Republic* (New York: W. W. Norton, 1969). John P. Diggins provides a stimulating historiographical critique of these debates in *The Lost Soul of American Politics* (New York: Basic Books, 1984).

19. See, for example, David Greenstone, "Political Culture and Political Development: Liberty, Union and the Liberal Bipolarity," *Studies in American Political Development* 1(1986): 1–49, espec. 6.

20. Gordon Wood describes both of these tendencies in detail. See *The Creation of the American Republic*, chaps. 1 and 2.

inadequacy of American republicanism as a basis for constitutional jurisprudence.

Unlike some radical versions of republican theory, the mainstream of republican constitutional thought in the United States presupposes that political and legal questions can be sharply distinguished. Political questions in republican theory are concerned with what is best for the whole community. A genuine political disagreement would then involve a dispute between two (or more) competing visions of the whole (*whole versus whole*). Republican theory recognizes that the government cannot be a neutral adjudicator between the parties in such conflicts. For this reason it proposes that disputes over the future direction of the whole community be resolved democratically, through elections followed by legislation that implements the will of the electoral majority. When elections fail to reconcile conflicting visions of the whole, republican theory permits the fallback options of secession and revolution. It does not, however, recognize any basis for the courts to resolve political disputes.

Legal questions in republican theory are concerned with whether one part of the community can legitimately benefit at another's expense (*part versus part*). In such disputes republican theory expects the state to remain neutral. This requires that official decisions that directly sacrifice the interests of one citizen to benefit another be made strictly in accordance with preexisting law. When two private parties fail to agree on the law, a republican constitution will require that their dispute be resolved by a court.

To the republican mind, legitimacy depends upon maintaining the distinction between these two kinds of disputes: conflating them is the essence of corruption. Corruption in politics consists of allowing one's view of the balance of advantage between the different parts of society to dominate one's vision of the whole. Here illegitimate bias consists of a conflict of interest. Legal corruption consists of allowing one's vision of the whole to influence the resolution of conflicts between the parts. Here illegitimate bias consists of an ideological conviction. Republican constitutional thought in this country is thus inordinately devoted to keeping political questions out of the courts and legal questions out of politics. It sees this task as a struggle against corruption, both in theory and in practice.[21]

Once political and legal issues are sharply distinguished, the republican view of government can be expressed in two familiar ideas. The idea of *popular sovereignty* applies to issues that call forth our visions of the whole community (whole versus whole). The *rule of law* applies to issues that call upon us to decide impartially between the different parts of the community (part versus part).[22]

---

21. The refusal to reduce law to politics is consistent with the high tradition of republican theory which has always viewed "who gets what?" as a question of "housekeeping" which should be kept out of politics. In our country this has been taken to justify consigning issues of distributive justice to the courts. See Hannah Arendt, *The Human Condition* (Chicago: University of Chicago Press, 1958); see also Hanna Pitkin, "On Relating Public and Private," *Political Theory* 9, no. 3 (1981): 327–52.

22. The locus classicus for all discussions of the role of popular sovereignty and the rule of law in U.S. constitutional thought is Edward Corwin, "The Basic Doctrine of Constitutional

The popular versions of republican theory in our political culture are a merger of these two ideas—which appear in *Dred Scott* as the claim that free Negroes could not be part of the sovereign "people" if upholding racially based slavery is required by the rule of law.[23] Let us now consider both ideas in more detail.

Popular sovereignty is the foundation of republican political rhetoric. It implies that "we the people" have created the state and that the legitimate power it exercises is ours, collectively. The origin of such political power lies in the natural rights that individuals would have against each other if there were no state. In the American conception of republican self-government we implicitly exercise our natural rights to promote our ends outside the state in order to create the power to transform ourselves collectively through the state. Once these natural rights are harnessed to create the public power, individuals cannot seek to enforce them directly against the state. Within the constitutional republic, claims to natural rights are thus transformed into straightforwardly political appeals to the purposes for which the government was constituted. These appeals, by distinguishing those rights pooled and rights expressly retained by individuals, sometimes serve to limit the powers of the state which claims to exercise popular sovereignty. Those who oppose such limitations argue with equal force that strong government is simply an expression of the natural rights of the majority.[24]

The consequence of popular sovereignty in American republican thought is that legitimate political conflicts can arise only between parties that lay claim to represent the public as a whole. To make good on such a claim, each side must represent itself as the best embodiment of the public interest. Democratic legislation then becomes the only authoritative way to settle conflicts over who really represents the whole. Although such legislation may be formally enacted by simple majority rule, from the standpoint of popular sovereignty the majority must not be seen to be making laws in its own self-interest at the expense of

---

Law," *Michigan Law Review* 12, no. 4 (1914): 247–76. (See also Corwin, "We, the People," in *The Doctrine of Judicial Review*.) My own thinking about republican theory and its relation to Marshallian jurisprudence was stimulated by interactions with Professors Duncan Kennedy and Morton Horwitz in 1979. At this stage I am not sure how many of my specific ideas were influenced by their rich interpretations of American legal history, although I doubt that either of them would agree with my overall theoretical framework. I am especially grateful for access to Professor Kennedy's unpublished manuscript, "The Rise and Fall of Classical Legal Thought" (1975), a prolegomenon to which has been published as "The Structure of Blackstone's *Commentaries*," *Buffalo Law Review* 28 (1979): 209.

23. Republican theory is notably silent on how membership in the political community is determined. Most accounts of popular sovereignty assume that the boundaries of the political community are fixed according to settled normative or geographical criteria. The rule of law is also centrally concerned with relations among citizens, although its protections extend to aliens and newcomers, and to potential citizens of communities in the process of formation and expansion.

24. See, for example, Robert Bork, "Styles in Constitutional Theory" *South Texas Law Journal* 26 (1985): 383; Cf. Ronald Dworkin, *Taking Rights Seriously* (Cambridge: Harvard University Press, 1977).

the minority.[25] The treatment of minorities who will remain part of the "people" is addressed by the concept of the rule of law.

The rule of law functions in American republican theory to prevent the majority from using its legislative power to take advantage of minorities. This is essential to the American meaning of popular self-government. "We the people" are a people because majority and minority alike are governed by law in their private disputes, not because law can be made by a temporary majority. In American republican theory the neutrality of government is required for the people to govern through law—and for law, as such, to be the result of majority decisions.

As a concept, the rule of law is initially more difficult to grasp than popular sovereignty, but no less important to our constitutional development. The present-day United States was originally settled by persons who moved westward claiming the full legal protection of rights that had vested under English law, federal law, or the laws of the states from which they came. How far were territorial governments required to respect preexisting rights? At what point could a local majority, whether as a territorial legislature or as a newly admitted state, divest a U.S. citizen of preexisting rights in the name of majority rule? How far does republicanism in the states, guaranteed in the federal Constitution, forbid majorities from appropriating the property of minorities on grounds that would not be approved by a nonpolitical court as a legitimate basis for redistributing wealth between two individuals?[26] In American constitutional thought the "rule of law" expresses the point that, even though democratic government presupposes our natural right to transform society collectively from within, the exercise of governmental power must be subject to restraints of process similar to those that would apply if we had to sue our neighbors to divest them of their legally established rights.

Respect for the rule of law means that the courts should always interpret legislation as though the majority were attempting to represent the public as a whole rather than to serve the majority's own particular interests. By adopting this principle republican courts translate the collective actions of the political majority into formally neutral law which can be applied to resolving disputes between part and part. Without the rule of law popular sovereignty would amount to an exercise by the state of the private power of the majority against the minority—a form of tyranny. To counteract such tyranny the rule of law requires that, at the stage of implementing legislation, the interest of two people be seen as intrinsically no more representative of the public than the interests of one.

As a merger of popular sovereignty and the rule of law, republican politics consists of a kind of double vision of government. From one perspective we rule

25. For a contemporary treatment of this issue, see Brian Barry, "The Public Interest," in Anthony Quinton, ed., *Political Philosophy* (Oxford: Oxford University Press, 1967), 112–26.

26. A metaphorical development of this problem of legitimating majority rule is in Robert Nozick, *Anarchy, State, and Utopia* (New York: Basic Books, 1974), especially the "Tale of the Slave," 290f.

the state. By assuming our role as citizens we exercise our natural rights to constitute a government which we control through popular sovereignty. Republicanism teaches us to speak in debating public questions as though we had no interests at heart but those of the public. From the second perspective, the state rules us. By reconstituting us as "The People," the state respects and enforces our private rights in relation to each other. In the republican model of government the people as a whole must be saved by the rule of law from the fluctuating opinions of temporary majorities.

The foregoing suggests that in a democratic republic the people are constituted twice over: once in order to rule, and once in order to be ruled. As rulers, the people are presumed to be united in aiming at the common good, even when they are deeply divided in their vision of that good. As ruled, the people are divided by their particular interests, but are presumed to be united in the demand that the state respect the vested rights of all individuals in society. Even before the American colonists sought to replace the monarchy with popular sovereignty, they were rhetorically constituted as a single people by the demand for governmental legality, including the independence of colonial magistrates from parliamentary politics. In this respect the American Revolution, like many others, originated in a rebellion by the ruled in the name of legality and ended in divisions among the new rulers over the nature of the public good.[27]

Republican theory implies that we can reconcile these two conceptions of the people by conceiving of any given issue in either the language of whole versus whole or the language of part versus part. In practice, however, republican politics pits these two rhetorical stances against each other in debate. If the politics of the whole corrupts disputes between the parts, we have the tyranny of the majority. But if the vested interests of the parts corrupt the politics of the whole, we are left with virtual anarchy—a government impotent to change preexisting economic expectations by means of legislation. These two forms of corruption correspond to the twin horrors of American political life—the fears that majoritarianism can lead to tyranny and that individualism can lead to anarchy. To avoid these horrors the rhetoric of republican politics constantly pushes us to extremes of language; by refusing to describe a given social conflict in both the language of popular sovereignty and the language of the rule of law, we attempt to preserve the purity of the political and legal processes.

As we shall see, American republican theory is conspicuously silent on whether the distinction between political and legal questions is itself a political or a legal question. Although judicially decidable conflicts in republican thought are usually between individuals, such conflicts often implicate the values and interests of groups, regions, and the ethnic, cultural, and religious minorities that exist in a diverse community. As we have seen, however, republican theory also requires that the conflicts of interest between groups or

27. See, for example, Bailyn, *Ideological Origins*, and Wood, *The Creation of the American Republic*. Cf. Michael Walzer, "A Theory of Revolutions," in *Radical Principles* (New York: Basic Books, 1980), 201–23.

factions in the community be resolved in terms of the common good. How far must the government remain officially neutral in these larger conflicts in order to uphold the rule of law in relations among individuals? Can the government be neutral on issues that affect the public good, if these can be resolved legitimately only through the democratic process?

In deciding *Dred Scott* the Supreme Court recognized that the issue of whether slavery should expand or contract in the United States raised issues central to both popular sovereignty and the rule of law—a point widely acknowledged in congressional debate and in previous judicial decisions. The willingess of the Court to decide the issue implied that the reconciliation of popular sovereignty and the rule of law was itself a legal, rather than a political, question.[28] For this reason those who objected to the Court's decision typically denounced it as a corrupt usurpation of political power, whereas those who welcomed the decision saw it as a vindication of the rule of law. Both political responses reflected republican notions of the role of "legality" in constitutional thought.[29]

Legality and the Politics of Rights: The Failure of Republican Constitutional Thought

We have seen that republican political legitimacy requires that the outputs of the state be legal, even though its inputs are political. In distinguishing between these, republican legal thinkers have tended to describe our community in two distinct ways, both of which use the language of rights. On the one hand, they see us as exercising our *natural rights* to transform society when we participate in politics as democratic citizens. On the other hand, they demand that courts respect our *vested rights* when we seek to enforce the settled expectations that are created by the political process. The constitutional idea of vested rights, however, refers not to the entire body of positive law but to only those expectations arising under positive law that are protected from subsequent changes brought about through legislation. In republican theory the respect for vested rights is required by the rule of law and does not in principle interfere with legislative expressions of natural rights.

The distinction between natural and vested rights gives republicanism its

28. Taney's opinion revolved around another issue on which Republican theory is silent— whether *membership* in the community is a political or a legal issue. Before *Dred Scott*, Congress had always assumed that both the naturalization of U.S. citizens and the initial terms of popular sovereignty in the territories were political questions to be addressed by federal legislation. Taney explicitly recognized that Congress was constitutionally limited by the Bill of Rights in legislating for the territories, even if it was acting in lieu of a state government, which would not, at that time, have been so limited. These issues are discussed more fully below.

29. See, for example, the fascinating discussion in Thomas Hart Benton, *Historical and Legal Examination of That Part of the Decision of the Supreme Court of the United States in the Dred Scott Case Which Declares the Unconstitutionality of the Missouri Compromise Act, and the Self-Extension of the Constitution to Territories, Carrying Slavery Along with It* (New York: D. Appleton and Co., 1857). See also the speech of Judah P. Benjamin, quoted in Hurd, *The Law of Freedom and Bondage*, para. 521ff.

logic of maneuver, allowing republican thinkers to suggest that some "rights" can be claimed politically through voting, revolution, or secession, but that these are not the same as the "rights" that are judicially enforceable under the rule of law. Under these circumstances, there will be considerable room to argue about which rights are which. By focusing political argument on the distinction between natural and vested rights, republican theory diverts attention from the question of whether popular sovereignty and the rule of law are really compatible. In one sense, republicanism allows us a right to change the political system through legislation or revolution, but in another sense it also allows us to retain all the particular rights that have already been granted by the system.[30] There need be no contradiction if we are talking about different rights, or if we are using the word "rights" in different senses.[31]

The republican distinction between natural and vested rights is intended to suggest that constitutional problems are analogous to a familiar distinction in the private law of contracts between the right we have to make a contract to begin with, and the right that becomes enforceable against us once a contract has been entered. The former right might be seen as a general legal power to undertake an obligation voluntarily; the latter is a specific entitlement that is vested against us and that we may not abrogate unilaterally as long as the contract remains in effect. The republican doctrine of vested rights implies that the question of whether a statute can be constitutionally changed is essentially similar to the question of whether rights under a contract have vested.[32]

To state this analogy is to see how misleading it is. The powers to make, revise, and void a contract are themselves artifacts of prior law, not natural rights, and the judgment that a contractual right has vested is a legal decision to cut off these powers. This decision—enforcing contractual expectations rather than upholding contractual powers—must itself be justified. It is no guide to answering the constitutional question of whether fresh legislation can override prior legal expectations.

Drawing on another analogy with the private law, it is equally possible to compare the constitutional status of legislation to the law of trusts and estates, the locus classicus for the doctrine of vested rights. A legal will can be seen as an act of private legislation disposing of property in the future. Under some

30. For a detailed and sympathetic discussion of American ideas of revolutionary legality in the late eighteenth century, see Wood, *The Creation of the American Republic*, and Bailyn, *Ideological Origins*.

31. There is something initially plausible in the republican distinction between natural and vested rights. At first glance it seems to capture the fact that we can make two quite different points in asserting our rights: sometimes we assert our rights to claim a powerful and universal reason for getting what we want; sometimes we assert our rights to deny the relevance of the otherwise valid reasons that might justify interfering with us. But, as I suggest above, this conceptual distinction can be made independently of the republican view that we are necessarily referring to different kinds of rights, distinguishable on the basis of whether they can be changed by fresh legislation.

32. For an elegant discussion of the pre-constitutional relationship between private and public law, see Duncan Kennedy, "The Structure of Blackstone's *Commentaries*."

circumstances it may also create present expectations on which people come to rely, but during the lifetime of the testator a will can be changed without violating the rights of those whose expectations are disappointed. The future interests created under a will become vested rights only upon the death of the testator.

In order to use the idea of vested rights as a constitutional doctrine we would need to be able to distinguish between laws that, like private contracts, create expectations that can vest immediately and laws that, like private wills, create expectations that can be changed whenever there is a change of policy or sentiment on the part of the testator. Yet republican theory is of no use in addressing this issue. It tells us only that, looking forward, the state has the power to change the law and that, looking backward, the state has the duty to deliver those benefits it has already promised.

The difficulty with this formulation is that lawmaking, the exercise of popular sovereignty, produces forward-looking laws, which necessarily have a differential impact on the settled expectation of present individuals. All new legislation purports to bring about a future result by altering behavior from this time forward. In doing so, however, legislation will inevitably affect the value of past holdings insofar as this depends upon expectations about the future state of the law. There is thus a general issue of what, if anything, people are entitled to expect about the future state of the law. Does the respect for vested rights imply a constitutional commitment to preserve the present value of all legal expectations, or only of some? Republican theory tells us nothing about when legislation is like a will which can be changed at the discretion of an immortal testator, the "sovereign people," and when it is like an enforceable contract between the government and individuals. As we shall see, this issue could be addressed only when republicanism in the states had been superseded by the federalism of the U.S. Constitution.[33]

The basic problem for a postrevolutionary constitution is to provide a structure under which a new government can legitimately change the law without violating preexisting rights. In order for republican theory to work at the level of constitutional reasoning it would need to address the problems that arise when changes in the law redistribute wealth and power in ways that restructure preexisting social relations. This republican theory could not do.

The weakness in the republican model of constitutional government became immediately apparent after the revolution. The American Revolution was not a social contract in which newly freed individuals met in the state of nature and decided to form a government. It was a political transition in which natural rights were claimed on the basis of having broken our tie with England, and in which vested rights were claimed on the basis of what the law would have been if we were still in England—an England uncorrupted by king and Parlia-

---

33. *Fletcher* v. *Peck* 6 Cranch 87 (1810) was the first case in which state legislation was invalidated under the U.S. Constitution. There, Chief Justice Marshall held that the repeal of prior state legislation granting title to land effectively violated a contract between the state and the grantees enforceable under the U.S. Constitution.

ment.[34] The burning constitutional question that emerged after the revolution was, how much of preexisting English law had created mere future expectations which could be changed by new legislation, and how much of it had created vested rights which could not be changed without paying off their holders.[35] This question was especially relevant to republican debate about the future of slavery in the early federal period.[36]

After the American Revolution the two models of republican discourse, based, respectively, on popular sovereignty and the rule of law, could no longer be compartmentalized and applied to different topics. They were revealed as mirror images that could reflect each other at every point. The public law model suggested that, since the revolution, everything had changed; the private law model suggested that nothing had changed except for the ultimate power to appoint and remove public officers. These two mirror images were not, however, perfect reflections. Each contained a distorted image of the other; yet, without the presence of the other, neither gave a clear picture in its own right. Instead of keeping law and politics distinct, republicanism in practice had both politicized law and legalized politics. Yet republican theory provided no way of reconciling these two alternative conceptions of the political community. Rather, the central concepts of popular sovereignty and the rule law tended to abstract from all of the difficult problems posed by imbalances of power in the government and society, respectively.

The basic flaw in the republican framework lay in its premise that government can distinguish between political issues, arising out of conflicting conceptions of the whole, and legal issues, arising out of demands for redistributions among the parts. But if all issues are simultaneously describable as disputes about the whole and as shifts in the balance between the parts, republican theory is at best a manner of speaking politically, which is no help in deciding real controversies. A constitution that addresses the flaw in republican theory must recognize that the struggle between competing visions of the whole is always also a struggle between the parts: all public policies affect the distribution of wealth and power in society. Such a constitution must also recognize that the conflicts between any two parts of society will always implicate competing visions of the whole: all legal rights are artifacts of public policy.

Constitutional thought about slavery between the revolution and the Civil War reflects the ways in which the federalist model of wholes and parts transcends and incorporates the republican conflict between natural and vested rights. The conceptual framework that made this possible was largely the work of John Marshall, who did not, however, fully apply it in his own decisions about slavery.[37] We now turn to the Marshallian framework.

34. For a discussion of English legal doctrine at the time, see Kennedy, "The Structure of Blackstone's *Commentaries.*"

35. These are the underlying issues in *Chisholm* v. *Georgia* 2 Dall. 419 (1793) and *Calder* v. *Bull* 3 Dall. 386 (1798).

36. See, for example, Fehrenbacher, chaps. 1–3.

37. See Donald M. Roper, "In Quest of Judicial Objectivity: The Marshall Court and the Legitimation of Slavery," *Stanford Law Review* 21 (1969): 532–39.

DRED SCOTT IN THE MARSHALLIAN FRAMEWORK

Marshall's Constitution

John Marshall interpreted the U.S. Constitution as an attempt to face the problems in republican theory discussed above. In his constitutional jurisprudence the conceptual distinction in republican thought between natural and vested rights was replaced by an institutional conflict between legislature and judiciary. This in effect transposed the outstanding problems in republican thought from the level of theoretical contradiction to the level of institutional conflict.

In Marshall's view of the Constitution, the Congress and the judiciary must each make their own attempt to reconcile the two distinct pictures of the sovereign people provided by republican thought. He anticipated that the two branches of government will often draw divergent conclusions about when to view differences among the people as legislatively relevant opinions and when to view them as legally enforceable entitlements. Yet the specifically constitutional issue this poses for the federal government would no longer need to be described directly as an opposition between natural and vested rights, but, rather, as a matter of institutional deference between the branches. How extensively may the legislature modify what the judiciary has done? How restrained must the courts be in reviewing the acts of the legislature? These are the now-classic problems of the separation of powers which define the balance of authority between the branches of government.

In Marshall's view of the separation of powers, legislation and adjudication were not merely distinctive governmental functions, each with its own proper domain; they were also mutual reflections of each other. In England parliamentary sovereignty amounted to the finality of legislative review of the judiciary. This meant that the High Court of Parliament had the ultimate power to alter the standards of proof, burdens of proof, and the jurisdiction of the courts to grant remedies that would be otherwise available under the common law. In the United States the plenary power of legislatures to review and modify judge-made common law was in principle continued at the state level, but under the federal Constitution, Congress was not a successor to the plenary powers of Parliament but a body with constitutionally enumerated powers. Marshall believed that in order to hold Congress within its constitutional limitations, the framers must have contemplated that, just as legislatures have final review of the courts on statutory matters, courts must have final review of legislation on constitutional matters. This conception of judicial review of legislation was a fundamentally novel constitutional doctrine, despite some precursors in powers of the English Privy Council over colonial legislation.[38] It meant that under our Constitution, Congress and the judiciary would be reinterpreting continually what the other had done in its own terms, each with its special claim to finality.

Beyond recasting the problems of republican politics in terms of the separa-

---

38. See Julius Goebel, Jr., *Antecedents and Beginnings to 1801*, vol. 1 of the Oliver Wendell Holmes devise, *History of the Supreme Court of the United States* (New York: Macmillan, 1971).

tion of powers, Marshall believed that our Constitution makes a further departure from the republican model. In creating a federal system of government it unavoidably recognizes that all disputes about the whole affect the balance of power between the parts, and that all disputes among the parts affect the future of the whole. A federal constitution thus implicitly rejects the republican assumption that disputes must be decided on the model of either whole versus whole or part versus part. Such a constitution must provide a way of resolving disputes of whole versus part.

Federalism, of course, presents a different initial problem about the relation of wholes and parts from the problem of factionalism in republican thought. Marshall's genius, however, was to use a logic of wholes and parts that was central to federalism as a key to understanding most constitutional conflicts. He saw the legal status of the federal Constitution itself—a sovereign act of the whole which left intact the sovereignty of the parts[39]—as a metaphor for interpreting the relations among the various powers recognized under the Constitution. By bringing most constitutional issues under the dominant paradigm of whole versus part, Marshall was then able to present a series of issues as analogous across the entire structure of government. When can the larger, more inclusive federal government make laws that have impact primarily on the smaller state government? When can the majority within a state legally discriminate against citizens of other states? When does the judicial enforcement of the Constitution itself take precedence over the will of the temporary majority?

Once these questions were seen to pose analogous issues of whole versus part, Marshall developed a series of constitutional doctrines for resolving them. We shall see, below, that sometimes these doctrines permit the whole to dominate the parts; sometimes they favor the parts over the whole; and sometimes they shift the issue to the question of which side represents the whole and which the part in a given controversy.

How would the novel conflicts of whole versus part be resolved under the federal Constitution? Clearly, it would not be enough to say "by legislation." Many such conflicts could foreseeably arise between the federal Congress and the state legislatures. Which legislative body could then be trusted to decide a conflict in which it was the real party in interest? Moreover, even in constitutional conflicts between state legislatures it was not obvious that the Congress should always have the last word.

The existence of a federal constitution that declared itself as "the supreme Law of the Land" implied that such conflicts between sovereign legislative bodies could in principle be resolved judicially on constitutional grounds. Moreover, in defining the federal judicial power, the Constitution explicitly gave the federal courts jurisdiction to decide disputes between the states and, implicitly, to decide disputes between state and federal government. The established judicial techniques for addressing such questions derived from the field

---

39. Before Marshall's tenure, the case of *Chisholm* v. *Georgia* had definitively interpreted the Constitution as the direct creation of a sovereign people rather than as a treaty among sovereign states.

of international law, where courts of a particular jurisdiction could entertain the claim that they were bound to enforce laws of another jurisdiction because of the need to recognize multiple sovereignties over the parties to a case. Under the U.S. Constitution the characteristic problem of international law—choosing which law to enforce in the context of conflicting claims to sovereignty— became a fruitful paradigm for the development of our federal law.[40] By the onset of the Civil War legal scholars such as John Codman Hurd could interpret the U.S. Constitution as a substitute for public international law (treaties) among the states, allowing the customs of private international law regarding the existence of multiple sovereignties to become formalized in the jurisprudence of federalism.[41]

Although John Marshall was developing the paradigm of whole versus part in a federal context, he tended to view state constitutions as Jeffersonian republican documents, a view consistent with the fact that many of the great state courts remained bastions of legal republicanism long after the adoption of the federal Constitution.[42] Such a division of labor would set the stage for *Dred Scott*, leaving most substantive questions of popular sovereignty and vested rights to the state courts, while directing the federal judiciary to constitutional questions of equalization and autonomy among the units of government.

Structure and Analogy

In *Marbury* v. *Madison*[43] Marshall suggests that the American Constitution is in effect a second declaration of independence from England, this time in the

40. We should not minimize the contribution to "Marshallian" jurisprudence made by Joseph Story, Marshall's colleague on the Court, and also the great antebellum American scholar on choice of law and conflict of law in the international context. An interesting test of the thesis above would be to compare the jurisprudential techniques of Story's *Commentaries on the Constitution of the United States* with those of his treatise on the conflict of laws. See Story *Commentaries on the Conflict of Laws, Foreign and Domestic* (Boston: Little, Brown, 1857).

41. Hurd argues that most federal law in the United States is an extension of the concept of domestic alienage under private international law to issues of civil rights under municipal law. In his view most domestic aliens, those who are citizens of other states and nations, may be accorded civil rights out of judicial respect for the positive law of other jurisdictions. By parallel reasoning, however, other domestic aliens, especially slaves, must be denied civil rights out of judicial recognition of their antecedent disabilities under the positive law elsewhere. Hurd's numerous scholarly objections to specific points in *Dred Scott* are frequently responses to the Taney Court's departure from the apparent evenhandedness of the model of "quasi-international" law in favor of the theory, discussed below, that the Constitution requires affirmative steps to equalize between slave and free states. (See *Law of Freedom and Bondage*, vol. 1, chaps. 2–9; vol 2, pp. 222ff.)

42. While all state constitutions embodied the separation of powers, the jurisprudence of whole versus part was developed in the federal context by John Marshall, and only later became a model of constitutional adjudication. For an example of the emergent problem of reconciling Marshallian jurisprudence with republican models of constitutional thought in the states, see James Kent, *Commentaries on American Law*, 4 vols. (New York: O. Halsted, 1826–30), and subsequent editions. Kent's discussion of Marshall's reversal of Kent's own opinion in *Gibbons* v. *Ogden*, 9 Wheat. 1 (1824), is especially interesting. See Lec. XIX, 404ff.

43. 1 Cranch 137 (1803).

realm of legal, rather than political, doctrine. If the United States were still part of England, he argued, the courts would have plenary power to grant Marbury a remedy against the king's officer, but the king in Parliament would also be the final interpreter of the Constitution. Marshall declares, however, that in contrast with the English legal system, American constitutionalism sometimes limits judicial oversight of the executive, while permitting judicial review of the legislature.

Marbury v. *Madison* was the first major case in which John Marshall articulated his basic jurisprudential technique of describing the major conflicts in constitutional law by analogy with an overall conflict between whole and part which legitimates the judicial interpretation of the Constitution itself. Without repeating the familiar facts of *Marbury*, a simple enumeration of the levels of controversy will illustrate how Marshall's method of structuring a constitutional argument is nothing less than an effort to transpose a judicial metaphor onto the republican political theory of this country, suggesting that even political questions can be turned by analogy into the sort of questions that a court decides when resolving cases between two individuals.

The first level of conflict was between *Marbury and Madison*. (Marbury sought a writ ordering Madison to deliver Marbury's signed commission as justice of the peace.) The parties were not, however, merely private individuals—Madison was sued in his capacity as the secretary of state. Thus, the second explicit level of controversy was between *individual and executive*. Given the peculiar conflicts of interest in the case,[44] Marshall must have been very much aware that there was also a third level of conflict implicit in the case—a conflict between *judiciary and executive*.

Marshall noted that the powers of the U.S. Supreme Court in cases of original jurisdiction were strictly enumerated in the Constitution, and since the Constitution had not given Congress the express authority to extend the original jurisdiction of the Supreme Court, he argued that the act of Congress that purportedly gave the Court jurisdiction to grant Marbury his remedy was unconstitutional. In reaching this conclusion Marshall invented a fourth conflict, also implicit, which had not been posed by the parties to the case: a conflict between *Court and Congress* over the interpretation of the Constitution. Article III, however, does not give the Court power to directly decide disputes between the branches of government, perhaps because, in openly deciding such cases, the Court would inevitably become a party. In order to preserve the legitimacy of his decision Marshall was anxious to avoid directly adjudicating a conflict to which the Court was a party, whether it be the implicit conflict between the judiciary and the executive, or that between the judiciary and Congress. Marshall, thus, based his decision in *Marbury* on resolving a fifth conflict raised by the case—the conflict between *the Constitution and a statute*. Amid all the unanswered questions posed by the case Marshall chose to decide whether a law repugnant to the Constitution can nevertheless be law.

---

44. Marshall's Court was being asked to intervene in this suit against Marshall's own successor as secretary of state, who was charged with failing to deliver a commission that Marshall himself had signed before leaving office.

This last issue, Marshall asserted, is "of great interest to the people, but is not of a complexity matching its interest."[45] The supremacy clause itself had declared the Constitution to be superior to any statute. Constitutional supremacy meant to Marshall that parliamentary sovereignty in England, under which Parliament can effectively change the Constitution by passing an unconstitutional law, had not been straightforwardly replaced by congressional sovereignty in the United States. Rather, the American conception of constitutionally limited government had changed the significance of sovereignty in ways that were alien to both British absolutism and American republican theory. In Marshall's view the enactment of the Constitution itself was the only indisputable expression of "we the people," acting as a whole. Thereafter, no single branch (or, as we shall see, level) of government could presume to be the constitutionally preferred representative of the sovereign people in all matters. The Constitution itself, according to Marshall, would determine which branch or level of government would be presumed to represent the will of the people as a whole on particular questions.

In *Marbury*, Marshall announced that the resolution of disputes about which part of government best represents the people as a whole had become a legal issue under our Constitution, and that this issue was intrinsically subject to judicial resolution using ordinary legal techniques. An apparent conflict between the Constitution and a statute would be no less judicially resolvable than an ordinary conflict between two sources of law. The simple constitutional issue was whether popular sovereignty was invested in laws made by the people as a whole or in laws enacted by a legislative majority of the people. On this issue, Marshall said, the text of the U.S. Constitution was decisive, declaring itself to be an act of popular sovereignty which is also supreme law.

The notion that a legislative majority is not automatically presumed to be the best representative of the people as a whole is essential to Marshall's view of constitutionally limited government. In Marshall's analysis, legislation was merely the act of a temporary majority unless it was fully in accordance with the Constitution—in which case the judiciary should defer to Congress as the valid representative of the people as a whole. If, however, Congress exceeded the scope of its constitutional authority, the Supreme Court must assume the role of defending popular sovereignty against legislative usurpations of power.

By appropriating the rhetoric of popular sovereignty in this way, Marshall's opinion obscured the fact that he had made the Court the final arbiter of which governmental entity represents the popular will in our political system. By presenting all issues in the case as analogous to a judicially resolvable conflict between the whole and the part, he implicitly equates the idea that the Constitution is superior to statutes with the idea that the Court is the authoritative interpreter of the Constitution. Yet in explicitly deciding whether a law repugnant to the Constitution is still valid, Marshall implicitly decides that the Court is the final authority on whether a law is indeed repugnant to the constitution. Building on the Court's previously acknowledged power to refuse to enforce a statute that the legislature *conceded* to be unconstitutional, Marshall's innova-

---

45. *Marbury* at 176.

tion lay in his undefended assumption that the Court, rather than Congress, must be the final authority in a dispute over whether a law *is* unconstitutional.[46]

Does Marshall's rejection of congressional sovereignty imply an assertion of judicial sovereignty, at least in relation to Congress? Interpretive finality in relation to statutes had been one of the characteristics of parliamentary sovereignty in England. Marshall, however, wished to distinguish interpretive finality in constitutional matters from an exercise of sovereign will. He believed that the legitimacy of courts depends upon their claim to defer to a sovereign will which lies outside their own. The Supreme Court must, thus, describe itself as deferring to the revealed will of the people when it applies the Constitution to invalidate a statute, just as it ordinarily defers to the revealed will of Congress in applying a constitutional statute.

In testing the constitutionality of legislation, the judicially decidable question, as Marshall posed it, was whether the will of Congress, as expressed in the statute, was consistent with the will of the people, as expressed in the Constitution—the very question that Congress had a constitutional duty to address in passing the statute to begin with. If the constitutional question before the Court makes sense, allowing Congress the final authority to review the Court's answer would make the question nonsense. In itself, of course, the notion that constitutional interpretation is a distinctively judicial function merely elaborates Marshall's view of the separation of powers; it does not conclusively answer the conventional argument that interpretive finality gives the Court supremacy over Congress. Many have argued that the practice of congressional deference to *Marbury* gives the Court, as final interpreter of the will of the people, a legally unreviewable power to change the meaning of the Constitution. But, provided that the sovereign authority remains located outside the judiciary, the Court can still claim a clear distinction between interpretive finality and its own sovereignty—a rhetorical advantage denied to Congress should it attempt to reverse the Court's interpretation.

The real significance of *Marbury* is not that the Court assumed the role of sovereign in our system but rather that under the Constitution debates about sovereignty were transformed into debates about the presumption of *equality* and mutual reviewability between coordinate units of government. Just as Marshall's Court interpreted and expanded its own powers in *Marbury*, the Court also proved willing to defer to congressional interpretation of congressional powers in *McCulloch*, as we shall see below. Although the Court would remain the final interpreter of the Constitution, it characteristically describes this task as one of deference to whichever branch of government it determines to be the best representative of the whole.

Marbury v. *Madison* was the only Supreme Court decision invalidating an act of Congress until *Dred Scott*.[47] We shall see below that a crucial issue in the latter

46. See Sylvia Snowiss, "From Fundamental Law to the Supreme Law of the Land: A Reinterpretation of Judicial Review," *Studies in American Political Development* 2 (1987): 1–67.

47. After *Marbury*, Marshall confined his exercise of federal judicial review to state legislation, focusing primarily on the contracts clause—a technical area in which the judiciary could make a special claim to legislative deference.

case is whether the U.S. Constitution could be considered an act of the whole if any members of a race that could be enslaved were considered part of the "sovereign people." Before considering the issues in *Dred Scott* that bear directly on the separation of powers, however, we must add a further element to our discussion of the Marshallian framework. The implied limitations on the powers of Congress in *Dred Scott* derive in part from the requirements of federalism. To this aspect of Marshallian jurisprudence we now turn.

Wholes and Parts

In the Marshallian jurisprudence of federalism we see Marshall's implicit critique of the republican theory of popular sovereignty developing into a constitutional theory of what is required to equalize between the whole and the part. Here, the underlying metaphors that govern Marshallian jurisprudence receive their fullest and most subtle development. Because in principle all members of the sovereign people were both federal citizens and citizens of the several states, Marshall believed that the U.S. government and the governments of the states, collectively, must be seen as alternative representatives of the people as a whole. Delimiting the respective powers of Congress and the state legislatures thus posed a problem of whole versus part at two levels. At one level the Court was obliged to ask whether the government of the whole (the United States) or the government of the part (the particular state) should prevail. At a deeper level the Court was obliged to argue that sometimes the national government and sometimes the states, collectively, are the proper constitutional representatives of the people as a whole under the U.S. Constitution.

Marshall's own views on these questions invariably favored expanding congressional authority over the states. He thus characteristically argued that under the Constitution the federal government represented the interests of the people as a whole in conflicts with individual states, which represented only a part of the people. He made this argument, however, using an analytical framework that suggested that, just as federal power was absolute within its sphere, there was a proper sphere of state power that must also be seen as an expression of popular sovereignty under the Constitution.[48] Under this second line of analysis, the whole would be considered to be the sum of the parts, and hence the collective sovereignty of the states would limit the powers claimed by a temporary legislative majority in Congress. Although Marshall never had the inclination (or occasion) to uphold state sovereignty in deciding a case, his jurisprudential framework of federalism was potentially at odds with his own judicial politics.[49] As we shall see, his successor, Taney, developed the implications of that framework in a series of cases culminating in *Dred Scott*—the first case in which an act of Congress was struck down as a violation of the sovereignty of the people embodied in the several states.

48. This concession is especially salient in *Gibbons* v. *Ogden* 9 Wheat. 1 (1824) at 196–212.
49. Marshall defended the neutrality of his analytical framework in a series of pseudonymous articles, reprinted in Gunther, ed., *John Marshall's Defense of McCulloch* v. *Maryland* (Stanford: Stanford University Press, 1969).

The fullest development of the Marshallian jurisprudence of whole versus part occurs in *McCulloch v. Maryland*.[50] As the particular facts of the case are well known, we can directly address the main constitutional issues. The first issue in *McCulloch* is whether Congress has the authority to imply further powers, here the power to create a bank, from those expressly enumerated in the Constitution. If Congress has such implied powers, the second issue is whether their exercise must preempt the exercise of the plenary powers of a state, here the power to tax.

In addressing the first issue Marshall argues that the "necessary and proper" clause in the Constitution provides a textual basis for deriving implied powers from express powers. In using this approach Marshall implicitly assumes that some of the enumerated powers in the Constitution, such as the power to regulate commerce, set limitations on constitutionally permissible ends and that other enumerated powers, such as the power to issue currency, are merely examples of the permissible means to those ends. If the Constitution does not provide an exhaustive list of the means Congress may employ to achieve permissible ends, then the "necessary and proper" clause must fill the gap.[51]

Having assumed a constitutional distinction between means and ends, and having asserted that Congress is expressly limited only in the ends that it may pursue, Marshall, in the first prong of his opinion in *McCulloch*, is mainly concerned with whether the reasonableness of the relation between means and ends is for the Court or Congress to decide. On this point he argues that if the ends asserted by Congress are legitimate and the means are not expressly prohibited by the Constitution, the Court may not impose its own standard of rationality on the legislative choice of the means appropriate to its end.

In Marshall's view, the "necessary and proper" clause is a grant of authority to Congress rather than an invitation for the Court to review the "necessity" and "propriety" of the legislative choice of means to a constitutionally permissible end. Although much of Marshall's language in *McCulloch* urges on the Congress a higher standard of reasonableness than any that the Court will impose, his constitutional point is that the choice among permissible means lies within the sphere of proper legislative authority. In this respect *McCulloch* limits the scope of judicial review originally articulated in *Marbury*. In *McCulloch* the Court confines itself to review of whether the Congress has chosen to promote an end that is constitutionally authorized (such as regulating commerce or providing for the national defense); in the choice of means to such an end, however, the Court denies that there is any judicial standard for interfering with legislative discretion unless there is an explicit constitutional prohibition.

The first prong of *McCulloch* provides the clearest expression of a premise

---

50. 4 Wheat. 316 (1819).

51. Charles Black, however, interprets this argument as a rebuttal to those who argued that the clause places judicially enforceable limitations on Congress. In Black's view Marshall believed that establishing a bank is an inherent power of Congress. See Charles L. Black, Jr., *Structure and Relationship in Constitutional Law* (Baton Rouge: Louisiana State University Press, 1969), 14.

that became fundamental in Marshallian jurisprudence: that each constitutionally authorized decision maker occupies a sphere of authority within which
its reasons are substantively unreviewable. According to this premise, the
unique role of the Supreme Court under the Constitution is not to review the
reasonableness of what other governmental entities have done but rather to
police the boundaries between the spheres of proper constitutional authority.
Within its proper sphere each constitutionally recognized decision maker
would exercise absolute power—a form of sovereignty analogous to that of the
king in Parliament. Yet outside its proper sphere, the actions of a constitutional
decision maker, no matter how reasonable, would be legally nugatory.

The second prong of the *McCulloch* decision was concerned with the potentially more difficult question of what happens when two spheres of constitutional authority overlap. This problem arose out of Marshall's need to accommodate the relation of federal and state authority to the model of cosovereign
spheres of absolute power, which was the core of Marshallian jurisprudence.
He recognized that taxation was one of the plenary powers left to the sovereign
states. If Congress was legitimately acting within the scope of federal power in
creating a bank, could the state burden such a federally created entity by
imposing taxes that would otherwise clearly fall within the scope of state
sovereignty?

In answering this question Marshall again wished to avoid the obvious move
of reviewing the reasonableness of the state tax and the degree to which it
burdened the federal entity. He believed that such an inquiry would inevitably
require the Court to decide legislative questions "unfit for the judicial department."[52] To Marshall the proper judicial question was whether the state had
the constitutional power to tax a federal entity, however slightly. If the state has
such a power under the Constitution, then it seemed plain to Marshall that the
federal courts had no authority to review and limit its exercise: "The power to
tax involves the power to destroy."[53] Rather than balancing state and federal
power, Marshall argued that the legitimate exercise of federal power must
always preempt state powers which would otherwise be absolute within their
sphere.

In *McCulloch*, Marshall suggests that in order to determine the division of
powers between federal and state legislatures he must first determine the
proper separation of powers between each type of legislature and the federal
courts. As we have seen, his crucial assumption is that a *court* would be usurping
legislative functions in reviewing the reasonableness of a legislative decision at
either the state or the federal level. For Marshall this presumed limitation on
the judicial function defines the central legal issue in the case as a conflict
between two claims to legislative power, each of which must be recognized as
absolute if it is recognized at all. Thus conceived, the issue before the Court is
whether the state power to tax could defeat all exercises of legitimate congressional power or whether an exercise of legitimate congressional power is
wholly immune from the state power to tax. In view of the fact that the

52. *McCulloch* at 430.
53. Marshall adapted this phrase from Webster's brief. Cf. *McCulloch* at 327, 427.

economic interests of the state are represented in Congress, Marshall concludes that this is a matter in which the representatives of a part of the people should not be allowed to defeat the representatives of the whole.

The preceding form of argument is typical of Marshallian jurisprudence. As suggested above, Marshall's genius was to conceive of the federal system as embodying a series of structurally parallel conflicts, all of which could be resolved simultaneously by resolving any of them. These conflicts were all presumed by Marshall to be judicially resolvable using either the traditional legal methods for deciding disputes between part and part or the emergent constitutional theory for dealing with conflicts between the whole and the part. Never, according to Marshall, would the Court properly decide a question of constitutional law on the basis of its own view of what is best for the whole. Instead, the Court would always describe itself as setting boundaries between the legitimate powers of these competing parties before it, whether these be ordinary individuals claiming their rights or governmental institutions claiming to act with the sovereign authority of a united people.

Marshall's technique for deciding constitutional cases depended upon his view that they each presented several levels of conflict to which the major institutions of government were implicitly or explicitly parties. Once the case was seen to involve the scope of authority of constitutionally recognized decision makers, the legal theory of overlapping sovereignties came into play. The central judicial function, described in Story's *Commentaries on the Conflict of Laws*, was to defer to different sovereignties on different issues, and to define the scope within which each competing claim to sovereign authority would be judicially recognized as absolute. The constitutional meaning of such absolute sovereign power in a domestic context was that the courts must not inquire into the reasonableness of any particular decision, but only into the authority of the decision maker to reach it.

In the years before *Dred Scott* the Marshallian jurisprudence of federalism provided the conceptual framework for much of the debate about American slavery. In *Groves* v. *Slaughter*,[54] for example, the Taney Court ruled that the federal commerce power preempts a slave state from forbidding the importation of slaves by persons who were not bona fide immigrants. On the other side, however, the doctrine of implied congressional powers seemed to suggest a potential strategy for the gradual abolition of slavery within the terms of the pre-Civil War Constitution. Alongside the commerce clause, established in *McCulloch* as the preeminent legislative end which authorizes wide congressional discretion over the choice of means, Marshallian jurisprudence clearly anticipated that other express powers in the Constitution could be cited in statutes as a grounds for implying congressional powers beyond those expressly enumerated. Among these were the power to regulate territories and perhaps also the power to admit new states. Before *Dred Scott* was decided in 1857 many abolitionists hoped that these powers, alongside the judicially acknowledged commerce power, could be exercised by Congress as a basis for limiting

54. 15 Pet. 449 (1841).

the spread of slavery beyond the original slave states.[55] In the territories the already substantial federal power to regulate economic activity within the sovereign states would be enhanced by the plenary powers which would inhere in Congress exercising the prerogatives of a future state government. Congress would then be subject only to the constitutional restraints that federalism imposed on each state to recognize the rights of out-of-state citizens—which did not include the right to permanently hold slaves who were domiciled in free states.

We are now in a position to describe a large part of the constitutional significance of *Dred Scott*, and especially of Taney's opinion for the Court, by locating the various issues presented by the case in the structure of Marshallian analysis described above.

Like *Marbury*, *Dred Scott* begins as a conflict between two individuals—here, a freedom suit brought by Dred Scott against Sanford. Under the formalities of the pleadings, Dred Scott's alleged slavery is invoked as Sanford's legal defense against the charge of assault and false imprisonment. A judicial rejection of this defense, either on the law or the facts, would have had the effect of freeing Dred Scott under Missouri law.

On another level *Dred Scott* is also a conflict between state and federal courts over the interpretation of state law in cases over which federal courts have jurisdiction. In *Swift* v. *Tyson*[56] Justice Story had ruled for the Taney Court that the federal judiciary could differ from state courts in the interpretation of state law—creating the possibility of divergent state and federal interpretations of state precedents and statutes. We have seen above that the Missouri Supreme Court, for reasons admittedly extrajudicial, overruled the established Missouri case that supported Dred Scott's claim to freedom. Was the U.S. Supreme Court as a matter of federal law bound to follow the Missouri Supreme Court in rejecting its own state precedent?

On still another level *Dred Scott* presents a conflict between state legislatures. Dred Scott had been taken as a slave to Illinois, which prohibited the importation of slaves and which refused to enforce the claims of masters who had voluntarily imported slaves into Illinois, contrary to the law. Must the extraterritorial effect of Illinois law be deemed to have freed Dred Scott upon his presumably voluntary return to Missouri? Or did Illinois law merely deprive a Missouri owner of certain remedies to recover slave property held in Illinois?

Yet another conflict in *Dred Scott* is between the limited powers of Congress and the plenary powers of state legislatures. In regulating federally administered territories, Congress presumably acted both with its full federal powers and as a surrogate for state governments yet to be established. Did the federal Constitution constrain the ways in which Congress could exercise the plenary

---

55. See William M. Wiecek, "Slavery and Abolition before the United States Supreme Court, 1820–1860," *Journal of American History* 65, no. 1 (1978): 34–59; and Bestor, "The Civil War" and "State Sovereignty."

56. 41 U.S. 1.

powers of states, especially in regard to questions of slavery? Or was Congress free to regulate slavery in the territories according to its political will, both when it passed the Missouri Compromise in 1820 and when it repealed part of the Missouri Compromise in the Kansas-Nebraska Act of 1854? What was the difference, if any, between administering federal territories under the Constitution and establishing federal colonies to which, arguably, the U.S. Constitution did not apply?[57]

Finally, *Dred Scott* is a conflict between the Supreme Court and Congress over the power to interpret the U.S. Constitution. The case itself directly concerns how the United States is to be constituted—ethnically, politically, and territorially—and whether such a fundamental question of political development is judicially reviewable. In *Luther v. Borden* the Taney Court had ruled that the clause in the Constitution that guarantees a republican form of government to the states is judicially unenforceable, stating for the first time the doctrine that "political questions" should not be reviewed by the courts.[58] Was the attempt of Congress to preordain certain aspects of the republican constitutions of newly admitted states a similarly political question in which the Court ought not to interfere? Or did the constitutional protection of popular sovereignty in the states require that Congress place no greater limitation on the sovereign power of newly admitted states than the Constitution had placed on the original thirteen?

In the mid-nineteenth century this issue was not considered to be merely academic: congressional regulation of territories during the initial period of settlement would largely determine the political composition of the people who would elect the territorial legislature and ratify the constitution of the new state. When the Kansas-Nebraska Act partially suspended congressional efforts to preempt popular sovereignty in the territories, there was a race between pro- and antislavery groups to populate the future states, leading to a sequence of violent acts and reprisals which are part of the lore of American history.

Dred Scott did not raise the issue of whether the Constitution required that the question of slavery be decided by popular sovereignty in the new states,[59] but it did determine that the Missouri Compromise was unconstitutional be-

---

57. Cf. the later rulings in the *Insular Cases*. These were published in vol. 182 of *U.S. Reports* with additional materials published separately as a book. See especially *De Lima v. Bidwill* 182 U.S. 1 (1901), which cites *Dred Scott* as authority for the proposition that the United States can have subjects who are not citizens. See also *Downs v. Bidwill* 182 U.S. 144 (1901). Note, however, that Taney's opinion in *Dred Scott* explicitly denies that Congress has the power to establish colonies (at least if bordering on the Unites States) which can be governed without the ordinary limitations imposed by the Constitution. See *Dred Scott v. Sandford* 19 Howard 393 (1857) at 446–48.

58. 7 How. 1 (1849). The Court's decision in effect upheld the power of Rhode Island to maintain severe limitations on suffrage that had been in effect since the colonial period, and long before "republican" government had been constitutionally required. See William Wiecek, *The Guarantee Clause of the U.S. Constitution* (Ithaca: Cornell University Press, 1972); [note] "Political Rights as Political Questions: The Paradox of *Luther v. Borden*," *Harvard Law Review* 100, no. 8 (1987): 1125–46.

59. Much to the disappointment of Stephen Douglas. See Fehrenbacher, 195–97, 206–07.

THE LOGIC AND LEGACY OF DRED SCOTT 227

cause, unlike Illinois law, it would necessarily have the effect of divesting Missouri slaveholders, such as Emerson, of their property in slaves, like Dred Scott, who might eventually return to Missouri. Why did Taney make this assumption, when the Missouri courts had viewed the extraterritorial effects of federal law prohibiting slavery as similar to the extraterritorial effects of state law such as that of Illinois? This question is not directly addressed by Taney, but the answer to it lies, I believe, in the framework of Marshallian jurisprudence which informs Taney's opinion throughout.[60] Taney believed that Congress, as such, was always subject to constitutional restraints, including the Bill of Rights, even when, in legislating for the territories, it acted on behalf of a future state government. If Congress indeed had the power to prohibit slavery in the territories, Taney assumed that this must be an implied federal power, deriving either from the territories clause or the power to admit new states.[61] In Marshallian terms the congressional exercise of such an implied federal power to prohibit slavery in the territories must inevitably preempt state legislation repugnant to it. To Taney there was apparently little question that the Missouri Compromise, if valid, must preempt state law and have the effect of freeing slaves who, like Dred Scott, returned with their former owners to slave states.

Thus far, our account of the Marshallian framework explains why Taney believed that Dred Scott's case required the Court to decide the constitutionality of the prohibition of slavery in the Missouri Compromise, despite the fact that this part of his opinion was dismissed as mere dictum by Curtis, who claimed that the majority had no legal basis to reach this issue after it decided that even a free Dred Scott would have no federal standing to sue. Under Taney's legal assumptions, the federal legislative power to free Dred Scott in Wisconsin Territory implied the power to free him in Missouri; and this implied the power to make Dred Scott a citizen of Missouri for purposes of federal law and, hence, a citizen of the United States. If the Missouri Compromise was presumed to be constitutional, then Taney's far more questionable claim that Congress had no power to naturalize a native-born Negro would have been the only remaining basis for his opinion.[62]

60. Taney explicitly embraced the Marshallian framework in *Dred Scott*: "The principle on which our governments rest, and upon which alone they continue to exist is the union of States, sovereign and independent with their own limits in the internal and domestic concerns, and bound together as one people by a general government, possessing certain enumerated and restricted powers delegated to it by the people of the several States, and exercising supreme authority within the scope of the powers granted to it." (*Dred Scott* v. *Sandford* 19 Howard 393 [1857] at 447–48).

61. Taney never went so far as to fully accept Calhoun's theory that in regulating the territories Congress was merely a trustee for the states. See Bestor, "State Sovereignty" and "The Civil War as a Constitutional Crisis."

62. On this point Curtis clearly has the better of the argument. See *Dred Scott* v. *Sandford* 19 Howard 393 (1857). See also 419–20, 571–78. Hurd confirms that some free Negroes were U.S. citizens in *The Law of Freedom and Bondage*, para. 371. For a capsule discussion of the state of law on this question leading up to *Dred Scott*, see Kent, *Commentaries*, 13th ed., vol. 2, [320]-[333].

I wish to argue, however, that Taney's opinion in *Dred Scott* was not merely a passive reflection of the framework of Marshallian analysis; rather, it focused on a problem in the Marshallian framework, using judicial innovations that have had a lasting effect on our constitutional thought. Those innovations concern the way in which we determine *which* state-created individual rights require special constitutional solicitude. To complete the Marshallian framework as it bears on *Dred Scott*, we must now consider the place of the individual in the federal system.

Individual Rights and the Crisis in Marshallian Theory

The interpolation of the model of state sovereignty into the resolution of intergovernmental disputes was the golden key to Marshall's constitutional jurisprudence. In international law a sphere of sovereign power was a claim asserted against the world—not a claim that arose out of relations with a particular party. The constitutional model of cosovereignty likewise suggested that the sphere of legitimate power exercised by any constitutional decision maker was an absolute limitation on the powers of any other decision maker in the federal system. Thus, in *McCulloch*, the federal judicial power was inherently the same in relation to both Congress and the states; the powers of state legislatures were the same in relation to both Congress and the Court. By attempting to sustain such a pattern of reasoning Marshall hoped to show that with the adoption of the U.S. Constitution the entire American legal system was in principle consistent. To establish this consistency he tried to demonstrate in case after case that the constitutional power of each decision maker—whether a court, a legislature, an executive official, or a private individual—was the same at every level of legal controversy in which that decision maker was engaged.

A partial list of the possible conflicts between governmentally recognized powers involved in many constitutional cases suggests the scope of Marshall's vision and the magnitude of his task:[63]

Federal legislative v. federal judicial
State legislative v. federal judicial
Federal executive v. federal judicial
State judicial v. federal judicial
Federal executive v. federal legislative
Federal executive v. state legislative
Federal executive v. state judicial

63. In "The Rise and Fall of Classical Legal Thought," Duncan Kennedy argues that, building on the post-Civil War jurisprudence of Cooley, late nineteenth-century legal thinkers such as Tiedeman attempted to constitutionalize the entire legal system by extrapolating from Marshall's reasoning as described above. I owe much of my formulation of the Marshallian model of "powers absolute within their sphere" to the Kennedy manuscript. See Thomas Cooley, *Treatise on Constitutional Limitations* (Boston: Little, Brown, 1868); Christopher Tiedeman, *A Treatise on the Limitation of Police Power in the United States* (St. Louis: F. H. Thomas, 1896); Tiedeman, *The Unwritten Constitution of the United States: A Philosophical Inquiry* (New York: G. P. Putnam's, 1890).

Individual v. federal legislative
Individual v. state legislative
Individual v. state judicial
(Individual v. individual)

Of course, no single case required the Marshall Court to address all these levels of conflicts at once—and some potential conflicts (such as those between Congress and the president) were never directly presented to the Marshall Court. Perhaps the fullest application of Marshall's framework during his lifetime lay in the removal of inconsistency between the exercise of federal and state judicial power. By allowing appeals of federal questions from state to federal courts,[64] Marshall in effect nationalized the judicial power while building deference to state sovereignty into the content of federal law.

The logic of Marshallian jurisprudence would seem to suggest that individual constitutional rights might also be viewed as spheres of absolute sovereignty: within their appropriate sphere the reasons of the right-holder would then be no more subject to judicial review than the reasons of a legislative body. Viewed in this way the sphere of individual rights would appear as the third level of popular sovereignty, coequal with the sovereignty embodied in federal and state power. Not even John Marshall, however, could plausibly make such a general claim about individual constitutional rights in the federal system. To have done so, he would have had to argue that the scope of individual rights protected by the federal courts is the same against Congress, the state legislatures, and other individuals.

Such an argument would have been at odds with Marshall's own interpretation of federalism, which presupposed that individual rights would be defined differently in each of these contexts. During the Marshall era the rights of individuals against each other were seen as artifacts of state law, interpreted primarily by state courts and subject to the plenary powers of state legislatures to revise the common law. In practice the state courts did not describe ordinary individual rights in the formalist language of spheres of absolute power, but rather in terms closer to today's instrumentalist language of competing interests which must be balanced case by case.[65] Such right-holders were difficult to regard as miniature sovereigns within their proper domains.

If the rights of individuals against each other were not constitutionally grounded in the Marshall era, these legal rights could not serve as a general

---

64. See, for example, *Cohens* v. *Virginia* 6 Wheat. 264 (1821). Note, however, that conflicts between the individual and the federal judiciary have never been fully integrated into the Marshallian scheme. Assertions that the courts must recognize constitutional defenses when individuals are charged with contempt of federal court orders continue to raise deep problems for the framework of the separation and division of powers. See *United States* v. *United Mine Workers* 330 U.S. 258 and *Walker* v. *City of Birmingham* 338 U.S. 307 (1967).

65. See Morton Horwitz, *The Transformation of American Law* (Cambridge: Harvard University Press, 1977). For an attempt at the state level to reconcile Blackstone's view of individual rights with a republican theory of popular sovereignty and a Marshallian view of federalism, see Kent's *Commentaries*.

source of individual rights against the states. Beginning with *Calder* v. *Bull*,[66] a pre-Marshall decision, the U.S. Supreme Court had upheld the sovereign power of state legislatures to change the legally enforceable expectations of individuals. Unless the right·to a legal remedy had already vested as a result of past adjudication or an executory contract, the *Calder* Court suggested that the legislature would have the plenary power to alter, vitiate, or perhaps even eliminate that remedy. State law, as such, would not provide a source of federally enforceable individual constitutional rights against state governments, except when the constitutional protection of individuals was necessary to preserve the separation of powers between state legislatures and the courts. In evoking the separation of powers to justify its conclusions, the *Calder* Court asserted that the state legislature was not really changing individual *rights* in exercising the legislative power to alter judicially enforceable *remedies*.

Even the limitations on Congress imposed by the Bill of Rights were never construed in the Marshall era to create a sphere of individual rights protected against the states and other individuals.[67] The Marshall Court explicitly held that the Bill of Rights was not enforceable against the states[68] and never decided a case that enforced the Bill of Rights against an act of Congress. Neither did the "privileges and immunities" clause prove to be a source of substantive individual rights.[69] Instead of viewing that clause as an invitation to draw up a charter of federally protected rights, the Marshall Court in effect viewed it as an adjunct to the principle of federalism—requiring the majorities of each state to give out-of-state citizens the same civil (but not political) rights they conferred upon themselves. In taking legislative majorities in the states to be the source of constitutionally protected civil rights, the Supreme Court used the "privileges and immunities" clause largely as a bar to legislative classifications that discriminate against out-of-state economic actors. In this respect it was merely an adjunct to the "full faith and credit" clause, requiring extraterritorial enforcement of state court judgments, and the "diversity" jurisdiction of federal courts, permitting out-of-state citizens to choose a federal alternative to state courts, even in cases arising under state law.

The only area in which Marshall sought to apply his model of cosovereignty to the protection of individual rights was in the interpretation of the contracts clause—a relatively technical legal area in which the Court could claim a special legitimacy in reviewing state legislation. In *Ogden* v. *Saunders* Marshall considered whether a state bankruptcy law violated the constitutional rights of future creditors under the contracts clause. Here he attempted to argue that the contractual rights of individuals in relation to each other limited the legislative powers of the state over individuals; thus, he provided a basis for federal

66. 3 Dall. 386 (1798).

67. Laurence Tribe, *American Constitutional Law* (Mineola, N.Y.: Foundation Press, 1978), chap. 6, sec. 32.

68. *Barron* v. *Mayor of Baltimore*, 7 Pet. 243 (1833).

69. For a discussion of the pre–Civil War cases on privileges and immunities up to and including *Dred Scott*, see Hurd, *The Law of Freedom and Bondage*, chap. 24.

judicial review of state legislation that infringed upon the constitutional rights of individuals.[70]

Marshall's analysis in *Ogden* was rooted in his claim that the power of individuals to make contracts is a natural analogue to the legislative power to create new law. He argued that, to the extent that state law altered the substantive powers of individuals entering contracts, there would be an unconstitutional "impairment of the obligations of contracts." From this he concluded that individual freedom of contract is a constitutionally protected right, drawing its substance from preexisting state law but enforceable in federal court against statutory revisions of that law by the states. In this way Marshall extended his own previous opinion in *Sturgis* v. *Crowninshield*[71] to invalidate not merely legislation that limits the enforcement of rights under preexisting contracts but also legislation that limits the scope of the right to contract as such. In making this argument, however, Marshall found himself in dissent for the only time in his career as chief justice.

The majority on the Court, best represented by the opinion of Trimble, wished to avoid asserting a judicial power to protect citizens of a state from efforts by their own state legislatures to change the laws governing relations between individuals. Trimble reasoned that the power to enter contracts was not a natural right but rather an artifact of positive state law that set the background conditions against which all contracts must be interpreted. Therefore, he argued, a change in the positive law of contract would necessarily affect the interpretation of all contracts concluded under the new law. In this interpretation such legislation would be a legitimate exercise of state sovereignty rather than an unconstitutional invasion of individual rights.

To Trimble, the main constitutional problem in *Ogden* was to make his theory of the contracts clause consistent with the Court's holding in *Sturgis*, forbidding the application of new state bankruptcy law to preexisting contracts: if the legislature could require the courts to apply new law in interpreting new contracts (*Ogden*), why not allow the legislature to require courts to apply new law to the interpretation of old contracts (*Sturgis*)? To resolve this issue Trimble's opinion attempted to limit *Sturgis* in a way that Marshall did not. Under *Sturgis*, he suggested, courts are merely bound to interpret contracts according to the law in effect when those contracts were made, regardless of subsequent legislation to the contrary. The individual rights protected under the contracts clause would thus be limited to those necessary under the separation of powers to protect the constitutional role of the judiciary from state legislatures. In distinguishing *Sturgis* in this way, Trimble evokes the distinction between rights and remedies in *Calder*.[72] Yet he makes no argument to explain why this

---

70. 12 Wheat. 213 (1827). For Marshall the threshold constitutional question was whether a state bankruptcy law, releasing debtors from the legal enforcement of contractual obligations, was valid legislation at all, rather than a legislative usurpation of judicial power.

71. 4 Wheat. 122 (1810).

72. According to Trimble (*Ogden* v. *Saunders*, 317–24, 327), state bankruptcy laws can *never* affect the natural obligations of contracts, since these arise out of the moral relation between

legislation affecting new contracts is merely an alteration of remedies, whereas similar legislation as applied to old contracts would be a violation of rights. Rather, Trimble simply assumes that once a contract has been concluded the remedies expected will have vested as rights for constitutional purposes.

Through this assumption Trimble implicitly concedes much of the logic of Marshall's dissent, while anticipating the impasse of Marshallian jurisprudence before the Civil War. In upholding the validity of *Sturgis*, Trimble recognizes positive law enacted by the sovereign states as the source of federally protected constitutional rights. Yet in limiting the effects of *Sturgis*, Trimble also argues that federal constitutional protection extends only to those legal rights that are presumed to have vested under state law.[73] He thus attempts to reconcile popular sovereignty and the rule of law at the state level where republican theory still applied: state law will be taken as the source of substantive constitutional rights, but only when this is necessary to protect the judicial power from legislative encroachment. Otherwise, the sovereign state retains the plenary power to change the substantive law that underlies the civil rights of individuals.

In *Ogden* v. *Saunders* Marshall and his colleagues had faced a dilemma presented by his general framework of constitutional analysis. In unsuccessfully attempting to extend his framework to cover federal protection of individual rights against incursions by state government, Marshall had been constrained to view the individual rights in question as natural powers to make contracts, which were a separate sphere of absolute sovereignty coordinate with, and preceding, the sovereign powers of states to legislate. Marshall's colleagues on the Court, here represented by Trimble, implicitly recognized that such a conception of federally protected individual rights would be incompatible with the equality and sovereignty of states in a federal system which had provided the central paradigm of Marshall's framework. Arguing that individual freedom of contract could not be described as an analogue to state sovereignty—another power absolute within its sphere—they concluded that remedies for breach of contract available under state law were not part of the vested rights of contracts for federal purposes.

If the majority on the *Ogden* Court had followed Marshall's interpretation of his own jurisprudence, there might have been little left of federalism: federal

---

debtor and creditor. Arguing that the state legislature has no role in this moral relation, Trimble concluded that contract law is merely concerned with when the moral obligations created by contracts will be enforceable through legal remedies. Note that nothing in this argument justifies the *Sturgis* Court in striking down the application of bankruptcy laws to preexisting contracts, a problem that Trimble takes pains to overcome in the remainder of his opinion.

73. The theory of vested rights was, thus, a severe limitation on the use of substantive state law as a source of federally enforceable constitutional rights, as Corwin points out in the three seminal articles cited in note 1 above. For a recent elaboration of Corwin's point, see James L. Kainen, "Nineteenth-Century Interpretations of the Federal Contract Clause: The Transformation from Vested to Substantive Rights against the State," *Buffalo Law Review* 31 (1982): 381–480.

courts could merely have paid lip service to state sovereignty by using old state law affecting contracts among individuals as a constitutional basis for striking down new state law. (As we shall see later, such a constitutionalization of preexisting state law was later to become the underlying basis for the jurisprudence of substantive due process, which can be viewed as a vindication of Marshall's position in *Ogden* v. *Saunders*.)[74]

To avoid such a conclusion the Marshall Court made federalism itself the main basis for judicial protection of individual rights against the states. Federal right-holders were seen quintessentially as out-of-state citizens, protected against discrimination by state legislatures. The substance of this protection lay in the "privileges and immunities" and commerce clauses of the Constitution. The procedure lay in the diversity jurisdiction of the federal courts. Under this conception the baseline of individual constitutional rights was still set by the individual state legislatures, and these, under their republican form of government, were in principle free to engage in vast social experiments using their sovereign power to change the law. If individual rights were the creation of state law, there were, in structural terms, only two constitutional justifications for protecting them in federal courts: to preserve the separation of powers between legislation and adjudication and to uphold the division of powers between state and federal legislatures. In Marshallian jurisprudence, U.S. citizens would have a constitutional right to protection against the states in federal courts whenever this was necessary to uphold the sovereignty of the states in a federal system.

In *Dred Scott* Taney achieved a perverse, but ingenious, synthesis of the competing views of Trimble and Marshall in *Ogden* v. *Saunders*. His underlying problem in *Dred Scott* was to show that the substantive state laws establishing slavery had created federally protected constitutional rights in slaveholders, while the state and federal laws prohibiting slavery had conferred no constitutional rights in the descendants of slaves to whom those laws applied. This asymmetry required Taney to adumbrate a new theory about when and why the adverse effect of a statute on individuals would trigger constitutional review.

DRED SCOTT AND CONSTITUTIONAL DEVELOPMENT

From a legal point of view, as already suggested, *Dred Scott* is generally considered a dead end in American jurisprudence, made obsolete by the nationwide abolition of slavery resulting from the Civil War. Commentators tend to assume that *Dred Scott* has had little impact on the law because seven separate majority opinions leave its holding unclear, and because it turns on substantive issues of slavery and procedural issues of pleading which no longer form part of our law. This assumption, although partially justified, ignores the fact that by attempting to preserve the state-created institution of slavery from legislative encroachment, Taney unintentionally devised the techniques by which the jurisprudence of slavery would be transcended in American constitutional law.

74. See Kennedy, "The Rise and Fall of Classical Legal Thought."

Having sketched the series of conflicts presented by *Dred Scott* in the Marshallian framework, we can now take up the two issues that Taney explicitly addressed in order to resolve the various Marshallian conflicts in the case without ever admitting that the Court had jurisdiction to reach the merits. In a sense both of these issues are jurisdictional. The first issue, sometimes considered to be procedural, is whether even a free Negro had standing to sue as both a state and a U.S. citizen under federal diversity jurisdiction.[75] The second issue, sometimes described as the "merits" of the case, is whether Dred Scott's suit should have been dismissed because he remained a slave in Missouri, despite the effects of his residence in Illinois and in federally administered free territory. A negative ruling on either issue would have finally required Dred Scott's case to be dismissed for lacking of standing; Taney gave a negative ruling on both.

In discussing these issues, Taney addresses two central problems of American constitutional jurisprudence. The first, which relates to the first part of this essay, concerns the hereditary character of slavery based on race under a republican form of government. The second, which relates to the second part, is the impact of Marshallian constitutionalism on the principles of international law which governed the ordinary relations of comity between the sovereign states that permitted, and those that prohibited, slavery.

Slavery and Republican Theory

The peculiarities of the American law of slavery are well-documented. Much has been written on the legal paradoxes of the notion of property in persons, and on how the resolution of these paradoxes taxed the American legal mind; we need not repeat these discussions here.[76]

---

75. Stated generally, this issue may have been spurious, as Fehrenbacher points out (pp. 277–78). In previous cases dealing with corporations the Taney Court had not required U.S. citizenship of those seeking federal diversity jurisdiction. Alien corporations were customarily allowed access to the federal courts in disputes with state citizens without claiming to be U.S. ctizens for all purposes. The clear implication was that the degree of U.S. citizenship necessary for federal diversity jurisdiction was less than that required for full protection under the "privileges and immunities" clause. Fehrenbacher suggests that the lower federal court may have had this distinction in mind in accepting jurisdiction of *Dred Scott*. Interestingly, Hurd also gives evidence that the general issue of diversity jurisdiction for Negroes may have been pretextual. He points out that, even after *Dred Scott*, free Negroes domiciled in the United States could be treated as citizens for purposes of federal diversity jurisdiction (but, presumably, only in cases where their freedom was not at issue.) See *The Law of Freedom and Bondage*, para. 371–72, including 1:437., *n* 1.

76. Modern scholarship on the laws of slavery rests heavily on the research of Caterall, *Judicial Cases concerning American Slavery and the Negro*. Her conclusions regarding *Dred Scott* are summarized in "Some Antecedents of the Dred Scott Case," *American Historical Review* 30 (1924–25): 56–71. See also Hurd, *The Law of Freedom and Bondage in the United States*. Further detailed discussions of the American law of race and slavery are in Kenneth M. Stampp, *The Peculiar Institution* (New York: Vintage Press, 1956); A. Leon Higginbotham, *In the Matter of Color* (New York: Oxford University Press, 1981); and Mark Tushnet, *The American Law of Slavery, 1810–1860* (Princeton: Princeton University Press, 1981). See also David Brion Davis, *The Problem of Slavery in the Age of Revolution* (Ithaca: Cornell University Press, 1975). The

The earliest forms of slavery in North America were penal servitude, indenture, and the conquest of American Indians. In these forms of slavery the putative rights of masters were grounded, respectively, in criminal law, contract law, and the laws of war. Mastery based on these legal models appeared as an enforceable entitlement (generally transferable) to the entire use of the slave's labor for a designated term, but not as an absolute right of dominion over the slave and his or her progeny.

Black slavery was not consistent with these models. The American black was considered to have been captured and enslaved elsewhere, and his status as a slave was presumed to be a result of the international and maritime law that allowed for his importation as property. Once a black person had been imported as a slave under laws presumed to be valid elsewhere, that person's descendants would continue to be deemed property under the American laws of slavery. In the North American colonies, black slavery was an inherited consequence of the law governing the slavers' ships, a law that did not protect the slaves themselves because they were presumed to be without nationality or citizenship when they arrived on American shores. Under the various American slave codes there were no rights to enslave a man whose ancestors had always been free, but the black in North America was considered to have been legally enslaved when he arrived, before the operation of any American law.[77] His owner's right to capture him was, thus, a legal consequence of his prior enslavement, rather than vice versa.[78]

---

peculiarities of the American law of race and slavery are put into comparative perspective in Orlando Patterson, *Slavery and Social Death* (Cambridge: Harvard University Press, 1982), and George Frederickson, *White Supremacy*.

77. The various Black Codes governing freed slaves did provide, however, for reenslavement under some circumstances. In some instances this reenslavement appears to have been a specific legal punishment, applicable only to blacks, which was a form of term bondage rather than chattel slavery. In other instances, however, the return to chattel slavery appears to have been the legally prescribed punishment for offenses applicable only to blacks, such as failing to leave the state after being freed. The possibility of reenslaving freed slaves is mentioned throughout Berlin, *Slaves without Masters*, chaps. 1–3, 6, 8–11, and the Epilogue. For cases, see the index to the five volumes of Caterall, *Judicial Cases*. For commentary, see the index to Hurd, *The Law of Freedom and Bondage*.

78. The conditions of one's entry into the United States continue to have constitutional significance for one's rights against being held in captivity under federal law. The recent treatment of the Mariel Cubans and Haitian refugees makes it clear that persons captured in the process of making illegal entry have few, if any, legal rights of due process against federal detention while they remain in the United States. Under the recently enacted immigration law, suspected illegal aliens apprehended in the United States who cannot prove birth, naturalization, or legal entry may also be subject to summary deportation proceedings. Such a shift in the burdens and presumptions regarding proof of citizenship raises issues of procedural due process similar to those addressed in *Dred Scott*, and in the fugitive slave cases discussed below—especially if summary deportation procedures are triggered by grounds of suspicion based largely on ethnicity and language. A state court, confronted with these issues, might conceivably view the use of summary proceedings predicated on race or ethnicity as a violation of the U.S. and state constitutions, and extend full due process rights under state law to persons who cannot prove their claim of birth in the United States, and who might

Although property in slaves was sometimes treated as realty for purposes of inheritance, in most respects slaves were treated as chattel. Chattel property, the source of our word *cattle*, is traditionally appropriate only to inanimate objects and to those animal species that could be domesticated. Once a member of such a species had been captured and domesticated, that animal and its offspring would always have a legal owner, as determined by the rules of property law. Animals that were chattel property could escape from their owner's possession, but if they were subsequently found they had in principle to be returned to their rightful owner. In the common law tradition, however, animal species that could not be domesticated could not be fully owned as chattel. They could be captured, sold, and stolen from their owners, but if they escaped from their owners' possession, they were deemed to have returned to their "wild" state and, hence, could become the property of whoever recaptured them. The traditional legal treatment of dogs and cats illustrates this distinction: runaway dogs must be returned if their rightful owners can be identified; runaway cats may be "adopted" by anyone who finds them. Significantly, early black slaves were frequently given names otherwise reserved for dogs or horses, common forms of chattel property.[79]

The common law distinction between property in domestic and wild animals provided much of the conceptual basis for the distinctions between black and Indian slavery in seventeenth-century North America. Indian slavery was a possible consequence of a treaty between colonists and an Indian nation, whereas black slavery was possible because its victims were presumed to lack nationality or citizenship.[80] In his study of a mulatto town in Massachusetts, Francis Hutchins shows how the offspring of escaped slaves and Indians were considered to be unowned and unreturnable by analogy to the offspring of wild and domestic animals. As Hutchins makes clear, the legal freedom available through intermarriage between blacks and Indians was not citizenship in the political community but merely the capacity to be free of ownership which was not grounded in direct contracts of indenture.[81]

---

otherwise be deported under federal law. In such circumstances the U.S. Supreme Court could find it difficult to overturn the state's interpretation of the U.S. Constitution without citing *Dred Scott* as valid precedent for the claim that naturalization cannot take place as an indirect effect of state laws and procedures (*Dred Scott* v. *Sandford* 19 Howard 393 [1857] at 405–08).

79. See, for example, Arthur Zilversmit, *The First Emancipation: The Abolition of Slavery in the North* (Chicago: University of Chicago Press, 1967), 7.

80. See Hurd, *Law of Freedom and Bondage*, vol. 1, para. 163–168; *Dred Scott* v. *Sandford* 19 Howard 393 (1857) at 403–04. Civil freedom in America has always been contrasted with the slavery of blacks, on the one hand, and the savagery of Indians on the other. See Gary F. Reed, "Freedom as the End of Civilization" (Ph.D. diss., University of California, Santa Cruz).

81. *Mashpee* (West Franklin, N.H.: Amarta Press, 1979) chaps. 1–5. In exercising this "freedom," many New England mulattos went to sea. The maritime jurisdiction of the federal courts covered the crews of ships in U.S. ports. In practice, however, federal courts were reluctant to protect free Negro seamen on U.S. ships from the operation of local law in southern port cities. The most vivid description of the seafaring mulatto is in Melville's *Moby Dick*.

The legal problems of manumission in the United States are largely explained by the extent to which the legal rationale of hereditary slavery was based on the common law of chattel property in animals. Roman law, which was based on a different model, could describe enslavement and manumission as largely reversible processes.[82] American law did not directly allow the enslavement of populations hitherto free; insofar as slaves existed they were not the creation of American law but the result of the operation of international law on persons whose racial identity made them citizens of no nation. If enslavement was an inherited attribute of their race, manumission as such could not reverse all the legal consequences of hereditary slavery.

The limited meaning of manumission was established as a matter of constitutional law in the case of *Prigg* v. *Pennsylvania*, the most important Supreme Court opinion on slavery until *Dred Scott*.[83] Here Justice Story considered the effect of the fugitive slave laws on the state-created legal protection of free Negroes from kidnapping by slave catchers under color of the federal Fugitive Slave Law of 1793. Despite his explicit opposition to slavery, Story upheld the constitutionality of the law and held that the state "personal liberty act" was repugnant to valid federal law. In reaching this conclusion Story tacitly admitted that a masterless Negro living in a free state was necessarily subject to the summary process of the Fugitive Slave Law. As long as slavery existed in any state, free Negroes could never be granted the procedural right to prove their freedom in the courts of the states in which they were "recaptured" as alleged escapees.

In *Dred Scott*, Taney devotes much attention to statutes and cases that demonstrate that free Negroes were systematically denied the civil rights of citizens, giving special attention to the laws of the states that had abolished slavery. Beginning with the early colonial period, he demonstrates the presumption of racial inferiority in American law, arguing that even apparent liberalizations of the law were enacted in the interests of whites rather than blacks. Essentially, Taney's argument follows *Prigg* in asserting that the constitutional provisions that protected slavery were part of a compact without which the Constitution would never have been ratified. If free Negroes were to have the full privileges and immunities of citizens of any state, then the Constitution would require that they be accorded the privileges and immunities of citizens in every state. To Taney such a result would violate the original intent of the framers of the U.S. Constitution. The Constitution, he argued, did not take a neutral position on whether slavery would continue, but was based, rather, on a commitment to preserve slavery in the original slave states. This meant that the Supreme Court could not take a neutral view of the effect of federal or state laws that might impede the preservation of slavery in particular states by extending civil rights to Negroes.

The republican phrasing of Taney's argument tends to obscure its point. Relying on the language of popular sovereignty, Taney argues on historical

82. See Patterson, *Slavery and Social Death*, chaps. 4, 10; and W. W. Buckland, *The Roman Law of Slavery* (Cambridge: Cambridge University Press, 1908).

83. 16 Pet. 539 (1842).

grounds that members of the Negro race could not be considered part of the "people" of the United States at the time of the founding. To this, Justice Curtis takes exception, correctly noting that some free Negroes had state citizenship, even in slave states, at the time the Constitution was ratified.[84] Taney's argument seems less peculiar, however, if we recognize that it is not at bottom historical but, rather, theoretical.

Taney's claim about the constitutional impossibility of U.S. citizenship for free Negroes rests on the potential irrelevance of state citizenship for membership in the "people of the United States."[85] It assumes a point, stressed later in his opinion, that the Constitution, unlike the Articles of Confederation, is not a treaty among states, each with its own criteria of citizenship, but a separate and coordinate act of popular sovereignty based on its own assumptions about who the "people" are. In *Dred Scott*, Taney believed, the Supreme Court was called upon to determine the specific identities through which the whole "people" could be divided into its "parts."

Such a decision was highly consequential for the sublimation of popular sovereignty that, as we have seen, formed the essence of Marshallian jurisprudence. If the states were to form the "parts" into which the people were divided, then the Court could equalize among the slave and free states by requiring all states to deny its free Negroes protection under the "privileges and immunities" clause of Article IV. If, however, free blacks and free whites could also be considered to be the "parts" of the "people," then requiring all states to accord such persons the full civil rights of its own citizens would undermine the institution of slavery in some states. Using the peculiar language of republicanism discussed above, Taney concluded that free blacks could not be part of the sovereign people under a federal Constitution that was based on the presumptive equality of slave and free states.

Curtis rejected this conclusion largely because, unlike Taney, he believed that protecting free blacks as U.S. citizens under the "privileges and immunities clause" would *not* require that blacks be accorded the same civil rights as white citizens when traveling out of state. With no intended irony, Curtis argued that the legal discrimination against free blacks who were U.S. citizens would be no less problematic than the discrimination against women and children—who were already recognized as U.S. citizens despite the varying legal disabilities imposed upon them by the states. To Curtis the "privileges and immunities" clause required only that out-of-state blacks, women, and children be treated no worse than the state's citizens in the same categories. If states remained free under the Constitution to discriminate against blacks who were U.S. citizens, then the mere coverage of blacks under the "privileges and immunities" clause would not necessarily jeopardize the legal repression of free Negroes in the states—provided that the states accorded the same civil rights to out-of-state blacks that they accorded to their own blacks. In this view Curtis was arguably less liberal, and certainly less prescient, than Taney who recognized that, as U.S. citizens, blacks like Dred Scott could claim, at the very least, the protection

84. *Dred Scott* v. *Sandford* 19 Howard 393 (1857) at 582.
85. Corwin first noted this in "The Dred Scott Decision," 67.

of the federal courts whenever they, or another party, were not citizens of the state that had passed the discriminatory law in question.

Slavery, State Sovereignty, and Constitutional Rights

To John Marshall and his colleague Joseph Story, slavery, like polygamy, was an unnatural and immoral institution that had to be recognized in domestic law only to the extent necessary to accommodate the sovereignty of other states. In this view, the existence of slavery in the United States was an unfortunate consequence of the fact that some persons were deemed to have entered the United States, or its predecessor colonies, as chattel property under international law.[86] Thereafter, Marshall and Story believed, the national recognition of the institution of slavery would be required legally only to the extent necessary to preserve the relations of comity among the sovereign states of the American union. By describing slavery in this way, the Marshall Court gave little reason to doubt that Congress could exercise its legitimate powers over interstate commerce and federal territories in order to limit the expansion of slavery, and perhaps also to create the economic and political conditions under which slavery might eventually become extinct in the states.

There were two general issues of international law that applied to Dred Scott's travel in and out of slave jurisdictions. The first was whether the laws of slavery or freedom followed him as he moved with his master. This posed a question of the choice of law which would arise in either jurisdiction. The second issue was whether, under either body of law, the status of slave could reattach to a person who had legally resided in another jurisdiction as a free man. This was the issue of whether freedom was "contagious," and, if so, whether a free black could be "reinfected" by slavery upon returning to slave soil.[87]

In addressing these issues American courts generally applied principles that had been first articulated in England and celebrated in Story's influential treatise on *Conflicts*. The *Somerset*[88] case established that the laws of freedom applied in free jurisdictions. In the United States this principle meant that a slave owner who had voluntarily brought his slave to reside in a free state could not resort to legal process in order to force his slave to return to a slave state. The potentially emancipatory effect of *Somerset* was later limited, however, by

---

86. For Story's view, see *Conflict of Laws*, sec. 114; *Commentaries on the Constitution*, vol. 3, chap. 40; and his opinion on Circuit in *La Jeune Eugenie* 26 F. Cas. 832 (No. 15,551) (C.C. Mass. 1822). For Marshall's view, see *The Antelope* 10 Wheat. 66 (1825). Marshall's opinions on slavery are discussed in Donald M. Roper, "In Quest of Judicial Objectivity," 532–39. For a broader discussion reaching into the Taney era, see Wiecek, "Slavery and Abolition." See also John T. Noonan, Jr., *The Antelope: The Ordeal of Recaptured Africans in the Administrations of James Monroe and John Quincy Adams* (Berkeley: University of California Press, 1987).

87. In Alexander Bickel's colorful phraseology. See "Citizen or Person," in *Morality of Consent* (New Haven: Yale University Press, 1975). Fehrenbacher (pp. 51–58, 396–98) provides an excellent account of the distinction between "reversion" and "reattachment." See, more generally, Robert Cover, *Justice Accused* (New Haven: Yale University Press, 1975), chap. 5.

88. *Somerset v. Stewart* 98 Eng. Rep. 499 (K.B., 1772).

the case of the *Slave Grace*.[89] Here the English court held that the status of slavery could reattach to a person who returned to a slave state after a temporary sojourn under the laws of freedom. This important qualification allowed American courts to apply the *Somerset* doctrine only to cases in which the slave was *domiciled* on free soil, while applying the *Grace* doctrine to slaves who were presumed to be in transit with their masters. Northern jurists, especially those unsympathetic to slavery, often interpreted these doctrines to mean that slave-holders and their agents could not resort to law to recover slaves who had not escaped while in jurisdictions that recognized slavery.

For northern judges cognizant of international law, the thorniest remaining problem was whether the free states could legally prevent the masters from resorting to self-help. On the one hand, the laws of freedom could not really "attach" to a Negro domiciled in a free state unless he could resist kidnapping by recourse to the law. On the other hand, the common law of free states recognized a self-help right of "recaption" for owners of escaped livestock and parents of escaped children. Moreover, the U.S. Constitution had directly forbidden states from enacting new statutes that would interfere with the return of fugitive slaves.[90] To northern judges, even those with abolitionist sentiments, these two considerations placed serious obstacles in the path of state legislatures that sought to extend the legal benefits of personal security to Negro inhabitants. Given these competing legal pressures, the civil rights available to blacks on free soil were tenuous at best. In *Commonwealth* v. *Aves*[91] the Massachusetts Supreme Judicial Court forbade the master to resort to self-help when there was no allegation of an illegal escape by the slave. In *Prigg* v. *Pennsylvania*, as we have seen, the U.S. Supreme Court placed severe limitations on the legal protection of Negroes in free states, while denying that those states had an affirmative duty to assist in recaption under the Fugitive Slave Law.

The foregoing cases followed the general view of Kent and Story that the laws of the forum state were always binding in international law, but that the laws of the forum state could incorporate the extraterritorial effects of foreign laws as a matter of comity. By invoking comity the Missouri courts had once ruled that residence in a free state or territory could free slaves such as Dred Scott upon their return to Missouri, and by rejecting comity, the Missouri Supreme Court later decided to withdraw its recognition of the effects of foreign law in *Dred Scott* v. *Emerson*. When the Taney Court denied that the Supreme Court had jurisdiction to review a state supreme court decision on the extraterritorial effects in slave states of laws prohibiting slavery elsewhere, Story's views on comity were directly followed.[92]

The foregoing discussion suggests that, except for the preemptive effects on local law of the fugitive slave clause, considerations of constitutional federalism

89. 166 Eng. Rep. 179 (High Court of Admiralty, 1827).

90. Art. IV., sec. 2.

91. 35 Mass. (18 Pick.) 193 (1836).

92. *Strader* v. *Graham* 10 How. 82 (1850). *Strader* formed the basis of Justice Nelson's concurring opinion in *Dred Scott* at 457 (Fehrenbacher, chaps. 12, 17).

did not have much effect on the application of ordinary principles of international comity in dealing with questions of slavery.[93] This would change with Taney's opinion in *Dred Scott*.

In histories of the Supreme Court, Taney is sometimes described as the Jacksonian antithesis to Marshall's federalism and sometimes as the faithful successor to Marshall's judicial legacy.[94] Both descriptions are true. Taney characteristically preserved the structure of Marshall's approach to jurisprudence while paying greater attention to reconciling the spheres of state and national sovereignty. To Taney, state sovereignty was not a claim to autonomy from national authority, as it would become in the later era of "states' rights," but rather a ground for asserting national authority, especially on questions pertaining to slavery. Taney believed that the states were the fundamental constituent units of the United States and that the overarching goal of constitutional law was to equalize for the historical differences between the states. The principle that states must be treated as equals would thus become a valid constitutional ground for asserting national authority.[95]

This principle received its clearest implementation by Taney two years after *Dred Scott* in *Ableman* v. *Booth*,[96] where the protection of state sovereignty provided the basis for a judicial decision restricting state autonomy. After the Wisconsin Supreme Court decided that the enforcement of the federal Fugitive Slave Act of 1850 was illegal in the state, state courts had issued a writ of habeas corpus to release from federal custody an abolitionist editor who had helped the fugitive to escape from federal authorities. Ruling on a federal appeal, Taney held that state courts could not grant habeas corpus to release federal prisoners. Under the Constitution the state of Wisconsin could not be allowed

---

93. For a view of how the conventional application of private international law would bear on *Dred Scott*, see the concurring opinion of Nelson at 457, 460–66. This was to have been the opinion of the Court after the case was originally argued, but Taney assigned to himself the majority opinion after reargument. For the dissenting view of the bearing of conventional principles of international law on *Dred Scott*, see the opinion of Curtis at 595–605. He differs from Nelson in believing the "international law" favors Dred Scott on the merits, and does not deny the U.S. Supreme Court jurisdiction to review the negative ruling of the Missouri Supreme Court on the merits.

94. For historical discussions of Taney and his Court, see Carl Brent Swisher, *The Taney Period, 1836–1864*, vol. 5 of the Oliver Wendell Holmes devise, *History of the Supreme Court of the United States* (New York: Macmillan, 1974). See also Swisher, "Dred Scott One Hundred Years After," *Journal of Politics* 19, no. 2 (May 1957): 167–83. The continuities between Taney and Marshall are stressed with special vigor by Benjamin F. Wright, *The Contract Clause of the Constitution* (Cambridge: Harvard University Press, 1938), and Felix Frankfurter, *The Commerce Clause under Marshall, Taney, and Waite* (Chapel Hill: University of North Carolina Press, 1937). A fine recent overview of the Taney Court's views on the issues addressed in this article can be found in Harold Hyman and William Wiecek, *Equal Justice under Law: Constitutional Development, 1835–1875* (New York: Harper & Row, 1982), chaps. 1–6.

95. I owe much of my account of this matter to Arthur Bestor, "State Sovereignty." He points out that the pre–Civil War doctrine of equal state sovereignty, embraced in *Dred Scott*, was an alternative to secession rather than a justification for it, and that, after secession, the constitution of the Confederacy had no further use for the doctrine (pp. 174–78).

96. 21 Howard 506 (1859).

to nullify the effect of a federal law that was designed to partially equalize for the deleterious effect of freedom in Wisconsin on the preservation of slavery in other states.[97] To Taney the supremacy of federal law was grounded in a Constitution that existed to protect the equal sovereignty of all states.

The grounding of national supremacy in the need to equalize among the states was also central to Taney's reasoning in *Dred Scott*. There he proposed the peculiar theory that Congress had more power to prohibit slavery under the Northwest Ordinance, originally enacted under the Articles of Confederation, than under the Missouri Compromise, enacted under the Constitution. Under the Articles, he reasoned, the states were directly exercising their sovereign powers when Congress passed legislation, much as states would exercise their sovereignty in adopting treaties. The original adoption of the restriction on slavery in the Northwest Ordinance could thus be viewed as an extension of a treaty in which administration of state territory was ceded to the authority of the national Congress. Unlike the Articles, Taney argued, the Constitution was not a treaty among sovereign states but rather, in Marshallian terms, a separate sphere of sovereign power alongside that of the states.[98]

The ratification of the Constitution by a "people" who were also citizens of sovereign states had for Taney a special significance. He assumed that the Constitution would not have been ratified without the assumption that the national government was bound to respect the historical differences between the political units that participated in it on a basis of sovereign equality. The foremost of those historical differences was the existence of slavery in some of the original states but not in others.

In *Dred Scott* Taney explains how this fundamental constitutional principle of equal sovereignty among the states acts as a constraint on both federal and state law. The implicit burden of his argument is to show why respect for the slavery laws of one state justifies striking down the liberty laws of another, but not vice versa. In order to carry this burden he devotes the bulk of his opinion to demonstrating that, given the facts of American history, the Constitution is not, and cannot be, neutral regarding the continuing existence of slavery—that from a constitutional point of view there is no such thing as federal noninterference with slavery.

The underlying form of his argument will be clear if we transpose it onto a problem that was not altogether hypothetical for Taney. With the proposed establishment of a Mormon state of Deseret, the possibility of accommodating polygamous marriages in the federal system had to be considered. Under the federal Constitution the laws of marriage, like the laws of slavery, fell within the police powers of the states and hence within the sphere of state sovereignty. Yet, in their discussions of international and interstate law, both Story and Kent viewed polygamy, like slavery, as immoral practices of sovereign states which

97. Ironically, Taney's defense of national authority against states' rights would be cited a century later against Governor Faubus's resistance to desegregation in *Cooper* v. *Aaron* 358 U.S. 1 (1958) at 18.

98. *Dred Scott* v. *Sandford* 19 Howard 393 (1857) at 432–42.

strained the principles of comity.[99] In the argument parallel to Taney's in *Dred Scott*, the affirmative protection of the sovereignty of the preexisting monogamous states would require active national intervention against the effects of polygamy law in undermining monogamous marriages.

Suppose that a monogamous husband travels with his wife into a polygamous state. At what point, if any, does she lose the legal right to be her husband's only wife? We can elaborate this hypothetical problem to parallel the stipulated facts of *Dred Scott*. Must the polygamous state give extraterritorial effect to the laws of monogamy, thereby denying her husband the rights of multiple marriage it accords to its own citizens? Or would the polygamy laws of the forum state have the effect of denying women the remedies available under the bigamy laws of the states in which they were married? Bearing in mind the fact that Dred Scott married as a free man while in Wisconsin Territory, we can also ask about the extraterritorial effects of a legally valid polygamous marriage when our original husband and wife return to a monogamous jurisdiction. Would there be a reversion to the laws of monogamy, effecting a constructive annulment of the husband's second marriage? Or would the laws of polygamy have extraterritorial effect, thereby allowing the husband, but not his wives, the legal benefits of multiple marriage without divorce? Varying the facts, we can imagine further legal problems that would arise when a polygamist enters a monogamous state. Is any woman that he marries there to be construed as his first and only wife for purposes of monogamy? Or do each of the wives he married polygamously have a right to sue for bigamy within the jurisdiction of the monogamous state?

Taney's reasoning in *Dred Scott* would make a difference in the way in which nineteenth-century American courts might have treated this hypothetical example. Before *Dred Scott*, under the constitutional principles directly borrowed from international law, each state's judiciary could decide for itself how far the laws of the other were to have extraterritorial effect in its courts. A common judicial compromise would have been to distinguish between couples who had changed their residence, and mere temporary sojourners in a polygamous state. Following his reasoning in *Dred Scott*, however, Taney would view the historical preexistence of monogamy laws in some states as effecting constitutionally enforceable limitations on the enactment of polygamy laws in other states. Otherwise, he would argue, some states could partially or totally dissolve the bonds of exclusive marriage created by other states.[100] If the Supreme Court believed it could merely take a position of "non-interference" regarding the preservation of monogamy, Taney would argue that it would implicitly abdicate its responsibility to equalize between the states. In order to fulfill this

99. Story, *Conflict of Laws*, sec. 114; Kent, *Commentaries*, vol. 2, Lec. 26. The issue was not finally decided until *Reynolds* v. *United States* 98 U.S. 145 (1878).

100. Interstate disputes over child custody today pose many of the conceptual problems of reversion, reattachment, and comity that appear in *Dred Scott*. Another related issue: can children who are legally emancipated under the laws of one state become again subject to their parents under the laws of another state?

responsibility the Court would have to view the wife in a monogamous marriage as carrying the principle of state equality on her back when she travels in a polygamous state, while asserting that the husband in a polygamous marriage would not be entitled to any constitutional protection for his state-created rights. In questions of polygamy versus monogamy the Constitution required a choice as to which was to be merely tolerated (if permitted at all), and which was to be preserved.

To continue our analogy with *Dred Scott*, we can now imagine that Congress passes legislation permitting polygamy in federally administered territory. Under the earlier principles of federalism emanating directly from international law, this legislation would be presumed to be a surrogate for state power that stopped at the territorial boundary rather than an assertion of an implied federal power to regulate the marriages of all state citizens who take up residence in the territory. In such an analysis there would be no inherent federal preemption of repugnant state law as a result of congressional regulation of marriage in the territories: the extrajurisdictional effects of federal laws regulating the territories would, rather, be determined by the courts of the several states.

Following his reasoning in *Dred Scott*, however, Taney would probably insist that whenever Congress acts legitimately it exercises a constitutional power that preempts the states. For this reason he would conclude that Congress cannot act constitutionally in passing a marriage law for the territories that would have the effect of dissolving the exclusive rights granted by the states to women already in monogamous marriages. The principle of equal state sovereignty would require that the preexisting state-created rights of monogamously married women be constitutionally enforceable, even if this meant invalidating acts of Congress. In contrast, no privileges or immunities resulting from federally created polygamous marriages would be entitled to constitutional protection.

In *Dred Scott*, of course, Taney goes further than this. He claims that blacks could not, through the force of any legislation, state or federal, become U.S. citizens. He reaches this conclusion because he is constrained to deny blacks the benefit of the only two forms of constitutional protection available to individuals under the Marshallian scheme: protection under the "privileges and immunities" clause of Article IV, and protection under the diversity jurisdiction of the federal courts. Taney's main purpose in *Dred Scott* is to establish that the only historical identity through which such constitutional rights can be claimed is state citizenship—and not race. Within the established Marshallian logic, the simplest way to accomplish this is to deny that blacks can be citizens of any state for federal purposes.

Under the U.S. Constitution Taney believed that the only freedom available to individual slaves was the absence of a vested right in the persons who would otherwise be their owners. Such divesting of legal ownership, according to Taney, could be properly determined only by the courts proceeding case by case, and not by legislation. Unlike the ownership of property, however, full civil freedom was not the kind of right that could be conferred according to the private law of states, and subsequently vested under the Constitution. To

Taney this meant that free Negroes in free states were not really citizens, but merely beneficiaries of the absence of certain legal remedies available under the laws of slave states. Any other conclusion, Taney suggested, would be incompatible with the equality of state sovereignty under federalism.[101]

We now have the rationale for Taney's implicit choice to give constitutional protection to the state-created interests of Emerson, but not to those of Scott. In his travels outside his state Emerson had carried on his back the constitutional protection of state equality: his property in Missouri could not be divested as a matter of federal law by the act of any sovereign body outside his own state. Yet because Dred Scott was a citizen of no state when he left Missouri, he was not protected by any constitutional principle of state equality. For this reason none of the remedies that might have been available to him in the course of his travels could vest as constitutionally protected rights.

Perhaps inadvertently, Taney's approach to *Dred Scott* solved the problem that had frustrated John Marshall in *Ogden* v. *Saunders*—that of distinguishing between those state-created rights that trigger constitutional protection and those that do not. The Marshall Court, following Trimble rather than Marshall, had given constitutional protection only to those state-created rights that had already vested through a legal judgment or a preexisting executory contract. In *Dred Scott* Taney found a new way to protect individual rights under the Marshallian scheme without jeopardizing state sovereignty. He gave constitutional protection to the substantive statutory rights of slaveholders because this was necessary to equalize among the sovereign states. Yet he viewed the claims of slaves against their masters as a matter of procedural rights which could be protected, if at all, only in the courts of the forum state.

Where the Marshall Court's doctrine of vested rights had grounded the federal protection of individuals mainly in the separation of powers, Taney was able in *Dred Scott* to finally articulate a Marshallian rationale for also grounding the constitutional rights of individuals in the division of powers: the constitutional protection of individual civil rights would be required whenever such protection was necessary to equalize for the original historical differences among states. Individual rights created by state law would thus be fully constitutionalized whenever there were also demands for political equality asserted through one's state identity.

The development of some of the reasoning behind *Dred Scott* as a basis for the constitutional enforcement of civil rights occurred only after the Civil War. By constitutionalizing slavery under the principle of equality for state citizens, the Supreme Court had for the time being eliminated the possibility that any slaves

---

101. This suggestion was picked up in Catron's concurring opinion, which summarized the implication of Taney's ruling for constitutional jurisprudence as follows: "We must meet the question whether Congress had the power to declare that a citizen of a State, carrying with him his equal rights secured through his State, could be stripped of his goods and slaves, and deprived of any participation in the common property. . . . The Missouri Compromise violates the most leading feature of the Constitution—a feature on which the Union depends, and which secures to their respective States and the citizens an entire equality of rights, privileges, and immunities" (*Dred Scott* v. *Sandford* 19 Howard 393 [1857] at 528–29).

could be gradually emancipated through the effect of congressional action that attempted to prohibit slavery in the territories or in interstate commerce.[102] By constitutionalizing the inferior status of free Negroes, the Supreme Court had warned that even emancipation in the states could not confer U.S. citizenship on Negroes for purposes of federal law—because only Congress could naturalize those not born as U.S. citizens, and Congress was forbidden from doing so for Negroes who had no citizenship of birth.[103]

Once slavery was constitutionally protected, its elimination would require a constitutional amendment that tracked Taney's logic in reverse. The *Dred Scott* opinion meant that there were two distinct problems involved in such constitutional emancipation—freeing the slaves and extending citizenship to free Negroes. Taney's reasoning in *Dred Scott* thus provided a negative template for the legal form of the amendments required to end slavery and all its consequences within the Marshallian scheme of constitutional interpretation. It would, however, take a civil war to pass such amendments.

DRED SCOTT AND THE FOURTEENTH AMENDMENT

Dred Scott was the first antebellum Supreme Court opinion that unequivocally recognized that, at root, the Marshallian framework of wholes and parts is concerned with equalizing among some of the foundational identities that make up the nation. Interests based on constitutionally favored political identities would, according to Taney, deserve affirmative protection from adverse changes of both state and federal law. Under the Marshallian interpretation of the separation of powers, the task of choosing the identities that trigger such constitutional protection must ultimately, and unavoidably, fall to the Supreme Court. Although Taney's apparent eagerness to make this choice in favor of white supremacy has raised persistent questions about his personal motivations and biases, these questions should not be allowed to wholly overshadow his innovative contribution to Marshallian constitutional logic.

Taney's innovation was to find an expanded basis for the constitutional protection of substantive individual rights within the core logic of Marshallian jurisprudence, but not in the way that many commentators suppose. In conventional glosses on *Dred Scott* Taney held that the Fifth Amendment incorporates a natural right to property into constitutional law, much as Marshall had argued, albeit unsuccessfully, that the contracts clause incorporates a natural

---

102. In *Dred Scott* the Court struck down the Missouri Compromise on these constitutional grounds without considering the statutory question of whether the prohibition on slavery above 36′30″ could be enforced by emancipation—and, if so, whether emancipation in the federal territory occurred as an automatic effect of the statute or only as the consequence of an adjudicated dispute in which the issue was raised. See Fehrenbacher, chaps. 5–7, 14, 21.

103. Taney treats this latter point as a constitutional limitation, but he offers highly unconvincing arguments based only on custom and usage, as Curtis points out in dissent (*Dred Scott* v. *Sandford* 19 Howard 393 [1857] at 419–20 and 571–82). Taney gives no reason for his apparent assumption that a Negro who was a citizen of another country could not be naturalized under existing federal law.

right to freedom of contract. This interpretation, which has scanty support in Taney's text, faces two conceptual problems: first, Taney was probably aware that slaves were not generally considered to be property under either the law of nations or federal common law;[104] second, Taney certainly knew that the theory of natural rights created a presumption in favor of the liberty of slaves,[105] and that the constitutional protection of slavery would be jeopardized if natural rights were incorporated into the meaning of the "liberty" and "property" of "persons" under the Fifth Amendment. A careful reading of *Dred Scott* reveals that Taney was not prepared to extend direct constitutional protection to a subset of the natural rights of all citizens, a point he implicitly acknowledged in accepting (at 422) Curtis's general argument that not all U.S. citizens are constitutionally entitled to legal equality with white male adults. Like Curtis, Taney was in the mainstream of the American republican jurisprudence which held that natural rights could not in general be constitutionalized without allowing the rule of law to swallow up the exercise of popular sovereignty. To reach his conclusion in *Dred Scott* Taney therefore sought some constitutional basis for selecting those interests created under positive law that deserve special judicial protection from adverse legislative change.

As we have seen, Taney drew his principle of selectivity from federalism itself, arguing that the equal protection of a founding minority of slave states placed substantive restraints on federal and state laws that adversely affected the preexisting legal interests of white U.S. citizens in relation to Negroes. In reaching this conclusion Taney went beyond the Marshall Court's practice of using the comity required by federalism as a direct basis for the judicial protection of out-of-state citizens against discriminatory state laws; in *Dred Scott*, as we have seen, the equalization implicit in Marshallian federalism became an indirect basis for the selective constitutional protection of specific groups against laws adversely affecting their interests. The connection between the need to equalize among wholes and parts and the nonneutrality of the Constitution on fundamental values is, ironically, the most important part of the legacy of *Dred Scott*.

Dred Scott represents a hitherto missing link in our constitutional jurisprudence, containing judicial innovations that fit the framework of both Marshallian federalism and more recent approaches to the constitutional protection of individual rights. In unmasking the apparent neutrality of individual rights recognized under Marshallian federalism, Taney anticipated the terms of debate over the apparent neutrality of the due process and equal protection clauses of the Fourteenth Amendment. On its face the Fourteenth Amendment directly overturns Taney's conclusion in *Dred Scott* on the question of Negro citizenship, conferring the protections of citizenship universally on all natural persons born in the United States. The effect of this language has been to preclude the Court from using the concept of citizenship, as Taney did, to choose the primordial political identities that trigger the constitutional protec-

104. As Hurd points out in *The Law of Freedom and Bondage*, para. 507.
105. The Supreme Court had already recognized this point in, for example, *The Antelope* 10 Wheat. 66 (1825) and *Prigg v. Pennsylvania* 16 Pet. 539 (1842).

tion of the civil rights of individuals. Yet the need for a judicial choice among political identities has remained under the Fourteenth Amendment, and the core judicial techniques that have been used in making such choices were first adumbrated by Taney in *Dred Scott*.

In order to uncover the continuing importance of *Dred Scott* in the history of debate over the Fourteenth Amendment, we must first briefly reflect on the constitutional significance of the Civil War.

The Civil War

Ironically, the secession of most of the slaveholding states reversed the political valence of *Dred Scott*. Before secession *Dred Scott* meant that the U.S. Constitution committed the federal government to the preservation of slavery (much as *Brown* would later commit the federal government to ending segregation). As late as 1860, Congress passed resolutions, introduced by Sen. Jefferson Davis, to implement *Dred Scott* by extending federal protection to the rights of slaveholders in every state and territory. In *Dred Scott* the Taney Court had made it abundantly clear that such legislation would be constitutionally favored and that any legislation, state or federal, that undermined slavery (in either effect or intent) would be constitutionally suspect. Such legal protections for slavery, however, were not sufficient to forestall secession once the 1860 presidential election brought the Republicans to power and destroyed the national political base of the Democratic opposition. After secession, the constitutional legitimacy of the federal effort to preserve the union presupposed that *Dred Scott* remained good law. The case that had committed the union to preserving slavery had become part of the legal rationale for preserving the union.

That rationale was never tested in court, despite the frequent resort to claims about legality on both sides of the military struggle. Taney himself remained on the bench until his death in 1864, but never had the opportunity to comment on the constitutionality of secession. The only prior Supreme Court pronouncement on the subject had been in the much earlier case of *Cohens* v. *Virginia* where, in dictum, Marshall suggested that the union could be effectively dissolved "if all states, or a majority of them, refuse to elect senators."[106] In a sense the Civil War was fought over the question of whether individual states (or a minority of them) could be the final legal authority on the question of whether the U.S. Constitution had been dissolved.[107] From a Marshallian perspective the obvious answer to this question was that the Constitution alone can be the final authority and that it must be interpreted by the Supreme Court. Yet the Civil War was conducted with few apparent qualms about the legality of action by a Congress that lacked representatives from a substantial minority of the states.

From the northern point of view the Civil War itself had no constitutional effect. The very legitimacy of the war effort depended on the assumption that no war needed to be declared; Congress merely needed to appropriate the

106. 19 U.S. 164 at 389–410.

107. For an extensive defense of the constitutional rationale of secession and the Civil War, see Alexander Hamilton Stephens, *A Constitutional View of the Late War between the States: Its Causes, Character, Conduct, and Results* (Chicago: Ziegler and McCurdy, 1868, 1870).

funds necessary for a police action to restore federal authority in states in which temporary majorities were acting illegally under the mistaken belief that they were no longer subject to the Constitution. Yet southerners, and their sympathizers, consistently described the Civil War as a "War between the States," or, eventually, between two nations, the Confederate States and the United States.

When Lincoln emancipated masterless slaves during the Civil War, he was careful not to exceed the constitutional limitations set by *Dred Scott*. Implicitly invoking his extraordinary powers as commander in chief, Lincoln grounded emancipation in the need to facilitate enlistment by runaway slaves in states under martial law during a national emergency. Moreover, the Emancipation Proclamation was an executive order, not an act of Congress which would have been directly covered by *Dred Scott*.

The "emancipation" that resulted from the proclamation was limited in many ways. Emancipation by executive decree applied only to occupied areas under martial law, not to territories and not to slave states that had remained within the union. Where it applied, it merely suspended the enforcement of slavery laws and said nothing whatever about whether the slaves who had been emancipated were thereby citizens of any state or of the United States. The legal status of these runaway slaves, whose masters no longer had the legal power to reclaim them, was thus left entirely open by the Emancipation Proclamation.

From a constitutional point of view the main significance of the Civil War was that the military defeat and occupation of the South created the extraordinary political conditions required for the passage of three constitutional amendments that reversed the legal effects of *Dred Scott*. The Thirteenth Amendment, adopted at the end of the war, abolished slavery nationwide. This expropriation of private property by constitutional amendment was deemed to be a direct act of "the people," rather than the temporary national majority, and was thus not subject to judicial review under the due process or "takings" clauses of the Fifth Amendment. The Fourteenth Amendment extended national and state citizenship to freed slaves, reversing the conclusion of *Dred Scott* in terms that tracked Taney's logic: "All persons born or naturalized in the United States . . . are citizens of the United States and of the State wherein they reside." Finally, the Fifteenth Amendment extended voting rights to freed slaves and their descendants.

The effect of the Civil War amendments was prospective: they freed slaves and extended citizenship and voting rights to native-born Negroes only from the moment of ratification. The perception that these amendments were necessary to accomplish Reconstruction reinforced the assumption that *Dred Scott* had been good law up to that point. In this sense the Civil War amendments implicitly reaffirmed the *reasoning* of *Dred Scott*, which had created a framework of jurisprudence that would implicitly guide their subsequent interpretation.

The Ghost of *Dred Scott*

Although there is no question that the Fourteenth Amendment was originally conceived by politicians who sought to advance the civil rights of free Negroes, it was interpreted by judges immersed in the logic of *Dred Scott*. These judges were to be the final authority on the constitutional meaning of the Civil War for the Marshallian framework of federalism.[108] To postwar constitutional jurists, trained in the opinions of Marshall and Taney, there were two major points of view on the constitutional meaning of the Fourteenth Amendment.

From the first point of view the Fourteenth Amendment was fundamentally discontinuous with the original Constitution, calling for a new beginning in constitutional interpretation. To holders of this view the presumed constitutionality of the military invasion and defeat of the South by the federal government meant that state sovereignty was no longer a barrier to federal protection of individual rights against the states: freed of the fetish of state sovereignty the U.S. Constitution now authorized the federal judiciary to protect the natural rights of individuals against incursions by state legislatures. Once federalism was no longer the basis of constitutionally protected individual rights, one no longer needed to be an out-of-state citizen to be subject to constitutional protection. Rather, all U.S. citizens could claim to be in some sense "out-of-state" whenever their nationally established rights were violated by state government. The same constitutional principles that were intended to empower federal courts to protect freed slaves against racist local majorities under the Fourteenth Amendment could then empower federal courts to protect property holders against socialist local majorities.

From the second point of view the Fourteenth Amendment was essentially continuous with the Marshallian framework of the pre–Civil War Constitution. To holders of this view the constitutionality of federal military action in the southern states presumed that those states were mistaken in thinking that they had ever seceded. If from a strictly legal point of view there had been no federal reconquest of the South, the structure of federalism remained intact, and the rights of U.S. citizens in the states were fundamentally unchanged by the war. The main effect of the Fourteenth Amendment was then to define U.S. citizenship in a way that would resolve the problems left by *Dred Scott*. Once slavery had been abolished in the states, there was no need to retain Taney's distinction between those state citizens who were and were not U.S. citizens: anyone born in the United States was now a citizen of the United States *and* of the state in which he resided. The constitutional rights of U.S. citizens, however, would still be tied to the rights that each state had granted to its own citizens, and only those state-created rights that had previously vested were entitled to constitutional protection against the usurpation of judicial power by state legislatures.

The issue between these two viewpoints was clear: did the South simply make a political and legal mistake in seceding, or did the federal resistance to the South's secession require the articulation of a new theory of national government based on principles fundamentally different than cosovereignty with the states? Resolving this issue would require the Supreme Court to reconcile the two elements in the Marshallian picture that Taney had sought to reconcile in *Dred Scott*—individual rights and federalism.

The Supreme Court was forced to address the conflict between these two

108. My discussion in this section draws on Kennedy, "The Rise and Fall of Classical Legal Thought," chap. 2.

viewpoints in the *Slaughterhouse Cases*,[109] where it interpreted the Fourteenth Amendment for the first time. The cases arose because a new populist majority in Louisiana, reflecting carpetbagger influence, decided to establish a state monopoly on slaughterhouses. Such legislation was generally regarded by pre-Civil War courts as a legitimate exercise of the police power,[110] but the Fourteenth Amendment raised new grounds for challenging this type of state action. In the *Slaughterhouse Cases* the Supreme Court was asked to decide whether the legislative ban on selling meat that had been slaughtered in a private facility was a violation by the state of the "privileges or immunities" of U.S. citizens in regard to private property. Did the new "privileges or immunities" clause mean that there were now federal property rights that could not be divested, or drastically reduced in value, by the state legislatures?

In this first case pitting individual rights against federalism after the Civil War, the Supreme Court ruled that the "privileges or immunities" clause of the Fourteenth Amendment did not add any substantive rights to those protected under the "privileges and immunities" clause of Article IV. Writing for the majority, Justice Miller argued that in order to retain federalism, the only basis for viable social experimentation, the federal courts must refrain from inventing out of whole cloth a set of rights of national citizenship, such as the right to private property, that could not be altered by state legislatures or even by Congress. According to Miller, the new constitutional protection for "privileges" and "immunities" simply reiterated the previous ban on discrimination against out-of-staters in the context of the new national citizenship, while leaving open the possibility that Congress might legislate additional new rights for national citizens as a matter of positive law. In the absence of congressional action the Fourteenth Amendment would continue to give a U.S. citizen a federally protected legal right to only those privileges and immunities that the state legislature provided its own citizens. In setting the baseline for constitutionally protected civil rights, the state legislature would remain free to prospectively alter the legal remedies protecting property for everyone under its jurisdiction without violating the constitutional right of any national citizen. The effect of Miller's interpretation of the Fourteenth Amendment was to incorporate into post–Civil War jurisprudence Trimble's view of the balance between federalism and individual rights in *Ogden* v. *Saunders*.

In his dissenting opinion in the *Slaughterhouse Cases* Justice Bradley wished to

---

109. 16 Wall. 36 (1873).

110. The exception was *Wynehamer* v. *People* 13 N.Y. 378 (1856) in which a state prohibition law was struck down as an invasion of the constitutionally protected property rights of distillery owners without due process of law. *Wynehamer* was decided while *Dred Scott* was being reargued, and may have influenced Taney to refer (at 450) to the due process clause of the Fifth Amendment in striking down the Missouri Compromise as a violation of individual property rights (as well as the sovereignty of the state that had established them). J. C. Hurd gives explicit consideration to, and rejects, the analogy between *Wynehamer* and *Dred Scott* in *The Law of Freedom and Bondage* (para. 512 n1, 520). For further discussions of *Wynehamer* and *Dred Scott* as precursors of the doctrine of substantive due process, see Corwin, "The Basic Doctrine" and "Dred Scott."

move beyond the antebellum limitations on the range of substantive individual rights that could receive constitutional protection. At this stage in his thinking, however, Bradley could see no way of expanding judicial protection for individual rights against the states without attacking federalism. He therefore argued that in opening the way for an amended Constitution the Civil War had united the nation as never before, allowing the federal courts to enforce a set of common national rights, whether or not these had been declared by Congress.

Although the progressive political thrust of Miller's position was soon to be reversed, its long-range significance was to persuade the Court, including Bradley, that federalism must remain the prototype of constitutional cosovereignty in the system of structure and analogy. Miller's view prevailed in this case because, at a time of great confusion about what the Constitution would mean in the absence of federalism, the majority on the Court was able to say that from a constitutional point of view federalism had survived the Civil War.[111]

In the so-called *Civil Rights Cases* Justice Bradley achieved a synthesis of the two opposing positions in the *Slaughterhouse Cases*, allowing him to reconcile the expanded judicial protection of individual rights made possible by the Fourteenth Amendment with the Marshallian framework of analysis based on federalism. As we shall see, Bradley's approach to this problem owed much, implicitly, to the logic of the debate between Taney and Curtis in *Dred Scott*.[112]

The *Civil Rights Cases* were a constitutional test of the very type of legislation that the framers of the Fourteenth Amendment sought to legitimate. The Civil Rights Act of 1866 had been passed under the authority of the Thirteenth Amendment to override the harsh Black Codes enacted in several southern states in 1865. There was reason to fear, however, that, in the absence of direct constitutional authority for the language of the Civil Rights Act, *Dred Scott* could still be successfully invoked to block congressional protection for the civil rights of free Negroes. By echoing the statutory language the Fourteenth Amendment was intended to avoid such a constitutional problem. A subsequent series of Civil Rights Acts, passed by Reconstruction Congresses, made it illegal to discriminate in various ways against former slaves and their descendants, even where such discrimination was carried out by private individuals, such as innkeepers, exercising their ordinary rights under state law. Such legislation declared itself to be valid under the enforcement clauses in the Civil War amendments—especially the Fourteenth which appeared to grant Congress direct legislative powers to protect the rights of individual citizens against discriminatory barriers existing through state action. Under the interpretation of congressional powers in *McCulloch* it seemed likely that the courts would give

---

111. As a consequence of the *Slaughterhouse Cases* constitutional "privileges" and "immunities" are still largely interpreted in a manner that is consistent with their pre–Civil War meaning. Despite periodic calls for a more expansive interpretation, the Fourteenth Amendment "privileges or immunities" clause is not to this day an active source of federally protected constitutional rights. See Tribe, *American Constitutional Law*, chap. 6, sec. 32–33 and chap. 7, espec. sec. 4.

112. 109 U.S. 3 (1883). The resemblance is strongly suggested by Justice John Marshall Harlan in dissent, at 30–37.

wide deference to the congressional choice of the means necessary and proper to accomplish such a constitutionally permitted end.

In the *Civil Rights Cases*, however, Justice Bradley struck down the Civil Rights Acts as unconstitutional. Claiming that the enforcement authority of the Fourteenth Amendment covered only questions of public law (state versus individual) and not questions of private law (individual versus individual), he argued that the Civil Rights Acts were an unconstitutional intrusion on the sovereign powers of the states to govern the private relations among state citizens. The constitutional ban on discriminatory "state action" did not, according to Bradley, authorize Congress to legislate in any area where the state could not discriminate. Over private law the states retained their full police powers, and the powers of Congress were nugatory. Bradley used the distinction between public and private law to define the sphere of state sovereignty into which Congress could not intrude. He thereby severely limited the possibility of congressional enforcement of the Fourteenth Amendment.

Bradley's reasoning implicitly followed the *Slaughterhouse Cases* (and *Dred Scott*) in viewing state sovereignty as the source of all constitutionally protected individual rights. Recognizing that the Thirteenth and Fourteenth Amendments reversed the conclusions of *Dred Scott*, he decided the *Civil Rights Cases* as though Curtis's dissent had become the law. The following passage from Bradley's opinion is a succinct, albeit unacknowledged, postwar restatement of Curtis's view of Negro citizenship in *Dred Scott*:

> There were thousands of free colored people in this country before the abolition of slavery, enjoying all the essential rights of life, liberty, and property the same as white citizens; yet no one, at that time, thought that it was any invasion of their personal *status* as freemen because they were not admitted to all the privileges enjoyed by white citizens, or because they were subject to discriminations in the enjoyment of accommodations in inns, public conveyances, and places of amusement. Mere discriminations on account of race or color were not regarded as badges of slavery.[113]

In this passage Bradley laid the groundwork for the view that blacks could enjoy the "same" rights as whites and still be discriminated against in the exercise of those rights—the doctrine of "separate but equal" that would be later enshrined in *Plessy* v. *Ferguson*.[114]

Having established in the *Civil Rights Cases* that Congress has no power under the Fourteenth Amendment to alter state-created private rights, the Supreme Court went on to decide a series of cases under the due process clause of the Fourteenth Amendment that denied the states the power to alter preexisting rights under state property or contract law. The effect of these decisions

---

113. The *Civil Rights Cases* at 27.

114. 163 U.S. 537 (1896). The source of the "separate but equal doctrine" was Massachusetts Chief Justice Lemuel Shaw's opinion upholding school segregation in *Roberts* v. *City of Boston*, 5 Cush. 198 (1849). In that opinion Shaw anticipated the views of Bradley (and Curtis) mentioned above. See Leonard W. Levy, *The Law of the Commonwealth and Chief Justice Shaw* (Cambridge: Harvard University Press, 1957), chap. 7, espec. p. 114.

was to use the due process clause of the Fourteenth Amendment to accomplish what Marshall had adumbrated in his dissent in *Ogden* v. *Saunders*—that broad areas of private law, such as contract or property, could become a source of federally protected constitutional rights against state government.[115] Through this ingenious dialectical reversal many of the same private law rights that were constitutionally immune from being changed by Congress, as a result of the *Civil Rights Cases*, became the basis of public law rights which could be enforced in federal courts against the states. The constitutional double bind that Taney had originally created to entrench the positive law of slavery was now generalized to protect much of the private law regulating economic relations from legislative reform at both the state and federal levels.

The constitutional theory that expressed this view is often described as "substantive due process." That phrase, however, has two different, if partially overlapping, meanings. Interpreted formally it is the use of the due process clause of the Fourteenth Amendment as a license for the courts to scrutinize closely the constitutionality of legislative ends. In taking this approach to the judicial review of legislation substantive due process follows the logic, but not the spirit, of *McCulloch*. The second, and deeper, meaning of substantive due process refers to the use of past judicial interpretations of private law in the states as the source of federally protected rights against the states. The jurists who developed substantive due process clearly recognized, as Marshall had not in *Ogden* v. *Saunders*, that constitutional rights were grounded originally in positive state law; yet they interpreted the due process clauses of the Fifth and Fourteenth Amendments as a constitutionalization of the final power of the courts to say what the law is under the Marshallian theory of the separation of powers. Legislative efforts to revise the judicial interpretation of property or contract law could then be described as unconstitutional usurpations of the judicial function. Through the development of such arguments the Marshallian system of jurisprudence was completed, rather than abolished, in the Court's early interpretations of the Fourteenth Amendment.

The unacknowledged link between Marshallian constitutionalism and substantive due process is the jurisprudence of *Dred Scott*. By the late nineteenth century, the ghost of *Dred Scott* haunted the corpus of American public and private law. Slavery, of course, was gone; but, just as Taney had anticipated, the rights that federal courts protected were presumed to have originated in past acts of state sovereignty, much as property in slaves had been earlier presumed to be an artifact of purely local law. The federal courts had meanwhile assumed a unique role in protecting many state-created rights against both Congress and the temporary majorities in the states themselves. In justifying that role, the courts claimed that they were simultaneously protecting the sovereignty of

---

115. The crucial cases in the development of this line of reasoning were *Munn* v. *Illinois* 94 U.S. 113 (1877), *Barbier* v. *Connolly* 113 U.S. 27 (1885), and *Allgeyer* v. *Louisiana* 165 U.S. 578 (1897). This development culminated in *Lochner* v. *New York* 198 U.S. 45 (1905), which is often taken to stand for the doctrine of substantive due process. The issues presented by using private law as a source of constitutional rights are sketched in Tribe, *American Constitutional Law*, chap. 8, and fully developed in Kennedy, "The Rise and Fall of Classical Legal Thought."

the states from encroachment by the federal government and the rights of individuals from encroachment by the state governments. Once slavery had been abolished nationwide, however, the courts no longer perceived a need to affirmatively equalize among the states. As a consequence, the constitutional protection of individual rights was merely a pro forma protection of state sovereignty which in reality gave the federal courts unlimited power to curb expressions of popular sovereignty in the states. By the early twentieth century the theoretical sublimation of republican thought into Marshallian jurisprudence was virtually complete.

The Legacy of *Dred Scott*

The jurisprudence of substantive due process is no longer with us, and the notion that state sovereignty can be the grounding of most constitutional rights is now widely, and properly, discredited. The reasons for this change are beyond the scope of this article. In this brief concluding section I shall, rather, consider the enduring legacy of *Dred Scott* in the recent jurisprudence of constitutional rights that has grown out of the decisions of the Warren Court. Those decisions were centered on, but not confined to, the part of Fourteenth Amendment jurisprudence most neglected during the era of substantive due process—the interpretation of the equal protection clause.

After the centenary of *Dred Scott*, it was common to compare that dark moment in the Court's history with the Warren Court's landmark decision in *Brown* v. *Board of Education*.[116] The two decisions were widely described as similar in their audacity as judicial interventions in political problems that had divided the nation sharply along regional lines. Yet *Dred Scott* and *Brown* were also taken to teach opposite lessons about the wisdom of the Supreme Court's departure from its normally restrained judicial role to exert moral leadership in society. Rarely, if ever, mentioned was the fact that both decisions view constitutional rights as intrinsically concerned with the problem of equalization among the primordial constituent groups that make up this nation.

For Taney, as we have seen, these primordial constituent groups were the original states, some slave and some free, which must always be accorded a position of equal sovereignty under the Constitution. In order to make this claim on behalf of the states, he had to deny strenuously that the primordial constituents of the American "people" were the three ethnic groups—white, black, and Indian—which originally came under the jurisdiction of the U.S. government on very different terms. In Taney's words, "The question is simply this: can a Negro, whose ancestors were imported into this country and sold as slaves, become a member of the political community formed and brought into existence by the Constitution of the United States, and as such become entitled to all the rights, privileges, and immunities, guaranteed by that instrument to the citizen?" He answered in the negative because, on his reading of American history, Negroes had been treated consistently as "beings of an inferior or-

---

116. 347 U.S. 483 (1954). See Carl Brent Swisher, "Dred Scott One Hundred Years After," *Journal of Politics* 19, no. 2 (May 1957): 167–83; cf. Alpheus T. Mason, "Understanding the Warren Court," *Political Science Quarterly* 81, no. 4 (1966): 523–63.

der."[117] Much of the extreme language in his opinion reflects not only his personal acceptance of the racism of his time but also a peculiarly modern perception that the Court must be prepared to give historical justifications for its view that certain political identities qualify for constitutional protection and that others do not.

The form of Taney's argument in *Dred Scott* is often most modern at precisely those points where its content is most embarrassing or outrageous to the modern legal mind. I am referring, especially, to his extremist history of race in America, in which none of the legally relevant facts appears as a moral compromise, and all are seen to reflect the conclusion that blacks counted for nothing in the minds of constitutional decision makers. If, however, racial identity, rather than state citizenship, becomes the basis of constitutional equalization, this very form of argument, citing similar facts, can justify treating the state-created expectations of whites less favorably than those of blacks under the equal protection clause.[118]

Recent discussions of equal protection and affirmative action frequently, and often tacitly, evoke a distinction between two kinds of rights. The first are rights that are the artifact of state laws and that can be altered without judicial protection until they have in some sense vested. Among these, for example, are the putative "rights" that white males have in the continuation of a particular set of eligibility standards that do not take account of race in distributing some scarce social good. The second type of right is asserted on behalf of some group identity or value through which an individual can sometimes demand that the adverse results of the political process be partially or totally offset by the courts. When individuals can successfully assert such an identity or value, then their claimed right to equalization from the courts entitles them to demand close judicial scrutiny of the means, purpose, and impact of state policies that affect their legal expectations.

Proponents of the Warren era jurisprudence frequently argue that only members of certain historically disadvantaged groups have rights in the strong constitutional sense that triggers judicial review of political decisions.[119] One eminent constitutional scholar has even argued that the idea of political equalization lies behind all the constitutional rights recognized by the Warren Court and that this "procedural" approach is more appropriate to the constitutional role of the judiciary than grounding rights in "substantive" values.[120]

I doubt that there is such a sharp distinction between the notion of equaliza-

117. *Dred Scott* v. *Sandford* 19 Howard 393 (1857) at 403, 407.

118. There is a voluminous literature on whether (and in what ways) the equal protection clause requires the judiciary to give special scrutiny to laws that have an adverse impact on blacks. See, for example, Ronald Dworkin, "Bakke's Case: Are Quotas Unfair?" and "How to Read the Civil Rights Act," in *A Matter of Principle* (Cambridge: Harvard University Press, 1985).

119. See, for example, Richard A. Wasserstrom, "Preferential Treatment, Color Blindness, and the Evils of Racism and Racial Discrimination," *Proceedings and Addresses of the American Philosophical Association*, supp. to 61, no. 1 (1987): 27–42.

120. John Hart Ely, *Democracy and Distrust* (Cambridge: Harvard University Press, 1980).

tion as a "procedural" or a "substantive" value, just as I doubt that there is any real difference between saying that Taney believed in equalizing between slave and free states and saying that he therefore saw slavery as an affirmatively protected constitutional value. My point here, however, is that in engaging these issues we have, perhaps unknowingly, inherited a different part of the conceptual legacy of *Dred Scott* than the jurists of substantive due process.

In the jurisprudence of the Fourteenth Amendment, Taney's interpretation of Marshallian federalism eventually became the underlying metaphor for the use of group identity to trigger the constitutional protection of individual civil rights. Constitutionally favored groups now stand in place of the original states as the primordial constituent identities of the republic, and the technique of equalizing between wholes and parts, originally developed in the context of federalism, has been generalized accordingly. To enforce the presumed equality of fundamental political identities (based primarily on race, religion, or gender), the Court now recognizes that the Constitution requires a judicial choice of fundamental values, much as we saw, above, in our hypothetical choice in favor of monogamy and in Taney's choice in favor of slavery.

Individuals whose civil rights have been protected by such choices are treated as virtual representatives of the right to sovereign equality which states had under the Marshallian constitution, much as if our federal system itself had been repartitioned to reflect some of the cleavages of our pluralistic society, giving special solicitude to citizens of minority parts who sojourn in the land of the whole. The grounding of American constitutional rights in the metaphor of federalism does much to explain why in our constitutional jurisprudence the political rights of majorities are deemed to be fully protected by legislation, while the civil rights of minorities can require that majoritarian legislation be constrained by the courts.

This point may illuminate some aspects of the continuing debate over *Roe* v. *Wade*.[121] To its critics the Burger Court's opinion in *Roe* bears the same relation to the Warren era jurisprudence of the Fourteenth Amendment that the Taney Court's opinion in *Dred Scott* bears to Marshallian federalism. When the Taney Court was asked whether Dred Scott was a person or property, it replied that he could not be a U.S. *citizen* in the sense that would qualify him for constitutional rights under the jurisprudence of federalism. When the Burger Court was asked whether the fetus is a person or a thing, it implicitly replied that it did not qualify as a member of a *group* that would be eligible for constitutional protection under the Fourteenth Amendment. The result of *Dred Scott* was that only whites could be protected under the "privileges and immunities" clauses in order to promote the fundamental value of constitutional equality for the slave states; the result of *Roe* was that only pregnant women could be protected under the Fourteenth Amendment in order to promote the fundamental value of privacy. In both cases the dominant constitutional framework seemed incapable of basing judicial protection on universal human identity—whether birth in the case of Dred Scott or life in the case of the fetus.[122]

---

121. 410 U.S. 113 (1973).

122. The fact that all humans are mortal would tend to exclude the dead, like the unborn,

Our desire to distinguish between a pregnant woman and a slaveholder, and between the moral character of Taney's and Blackmun's reasoning, should not obscure the insight that our dominant constitutional legacy is concerned with equalizing between wholes and parts, and that this generally excludes universal human claims from protection through the courts rather than the political process unless the rights of specially favored minorities are clearly in jeopardy. From the perspective of modern Fourteenth Amendment jurisprudence, the problem with *Dred Scott* is not that Taney denied judicial protection to constitutional rights based on birth alone but that he denied that race is a legitimate historical basis for constitutional equalization.

Taney's legacy in *Dred Scott* is also reflected outside the jurisprudence of the Fourteenth Amendment. In the area of freedom of religion the Supreme Court has recently shown a willingness to accommodate the religious expression of some minorities, even if this means giving them legal benefits or privileges not available to others who may have nonreligious reasons for engaging in similar conduct. The basic assumption behind these liberal rulings is that religious minorities are historically among the primordial constituent identities which our constitution purports to equalize. In *Sherbert* v. *Verner*, for example, the Warren Court decided that the expression of minority religious preferences, unlike other preferences, must be affirmatively protected by the state, even if this increases the cost of public programs.[123] As the dissenters point out, the majority thereby chose in effect to discriminate against the claims of nonreligious persons rather than permit the state to discriminate against a minority religion. Since *Sherbert*, the First Amendment can require government to give preferential treatment to religious persons in order to promote the free exercise of minority religions.

Only recently, however, have conservative justices begun to articulate the key premise behind the religious accommodation cases—that the political regime is not neutral between religion and nonreligion, especially where minority religions are concerned.[124] The clear implication is that religious minorities may be entitled not merely to special privileges or to special exemptions but to accommodations that may restrict the powers of local governments in various ways. Why should a religious minority that is constitutionally entitled to provide its own schools or to be released from public schools without providing an alternative not also be entitled to exemption from certain school assignments or even to censor the school curriculum required of others?[125]

---

from consideration as a group that deserves constitutional protection. Among the living, however, age-based discrimination might be constitutionally disfavored under the due process clause, even if age groups, as such, could not be constitutionally protected under the equal protection clause.

123. 376 U.S. 398 (1967). State unemployment benefits may not be withheld from a person refusing a job requiring work on the Sabbath.

124. See, for example, Rehnquist, dissenting, in *Wallace* v. *Jaffree* 472 U.S. 38 (1985).

125. See *Wisconsin* v. *Yoder* 406 U.S. 205 (1972). Amish children have a right to exemption from the last two years of the compulsory school attendance requirement. Also see *Pierce* v. *Society of Sisters* 286 U.S. 510 (1925). These issues are discussed in *Mozert* v. *Hawkins County Public Schools* 827 F. 2d. 1058 (1987), cert. denied 56 U.S.L.W. 3569 (1988).

Many of the claims recently made about the constitutional requirements of accommodating religious minorities in secular public schools directly parallel the claims made in the aftermath of *Dred Scott* about the legal changes necessary to accommodate the rights of slaveholders in free states. Just as Taney saw the abolition of slavery as an unconstitutional discrimination against out-of-state property holders, Judge Brevard Hand has recently described "secular humanism," the intentionally nonreligious approach to education, as an unconstitutional discrimination against fundamentalist religious beliefs.[126]

To point out parallels with *Dred Scott* is not necessarily to criticize a constitutional argument. We are living in a state that is conceded to be nonneutral in its policies, and most constitutional rights are efforts by the courts to offset selectively the nonneutrality of the state in order to provide affirmative protection to certain values or groups. Arguments about which values and groups are deserving of such special constitutional protection are inevitably based in part on American history and require an authoritative judicial description of the constitutive identities that make up our political system.

Dred Scott is one such argument—a bad one, but perhaps for that very reason an argument that can teach us some surprising things about the structure and stakes of other such arguments today, whether in the United States, South Africa, Israel, or any other ethnically and culturally divided democracy. Among the lessons for students of American political development will be the insight that American democracy has not been exempt from the constitutional problems of regional and ethnic consocialism that have plagued other societies. For students of other societies our reconstruction of *Dred Scott* may provide a parallel insight: American constitutional law, building as it does on the sophistication and complexity of the Marshallian framework, can contribute significantly to the analysis of political systems scarred by continuing historical cleavages from which we are too often thought to be immune.[127]

Indeed, the framework of analysis developed in this essay provides a perspective on the problems facing many societies not usually compared with our own. Throughout recent history, revolutionary claims to political sovereignty have been used in pluralistic societies to promote (or deny) the rights of minority groups. Whether these claims involve the partition of existing states or the reunion of separate polities, they commonly propose to recast indigenous group conflicts by turning citizens into foreigners or foreigners into citizens. Our analysis above points to a common constitutional assumption behind many of these struggles: that conflicts between part and part can be overcome by changing the boundaries, both physical and conceptual, between those areas appropriate to popular self-determination and those protected by international law. In this way each minority part of a given society might be seen to represent an alternative whole, achieving a kind of toleration guaran-

---

126. See, for example, *Jaffree* v. *Board of School Commissioners of Mobile County* 544 F. Supp. 1104 (1983), and *Smith* v. *Board of School Commissioners of Mobile County* 665 F. Supp. 939 (1987).

127. For some further thoughts on this general subject in the context of a comparison of reverse discrimination polices in the United States and India, see Robert Meister, "Discrimination Law through the Looking Glass," *Wisconsin Law Review*, no. 4 (1985): 937–88.

teed by the mutual respect of sovereign states, each of which practices majority rule.

Our discussion of the American constitutional experience reveals that the fulfillment of this expectation is by no means automatic: problems of political identity and group equality will continue to arise even after problems of the division and reunion of sovereignty have been apparently settled. We have seen how the development of federal law under our Constitution began as a formal effort to interpolate the constraints of international law into a revolutionary ideology of popular sovereignty. Within the resulting framework of cosovereignty, however, the constitutional rights of individuals and groups remained problematic. *Dred Scott* was a decisive moment in the extension of the logic of wholes and parts, developed in the context of federalism, to address the general problem of minority political identities. The logic of that case prefigured much about the possibilities of using dual citizenship, foreign citizenship, and noncitizenship to both protect and limit the civil rights of minorities in pluralistic societies. In *Dred Scott* we can see the constitutional jurisprudence of cosovereignty as both a laboratory and a metaphor for the problems of social equalization that continue to arise among and within sovereign states.

RESEARCH NOTES

KRISTI ANDERSEN AND STUART J. THORSON
Syracuse University

Public Discourse or Strategic Game? Changes in Our Conception of Elections

Much has been written about the "new technology" of U.S. elections: computerized letters, data banks of potential contributors, advanced video advertising techniques, speedy transportation and communication, and instant analysis of polling data. If one examines these discussions for a sense of how the growing use of these new technologies has changed the politics of elections, one finds several themes. Many scholars and journalists have described, for example, the high dollar costs of technology-dependent campaigns, the consequent influence of political action committees, how presidential candidates in particular are "marketed," via the media, like toothpaste or breakfast cereal, and the prevalence in campaigns of superficial image rather than issues.[1] We argue here that these changes in the way elections are conducted are associated with a deeper change in the conception of elections. The core of this argument is that changes in election technology have made possible the conduct of campaigns in which "strategy" has taken on a new meaning, and that leaders and the public share a view of elections that has progressively less to do with education, public discourse, or participation.

Although most modern accounts of democracy view elections as a central feature of democratic life, they differ in their interpretations of the purpose of

An earlier version of this essay was presented to the core faculty of the Center for the Study of Citizenship of the Maxwell School, and we are grateful for the resulting thought-provoking discussion. We also thank John Agnew, Larry Herson, Ralph Ketcham, Tom Patterson, Roger Sharp, Manfred Stanley, and David Sylvan for their comments and suggestions.

1. See, for example, Herbert Alexander, *Financing Politics: Money, Elections, and Political Reform* (Washington, D.C.: Congressional Quarterly Press, 1982); Robert Agranoff, *The New Style in Election Campaigns*, rev. ed. (Boston: Holbrook, 1976); Elizabeth Drew, *American Journal: The Events of 1976* (New York: Random House, 1982); Larry Sabato, *The Rise of Political Consultants* (New York: Basic Books, 1981); Joe McGinnis, *The Selling of the President, 1968* (New York: Trident Press, 1969); Thomas E. Patterson, *The Mass Media Election* (New York: Praeger, 1980).

elections. One view is that elections provide a means of collectively choosing among some socially defined set of alternatives. A citizen, by casting a vote, registers a preference for one or another candidate. The electoral process, by aggregating together individual expressions of preference, identifies a winner. Further, this choice (or, more precisely, popular participation in making this choice) serves a *protective* function, constraining elected leaders so that they do not act in ways that grossly violate the public's interest.

Another tradition in democratic theory offers a different kind of justification for democracy. We might call this tradition "participatory democracy." Rousseau, for example, saw the ideal system as one that developed individuals' capacity for responsible social and political action through public participation. Similarly, John Stuart Mill defended democratic governments because "in theory, at least, they are most capable of creating the conditions for progressive moral development."[2] Under this view an actual election (the voting itself) is a ratification of a *process* of learning and discussion. As a consequence of participating in this discussion, the citizen (both as voter and as candidate) learns something about politics and, at least as important, something about himself: the citizen, as a consequence of having participated in the selection of representatives, has had an experience that makes him into a different and, perhaps, a better person.

In this essay we argue that Americans' understanding of elections is increasingly colored by the utilitarian view, and that an educative understanding of elections is, conversely, on the decline. To demonstrate this, we need to ask first: what characteristics of campaigns follow from each of the above two views of the role of elections in a democracy? From the utilitarian view, election campaigns must be waged by ambitious candidates who fear losses at the polls; they must offer apparent choices on matters the public perceives to be important; the public needs to have abundant and accurate information about the candidates. Also important, from the utilitarian perspective, citizen preferences are likely to be taken as givens. The task of the candidate, during a campaign, is to position herself in such a manner as to maximize her appeal to the likely voters. To the extent that these conditions are met, citizens can translate their preferences for policies into candidate choices.

A developmental perspective speaks to different aspects of the campaign. An election campaign should provide the opportunity for intellectual and moral development of citizens and leaders, and should convey the sense, to citizens, that they are serious participants in a social process. In contrast to the utilitarian view, the developmental perspective is unlikely to view citizen preferences as given and, instead, sees campaigns as providing an opportunity for citizens to develop and question their positions and understandings of socially relevant issues.

In the next two sections we describe an important shift in the way Americans understand the purpose of elections and their own role in elections. Since we cannot talk with the voters of the 1890s or the 1920s, our reconstruction of

2. Quoted in Brian R. Nelson, *Western Political Thought: From Socrates to the Age of Ideology* (Englewood Cliffs, N.J.: Prentice-Hall, 1982), 277.

these changes is necessarily indirect and, at this point, suggestive. We develop two lines of argument, the first having to do with the way technological changes have affected campaigns and helped to change the accepted definition of "strategy" and the second, with how changes in our understanding of elections are reflected in changes in the way election campaigns are described by the press.

TECHNOLOGICAL CHANGES AND CAMPAIGN STRATEGY

The presidential campaign was institutionalized in the 1830s and 1840s, with the advent of the national nominating convention, the party platform, and the "campaign as sport and spectacle" which Tocqueville described so vividly.[3] Since then, technological changes of all kinds have been rapidly incorporated into the practice of campaigning. As printing technology improved, and printing costs declined, for example, politicians could more easily produce leaflets and posters; as transportation improved, the whistle-stop tour and the big urban rally became popular campaign techniques. In the second half of the nineteenth century, the revolutions in communication and transportation fundamentally changed the press and its role with regard to politics. "Corporatization" of the press freed the papers from the direct party influence that had been characteristic of the early nineteenth century. Presidential campaigns thus were described by the press in a less fiercely partisan manner, and the expansion in telegraph and telephone communications meant that speeches and other campaign events could be instantly communicated to the large population of newspaper readers.

Radio was first used by presidential candidates in the 1920s. The Smith and Hoover campaigns in 1928 each spent a half million dollars to reach the nine million radio sets then in use. The consensus among commentators at the time appeared to be that as the traditional old-fashioned spellbinder was replaced by the exposure of individual listeners to the candidates' ideas (the use made of radio in 1928 was simply the live broadcasting of speeches), the level of political discussion would be raised. "The radio audience does not tune in for hokum. Radio demands thought," said one *New York Times* writer in 1928.

As the number of radio sets doubled in the next ten years, Roosevelt began to make even more extensive and effective use of this medium. The dramatic growth in the number of radios presaged a similar increase in the use of television in the 1950s, and presidential campaigns became more and more dependent on the new medium, through both news and political advertising. The specific implications of television technology for campaigns have been discussed by a number of scholars.[4]

3. State and local campaigns differ in many ways from presidential campaigns, but the centrality of the presidential elections in American political life, and the disproportionate emphasis of the mass media on them, means that our collective understanding of all elections is very much shaped by the way we see presidential elections.

4. For example, Patterson, *The Mass Media Election*, and Thomas E. Patterson and Robert D. McClure, *The Unseeing Eye: The Myth of Television Power in National Politics* (New York: G. P. Putnam's Sons, 1976).

Meanwhile, the early twentieth century had also seen the development of sampling theory and the notions of direct, structured interviewing and standardized question wording. Together these innovations allowed the growing use of the social survey as a means of obtaining information about demographics, behavior, and opinions; the 1930s marked the advent of "modern" survey research in the United States.[5] George Gallup, Lou Harris, Elmo Roper, and others began regularly (if infrequently, by current standards) to poll samples of the public on their opinions and voting intentions. By the 1950s presidential candidates were commissioning polls, and by the next decade polling had become a central part of presidential election campaigns. At the same time, media organizations of all sizes began routinely to commission and publish results of surveys at frequent intervals during campaigns. As high-speed computers and computer-assisted interviewing techniques have become steadily more and more available, the analysis and dissemination of poll results have become almost instantaneous.

The growing ability to catalog and analyze mountains of survey data, as well as voting records and demographic information such as census data, provided campaign planners with a new capability to act strategically in the service of victory. American political parties, in contrast to European parties, have always been described as more pragmatic and election-oriented than ideological and mobilizational. They are said to be primarily concerned with winning elections. In nineteenth-century America, campaigns were certainly "strategic" in the dictionary's sense—"devising or employing plans or stratagems toward a goal." Candidates then, as now, aimed to win. In consultation with members of their party, advisers, and financial backers, they constructed and implemented what they hoped would be winning strategies. Those who ran campaigns were able to get a general sense, from crowds, editorials, and so forth, of how the campaign was going; but they did not have the kind of technology-supported feedback that today makes it possible for candidates to minutely adjust and readjust their appeals with an eye toward the maximization of their eventual plurality. Thus when we talk about "strategies" in the context of campaigns of a hundred years ago, we are using the term in quite a different sense than it is used to describe modern campaigns.

What did "campaign strategy" appear to mean, for example, to the candidates and their advisers in the 1896 election race between William McKinley and Williams Jennings Bryan? One aspect of campaign strategy was clearly *how* to campaign. The Republicans, under the stewardship of Mark Hanna, had much more money than the Democrats; hence one important difference between the two campaigns was that the Republicans implemented a tremendously expensive, literature- and speaker-based campaign, whereas Bryan, traveling eighteen thousand miles and delivering six hundred speeches to five million people, took the Democrats' message directly to the public himself.

5. For interesting notes on earlier surveys, see Catherine Marsh, *The Survey Method* (London: George Allen & Unwin, 1982), as well as Richard Boyd and Herbert Hyman, "Survey Research," in F. Greenstein and N. Polsby, eds., *Handbook of Political Science*, vol. 7 (Reading, Mass.: Addison-Wesley, 1975).

McKinley, of course, chose to stay home in Ohio, where he conducted a "front-porch campaign," speaking to as many as eighty thousand people gathered there in a single day. In reading historians' accounts, one gets a clear sense that the two campaigns made conscious strategic choices based on constraints such as money, the convictions and perceived strengths of the candidates, and the voters' assumed preferences. They are described as making strategic errors: McSeveney, for example, argues that "by harping on free silver, Bryan lost precious opportunities to discuss an issue of potentially greater interest to workers—federal intervention in labor disputes." Their strategies are also sometimes described as having audience-specific components: "The G.O.P. tailored its arguments to the assumed needs of northeastern farmers; Bryan did not."[6]

Certainly the two campaigns dealt consciously with strategic (goal-directed) decision making by answering questions like these: What kind of organization shall they use or construct? Where shall they campaign? How much time shall they allocate to the various regions and states? What kinds of appeals shall they make to what voting groups? But for practical purposes these questions were asked and answered, in 1896, only once—early in the campaign. Information taken in during its course was unlikely to change the answers substantially. In today's campaigns, in contrast, candidates "take soundings from various sources to modify their behavior as seems best suited to make the most of opportunities as they arise."[7] In particular, tracking polls, samplings of opinion taken every day or so, can monitor changes in support, changes in opinions of various groups, changes in the public agenda; and constantly reworked political advertisements can respond to the observed changes.[8] In nineteenth- and early twentieth-century campaigns, strategy appears to have comprised a series of decisions made by the candidate and his advisers early in the season; in today's campaigns, technological changes have made possible a strategy that may involve numerous adjustments, as the campaign progresses, in theme, style, and emphasis.

Even the initial decisions that make up general strategic choices appear more complex than the same kinds of decisions years ago—primarily because technology has generated more data that have to be taken into account in making the decisions. Campaign strategists themselves provide a clear picture of the constant information monitoring and consequent slight adjustments that characterize a modern presidential campaign. For example, Richard Wirthlin, Ronald Reagan's pollster, wrote a 1981 article titled "Campaign Chronicle," which describes in detail how the Reagan strategists "constructed a landslide." As did

6. Paul W. Glad, *McKinley, Bryan and the People* (Philadelphia: J. B. Lippincott, 1964), 176–79; Samuel McSeveney, *The Politics of Depression: Political Behavior in the Northeast, 1893–1896* (New York: Oxford University Press, 1972), 179.

7. Nelson Polsby and Aaron Wildavsky, *Presidential Elections*, 5th ed. (New York: Charles Scribner's Sons, 1980), 163–64, 185.

8. See, for example, the discussion of tracking polls in Stephen E. Salmore and Barbara G. Salmore, *Candidates, Parties and Campaigns* (Washington, D.C.: Congressional Quarterly Press, 1985), 168–72.

the Jimmy Carter campaign, they began with a detailed set of goals ("Focus campaign resources to reinforce the Governor's image strengths that embody the presidential values a majority of Americans think are important"; "Position the campaign to pick up as much of the Anderson vote as possible as Anderson fades in the stretch"). Target groups were developed from voting returns and polling data. Modifications and refinements in goals and targets were made as the fall progressed. Early in the campaign, for example, the strategists discovered, from survey data, that although "Reagan was well known . . . he was not known well," and consequently ads were designed to "fill that information gap." Among the principal functions of a strategist in a modern election campaign, according to Wirthlin and his associates, is to "dynamically adjust the intermediate objectives and allocation formulae to changing political circumstances without abandoning the overall *strategic* [our italics] objectives of the campaign."[9]

In summary, this brief examination of accounts of presidential campaigns suggests that "campaign strategy" until the turn of the century (and perhaps later) connoted a series of one-time decisions about how the ensuing campaign would be structured. In contrast, "campaign strategy" now implies a constant willingness to alter such decisions, to make new decisions about image, appeals, and targets, contingent on feedback generated as the campaign progresses. The capability to generate and monitor such feedback and to finely adjust campaign appeals is, of course, based on the technology modern campaigns have at their disposal. The changes in the strategic capabilities of candidates, however, are not as significant as another shift which has occurred more or less simultaneously. This is the shift from a view of the election campaign as (importantly if not wholly) a dynamic interchange in which candidates' reasoned and perhaps changing arguments were important to a situation in which candidates attempt to learn a more or less fixed preference distribution of the electorate and adapt their campaign style accordingly. In other words, while present-day elections may or may not demonstrate the characteristics that are desirable from a utilitarian point of view, they decreasingly meet the criteria established by a developmental or educative perspective. We do not mean to idealize the nineteenth or earlier twentieth century: candidates wanted to win, behaved in sometimes manipulative or corrupt fashion in the service of victory, and not all citizens were sophisticated consumers of candidates' arguments. Nonetheless, historians have argued convincingly that at least some of the conditions essential to the educative ideal obtained. A recent article, for example, states that "one of the fundamental distinctions between the modern political universe and that of a century ago is that the nineteenth-century electorate was more committed, more informed, and more issue conscious."[10] James Bryce, writing in 1884, said:

9. Richard Wirthlin, Vincent Breglio, and Richard Beal, "Campaign Chronicle," *Public Opinion*, February-March 1981.

10. William E. Gienapp, "Politics Seem to Enter into Everything," in S. E. Maizlish and J. J. Kushma, eds., *Essays on American Antebellum Politics, 1840–1860* (College Station: Texas A & M University Press, 1982), 61.

It is not that voters are incapable of appreciating good arguments, or are unwilling to receive them. On the contrary, and this is especially true of the working classes, an audience is pleased when solid arguments are addressed to it, and men read with more relish the articles . . . which contain the most carefully sifted facts and the most exact thoughts.[11]

Thus changes in technology have been associated with changes in the way elections are perceived by candidates and citizens. The next section suggests how such changes in understanding have been both shaped and reflected by journalistic descriptions of campaigns.

HOW CAMPAIGNS ARE DESCRIBED

If we want to argue that our *collective* view of the meaning and purpose of elections—the view shared by leaders and the public—has changed substantially during the past hundred years, we need to look at the way election campaigns are presented and described in the news media. Patterson has said of modern campaigns that "for the large majority of voters, the campaign has little reality apart from its media version."[12] This was true in previous eras as well. During the presidential election of 1896, for example, with the exception of those voters who journeyed to Canton, Ohio, to experience McKinley's front-porch campaign and those who happened to reside along Bryan's whistle-stop route, the presidential campaign existed mostly in the newspapers and party literature.

In order to make comparisons with regard to how the print media described and presented various election campaigns, we examined closely six days of the *New York Times* prior to the presidential elections of 1896, 1928, 1960, and 1984. The papers studied were those of the Monday and Tuesday after Labor Day, and the Saturday, Sunday, Monday, and Tuesday beginning ten days before each election. We read, counted, and coded all stories having to do with the presidential election that were more than one paragraph in length.[13]

The number of election stories and the proportion of space devoted to the four elections varied considerably. During the six days studied in each year, there were sixty-three election stories in 1896, ninety-two in 1928, seventy-two

11. James Bryce, *The American Commonwealth*, 1894, vol. 2 (London, 1894) 250; cited in Richard Jensen, *The Winning of the Midwest* (Chicago: University of Chicago Press, 1971), 4.

12. Patterson, *The Mass Media Election*, 3.

13. We used a conventional interpretation of "having to do with the presidential election," which meant that we selected stories that dealt mainly with the candidates, their speeches and travels, predictions about the vote, and the election itself. Thus although a story about the state of the economy might well have had an impact on perceptions of the campaign, we did not include it in our sample. The stories were categorized according to their primary emphasis: (1) a campaign event (trips, plans, rallies); (2) a candidate's or supporter's speech; (3) predictions, assessments of strength; (4) an endorsement or repudiation of candidate by individual or group; (5) an accusation or defense; (6) the election campaign as a whole, a summary or analyais; (7) plans/finances/strategy of one or more campaigns; (8) focus on voters, reasons for vote, voting behavior of population groups.

in 1960 and forty-two in 1984. Of course, the percentage of space devoted to election-related news has decreased drastically over this period as the *Times*, along with other print media, has included more and more advertising, human-interest stories, news analysis, and so forth.

In all years except 1984, approximately a fifth to a third of the stories were mostly reports or transcripts of campaign speeches given by the presidential or vice-presidential candidates or by their supporters (in 1984 12 percent of the stories fell into this category). Substantial numbers of stories were primarily or secondarily concerned with the campaign itself—travels of the candidates, the size of crowds, the nature of rallies, and so forth. The urge to claim victory was strong in the early years; more recently, there have been fewer stories that were primarily predictions. Some stories in each year (1984 in particular) dealt with the accusations, charges, and countercharges that have always characterized American politics, whether they concerned silver mine owners' contributions to Bryan's campaign, the sources of anti-Catholic propaganda in 1928 and 1960, or the finances of Geraldine Ferraro's husband in 1984.

Two kinds of stories that simply did not exist in 1896 were those dealing primarily with the campaign strategy of one or both candidates (in 1984 this category accounted for 29 percent of the stories we read) and those focusing on the voters—through the use of survey data or interviews with particular voters. Conversely, stories consisting primarily of endorsements of one candidate or the other by prominent individuals or groups have become a much less important part of the press's description of a campaign.

There are a number of deeper differences in the way campaigns are presented and described to the public. First, whereas candidates (and their supporters or detractors) used to be allowed to speak for themselves, the press now *describes* what they say and often *analyzes* it along with the description. In 1896, stories that focused on a campaign speech followed a consistent formula: the story began by setting the scene (how many delegations had come to Canton that day, or how many people were in a crowd to hear Bryan) and then consisted simply of long quotes from the speech. If the speech was by the candidate himself or by another leading political figure, virtually all of it was reported. In many other cases, speeches were excerpted, but they were rarely, if ever, paraphrased. Transcripts of major speeches were included on almost a daily basis in the 1928 *Times* as well, and candidates' views (as exemplified in their speeches) were still presented with a minimum of paraphrasing or interpretation.

By 1960, however, the reporting of speeches had changed in several ways. Although in the case of some addresses full transcripts were included, they were now separate from the main story reporting on the speech (this separation had been made occasionally in 1928). Moreover, relatively fewer speeches were considered important enough, in 1960 and 1984, to warrant the inclusion of a transcript. Even more striking is the extent to which candidates' speeches were no longer presented at all but were described and paraphrased by reporters. This happened in relatively small ways: a quote from Kennedy was prefaced by the phrase, "He poked fun at Mr. Nixon by saying that . . ." (Oct. 23, 1960). We can also see this change at more critical junctures. After summarizing part of a Nixon speech on foreign policy, the story continued, "Mr. Nixon's statement of the Kennedy position on Qemoy and Matsu did not appear to coincide with Mr. Kennedy's own statement of his position" (Oct. 23, 1960). This change from news as "just the facts" to news as analysis is described more generally by Michael Nelson as "evaluative journalism."[14]

Second, whereas earlier news stories (those in 1896 and 1928) almost without exception focused on one candidate, in the two later years stories were increasingly "synthetic"—that is, they presented arguments, and sometimes quotes, from both sides and attempted to make comparisons and draw conclusions. In 1896, for example, during the period covered, a controversy erupted over whether the Republicans had urged employers to coerce workers to vote for McKinley and whether Bryan had told workers to ask for a contract ensuring stable wages in case of a McKinley election. Each day for a week or so there was an accusation or a defense in this matter, but each stood by itself—Hanna defended himself at length against the Democrats, and then a day or so later, Bryan, under the head "Bryan to His Accusers," was allowed, through the vehicle of several lengthy excerpts from his speeches, to rebut various critics.

In contrast, a controversy in 1960 centered on some advertisements produced for Kennedy. Although the headline read "Nixon Aide Scores Film for Kennedy," the story recorded responses from Herb Klein, Nixon's press secretary; Robert Finch, his campaign director; John Denove, in charge of Kennedy's television campaign; and Pierre Salinger, Kennedy's press secretary. Furthermore, the *Times* took pains to explain the references these people made and to point out areas of agreement and disagreement (Oct. 22, 1960). This tendency toward synthesism was even more pronounced in 1984. A relatively trivial example is provided by Mondale's claim that the president had failed to mark the anniversary of the death of 241 Marines in Lebanon. Reagan's lack of reaction to this assertion was noted by the *Times*, as was the fact that he did order federal flags flown at half-staff (Oct. 24, 1984). Many stories combined and synthesized information from speeches, interviews with campaign staff members, and polls. When Mondale called a Reagan remark "despicable," the paper quoted him but noted in the next paragraph, "At the same time Mr. Mondale brushed aside new polls that show him substantially behind Mr. Reagan in the Presidential contest" (Oct. 28, 1984). A story whose headline referred to the Republicans' penchant for "invoking Democratic heroes" such as FDR and Truman scrutinized polls for evidence of possibly defecting Democrats, looked at the *Times*'s own survey and quoted from Republican campaign managers (Oct. 27, 1984). A story purportedly focusing on a Reagan speech about anti-Semitism also included descriptions of the community where he spoke, analysis of past administration actions with regard to Jews and Israel, and even discussed things that Mr. Reagan could have said but did not (Oct. 27, 1984).

A third change has to do with candidate strategy. Changes in the *New York Times*'s discussion of candidates' strategies reflected the changes discussed

14. Michael Nelson, "Evaluative Journalism: A New Synthesis," *Virginia Quarterly Review* 58 (Summer 1982): 419–34.

above in insiders' and outsiders' descriptions of presidential campaigns. In the *Times* of 1896, "having a strategy" seems to have been closely akin to "wanting to win and working hard at it". Thus the "sound money" Democrats talked about "hard work still to be done" (Sept. 15, 1896); Hanna was "calmly confident" and believed that "our triumph depended solely upon a fair and thorough discussion of our platform" (Oct. 25, 1896). In the sixty-three stories we examined, there was no discussion of the strategic implications of particular speeches, trips, appearances, or other actions, on the part of either the candidates or the press.

In 1928, some straightforward connections were made between what the candidates were doing and their goals— that is, goals more specific than winning the election. Thus on October 27, Smith's trip to Pennsylvania was described as an attempt to garner the uncertain Pennsylvania electoral votes. In general, however, candidates' strategies were described in the news strories essentially as their doing the best they could, especially in states where the outcome of the vote was not certain. "With the start of his campaign tour only a week away, Governor Smith is laying plans to use the power of his words and personality to their fullest extent to win the farmers of the West" (Sept. 10, 1928).

One way in which 1928 differed appreciably from 1896, however, involved the media coverage of the election. By the latter year, the Sunday paper had evolved into more or less the form we know today, with numerous special sections, including some offering general analysis of the election campaign. On Sunday, October 28 the *Times* ran a map showing state voting in 1916 and 1924, several stories based on interviews with party leaders, and a story that did touch upon campaign strategy. That week Hoover had accused Smith of favoring "state socialism." The analysis argued that this "opened the floodgates of controversy" and provided an opportunity for Smith to attack Hoover, who had previously been ignoring Smith and criticizing the Democratic stance on the tariff. The story went on, "from the early days of the campaign the strategy of the Democratic leadership, it is said, has been to arouse Mr. Hoover and obtain a statement which would put him on the defensive in a controversy over an issue which the country could grasp" (Oct. 28, 1928). One might suggest, then, that in 1928 the notion of "strategy" as "developing persuasive counterarguments against your opponent" was perhaps clearer than in 1896.

In the *Times'* coverage of the 1960 election, discussions of strategy had moved out of the Sunday special sections and into pieces labeled "News Analysis." During the six days covered, one of these articles discussed the potential impact of the fourth televised debate; in another, James Reston wrote about a trip with Nixon. Reston commented that Nixon's "speech could almost be reduced to a mathematical formula. . . . Is it effective? Of course it is" (Sept. 13, 1960). Other articles, in the "News of the Week" section of the Sunday paper, dealt directly with the candidates' presumed strategies. In the debate, for example, "aside from [Cuba], the images of themselves that the two men have been seeking to project . . . were much as they had been. Nixon has been trying to depict himself as a man with wide experience in foreign affairs. . . . The image Mr. Kennedy has tried to create is that of a fresh and challenging force in American politics" (Oct. 23, 1960).

The Sunday magazine of October 23 had an article on the vice-presidential candidates, Johnson and Lodge, and concluded that their very different styles "color their strategic approaches to the campaign." The candidates themselves also could be heard to talk about their strategies in this sense. Nixon told an interviewer that Eisenhower had helped him change his campaign style and that he hoped he would now create a better impression (Sept. 13, 1960). Thus although some of what is meant by "strategy" would be familiar to followers of the two earlier campaigns—the allocation of campaign resources to states depending on their predicted electoral vote, for example—there was clearly an additional sense of "strategy" present in 1960: a strategy involving "images," "styles," and "impressions."

By 1984 a focus on strategy (with an emphasis on image-based strategy) characterized many regular news stories as well as designated "news analyses." On September 9 Reagan made a campaign stop at a Roman Catholic shrine in Pennsylvania, and the report read in part

> The mixture of religious symbolism and partisan political statements today appeared to contradict the recent assertions of top Reagan campaign aides that the President would ease up on his use of religion in his re-election effort. . . . some of Mr. Reagan's advisers have said that it was a mistake for him to denounce opponents of government-mandated school prayer as "intolerant of religion." (Sept. 10, 1984)

This paragraph illustrates the press's tendency to analyze— Reagan did not simply speak; his speech was characterized in terms of its partisanship and symbolism—and synthesize—the story is not only about this particular speech but about others and about Reagan's advisers. Equally clearly it shows the ease with which modern journalists infer strategic intentions from candidates' actions.

Our examination of campaign stories revealed at least three ways in which the 1984 campaigns appear to have differed from previous ones, including those of 1960, with regard to strategy. One of these clearly related to changing technological capabilities. That is, the campaign pollsters' ability to constantly track not only voters' opinions on the issues but also their less cognitive feelings about the candidates was reflected in the accounts of how the campaign was proceeding. Moreover, it was assumed that data from these tracking polls were being used to evaluate and modify campaign behavior. Analysis of a *New York Times*/CBS poll discussed on October, 10 1984, for example, pointed out which issues favored Reagan and which favored Mondale, showed exactly where (demographically) support and opposition to each lay, and argued that Mondale had "lost ground *in the past 10 days* [our italics] on what many political strategists consider the two most important personal indicators: the public's perception of a candidate's leadership and its general reaction to a candidate." In the same edition, Mondale's staff was described as being in an "upbeat mood" only a few days previously, until they found that "polls in the state

[California] that track shifts in voters' positions have detected a drift toward Mr. Reagan." The precision with which opinions could be tracked and the growing expertise of pollsters at dealing with more ephemeral personality- and image-related concerns of the electorate had produced a situation in which campaign staffs had constantly to react to a changing electoral context.

Campaign advisers in the eighties appeared to be very comfortable talking with the press about their strategies ("Our purpose is to get Democrats," said Edward J. Rollicks, the Republican campaign manager, on October 27, 1984, and went on to talk of "targeted" groups). Moreover, the press frequently framed their stories in terms of campaign strategy. The story cited above about Reagan's visit to a Catholic shrine, which gave the *Times* an opportunity to talk in general about Reagan's strategy with regard to the issue of religion, is a good example. An even better one is a "News Analysis" on September 11, which discussed Mondale's "poor strategy": "Sometimes bad ideas get imbedded in the strategic thinking of a Presidential campaign. A faulty central concept can either kill a candidacy outright or cripple it."

This last quote marks the third and most important way in which 1984 was different: put briefly, candidates' words and actions were *assumed* to be primarily, if not wholly, motivated by strategic considerations. Thus the "ideas" and "central concepts" of a campaign were not policy positions or ideological convictions. Rather, they had become a matter (as in the example just cited) of whether a candidate was portraying himself as "tough" or was conveying precisely the right image of leadership.

STRATEGY, ARGUMENT, AND THE MEANING OF ELECTIONS

Let us consider again the participatory justifications for democratic elections. If the act of voting is to be the ratification of a process of individual and social discussion and learning, the election campaign must foster such discussion and learning, by citizens and also by candidates. If politics has to do with conflict over the proper uses of collective authority to solve societal problems, a campaign should establish the context for thoughtful discussion of alternative solutions to these problems. Moreover, there must be opportunities for members of the public to engage in political discussion and to learn about issues raised by the campaign; there must also be appropriate settings for candidates to make reasoned arguments. These two points are not unrelated: citizens presumably will be more likely to learn from the campaign if they believe that they, as citizens, are being taken seriously. This does not merely require that they believe their vote "counts" but also that they see themselves being appealed to as persons who are part of an important social discourse. We would argue that people are likely to have this view of election campaigns to the extent that candidates present *arguments* that they themselves take seriously.

There are two ways in which campaign appeals—whether pamphlets, speeches, slogans, or primarily visual spots on television—can be seen as "arguments." First is what we conventionally think of as an argument: a series of sentences that set out premises, supporting evidence, and conclusions. Obviously people often make arguments that are not so extensive; rather, they consist, wholly or in part, of what we might call "pointers" to arguments. In politics, if someone says "abortion is murder," that can be seen as a pointer to an argument based on assumptions about when human life begins, what actions are immoral, and so forth. In this sense even implicit arguments pointed to by single words or images may be more or less public arguments if most people in a community agree that a particular argument is being pointed to. In the earlier campaigns we considered (those of 1896 and 1928) the press generally presented in their entirety even long and complex arguments made by the candidates (as well as the ever-present accusations, claims of support, and so on).

On the other hand, candidates' appeals may be primarily based not on arguments—of either the explicit or implicit kind—but on slogans or candidate images that do not appear even to be pointing to an argument. This is frequently the case in present-day campaigns. The relative dearth of explicit arguments in the campaign may be due partly to the perception of candidates and their staffs that the citizens—contrary to Bryce's claim about past generations of Americans—will be bored or turned off by complex arguments. In addition, as we have noted, changes in the canons of journalism have made it less likely that such arguments will be presented in the media even if they are made.[15] But one might contend that candidates in 1984 were often making well-understood implicit or pointed-to arguments. Undoubtedly this was sometimes true, but convincing evidence that it is more often not true can be found in the public opinion data. Repeatedly, surveys have found that many of those people who like Ronald Reagan and voted for him disagree strongly with him on such things as whether particular social programs should be cut, how important it is to reduce the deficit, or whether military spending should be increased. For example, despite the patriotic symbolism prevalent in Reagan's campaign, a *New York Times*/CBS poll found only seventeen percent of a national sample agreeing with Reagan that military spending should be increased, even though Reagan's approval rating was at a remarkable high of sixty five percent. (Jan. 28, 1986). Writing just after the election, Light and Lake interpreted pre- and postelection polls in 1984 as suggesting that "the election was being decided by voters much more on candidate images than issues."[16]

To the extent that modern campaigns are thus based decreasingly on arguments, people may not perceive that they are participating in a process of collective discussion and learning, for two reasons. First, it is impossible to argue about or talk much about a slogan or an image: we can dislike a candidate's macho image, but that does not constitute the basis of an argument of the

---

15. See also Thomas E. Patterson and Richard Davis, "The Media Campaign: Struggle for the Agenda," in Michael Nelson, ed., *The Elections of 1984* (Washington, D.C.: Congressional Quarterly Press, 1985).

16. Paul L. Light and Celinda Lake, "The Election: Candidates, Strategies and Decisions," in *The Elections of 1984*, 100.

sort that John Stuart Mill had in mind. Second, people will not feel they are being taken seriously when candidates are apparently willing to alter their appeal for short-term strategic reasons; and it is much easier to manipulate a more or less free-floating image or slogan than to make changes in a serious, developed argument.

These kinds of perceptions on the part of citizens are reinforced by the way social scientists describe and interpret elections (approaches that are increasingly reflected in the press). Before the 1950s, political scientists' and historians' accounts of campaigns were virtually indistinguishable: both accepted the notion that election campaigns were historical events which could be understood best by a particularistic case-study approach. Parallels might be drawn with other campaigns, of course, but generally scholars tried to understand the campaigns by placing them into a particular historical context.

The behavioral revolution in the 1950s and 1960s meant above all that social scientists, like natural scientists, saw their goal as the development of generalizations. "Idiographic" approaches came to be considered by many as inferior to a "nomothetic" orientation which attempted to develop general propositions. Thus, phenomena that had been seen as distinct were now placed in equivalence classes like "party systems," "political agendas," "public policies," or "campaigns." Research since the mid-sixties communicates the idea that campaigns are considered a phenomenon to be explained by a single theory. One description of candidate behavior, for example, concludes that "the basic question of *election game strategy* is how the candidate wishes to distribute his *strategy emphases*. . . . therefore a strategy vector can be written for each candidate."[17] From this example we can see how social scientists' methods and words might well reinforce the assumption that election campaigns are *games*: that the only concern of candidates is the final vote total, and that they are willing to make numerous alterations in their campaign appeals if it will help them win. At a deeper level, the very fact that "campaigns"—or even just "presidential election campaigns"—are all placed into an equivalence class implies that they can all be analyzed using the same framework. Thus whether viewed as games or not, campaigns are all fundamentally alike. This perspective shifts attention sharply away from necessarily context-laden issues, arguments, and political discourse and toward a utilitarian (results-based) view of elections.

Argument, on the other hand, is central to a participatory justification for elections. Benjamin Barber, in his recent *Strong Democracy*, makes a related point having to do with the importance of "political talk":

> Strong democratic talk entails listening no less than speaking; . . . one finds it easy enough to see how talk might be confused with speech and speech reduced to the articulation of interest by appropriate signs. Yet talk as communication obviously involves receiving as well as expressing. . . . The secret ballot allows the voter to express himself but not be influenced by others or to have to account for his private choices in a public language.

17. John H. Kessel, "A Game Theory Analysis of Campaign Strategy," in M. K. Jennings and L. H. Zeigler, eds., *The Electoral Process* (Englewood Cliffs, N.J.: Prentice-Hall, 1966), 291.

"Talk is ultimately a force with which we can create a community capable of creating its own future," says Barber.[18] He is arguing that elections are at the core of "thin democracy," and that "strong democracy" requires unmediated self-government by the citizenry. But even those who see more virtue in elections may be willing to accept the importance of political talk (what we have been calling reasoned argument) in building individual political efficacy and in creating a sense of *public* discourse and purpose.

Unfortunately for those who hold this view, the present analysis supports the conclusion that changes in political campaigns over the past ninety years have moved them away from political discourses and toward strategic games. The thirty-second spots and the "bits-and-pieces" descriptions of speeches in the newspapers and on television constitute, for the citizen, a campaign of assertions, slogans, and punch lines rather than one of sustained arguments. The mass media's preoccupation with strategy and tendency to infer strategic intentions from virtually any statement or action clearly conveys the impression of candidates whose primary goal—winning the election—takes precedence over all but the most fundamental of their political convictions. The frequently stated emphasis, on the part of the candidates in 1896 and 1928, on their arguments and persuasive abilities is consistent with the press's greater concentration on candidates' arguments in these years. Since 1960, and even more clearly in 1984, the presidential candidates have been described by the mass media and perceived by citizens not primarily as trying to *make arguments* or *persuade* but as trying to *calculate* public reactions to statements, speeches, or ads and *reposition* themselves accordingly.

It is easy in this situation for citizens to assume that they are seen merely as voters. The constant publicizing of polls may reinforce this view: citizens are merely numbers to be counted and aggregated. One possible consequence of this is a decline in electoral participation—voting turnout has steadily declined ever since the 1890s. Although there are numerous plausible explanations for the decline, it seems reasonable that the conceptual change we have been describing has contributed to decreasing political involvement, at both the level of participation and the level of emotional and intellectual commitment to politics. Furthermore, the conceptual change we have described is something that we might expect to be most strongly marked in people with more education; this could account for the apparent anomaly that while education levels have increased, voting turnout has gone down.

For both democratic theorists and ordinary citizens, those living in the nineteenth century as well as those living now, there are elements of both educative and utilitarian justifications in their self-understandings of elections. Nonetheless, the mix of these elements has shifted toward the utilitarian over the past hundred years, for the reasons we have discussed above. Those observers bemoaning this conceptual shift, as we do, might well be accused of elitism—as endorsing a kind of campaigning where the level of discourse is so high that only those few people who (voting behavior studies tell us) are able to perceive

18. Benjamin Barber, *Strong Democracy: Participatory Politics for a New Age* (Berkeley: University of California Press, 1984), 174–75, 198.

clear between-candidate differences could participate meaningfully. But an argument based on the need for accurate perception of candidate differences is itself an argument from a utilitarian perspective. If, on the contrary, one is convinced, like James Bryce, that both the right to rule and the capability to participate in political discourse are fairly uniformly distributed, considering elections from an educative point of view is an emancipating rather than an elitist position. Even more emancipating might be a move to deemphasize the importance of elections, since it is hard to imagine how this conceptual change could be reversed easily. Thus the development and strengthening of nonelectorally focused opportunities for political discourse and citizen participation might help to move us away from the purely utilitarian conception of the democratic process.

RONALD KAHN
Oberlin College

Polity and Rights Values in Conflict: The Burger Court, Ideological Interests, and the Separation of Church and State

I seek to counter a view commonly held by scholars that the Burger Court is pragmatic in its constitutional choices in contrast to the Warren Court, which is viewed as ideological.[1] I propose a methodology to study the effects of process values and rights values held by members of the Burger Court on their decision making. To view its decision making as pragmatic, without awareness of underlying values of process and rights, results in an oversimplified view and leads to the unwarranted conclusion that the Burger Court is case-specific in making constitutional choices. I limit my discussion to separation of church and state cases, primarily in the area of aid to parochial education, because traditionally scholars have emphasized the pragmatic nature of Burger Court choices in this area. A finding of consistency of values in justices' orientations in this area suggests that the methodology reported here might have general utility in the study of Supreme Court decision making.

Analysis of process and rights values principles in Supreme Court decision making allows for the systematic organization of judicial choices in specific areas of constitutional law and can account for group momentum in the shaping of constitutional doctrine. It points us to *definable limits* on the range of values that individual justices use in developing innovative Court doctrine. Such principles in flux do not indicate simplistic bargaining as the hallmark of its activity, but instead reveal an "ideological jurisprudence"—highly motivated and highly competitive—by justices who hold these principles as essential to an informed interpretation of an increasingly complex polity.[2]

1. See Vincent Blasi, *The Burger Court: The Counter-Revolution That Wasn't* (New Haven: Yale University Press, 1983), for essays by major constitutional scholars supporting this view.
2. See John Brigham, *Cult of the Robe* (Philadelphia: Temple University Press, 1987), chaps. 1, 2. Brigham argues that behavioralism as a tenet practiced by political scientists is

Before proceeding it would be useful to define our terms. Generally speaking, process principles include justices' beliefs about the jurisdictional questions of where in the polity constitutionally authorized decisions should be made. Such values include questions about whether federal courts or electorally accountable institutions should make choices; the *degree* of autonomy granted to state and local authority in our federal system; what role interest groups should play; and finally, how much weight polity principles should be given when balanced against rights arguments of a less defined, potentially more substantive nature. At their most persuasive, judicial choices based on process values are grounded *structurally*, on powers enumerated in the Constitution. For some justices these values imply judicial self-restraint, reliance on existing political power structures, and a firm faith in participational and access norms—as the main legacy of the past—to ensure a normally functioning democratic system.[3]

Rights principles are views held by justices about claims that individual citizens may legitimately make for enforceable privileges or immunities under the Constitution, statutes, and laws. Many rights relate to "cocoons" that shield citizens from government intrusion—"positive libertarian" interests embodied in the Bill of Rights. Such rights do not generally involve questions of relations *among* distributional arenas or agencies or "of jurisdictional boundaries on decision-making authority," for example, among branches of majoritarian political processes, so much as they do the nature of entitlements that individuals deserve as citizens and human beings within such arenas.[4] Historically, the clash between process and rights principles extends back to the founding period, when the Article VII structural credo necessary for ratification of the Constitution at the Philadelphia Convention was countered by the first ten amendments. The Federalist/anti-Federalist debate is informative in tracing the arguments for and against strict adherence to constitutional doctrines such as separation of powers, federalism, and characteristics of constituencies, and on the nature of and need for rights to be explicitly stated in the Constitution.[5]

---

undercut by ideologies of authority upon which the Supreme Court relies within its institutional framework and which impose constitutive characteristics on the values that motivate judicial action. Also see R. Jeffrey Lustig, *Corporate Liberalism* (Berkeley: University of California Press, 1982), chaps. 6 and 8, for an excellent analysis of pragmatism and ideology.

3. See Ronald Kahn, "The Burger Court, Boundary Setting, and State and Local Power," *Proteus* 4 (1987): 37–46, on evidence that process-based norms supporting state and local authority are central in the jurisprudence of Justices Burger, White, Rehnquist, Powell, and O'Connor in the areas of federalism, First Amendment speech, standing to sue, and equal protection.

4. See Frank I. Michelman, "Forward: Traces of Self-Government," *Harvard Law Review* 100 (1986): 4–77. Michelman describes the judicial role as imperial, enumerating "positive" and "negative" libertarian interests in the republican juridical tradition. In scope, these interests are based on assumptions by justices about process and rights values in the polity similar to the ones sketched below.

5. See Herbert Storing, *What the Anti-Federalists Were For: The Political Thought of the Opponents of the Constitution* (Chicago: University of Chicago Press, 1981). For an analysis of process and polity principles extending back to the founding period, see Ronald Kahn, "The Intersection of Polity and Rights Principles on the Burger Court: Towards a Social Science of Jurisprudence," *Legal Studies Forum* 11 (1987): 5–28.

With only slight contextual modification, these arguments resound with unsettling poignancy today. Because of their consideration by the Founders in the constitutional debate, however, establishment clause questions have a stronger constructionist basis than is found in modern innovations such as privacy rights or procedural guarantees such as the expanded right to vote.

IDEOLOGIES ON THE BURGER COURT: TOWARD A METHODOLOGY FOR THEIR STUDY

As a heuristic device, I posit that each justice has an individual set of process and rights principles, ranges of priorities from which they choose when they decide a specific case and which set limits on their choices. I do not claim that these are absolutes from which one can predict future choices by deduction from clear principles. Through the analysis of cases I will assess to what extent each justice has a set of process and rights priorities. From such analysis we can see differences in the manner in which various justices make principled choices, and the implications of different types of principles for the justices' constitutional choices, for the development of constitutional principles. In particular, this approach allows the pinpointing of differences among the justices as to the degree to which they view constitutional law as prescriptive of public official and citizen action, and whether they trust political institutions or other venues, such as churches, to make choices of constitutional significance.

Such inductive analysis allows the scholar to identify turning points or lacunae in a given justice's values, and thereby explore the possibilities for constitutional change in the future. The benefits of the "Gutman"-like bloc analysis employed is that, unlike traditional voting bloc analysis, it does not place an undue quantitative weight on case outcomes as an indicator of a justice's ideology, nor does it simply average agreement scores among justices. This approach allows the comparison of rights and process-based constitutional principles of each justice and groups of justices, so we can see what cross-cutting values exist and are in conflict in Supreme Court decision making.[6]

In Burger Court decision making on questions of the separation of church and state and aid to parochial education, we can expect to observe that justices' ideological interests as shown in different process and rights values have manifested themselves in the following ways: (1) at crucial times justices have made clear statements as to past and future directions of the Court and have signaled turning points for them in long-held process and rights values, and resulting constitutional choices; (2) justices have differed as to whether, and to what degree, strong notions of individual freedom of religious conscience or free exercise are the guiding norms for establishment clause doctrine, as opposed to reliance on process values such as the entanglement between church and state institutions or political divisiveness; and (3) groups of justices have differed as to whether process or rights values are to be considered and on the content of those values, leading to consistent patterns among groups of justices on the

6. See Herold J. Spaeth and Stuart H. Teger, "Activism and Restraint: A Cloak for the Justices' Policy Preferences," in Stephen C. Halpern and Charles M. Lamb, *Supreme Court: Activism and Restraint* (Lexington, Mass.: D. C. Heath, 1982), 277–99.

range of values to be considered, even when they are not necessarily in agreement about case outcomes.

The approach proposed is different from that of modern constitutional scholars who see their underlying objective as *advocacy* of a rights- or process-based interpretation of the Constitution and Supreme Court decision making. For example, John Hart Ely views the Constitution as consisting of process values to allow groups equitable participation in political structures. He advocates judicial review to allow equal respect of all discrete and insular minorities and analyzes Supreme Court choices with primarily this goal in mind. In contrast, Laurence Tribe and Michael Perry advocate a wider non-process-based rights creation by individuals on the Court.[7] This methodology asks the scholar to explore empirically the actual reliance on and relationship among process and rights norms used by justices in deciding cases before considering the normative and policy implications of basing constitutional choices on process and rights values.

The findings below challenge those who argue that Burger Court justices are primarily pragmatic in their choices. Vincent Blasi, for example, has argued that the Burger Court has been dominated by a pragmatic middle, consisting of Justices Stewart, Blackmun, Powell, White, and Stevens, who are described as logical, compassionate, disinterested, sensible, and dominant, "transcending most ideological divisions, but essentially pragmatic in nature, lacking a central theme or agenda."[8] This formulation, however, confuses an increased *complexity* of constitutional values as bases for Court choices with pragmatism. My objective is to make sense of this new complexity by showing consistencies in principles applied by Burger Court justices. Rooting scholarly analysis of constitutional law once again in values can also serve as a response to what might be labeled a rebirth of the relativism and empiricism of postwar scholarship. We need to understand that Supreme Court justices are moved by "ideological interests," just as are political officials such as mayors, even though the substance of these interests is different and their staying power may be greater.[9]

---

7. See John Hart Ely, *Democracy and Distrust* (Cambridge: Harvard University Press, 1980); Laurence H. Tribe, *American Constitutional Law*, 2d ed. (Mineola, N.Y.: Foundation Press, 1988), and *Constitutional Choices* (Cambridge: Harvard University Press, 1985); Michael Perry, *The Constitution, the Courts, and Human Rights* (New Haven: Yale University Press, 1982). Also see Ronald Kahn, "Process and Rights Principles in Modern Constitutional Theory," *Stanford Law Review* 36 (1984): 253–69, for a discussion of the consequences of viewing the Constitution in primarily process terms.

8. See "The Rootless Activism of the Burger Court," in Blasi, *The Burger Court*, 211–12.

9. See David Greenstone and Paul E. Peterson, *Race and Authority in Urban Politics* (New York: Russell Sage Foundation, 1973), 125–26, and Paul E. Peterson, *School Politics Chicago Style* (Chicago: University of Chicago Press, 1976), chap. 2, for explanations of how the "ideological interests" of big-city mayors for or against citizen participation led to choices that were not in their pragmatic electoral and organizational interests. Justices, professionally disciplined to think in terms of constitutional values, are far less prone than elected officials to make choices on raw pragmatic grounds.

Table 1. Burger Court Aid to Religious School Cases, 1970–85

Case Number	Date Decided	Name
1.	May 4, 1970	*Walz* v. *Tax Commission of New York* (397 US 664)
2.	June 28, 1971	*Lemon* v. *Kurtzman* (403 US 602)
3.	June 28, 1971	*Tilton* v. *Richardson* (403 US 672)
4.	June 25, 1973	*Comm. for Public Ed. & Rel. Lib.* v. *Nyquist* (413 US 756)
5.	June 25, 1973	*Levitt* v. *Comm. for Public Ed. & Rel. Lib.* (413 US 472)
6.	June 25, 1973	*Sloan* v. *Lemon* (413 US 825)
7.	June 25, 1973	*Hunt* v. *McNair* (413 US 734)
8.	May 19, 1975	*Meek* v. *Pittenger* (421 US 349)
9.	June 21, 1976	*Roemer* v. *Board of Public Works of Maryland* (426 US 736)
10.	June 24, 1977	*Wolman* v. *Walter* (433 US 229)
11.	Feb. 20, 1980	*Comm. for Public Ed. & Rel. Lib.* v. *Regan* (444 US 646)
12.	June 29, 1983	*Mueller* v. *Allen* (463 US 388)
13.	July 1, 1985	*Grand Rapids School District* v. *Ball* (473 US 373)
14.	July 1, 1985	*Aguilar* v. *Felton* (473 US 402)

BURGER COURT VOTING IN AID TO RELIGIOUS EDUCATION CASES

It will be seen that voting patterns in aid to parochial education cases do not support the "pragmatic middle" thesis. Table 1 lists chronologically the fourteen major cases on aid to religious schools during the Burger Court years 1970–85; Table 2 details majority opinion policy choices in these cases. Table 3 lists the justices in ascending order of the number of dissents from majority opinion policy choices except Justice O'Connor. She is listed last because of her late arrival to the Burger Court, the relatively few policy choices she made on aid to parochial education cases, and for comparison with the voting of contemporary Burger and Rehnquist Court justices.

There were two major groups with similar voting patterns on the Burger Court: one consisting of Justices Brennan, Marshall, Stevens, and Blackmun (to be called the Brennan group), and another consisting of Justices Rehnquist, Burger, and White (the Rehnquist group). Marshall and Brennan voted the same in all choices, joined by Justice Stevens in all but one case. Blackmun voted with Marshall and Brennan in all choices from 1980. Justices Rehnquist and White have disagreed in only two of eighteen choices. Chief Justice Burger disagreed with Rehnquist in only one of eighteen choices, and with White in five choices, but in only one since 1973.

In establishment clause cases decided since she joined the Court in 1981, Justice O'Connor has voted with the Rehnquist group in three of the four aid to parochial education choices and in two of the three major nonaid to education cases. She voted with the Rehnquist group in *Marsh* v. *Chambers* (463 U.S. 783 [1983]), a case upholding the right of prayer in state legislative chambers, and *Lynch* v. *Donnelly* (465 U.S. 668 [1984]), a case upholding the constitutionality of a crèche in a city-sponsored holiday display, but not in *Wallace* v. *Jaffree* (472 U.S.

Table 2. Substance of Parochial School Aid Majority Opinions

Case Number
1. Permits property tax exemption for church property.
2. A. No reimbursement to nonpublic schools for teacher salaries and instruction materials.
   B. No 15% state salary reimbursement directly to church school teachers for teaching secular subjects.
3. Permits federal aid for secular buildings at parochial universities.
4. A. No aid for maintenance and repair of nonpublic schools, including parochial grammar and secondary schools.
   B. No tuition reimbursement for low-income parents of parochial school children.
   C. No income tax benefits to parents of children attending nonpublic, including parochial, schools.
5. No aid for direct payment to parochial schools for test grading, including teacher-prepared tests.
6. No reimbursement for tuition to parents of children attending nonpublic, including parochial, schools.
7. Permits states to secure less expensive financing of parochial college buildings through allowing use of state bonding power.
8. A. Provides aid to parochial school children through the loan of secular textbooks.
   B. No direct aid to parochial schools for instructional materials/remedial teaching.
9. Allows annual state fiscal subsidy to nonpublic, including parochial, colleges and universities.
10. A. Permits state aid for textbook loans and testing/scoring of state-provided tests.
    B. Permits aid for out-of-parochial-school (off-premise) remedial, guidance, therapeutic services by staff hired by public school officials.
    C. No aid for instructional materials (maps, projectors) even if loaned to students and parents.
    D. No aid for field trips.
11. Allows direct payment to parochial schools for paying salaries of teachers for attendance record keeping, state standardized tests, including tests that have subjective element in grading.
12. Allows parents of children in all nonprofit public and nonpublic schools, including parochial schools, to deduct expenses for tuition, textbooks, and transportation.
13. A. Forbids a Shared Time Program: state-provided secular classes and guidance services in parochial schools to parochial school children.
    B. Forbids a Community Education Program: state-provided classes after school for students and adults in parochial schools.
14. Forbids use of federal funds to pay for public school teachers to teach in parochial school buildings remedial reading and math courses to economically disadvantaged children attending parochial schools, even when close state supervision of content is provided.

Table 3. Burger Court Voting on Aid to Religious School Cases

Justices	1.	2.A.	2.B.	3.	4.A.	4.B.	4.C.	5.	6.	7.	8.A.	8.B.	9.	10.A.	10.B.	10.C.	10.D.	11.	12.	13.A.	13.B.	14.
Harlan	M	M	M	M																		
Black	M	M	M	D																		
Stewart	M	M	M	M	M	M	M	M	M	M	M	M*	M*	D	M	M	M	M	M			
Powell					M*	M*	M*	M	M*	M*	M	M	M	M	M	M	D	M	M	M	M	M
Blackmun	M	M	M	M	M	M	M	M	M	M	M	M	M*	M*	M*	M*	M*	D	D	M	M	M
Stevens													D	M	M	M	M	D	D	M	M	M
Douglas		M	M	D	M	M	M	M	M	D	D	M										
Marshall	M	M	M	D	M	M	M	M	M	D	D	M	D	D	D	M	M	D	D	M	M	M
Brennan	M	M	M	D	M	M	M	M	M	D	D	M	D	D	D	M	M	D	D	M*	M*	M*
Burger	M*	M*	M*	M*	M	D	D	M*	D	M	M	D	M	M	M	D	D	M	M	D	M	D
Rehnquist					M	D	D	M	D	M	M	D	M	M	M	D	D	M	M*	D	D	D
White	M	D	D	M	D	D	D	D	D	M	M	D	M	M	M	D	D	M*	M	D	D	D
O'Connor																			M	D	M	D

* designates Justice writing the majority opinion.
M represents a majority vote.
D represents a dissent.

38 [1985], a case overturning an Alabama moment of silence law (all non-school aid cases); she also opposed the Rehnquist group in *Grand Rapids* v. *Ball*, a case that forbade state aid for parochial school personnel to teach secular subjects after school hours.

Data on dissents from majority opinions further suggest that the alleged pragmatic-middle bloc of justices did not perform a coherent moderating role of the Court. When they are compared for percentages of dissenting votes from majority opinions between 1970 and 1985 they appear at *all* points on the spectrum: under 10 percent (Powell, Stewart, and Blackmun, along with Harlan); 25 to 36 percent (Stevens, along with Black, Douglas, Brennan, Marshall, and Burger); and 50 percent and over (White, along with O'Connor and Rehnquist). Moderate middle justices are in all three groupings. In fact, Justice White, rather than any liberal justice, had the highest percentage of dissents of any justice on the Burger Court. Justice Stevens represents a median.

In summary: so called pragmatic-middle justices are represented in all the voting groups; the groups are stable; once justices join a group they tend to continue to vote with it; there are wide differences as to how often they voted with the majority—all these facts attest that something other than case-by-case, ad hoc, pragmatic decision making is occurring on the Burger Court. Nor can it be said that the Burger Court is dominated by a coherent group of middle justices. To see what accounts for the similarity and differences in voting among the groups of justices, qualitative case analysis is required.

PROCESS AND RIGHTS VALUES IN THE ESTABLISHMENT CLAUSE

First Amendment principles under the establishment clause involve both a general public *process* value that the state must not establish religion and a private *rights* imperative that the individual be allowed free exercise of religion uninhibited by state action. In an attempt to provide clarity by disassembling general establishment clause principles, the Burger Court in *Lemon* v. *Kurtzman*, a case in which the Court banned state reimbursement for parochial school teacher salaries and instruction materials, offered what has since become known as the *Lemon* standard. This standard, as applied, turned out to be a set of loosely defined scrutiny rules that accommodate the justices' process and rights values.[10] For a statute or government action to pass muster under this standard: (1) it must have a secular legislative purpose; (2) its principle or primary effect must be one that neither advances nor inhibits religion; and (3) it must not foster an excessive government entanglement with religion. I will use the internal structure of the *Lemon* standard to guide the argument made here about the relevance of process and rights principles to Burger Court establishment clause choices.

In addition to the essentially process-oriented *Lemon* standard, rights norms of free exercise of religion have been found to reside in the establishment clause. These may be conceived of as rights of citizens who may be either *external* or *internal* in their relation to the religious institution or activity in question. Citizens external to a religious institution should have the expectation that the state is not endorsing religious or nonreligious thought or institutions. Children and teachers internal to secular or sectarian institutions should have the expectation that the state does not interfere with the thinking of a child either for or against a religion or religious ideas. Thus, rights issues involve state entry into the cocoon that surrounds both believer and nonbeliever.

The groups of justices differed significantly over whether they view establishment clause issues in primarily process terms, such as the definition of secular purpose, the atmosphere of religious schools as forums for secular instruction, and entanglement, or in prescriptive rights terms, which limit state choices in this area.

The terms *pluralist* and *critical-pluralist* may be used to indicate differences among the justices with regard to process values. Support of pluralist process values suggests a trust of legislatures and electorally accountable political institutions to make choices about aid to parochial schools and other issues relating to the separation of church and state. Holding critical-pluralist process norms, on the other hand, suggests an underlying distrust both of these majoritarian institutions and also of other forums such as religious organizations protecting establishment clause principles.[11] I will use the term *rights, weak rights*, and *nonrights* to differentiate among the justices as to whether they

10. 403 U.S. 602, at 623–24 (1971).

11. See Kahn, "The Burger Court, Boundary Setting, and State and Local Power," for a review of the pluralist/critical-pluralist debate in modern political and constitutional theory.

expressed concern for establishing a cocoon around parochial school children and those external to religious institutions, including nonbelievers. They also differed on how these process and rights norms were to be interpreted.

Qualitative analysis of the cases along these dimensions shows that the Burger Court possessed a variety of judicial outlooks in the establishment clause cases that complement the voting alignments reported above. They range from a pluralist process/nonrights emphasis by Justices Rehnquist, White, and Burger, to pluralist process/weak rights values by centrist Justices O'Connor and Powell, to a critical-pluralist/rights approach by Justices Blackmun, Brennan, Marshall, and Stevens. Strong free exercise rights values is the major component of the Brennan group's call for a wall of separation between church and state. Here the rights component is less subject to contextual comparison, and thus more prescriptive and limiting of government behavior, than are the process values in the establishment clause. Every justice with strong rights values also had strong critical-pluralist process values. Process values in the establishment clause, however, operated as separate and distinct from the free exercise rights values. Justices with pluralist process values, usually trusting of the political system, had quite different views about whether free exercise rights of children were violated by government aid to parochial schools. These differences proved decisive in the development of the line of separation between church and state.

PLURALIST AND CRITICAL-PLURALIST PROCESS VALUES: CONFLICT OVER CONTEXT

The Brennan Group: Critical-Pluralist Process Values

Justices Brennan, Marshall, Stevens, and Blackmun, since 1980, have invoked process values—political divisiveness, religious or secular effects, and entanglement—to argue their critical-pluralist position, which distrusts the ability of government policy to ensure the separation between church and state that they viewed as the paramount requirement of the establishment clause. The prong of the *Lemon* standard most debated in establishment clause decisions was the entanglement of political and religious pursuits through state involvement in sectarian affairs. A concern for political divisiveness, then, became the focus of critical-pluralist/rights-oriented justices in their effort to bolster the *Lemon* standard against state support for religious institutions. For example, Justice Brennan, dissenting in the *Lynch* case, which allowed a city-provided crèche in a holiday display, warned that the "religious chauvinism" in this excessive entanglement could cause political antagonism from minority dissident religious groups.[12] With a strict assertion of the potential for political divisiveness as their standard and their fear of religious groups vying for state funds, the Brennan group sought to reintroduce prohibitive aspects into the establishment clause that they felt the loose application of the *Lemon* standard by the Burger Court had helped erode.

12. 465 U.S. 668, at 701 (1984).

Justice Blackmun's voting record in the establishment clause cases, his move to the Brennan group, revealed an abrupt change. This is an example of how our methodology highlights strategic turning points in individual justices' jurisprudence. Blackmun had voted with the pluralist, weak rights–oriented Powell and Stewart through *Wolman* v. *Walter*, a case allowing state aid for textbook loans, off-school therapeutic services, and the administering of state-provided tests for parochial school children.[13] Fearful that he had gone too far in subscribing to the majority's flexible reading of the *Lemon* standard since *Hunt* v. *McNair*, a case that upheld state financial support of parochial school construction, he dramatically joined the rights-oriented group in dissent in *Regan*, a case allowing direct payment to parochial schools to pay teacher salaries for "secular" tasks such as taking attendance. Blackmun has stayed with the rights values group ever since.[14]

Justice Stevens has embarked on a crusade to reintroduce watertight rights principles in establishment clause adjudication. Stevens has written typically terse (even austere) opinions about reintroducing an inviolable "wall of separation," lamenting the decline of the *Lemon* standard as a guide for stringent scrutiny. He has ruled with the Brennan group against aid to parochial schools, *except* aid that would afford parochial school children remedial, guidance, and therapeutic services that were *off* school premises and implemented by non–parochial school employees. Thus the Brennan group leaned toward a hermetically sealed church and state relationship of the most limited variety, with the Court policing the integrity of that relationship *preventively*.

The Rehnquist Group: Pluralist Process Values

Justices Rehnquist, White, and Burger share the process value of Court deference to legislatures and to the pluralist bargaining arena more generally. Characteristically to the point, Justice White said in *Lemon* v. *Kurtzman*, "It is enough for me that the States and the Federal Government are financing a separable secular function of overriding importance in order to sustain the legislation here challenged. That religion and private interests other than education may substantially benefit does not convert these laws into impermissible establishments of religion."[15]

The Rehnquist group worked to do away with a stringent *Lemon* test, especially that part which seeks to ensure that the primary effect of government aid is not to advance or inhibit religion. They rejected the notion that parochial schools have a pervasive religious atmosphere, and they have determined that almost all effects of government aid are incidental when considered within the broader context of a complex society in which religion plays an integral role. Aid to education was not viewed in prescriptive constitutional process or rights terms. They did not fear entanglement, that the state might corrupt the church or vice versa, nor did they fear there will be a denial of the free exercise rights of parochial school children or of believers and nonbelievers in the wider society.

13. 433 U.S. 229 (1977).
14. 413 U.S. 734 (1973); 444 U.S. 646 (1980).
15. 403 U.S. 602, at 664 (1971).

Beginning in 1973, Chief Justice Burger no longer displayed concern, as he had earlier, for a strict entanglement standard. His consequentialist application of the *Lemon* standard in *Lynch*, the crèche case, was representative of the Rehnquist group's presumption of secular purpose and good faith in state actions directed at the support of religious values, drawing the line only at the establishment of a state religion.[16]

The Centrist Justices: Powell and O'Connor

We also see "ideological interests" in process and rights values, rather than a disinterested pragmatism, when we consider Justice O'Connor's innovative, adaptive, but coherent responses to constitutional questions before the Court. Justice O'Connor emphasized an initial presumption of good faith on the part of government in dealing in church affairs. Evidence for this is provided in O'Connor's dissent in *Aguilar* v. *Felton* in which she declared her support for the ability of public school teachers to keep the potential of indoctrination out of the sectarian classroom.[17] In the Court's reevaluation of entanglement in *Lynch* v. *Donnelly*, the crèche case, Justice O'Connor advocated a more rigorous entanglement test than that found in *Regan*. She advocated there must be *proof* of entanglement, rather than merely a fear of it as advocated by the Brennan group. Nor would she support the latter's standard of political divisiveness based on potential. Entanglement problems that actually encroach on students' free exercise rights were, according to O'Connor, to be policed after the fact.[18] She sought to separate process from rights values, thus undercutting a strong rights-based jurisprudence.

Justice Powell has voted with the majority in all cases. This implies that he considered each case on its merits. A closer look at his opinions finds Powell swayed by particular contexts and by the opinions of both his process- and rights-oriented colleagues on the Court. This led to contradictory outcomes. For example, in 1973, Powell wrote the *Nyquist* opinion disallowing aid for facility maintenance and tuition reimbursement and tax benefits for parents of children attending parochial schools.[19] Ten years later, he voted with the majority in *Mueller* which allowed parents of parochial school children virtually the same benefits—tax deductions for tuition, textbooks, and transportation.[20] Also, in the *Wolman* case, Justice Powell rejected political divisiveness as a standard for the Court, arguing that in the modern era we need not fear religious control over democratic processes or deep religious divisions in politics.[21] In a dramatic reversal eight years later in *Aguilar* v. *Felton*, however, Justice Powell reasserted the "political divisiveness" standard in a move that indicated a reevaluation of his position.[22]

16. 465 U.S. 668, at 680, 686 (1984).
17. 473 U.S. 402, at 424–25 (1985).
18. 465 U.S. 668, at 689–90 (1984).
19. 413 U.S. 756 (1973).
20. 463 U.S. 388 (1983).
21. 433 U.S. 229, at 263 (1977).
22. 473 U.S. 402 (1985).

A comparison of O'Connor and Powell demonstrates that O'Connor, unlike Powell, has been concerned to develop consistent process norms. Even Powell, however, unlike the Rehnquist group, takes as a starting point a range of both process and rights values, and unlike the Brennan group, he did not support only process norms that would result in a wall of separation.

CONFLICTING RIGHTS PRINCIPLES: THE WALL OF SEPARATION

In regard to rights principles embedded in the establishment clause, we have already seen that the Brennan group consistently relied on process arguments to bolster their rights values, and vice versa, in a quest for a "high and impregnable" barrier between church and state. The addition of adherents to the rights-oriented camp in Justices Blackmun and Stevens, and the acknowledgment of free exercise rights as limitations on state support of religion by Justice O'Connor, have allowed a reconsideration, if not a rebirth, of a rights-oriented approach.

The Brennan group's objective was to keep Court discretion at a minimum by creating standards that produce a principled separation between church and state. Clear principles reduce the factors to be considered, factors that permit accommodation between church needs and majoritarian state interests. The external and internal free exercise components of the establishment clause were articulated by Justice Brennan in the majority opinion in *Aguilar* v. *Felton*:

> The principle that the state should not become too closely entangled with the church in the administration of assistance is rooted in two concerns. When the state becomes enmeshed with a given denomination in matters of religious significance, the freedom of religious belief of those who are not adherents of that denomination suffers, even when the governmental purpose underlying the involvement is largely secular. In addition, the freedom of even the adherents of the denomination is limited by the governmental intrusion into sacred matters.[23]

Concern for both internal and external free exercise rights, that is, of believers in sectarian institutions and nonbelievers as well, was also captured in Justice Brennan's "symbolic union" thesis, stated in his majority opinion in the *Grand Rapids* case, that state and federal programs might be perceived both by adherents of the controlling denominations as an endorsement of their religious beliefs and by nonadherents as a disapproval of their religious choices.[24]

As already indicated, the rights principles of the Brennan group promoted rigidity in the Court stance toward state aid to religious institutions and worked against the position of benevolent neutrality based on the magnanimous reading of free exercise as in the Rehnquist group. Relying upon principled separation arguments, those in the Brennan group have sought to use clear prescriptive process and rights values in the establishment clause to protect the specific

23. 473 U.S. 402, at 409–10 (1985).
24. 473 U.S. 373, at 389 (1985).

free exercise value, viewed as the right to be left completely alone in one's religious thought and practice. Accordingly, adjudication based primarily on consequences—as in Court leniency toward political bodies supporting religious aspects of holidays such as Christmas—did not fit their stance well. These process and rights predispositions of the Brennan group on the Court, more than the open-ended *Lemon* test, provided definitive answers to many otherwise subtle choices that had to be made in exploring what constitutes the establishment of religion.

Justice O'Connor, unlike the Rehnquist group, has been sensitive to protecting "internal" free exercise rights. In her concurrence in *Grand Rapids*, she relied in substance on Brennan's "'symbolic union" thesis. She determined that when parochial school instructors teach secular subjects after school in their regular classrooms, there was a significant chance that it would infringe on the free exercise right of children to make up their own minds about religion. O'Connor's fear was that identification of children with their parochial school teachers, furthered by being in regular classrooms, would lead to a mixing of secular and religious messages, and thus a constitutionally impermissible belief by the students that the state endorses their religion. Furthermore, there would be no way of monitoring this without entangling the state deeply in religious school activities.[25] Unlike the Brennan group, O'Connor did not view the use of state funds in religious schools surroundings as a per se violation of the establishment clause.

Similarly, O'Connor was concerned that free exercise values within the establishment clause would be protected in the public school context. In *Wallace* v. *Jaffree* she joined the Court in declaring that an Alabama law authorizing a period of silence for "meditation or voluntary prayer" in public schools was an impermissible establishment of religion. She opposed the Rehnquist group's view that free exercise principles should be evaluated on the basis of the framers' preference for prayer and religion. She argued that the *Lemon* standard is not to be applied ahistorically, noting that public education was nonexistent in the eighteenth century. She also took issue with the Brennan group's wholesale removal of questions of state support of religion from Court scrutiny by erecting a wall between church and state. For O'Connor, the effects of state policy need not be religiously neutral, but the policy must be free of religious content—a requirement that Alabama's actions could not meet.[26]

Thus, O'Connor viewed school children as having a right to choose prayer, meditation, or neither, without government interference in their choice. O'Connor's rights component was more clearly stated than that by her fellow centrist Powell.[27] O'Connor's centrism was not a search for pragmatic policy determinations, but rather a search for both process and rights guides to a

25. 473 U.S. 373 (1985).
26. 472 U.S. 38, at 80 (1985).
27. See Paul W. Kahn, "The Court, the Community and the Judicial Balance: The Jurisprudence of Justice Powell," *Yale Law Journal* 97 (1987): 1–60. Kahn argues that Powell has been too deferential to community values.

principled jurisprudence, in light of her interpretation of the Constitution, precedent, and allowable rights definitions under the Court's power of judicial review.

CONCLUSION

In this research note the following arguments have been presented: that the pragmatic middle thesis is not borne out by evidence from Burger Court decision making on establishment clause cases; that the substantive bases of judicial choice were not case-specific, outcome-oriented, or pragmatic, but instead rested on coherent process and rights values; and that an ideological jurisprudence methodology might be suitable for the analysis of other areas of Supreme Court decision making.

Justice Powell's retirement and the appointment of Justices Scalia and Kennedy to the Supreme Court suggest that a Court dominated by a pragmatic middle is also not likely in the future. Although Justice Kennedy seems to be inclined to weigh process and rights values in line with precedent, as Powell did, the other Court members are fixed and consistent in the range of process and rights values they envision in the establishment clause.

The Burger Court's definition of the process and rights values and the lack of a rights-oriented majority have led to the approval of direct government support of religious symbols and of aid programs for parents of parochial school children. The Burger Court, however, has stopped short of allowing schools and legislatures to affirmatively support religious fundamentalism as a right of children in secular schools. The Burger Court has thus said that religion is an important value in our liberal society, but not one that will replace the objectives of our schools to educate in a secular rather than a sectarian manner.

The fact that there is no universal judicial stance, but rather justices animated by clear positions who form groups in support of different process and rights values, reveals that the institutional momentum in our polity provided by the Supreme Court is fueled by a timely *convergence* of views. This changing dynamic of Supreme Court jurisprudence is a sliding scale of sorts—in which process or rights values, or a combination of them, serve to captivate a dominant coalition of individual members on the Court for sustained periods of time. The distinction between valueless pragmatism and convergence of value hierarchies of like-minded justices may appear small against the outcomes of judicial practice, but it is a factual and theoretical difference of the greatest magnitude. It is around this convergence that Supreme Court decisions revolve and doctrinal change centers—with differing values providing the problematic in specific cases rather than simply stare decisis or past precedent.

The conflict and, perhaps more important, the *relationship* of process and rights principles that inform judicial choices are strongly manifest in First Amendment cases where rights guarantees mesh in an uneasy equilibrium with the structural or process guarantees of the Constitution. Ultimately, some accord must be reached to keep the shifting alliance intact; it is the justices who, relying on conviction about a particular mix of values, will try to stretch the common ground or, in another case, try to erect some permanent barrier in the law. We are forced to disagree with Anthony Lewis who, drawing on the words of Justice Holmes, described the Burger Court era as "that period of dry precedent which is so often to be found midway between a creative epoch and a period of solvent philosophical reaction."[28] While reflecting societal debate about the proper institutional role of the Supreme Court, the Burger Court did more than refine Warren Court doctrine in an activist but rootless manner. It was, in Justice Holmes's terms, reactive and creative in forging a new—if complex—ideological course. The reconstitution of doctrine, rather than merely a reaction to past precedent, will continue into the Rehnquist era.

28. See Anthony Lewis, Foreword to Blasi, *The Burger Court*, ix.